Supply Chain Management: Innovations for Education

M. Eric Johnson
David F. Pyke

Editors

Production and Operations Management Society

Copyright©2000 by Production and Operations Management Society

All rights reserved. Except as permitted under the United States Copyright Act of 1976, no part of this book may be reproduced or distributed in any form or by any means, or stored in a data base or retrieval system, without the prior permission of the publisher.

POMS Series in Technology and Operations Management

Founder and Editor-in-Chief: Kalyan Singhal
Co-Editor-in-Chief: Jaya Singhal

Volume 2, 2000: Supply Chain Management: Innovations for Education

ISBN 0-9663725-1-4

Published by
Production and Operations Management Society
Executive Director: Sushil K. Gupta
College of Engineering
Florida International University
EAS 2460, 10555 West Flagler Street
Miami, Florida 33174, USA

Contents

M. Eric Johnson and David F. Pyke
Preface 1

Foreword from Dean Paul Danos 3

I. Introduction

M. Eric Johnson and David F. Pyke
A Framework for Teaching Supply Chain Management 4

II. Integration and Frameworks

Michael T. Sweeney and Robin Lane
Leveraging Service Quality through Supply Chain Management 21

Ananth Raman
Coordinating and Managing Supply Chains: The General Manager's Role 31

David J. Closs, Steven A. Melnyk, Theodore P. Stank, and Morgan Swink
An Integrated Curriculum For Teaching Supply Chain Management at Michigan State University 43

Raymond K. Cheung, Jiyin Liu, and Yat-Wah Wan
Education Initiatives on Logistics and Supply Chain Management for Service Providers in Hong Kong 57

III. Games and Exercises

Fangruo Chen and Rungson Samroengraja
The Stationary Beer Game 68

F. Robert Jacobs
Playing the Beer Distribution Game Over the Internet 80

Kathleen E. McKone
Teaching Supply Chain Management Principles: The Otogel Simulation Exercise .. 89

Joyce S. Mehring
A Practical Setting for Experiential Learning about Supply Chains: Siemen's Brief Case Game Supply Chain Simulator 100

Guenther Zaepfel and Bartosz Piekarz
The PC-Based Simulation Game, Lean Production, for Controlling the Supply Chain of a Virtual Bicycle Factory 110

Edward G. Anderson and Douglas J. Morrice
A Simulation Game for Teaching Service-Oriented Supply Chain Management: Does Information Sharing Help Managers with Service Capacity Decisions? 125

Ram Ganeshan, Tonya Boone, and Alan J. Stenger
The Integration Aspect of Supply Chain Management: A Framework and a Simulation.. 141

Burak Kazaz and Herbert Moskowitz
An Active Learning Exercise: Supplying Hoop Dreams 157

Nils Rudi and David F. Pyke
Teaching Supply Chain Concepts with the Newsboy Model.................... 170

IV. Running Supply Chain Projects

Laura Rock Kopczak and Jan C. Fransoo
Teaching Supply Chain Management through Global Projects with Global Project Teams... 181

F. Barry Lawrence
Warren Electric Group: An Industry Alliance to Teach Logistics Theory Meets Practice.. 194

V. Industrial Perspective on Teaching Supply Chain Management

Andre Kuper and Dwight Branvold
Innovation Diffusion at Hewlett-Packard 205

VI. Supply Chain Software

Ann Campbell, Jarrod Goentzel, and Martin Savelsbergh
Experiences with the Use of Supply Chain Management Software in Education ... 219

R. S. M. Lau, Robert E. Rosacker, and Stephen L. Tracy
Teaching Supply Chain Management with an Integrated Business Curriculum and SAP Client/Server Paradigm.. 233

VII. Executive Education

Thomas E. Vollmann, Carlos Cordon and Jussi Heikkila
Teaching Supply Chain Management to Business Executives................... 245

Peter Gilmour
Integration, Globalization and Customization: Logistics Management Education in Asia Pacific.. 255

PREFACE TO SUPPLY CHAIN MANAGEMENT: INNOVATIONS FOR EDUCATION

M. ERIC JOHNSON AND DAVID F. PYKE

Tuck School of Business, Dartmouth College, Hanover, New Hampshire 03755, USA

Few topics in production and operations management have had the impact, both on industry and academia, as supply chain management. Managers in nearly every industry have begun to realize that competition in the 21st century will no longer be firm against firm, but supply chain against supply chain. Spawning an entire industry of supply chain software and consulting companies, demand for supply chain expertise exploded in closing years of the 2nd millennium. As late as 1995, few business or engineering schools had courses dedicated to supply chain management. Now nearly every top business and engineering school has at least one dedicated course, and many more have integrated supply chain topics into core curricula.

In this book we explore some of the leading-edge thinking around supply chain education. We introduce the book with our paper that examines how supply chain management is being taught, both in management and engineering schools. From that point, the book is broken into six major sections. The first three sections concentrate on the educational initiatives within a traditional degree-based setting. We begin with four papers that examine how supply chain concepts are being integrated into curricula in the United States, Europe, and Asia. The next section presents many advances in experiential learning techniques. By far our largest section, the nine papers in this section provide a wide range of games and exercises, emphasizing the importance of experiential learning techniques. This is naturally followed by two papers discussing the role of industrial projects in supply chain education.

The last three sections look at educational ventures that interface directly with industrial needs and applications. The first paper looks at supply chain education within Hewlett-Packard, a recognized leader in supply chain innovation. In the next section, two papers describe how industrial supply chain software has impacted university education. Finally, we conclude with two papers that focus on executive and professional education.

We hope that this book will be a valuable resource for instructors of supply chain management, both in industry and academia. We wish to thank the many people who have contributed to the success of this book. In particular, we wish to thank Hau L. Lee and the Supply Chain Thought Leaders Roundtable for the early recognition of the importance of sharing teaching ideas. We also wish to thank Kalyan Singhal, Editor-in-Chief and Jaya

Singhal, Co-Editor-in-Chief of the POMS Series in Technology and Operations management for their vision and encouragement. Finally, we acknowledge the substantial financial support of this book project from Owen School of Management, Vanderbilt University and the Tuck School of Business at Dartmouth College.

We also wish to thank the hard work of the over one hundred authors and referees, whose dedication has produced this high quality volume that will impact our community for years to come.

Edward Anderson, University of Texas; Ravi Anupindi, Northwestern University; Bob Blanning, Vanderbilt University; Tonya Boone, Ohio State University; Dwight Branvold, Hewlett-Packard; Alex Brown, Vanderbilt University; Gérard Cachon, Duke University; Ann Campbell, Georgia Tech; Kyle Cattani, University of North Carolina; Fangruo Chen, Columbia University; Raymond Cheung, Hong Kong University of Science and Technology; David Closs, Michigan State University; Carlos Cordon, IMD; Ricardo Ernst, Georgetown University; Geraldo Ferrer, University of North Carolina; Jan Fransoo, Eindhoven University of Technology; Ram Ganeshan, University of Cincinnati; Amit Garg, IBM; Peter Gilmour, Macquarie Graduate School of Business; Jarrod Goentzel, Georgia Tech; Skip Grenoble, Penn State University; Mark Hanna, Miami University; Jussi Heikkila, IMD; Mary Holcomb, University of Tennessee; Alan Stenger, Penn State University; Bob Jacobs, Indiana University; Ziv Katalan, University of Pennsylvania; Burak Kazaz, Loyola University of Chicago; Craig Kirkwood, Arizona State University; Laura Kopczak, Stanford University; Daniel Krause, Michigan State University; Ravi Kumar, University of Southern California; Andre Kuper, Hewlett-Packard; Robin Lane, Cranfield School of Management; Marty Lariviere, Duke University; R.S.M. Lau, University of South Dakota; Barry Lawrence Texas A&M; John Leschke, University of Virginia; Janny Leung, Chinese University of Hong Kong; J. Liu, Hong Kong University of Science and Technology; Karl Manrodt, University of Tennessee; Dale Masel, Ohio University; Kathleen McKone, University of Minnesota; Joyce Mehring, University of Massachusetts at Lowell; Russ Meller Auburn University; Steven Melnyk, Michigan State University; Richard Metters, Southern Methodist University; Douglas Morrice, University of Texas; Herbert Moskowitz, Purdue University; Liam O'Neill, Cornell University; Nick Petruzzi, University of Illinois; Bartosz Piekarz, University of Linz, Austria; George Polak, Wright State University; Ananth Raman, Harvard University; Robert Rosacker, University of South Dakota; Nils Rudi, University of Rochester; Joyce S. Mehring (Univ. Mass); Rungson Samroengraja, Booz, Allen & Hamilton; Martin Savelsberg, Georgia Tech; Ken Schultz, Indiana University; Medini Singh, Dartmouth College; Theordore Stank, Michigan State University; Alan Stenger, Penn State University; Michael Sweeney, Cranfield; Morgan Swink, Michigan State University; Stephen Tracy, University of South Dakota; Gene Tyworth, Penn State University; Thomas Vollmann, IMD; Y. Wan, Hong Kong University of Science and Technology; Ed Watson, Louisiana State University; Elliot Weiss, University of Virginia; Lisa Williams, Penn State University; Enver Yucesan, INSEAD; Gunther Zapfel, University of Linz, Austria

FOREWORD FROM DEAN PAUL DANOS

DEAN, TUCK SCHOOL OF BUSINESS, DARTMOUTH COLLEGE

Supply Chain Management is a topic of immense importance to world business, not only in "bricks and mortar" enterprises but just as importantly in the critical aspect of order fulfillment in the new world of e-commerce.

Supply chains move materials, information and money across a network of partners. In order for materials, components, semi-finished products and finished products to be moved in a low-cost, timely manner, all parties must be willing and able to share information.

This book gives instructors the up-to-date perspectives and concepts they need to teach the next generation of managers the essentials of supply chain management in the information age.

At the Tuck School of Business we believe that the leaders we educate should know the latest developments in supply chain management along with other important topics such as strategy, marketing and finance. We, therefore, commend the Production and Operations Management Society for publishing such an important and timely book on this crucial topic in management education.

Paul Danos
Dean, Tuck School of Business
Dartmouth College

A FRAMEWORK FOR TEACHING SUPPLY CHAIN MANAGEMENT*

M. ERIC JOHNSON AND DAVID F. PYKE

Tuck School of Business, Dartmouth College, Hanover, New Hampshire 03755, USA

The rise of global markets and increasingly virtual companies has focused management attention on competition between supply chains. Many schools of management and engineering are adopting integrated curricula that prepare students to design and manage the resulting complex global web of material and information flows. In this paper, we examine the curricula used by many top engineering and graduate business schools for courses in supply chain management. We present a framework for supply chain management and highlight supporting material and pedagogy. We also classify popular supply chain case studies within our framework and provide useful references to recent business press treatment of these issues.
(SUPPLY CHAIN MANAGEMENT, EDUCATION)

Introduction

In April, 1995 a panel of academics gathered at the Spring INFORMS meeting to discuss the emerging interest in supply chain management. At that time, only a handful of universities taught a course with the title "supply chain management," although some were teaching supply chain concepts in courses under the label "logistics" or "operations management." Today, many top business schools along with some engineering programs have courses titled "supply chain management" and more are added each year. In nearly all of the top MBA programs, core operations management courses have been augmented with significant content on supply chains (van Wassenhove and Corbeyz 1998).

Skeptics would argue that this rush to change curriculum was little more than a repackaging of topics long covered in operations management such as logistics, inventory control, and facility location. Or that, as with quality control in the 1970s and lean manufacturing in the 1980s, supply chain was the popular management fad of the late 1990s. But a closer look at both business practice and MBA programs reveals stronger forces at work, creating an environment ripe for supply chain concepts. Integration, long the dream of management gurus, was slowly sinking into the minds of western managers and business school deans. As we shall see, integration may be the key unifying theme behind supply chain curriculum and practice. For example, product design, manufacturing, and logistics are coming head-to-head with channel design and category management; traditional functional silos of marketing, R&D, manufacturing, and logistics are consolidating into the integrated supply chain.

---

*Names of the authors in this paper appear in alphabetical order. Reprinted from *Production and Operations Management*, Vol. 9, No. 1, Spring 2000, pp. 2–18.

Others would contend that managers have long been interested in integration, but the lack of information technology made it impossible to implement a more "systems-oriented" approach. Clearly industrial dynamics researchers dating back to the 1950s (Forester 1958, 1961) have maintained that supply chains should be viewed as an integrated system. With the recent explosion of inexpensive information technology, it seems only natural that business would become more supply chain focused. However, while technology is clearly an enabler of integration, it alone can not explain the radical organizational changes in both individual firms and whole industries. Changes both in technology and in management theory set the stage for integrated supply chain management.

While integration and information technology may have been key catalysts in the surge of interest surrounding supply chains, eBusiness is fueling even stronger excitement. eBusiness facilitates the virtual supply chain, and as companies manage these virtual networks, competition is increasingly no longer business-to-business but rather supply-chain-to-supply-chain. In other words, the importance of integration is magnified.

Still many would argue that the language and metaphors are wrong. "Chains" evoke images of linear, unchanging, and powerless. "Supply" feels pushy and reeks of mass production rather than mass customization. Better names, like "demand networks" or "customer driven webs" have been proposed by many a potential book author hoping to invent a new trend. Yet, for now, the name "supply chain" seems to have stuck. And under any name, the future of supply chain management appears bright.

In this paper, we examine the curricula used by many top engineering and graduate business schools for courses in supply chain management. We first present a framework comprising 12 key components of a "typical" supply chain management course. Next we discuss how each of the components is taught and present references that are useful as student reading assignments. Using our framework, we categorize popular teaching cases and recent business news stories related to supply chain management. We also briefly discuss pedagogy and the use of games, projects, and simulations. Finally, we examine the structure of several courses at U.S. institutions.

Key Components of Supply Chain Management

Supply chain management is an enormous topic covering multiple disciplines and employing many quantitative and qualitative tools. In our survey of class syllabi we observed a wide range of topics and a great diversity in the detail with which those topics were examined. Most of the graduate level classes did not use a textbook but rather relied on case studies and on articles from managerial journals. Within the last 3 years, several textbooks for supply chain have arrived on the market providing both managerial overviews and detailed technical treatments. For examples of managerial introductions to supply chain management see Copacino (1997), and Handfield and Nichols (1998), and for logistics texts see Lambert et al. (1997) and Ballou (1998). For more technical, model-based treatments see Silver, Pyke, and Peterson (1998) and Simchi-Levi, Kaminsky, and Simchi-Levi (1998). Also, there are several casebooks that give emphasis to global management issues including Taylor (1997), Flaherty (1996), and Dornier, Ernst, Fender, and Kouvelis (1998). In this paper, we will concentrate on courses that are primarily supported by recent articles and cases.

Since integration is an overriding theme in supply chain, many different functional areas are addressed within a single course. At most U.S. business schools, supply chain management is taught from an operations or logistics perspective. This paper is most closely tied to such a perspective. To enhance the theme of integration, some schools employ the participation of several instructors from different functional perspectives—most frequently from operations, logistics, marketing, and organizations. In courses taught by a single faculty member, this same idea may be accomplished by guest lectures or by the instructor actively presenting different perspectives. By its very nature supply chain is integrative, so it might seem inappropriate to "dis-integrate" it when presenting it to students. However, it is impossible to address all the dimensions of supply chain management at one time. Therefore, most instructors discuss certain dimensions in depth before moving on to others. Integration, of course, can be addressed in each category.

To help order our discussion, we have divided supply chain management into 12 areas. We identified these 12 areas from our own experience teaching supply chain management, from analysis of syllabi of many supply chain courses, and from our discussions with other instructors. Each area represents a supply chain issue facing the firm. For any particular problem or issue, managers may apply analysis or decision support tools. For each of the 12 areas, we provide a brief description of the basic content and refer the reader to recent articles that make suitable class reading assignments. We also mention likely operations research–based tools to aid in analysis and decision support. In the subsequent section, we present an extensive list of recent (since 1990) teaching cases, each categorized within our framework (Table 1). We will also present a list of recent news articles classified into the 12 areas.

The 12 categories we define are as follows:
- location
- transportation and logistics
- inventory and forecasting
- marketing and channel restructuring
- sourcing and supplier management
- information and electronic mediated environments
- product design and new product introduction
- service and after sales support
- reverse logistics and green issues
- outsourcing and strategic alliances
- metrics and incentives
- global issues.

Before launching into a particular selection of topics, most courses begin with an introduction to supply chain, often emphasizing the importance of integration. There are numerous suitable first day readings including Cooper, Lambert, and Pagh (1997a), Davis (1993), Johnson (1998a), and Lee and Billington (1992).

Location pertains to both qualitative and quantitative aspects of facility location decisions. This includes models of facility location, geographic information systems (GIS), country differences, taxes and duties, transportation costs associated with certain locations, and government incentives (Hammond and Kelly 1990). Exchange rate issues fall in this category as well, as do economies and diseconomies of scale and scope. Decisions at this level set the physical structure of the supply chain and therefore establish constraints for more tactical decisions. Optimization models play a role here, as do simple spreadsheet models and qualitative analyses. There are many advanced texts specially dedicated to the modeling aspects of location (Drezner 1996) and most books on logistics also cover the subject. Simchi-Levi, Kaminsky, and Simchi-Levi (1998) present a substantial treatment of GIS, whereas Dornier, Ernst, Fender, and Kouvelis (1998) dedicate a chapter to issues of taxes, duties, exchange rates, and other global location issues.

The transportation and logistics category encompasses all issues related to the flow of goods through the supply chain, including transportation, warehousing, and material handling. Depending on the intent of the instructor, this may include many of the current trends in transportation management, including vehicle routing, dynamic fleet management with global positioning systems, and merge-in-transit. Also included are topics in warehousing and distribution, such as cross-docking and materials handling technologies for sorting, storing, and retrieving products. This category contains much of what was traditionally taught in logistics courses, and there are many excellent texts on the subject. Useful short articles

TABLE 1
Recent Cases in Supply Chain Management

Case (School, Contact person or author)	Location	Logistics	Inventory	Marketing	Sourcing	Information	Product Design	Service	Reverse SC	Outsourcing	Metrics	Global Issues
7-11 Japan (Stanford, 1997, Seungjin Whang)			●			●						
Amhall Paper Products (Stanford, 1997, Seungjin Whang)			●			●						
A Note on the U.S. Transportation Industry (HBS, 1995, Jan Hammond and J. Morrison)		●										
A Tale of Two Electronic Components Distributors (HBS, 1997, Bharat Rao and Ananth Raman)					●							
Alden Products - European Manufacturing (HBS, 1989/98)	●											●
Apparel Exports and the Indian Economy (HBS, 1995, Ananth Raman),					●							
Apple Computer's Supplier Hubs (Stanford, 1996, Laura Kopczak)		●								●	●	
Applichem (HBS, 1986, Therese Flaherty)					●						●	●
Barilla SpA (HBS, 1994, Jan Hammond)			●	●								
Baxter Healthcare: North American Supply Chain Management Experience (CLM, 1996, Kevin Boberg and Arnold Maltz)		●										●
Benetton (HBS, 1989, Howard Stevenson)				●				●				
Bose: JITII (HBS, 1994, Roy Shapiro)					●	●						
Bradco/Taylor (Tuck, 1999, Dave Pyke)	●	●										
Brueggers and Chesapeake Bakeries (Duke, 1997, Gerard Cachon)				●								
Burlington Northern (HBS, 1989, Jan Hammond)		●										
Campbell Soup: A Leader in Continuous Replenishment (HBS, 1994, Theodore Clark)				●	●							
Cummins Engine Co: Starting up "B" Crankshaft Manufacturing at the San Luis Potosi Plant (HBS, 1994, Robert Hayes)							●					●
Ergonomics, Inc (CLM, 1997, Omar Helferich and Robert Sroufe)			●						●			
Emerson Electric Co. ACP Division: The Fan Subpack Sourcing Decision (Darden, 1993, Keith Paige and Edward Davis)					●							●
Frito-Lay: The Backhaul Decision (HBS, 1992, Jan Hammond)		●										
General Appliance (Wharton, 1994, Morris Cohen)	●				●							

include Kopczak, Lee, and Whang (1995) and Hammond and Morrison (1995). Because of globalization and the spread of outsourced logistics, this category has received much attention in recent years. However, we will define a separate category to examine issues specifically related to outsourcing and logistics alliances. Again, optimization models can be used here, as can spreadsheet models and qualitative analysis. Recent management literature has examined the changes within the logistics functions of many firms as the result of

TABLE 1 (cont'd)

	Location	Logistics	Inventory	Marketing	Sourcing	Information	Product Design	Service	Reverse SC	Outsourcing	Metrics	Global Issues
Glu Lam (Tuck, 1993, Dave Pyke)			•									
Heineken Netherlands BV: Reengineering IS/IT to Enable Customer-Oriented Supply Chain Management (IMD, 1997, D. Marchand, T. Vollmann, K. Bechler)				•		•						
H.E. Butt Grocery Company: A Leader in ECR (HBS, 1991, Theodore Clark)			•	•								
Hewlett Packard Spokane Division: Order Fulfillment and Inventory Control (Vanderbilt, 1995, Eric Johnson)			•									
HP Deskjet Printer Supply Chain (Stanford, 1993, Hau Lee and Laura Kopczak)			•				•					
HP's da Vinci Project (Stanford, 1996, Glen Schmidt, Hau Lee, Seungjin Whang)							•					
HP Universal Power Supply (Stanford, 1997, Hau Lee)			•				•					
IBM After Sales Service (HBS, 1995, Andrew Dutkiewicx and Jan Hammond)								•				
Information Flows under SAP/R3 (Stanford, 1996, Seungjin Whang and Hau Lee)						•						
Intercon (HBS, 1991, K. Mishina and M. Flaherty)					•							
International Sourcing in Athletic Footware: Nike and Reebok (HBS, 1994, Philip Rosenzweig)					•							
Kodak Business Imaging Systems Division (HBS, 1992, Steve Wheelwright)					•							•
Laura Ashley and Fedex Strategic Alliance (HBS, 1996, Robert Anthony and Gary Loveman)		•								•		
LL Bean (HBS, 1993, Arthur Schleifer)			•									
Massimo Menichetti (HBS, 1988, Ramchandran Jaikumar)					•						•	
Mattel: Vendor Operations in Asia (Vanderbilt, 1998, Eric Johnson)	•											•
Merloni Elettrodomestici SpA (HBS, 1996, Jan Hammond)		•										
National Bicycle (Wharton, 1993, Marshall Fisher)							•					
National Wine and Spirits (A&B) (Vanderbilt, 1994/1998, Eric Johnson)	•											
Nike - Global Supply Chain (Stanford, 1998, Ann-Kristen de Verdier and Seungjin Whang)					•							•
Nike in China (HBS, 1993, Jame Austin)					•							•
Orange Juice Logistics: Oceana Fruit Juice Co. (Stanford, 1994, Seungjin Whang) and The Orange Juice Logistics Case Study Florida, Richard Beilock)	•											

functional integration (Greis and Kasarda 1997) and the role of logistics in gaining competitive advantage (Fuller, O'Conor, and Rawlinson 1993).

Inventory and forecasting includes traditional inventory and forecasting models. Many business school instructors had been teaching this material for years until, about 10 years ago, it seemed to fall out of favor as qualitative approaches came to dominate operations courses. However, because of the advent of supply chain management, these models have reemerged in the classroom. Inventory costs are some of the easiest to identify and reduce when

TABLE 1 (cont'd)

Case	Location	Logistics	Inventory	Marketing	Sourcing	Information	Product Design	Service	Reverse SC	Outsourcing	Metrics	Global Issues
P&G - Wal-Mart (Darden, 1994, Mark Parry)				●								
P&G: Improving Consumer Value Through Process Redesign (HBS, 1995, Theodore Clark)				●								
Partnerships in the Supply Chain: Introducing Co-Managed Inventory at Guinness GB (CLM, 1998, Helen Peck)			●	●								
Pellton International: Partnerships or Tug of War? (UCLA, 1997, Charles Corbett and Luk van Wassenhove)					●							
Polaroid Europe (HBS, 1995, Afroze Mohammed)	●											●
Rosenbluth: Supply Chain Management in Services (Western Ontario, 1993, Allan Kamauff)						●	●					
Sara Lee: QR at Hanes (HBS, 1993, Benn Konsynski and Jiro Kokuryo)					●							
Saturn Corporation: Improving the Plant-Retail Link in the Auto Industry Supply Chain (CLM, 1996, Brian Gibson)		●										
Sof-Optics (HBS, 1991, W.E. Sasser, R. Jaikumar, D.C. Rikert)								●				
Sport Obermeyer (HBS, 1996, Ananth Raman)			●		●							
StWork (Northwestern, 1997, David Simchi-Levi)	●											
Supplier Management at Sun Microsystems (Stanford, Charles Holloway, David Farlow, Glen Schmidt, and Andy Tsay)					●							
Tenko (Stanford, 1997, Warren Hausman)							●					
The Jewel Box: A Life Cycle Case Study (CLM, 1996, Omar Helferich and Robert Sroufe)									●			
Tong Yang Cement (Stanford, 1997, Seungjin Whang, Hau Lee, Glenn Schmidt)			●									●
Toys "R" Us Japan (A&B) (CLM, 1996, Mark Kay)		●		●								
Toyota Motor Manufacturing, U.S.A., Inc. (HBS, 1995 K. Mishina, K. Takeda)					●							
Vandelay Industries (HBS, 1997, David Upton)						●						
Vanity Fair Mills (HBS, 1993, Robert Buzzell)				●								
Walls (China) Co., Ltd (CLM, 1997, Peter Gilmour)		●	●									●
Whelan Pharm. (Washington Univ., 1997, Panos Kouvelis)	●											●

attacking supply chain problems. Students need to be facile with simple models that can identify the potential cost savings from, for example, sharing information with supply chain partners (Lee and Nahmias 1993). Many schools teach some inventory theory before discussing broader supply chain issues. Of course there are many full texts on the subject such as Silver, Pyke, and Peterson (1998) and Graves, Rinnooy Kan, and Zipkin (1993). Useful managerial articles focusing on inventory and forecasting include Davis (1993) and Fisher, Hammond, Obermeyer, and Raman (1994).

Marketing and channel restructuring includes fundamental thinking on supply chain structure (Fisher 1997) and covers the interface with marketing that emerges from having to deal with downstream customers (Narus and Anderson 1996). While the inventory category addresses the quantitative side of these relationships, this category covers relationship management, negotiations, and even the legal dimension. Most importantly, it examines the role of channel management (Anderson, Day, and Rangan 1997) and supply chain structure in light of the well-studied phenomena of the bullwhip effect (Lee, Padmandbhan, and Whang 1997). These include, for example, issues related to pricing and trade promotions (Buzzell, Quelch, and Salmon 1990) and channel initiatives, such as vendor managed inventory, coordinated forecasting and replenishment, and continuous replenishment (Fites 1996; Waller, Johnson, and Davis 1999). Because many of these initiatives involve channel partnerships and distribution agreements, this category also contains important information on pricing, along with anti-trust and other legal issues (Train 1998). The opportunities for interacting with marketing faculty are, of course, the greatest here.

While marketing focuses downstream in the supply chain, *sourcing and supplier management* looks upstream to suppliers. Make/buy decisions (Venkatesan 1992; Carrol 1993; Christensen 1994; Quinn and Hilmer 1994; Kelley 1995; Robertson and Langlois 1995) fall into this category, as does global sourcing (Little 1995; Pyke 1994). The location category addresses the location of a firm's own facilities, while this category pertains to the location of the firm's suppliers. Supplier relationship management falls into this category as well (McMillan 1990; Womack, Jones, and Roos 1991). Some firms are putting part specifications on the web so that dozens of suppliers can bid on jobs. General Electric (GE), for instance, has developed a trading process network that allows many more suppliers to bid than was possible before. The automotive assemblers are developing a similar capability. Other firms are moving in the opposite direction by reducing the number of suppliers, in some cases to a sole source (Helper and Sako 1995; Cusumano and Takeishi 1991). Determining the number of suppliers and the best way to structure supplier relationships is becoming an important topic in supply chains (Cohen and Agrawal 1996; Dyer 1996; Fine 1998; Magretta 1998; Pyke 1998).

The information and electronic mediated environments category addresses long-standing applications of information technology to reduce inventory (Woolley 1997) and the rapidly expanding area of electronic commerce (Benjamin and Wigand 1997; Schonfeld 1998). Often this subject may take a more systems orientation, examining the role of systems science and information within a supply chain (Senge 1990). Such a discussion naturally focuses attention on integrative ERP software such as SAP (Whang, Gilland, and Lee 1995), Baan, and Oracle, as well as supply chain offerings such as i2's Rhythm and Peoplesoft's Red Pepper. To stay abreast of this rapidly changing field, many instructors supplement class readings with guest lectures from industry. Much of the teaching related to specific software is limited to developing an awareness of what the applications claim to do and the experience of firms that spend up to $200 million to implement them. Finally, the many supply chain changes wrought by electronic commerce are particularly interesting to examine, including both the highly publicized retail channel changes (e.g., Amazon.com) and the more substantial business to business innovations (such as the GE trading process network). It is here that we interface most directly with colleagues in information technology and strategy, which again creates opportunities for cross-course integration (Lee and Whang 1999).

Product design and new product introduction deals with design issues for mass customization, delayed differentiation, modularity, and other issues for new product introduction. With the increasing supply chain demands of product variety (Gilmore and Pine 1997; Fine 1998) and customization (McCutcheon, Raturi, and Meredith 1994), there is an increasing body of material to cover. One of the most exciting applications of "supply chain thinking" is the increased use of postponed product differentiation (Feitzinger and Lee 1997). Here we find an interface with engineering and development, with clear implications for product cost and inventory savings. Inventory models are often used to identify some of the benefits of these initiatives (Lee, Billington, and Carter 1993). Also important are issues related to managing new product introduction and product rollover (Billington, Lee, and Tang 1998).

Many excellent cases illustrate these issues, and we find that students can easily identify with many of the examples.

The service and after sales support category addresses the critical, but often overlooked, problem of providing service and service parts (Cohen and Lee 1990). Some leading firms, such as Saturn and Caterpillar, build their reputations on their ability in this area, and this capability generates significant sales (Cohen, Zheng, and Agrawal 1997). Some instructors teach inventory models for slow-moving items in this category.

Reverse logistics and green issues are emerging dimensions of supply chain management (Marien 1998). This area examines both environmental issues (Corbett and van Wassenhove 1993; Herzlinger 1994) and the reverse logistics issues of product returns (Padmanabhan and Png 1995; Clendenin 1997; Rudi and Pyke 1998). There are few teaching cases, and not many models available for this area (Fleischmann et al. 1997). Nevertheless, because of legislation and consumer pressure, the growing importance of these issues is evident to most managers. Managers are being compelled to consider the most efficient and environmentally friendly way to deal with product recovery.

Outsourcing and strategic alliances examines the supply chain impact of outsourcing logistics services. With the rapid growth in third party logistics providers, there is a large and expanding group of technologies and services to be examined. These include fascinating initiatives, such as supplier hubs managed by third parties. The rush to create strategic relationships with logistics providers and the many well-published failures have raised questions about the future of such relationships. (See Bowersox 1990; SCMR 1998), and the news stories in Table 2.) In any case, outsourcing continues to raise many interesting issues (Cooper et al. 1997b).

Metrics and incentives examines measurement and other organizational and economic issues. This category includes both measurement within the supply chain (Meyer 1997) and industry benchmarking (CLM 1994; PRTM 1997). Because metrics are fundamental to business management, there are many reading materials outside of the supply chain literature, including accounting texts for instance. Several recent articles concentrate on the link between performance measurement and supply chain improvement (O'Laughlin 1997; Johnson and Davis 1998).

Finally, *global issues* examines how all of the above categories are affected when companies operate in multiple countries. This category goes beyond country specific issues, to encompass issues related to crossboarder distribution and sourcing (Arntzen, Brown, Harrison, and Trafton 1995). For example, currency exchange rates, duties and taxes, freight forwarding, customs issues, government regulation, and country comparisons are all included. Note that the location category, when applied in a global context, also addresses some of these issues. As we mentioned earlier, there are several texts devoted to global management and a growing number of cases probe specific issues. Many recent articles also examine challenges in specific regions of the world [e.g., for Asia see Lee and Kopczak (1997) or for Europe see Sharman (1997)].

Course Structure and Pedagogy

As with other courses, instructors are rapidly innovating in the classroom. In our survey, we observed many different teaching tools and approaches. In most business school classes, the overall approach is still case dominated, with more than half of the sessions dedicated to case discussions. Table 1 provides an extensive list of recent (since 1990) cases used by instructors to illustrate supply chain concepts. The cases are classified within our framework of 12 areas. Since many cases cover multiple areas, we limited the classification to 2 or 3 of the most important points. As can be seen from the table, there are some areas where cases are lacking—specifically in areas of service and after-sales support, reverse logistics and green issues, outsourcing and strategic alliances, and metrics and incentives. Besides the

TABLE 2

Supply Chain News Clippings

1. Location

"Green is Good," *Economist*, May 17, 1997.
"Shape of Supply Chain," *Traffic World*, June 8, 1998.
"Texas Instruments' Global Chip Payoff," *Business Week*, August 7, 1996, 64.

2. Logistics and Transportation

"Just Get it to the Stores on Time," *Business Week*, March 6, 1995, 66.
"More Often, Delays and Snafus Grip America's Rail Freight," *Wall Street Journal*, May 29, 1998.
"Logistics for Profit," *Fortune*, April 1, 1996.
"Frito-Lay Devours Snack Food Business," *The Wall Street Journal*, October 27, 1995.
"Logistics Revolution Spreads Stealthily," *Chicago Tribune*, November 12, 1995.
"U.S. Questions Sales Practices at Frito Lay," *Wall Street Journal*, Friday May 24, 1996.
"Next-Day Delivery: Cadillac Lowering Costs and Raising Satisfaction by Getting Cars to Consumers Faster," *Chicago Tribune*, April 2, 1998.
"Delivering the Goods," *Fortune*, November 28, 1994.

3. Inventory and Forecasting

"Global Pile-Up," *Economist*, May 10, 1997, 21.
"Burned By Busy Signals," *Business Week*, March 6, 1995, 36.
"Capacity Boosts Take Toll on Many Firms," *Wall Street Journal*, October 21, 1996.
"Hot Wheels," *Business Week*, September 15, 1997, 56.
"Autos: How Do You Get a Hot GMC Suburban? You Wait for a Computer to Dole One Out," *Wall Street Journal*, April 10, 1996.
"Publishing Industry's Focus Shifts To Limiting Returns," *New York Times*, July 27, 1998.
"At Christmas, Retailers Are Like Kids Who Ask Santa Claus for a Pony," *Wall Street Journal*, October 27, 1997.
"Beetlemania Hits America Again Fueling Gray Market, Waiting Lists," *Wall Street Journal*, May 1, 1998.
"Tired of Renting 'Shanghai Surprise'? Blockbuster, Hollywood Hope to Help," *Wall Street Journal*, March 25, 1998.
"Sold Out: Corvette's 6-Speed Manual More Popular than Expected," *Chicago Tribune*, April 12, 1998.
"Laptop Buyers Struggle with Shortages," *Wall Street Journal*, November 20, 1996.
"Compaq Shuts Down Its Biggest Plant To Rid Inventory of Unsold Computers," *Wall Street Journal*, April 24, 1998.
"Market Place: Sales Gain for Sunbeam Is Costly to Investors," *New York Times*, May 7 1998.

4. Marketing and Channel Restructuring

"The Gap Plots Panty Raid on Victoria's Secret," *Wall Street Journal*, October 1, 1998.
"P&G, Seeing Shoppers Were Being Confused, Overhauls Marketing," *Wall Street Journal*, January 15, 1997.
"Some Companies Let Suppliers Work on Site And Even Place Orders," *Wall Street Journal*, January 13, 1995.
"Chain Reaction: Book Superstores Bring Hollywood-Like Risks to Publishing Business," *Wall Street Journal*, May 29, 1997.
"In Publishing, Bigger is Better," *New York Times*, March 31, 1998.
"PepsiCo Chief's Stand on Exclusive Pacts Adds to Cola Wars' Charged Atmosphere," *Wall Street Journal*, May 15, 1998.
"How Magazines Make It to Stores—And Why They Soon May Not," *Wall Street Journal*, February 26, 1998.
"The Dumbest Marketing Ploy," *Fortune*, October 5, 1992.
"Anheuser-Busch Chugs On Amid Probe of Distribution," *Wall Street Journal*, March 9, 1998.
"New World, Ordered," *INC*, (Solomon) December, 1995.
"The $30 Billion Promise," *Traffic Management*, December, 1993, J.A. Cooke.
"Efficient Consumer Responses," *Food Processing*, February, 1994, F. Crawford.

5. Sourcing and Supplier Management

"Is this the Factory of the Future," *New York Times*, July 26, 1998.
"Strange Bedfellows: Some Companies let Suppliers Work on Site and Even Place Orders," *Wall Street Journal*, January 13, 1995.
"VW, Suppliers Work Side By Side, Seek Big Gains in Productivity, At 'Factory of the Future', in Brazil," *Automotive News*, June 9, 1997.
Walton, M. "When Your Partner Fails You . . . ." *Fortune*, May 26, 1997, 151–154.
"How IBM Turned Around Its Ailing PC Division," *Wall Street Journal*, March 12, 1998.
"GM, in Possible Blow to U.S. Steel Firms, Is Broadening Its Suppliers World-Wide," *Wall Street Journal*, April 14, 1998.
"Gibson Greetings Plans to Outsource Manufacturing of Cards, Gift Wraps," *Wall Street Journal*, April 1, 1998.

TABLE 2 (cont'd)

6. Information and Electronic Mediated Environments
"It's a Wired, Wired World," *CFO*, September 1997, 63–68.
"High-Tech Inventory System Coordinates Retailer's Clothes With Customers' Taste," *Wall Street Journal*, June 12, 1996.
"On-Line Investors Don't Sing Praises of Music Seller N2K," *Wall Street Journal*, March 6, 1998.
Electronic Commerce. *The Economist*, 1–18, May 10, 1997.
Engardio, P. "Souping Up the Supply Chain." *Business Week*, August 31, 1998, 110–112.
Gross, N. "Leapfrogging a Few Links." *Business Week*, June 22, 1998, 141–142.
Hof, R. D., McWilliams, G., and Saveri, G. "The 'Click Here' Economy," *Business Week*, June 22, 1998, 122–128.
Stepanek, M. "Rebirth of the Salesman," *Business Week*, June 22, 1998, 146–147.
"A Small Card Maker Finds Itself Atop the Web," *New York Times*, June 4, 1997.
"Online Sellers Learn How to Get Packages to Consumers," *New York Times*, March 30, 1998.
"Cyberspace Grocery Shoppers Can't Squeeze Produce," *New York Times*, May 12, 1998.
"An Online Grocer Bets Against Bananas and Meat," *New York Times*, May 4, 1998
"Whirlwind on the Web," *Business Week*, April 7, 1997.
"Spain's Zara Cuts a Dash With 'Fashion on Demand," *Wall Street Journal*, May 29, 1998.

7. Product Design and New Product Introduction
"Can Butterfly Help IBM Fly Higher?," *Wall Street Journal*, June 6, 1995.
"Can Honda Build a World Car," *Business Week*, October 8, 1997, 100.
"Goodyear Posts Small Profit, Unveils Improvement Plans," *Wall Street Journal*, February 10, 1998.
"Ford Motor Reaches Agreement To Create Retail Network in Utah," *Wall Street Journal*, May 19, 1998.

8. Service and After Sales Support
"You Need It, We Got It," *Forbes*, May 20, 1996.

9. Reverse Logistics and Green Issues
"Some Vendors Pay Big Sums to Get Competing Goods Off Store Shelves," *Wall Street Journal*, May 15, 1998.
"The Greening of the Supply Chain," *Supply Chain Management Review*, Summer, 1998, 76–86.

10. Outsourcing and Strategic Alliances
"Messy Divorce," *American Shipper*, March, 1998, 22–26.
"Driving Force: In Today's Economy, There is Big Money to be Made in Logistics," *Wall Street Journal*, September 6, 1995.
"New Dana Illustrates Reshaping of Auto Parts Business," *Wall Street Journal*, September 2, 1997.
"Dell to Outsource all its Shipping to Roadway Unit," *Wall Street Journal*, February 15, 1995.
"Short Supply: Success of AIDS Drug has Merck Fighting to Keep up the Pace," *Wall Street Journal*, November 5, 1996.
"Ryder Sys Unit To Manage Ford Motor N. Amer Supply Chain," *Wall Street Journal*, July 21, 1998.
"Carpet Makers Confront Era That Extols Wood Floors," *Wall Street Journal*, March 31, 1998.
"What is the future for Third-Party Logistics?" *Supply Chain Management Review*, 1998.

11. Metrics and Incentives
"Give Them What They Want," *Management Review*, November, 1998.
"Seven Greatest Myths of Measurement," *Management Review*, May 1997, 29–32.

12. Global Issues
"Gillette Won't Meet Certain Goals While Emerging Markets Face Turmoil," *Wall Street Journal*, September 30, 1998
"Whirlpool Found U.S. Methods Didn't Always Apply in Europe," *Wall Street Journal*, April 10, 1998.
"Orient Express: Just How Hard Should A U.S. Company Woo Foreign Markets?" *Wall Street Journal*, April 6, 1998.
"Nike Plans Changes at Asia Plants, Raising Workers' Minimum Age," *Wall Street Journal*, May 13, 1998.
"Levi Strauss, Citing Rights Gains, to Expand Role in China," *New York Times*, April 9, 1998.
"Trying to Avoid Tariffs, Old World Pasta Makers Go American," *New York Times*, February 28, 1998.

listed cases, there are several texts that contain cases including Flaherty (1996), Dornier, Ernst, Fender, and Kouvelis (1998), and Cavinato and Young (1996). Additionally, the Council of Logistics Management (CLM) publishes cases related to logistics. To supplement case discussions, some instructors use recent business press stories to update issues in the

TABLE 3

Class Structures for a Selection of Successful Supply Chain Classes and Supply Chain Modules within Other Classes

Session	Topic	Case
Stanford University, GSB (Winter 99, Whang/Lee)—Graduate Engineering/MBA Elective		
1	What is Integrated SCM?	
2	Information Distortion	
3	Inventory Models	
4	Countering Bullwhip	Barilla
5	Postponement	HP Deskjet
6	Product Universality	HP Network
7	Mass Customization	National Bike
8	Accurate Response	Obermeyer
9	Data-Driven SCM	Seven Eleven Japan
10	SCM Performance Measures	
11	SC Restructuring	Amhall
12	Supplier Hub	Apple Computer
13	Supply Chain Design	Mattel Inc.
14	Information and Logistics Restructuring	
15	E-Commerce and SCM	
16	Distribution Network	Polaroid
17	After Sales Service Support	
18	Right SC for Right Product/Time	
19	SC Integration	
Vanderbilt University (Fall 98, Johnson)—MBA Elective		
1	Introduction	
2	Supply Chain Metrics	Guest Speaker
3	Inventory	HP: Spokane Division
4	Inventory Laboratory	
5	Mass Customization/Postponement	HP: Deskjet
6	Short Product Life	L.L. Bean
7	Global Facility Location	Mattel: Vendor Operations in Asia
8	Transportation and Distribution	
9	Distribution System Design	National Wine and Spirits: A
10	Distribution System Implementation	National Wine and Spirits: B
11	Product Introduction and Rollover	
12	Optimizing Logistics Flow	General Appliance
13	Information, EDI, and VMI	Vanity Fair Mills
14	Plant Trip—FedEx Midnight Sort	
15	Outsourcing logistics services (3PL)	Apple Computer
16	E-Commerce and Direct Distribution	
Ohio State University, (Spring 98, Cooper)—MBA Elective		
1	Introduction	
2	Integration: Process and Function	
3	Interfirm Integration	Guest Speaker
4	Beer Game	
5	Beer Game Debrief	
6	Military Logistics	
7	Economics of Integration	Guest Speaker
8	Cost Issues	
9	Consulting in SC	Guest Speaker
10	Opportunities and Pitfalls	
11	Managing Components	
12	Changing Role of Purchasing & Sales	
13	Outsourcing	
14	Japanese Keiretsu	Guest Speaker
15	Reverse Logistics and Recycling	

TABLE 3 (cont'd)

Session	Topic	Case
Ohio State University, (Spring 98, Cooper)—MBA Elective (cont'd)		
16	GIS and Modeling	Guest Speaker
17	Symposium	
18	International Issues	
19	Future Perspectives	
Duke University (Fall 98, Cachon)—MBA Elective		
1	Introduction	
2	Transportation	Frito-Lay
3	Incentives, Contracts & Legal Issues	
4	Postponement	HP: Deskjet
5	Managing Product Variety	Brueggers and Chesapeake Bakeries
6	Transit point and cross docking	Merloni SpA
7	Vendor Managed Inventory	Barilla
8	Accurate/Quick Response	Sport Obermeyer
9	Procurement/Supplier Management	Supplier Management at Sun
10	Outsourcing	
11	International SC	International Sourcing in Athletic Footwear
12	Electronic Commerce	
Northwestern University (Fall 98, Simchi-Levi)—Graduate Engineering/MBA Elective, Three-hour sessions [based on textbook: Simchi-Levi et al. (1998)]		
1	Introduction, Information, and DSS	
2	Network Planning and Design	StWork Corp.
3	Inventory Management	Sport Obermeyer
4	SC Integration	Computerized Beer Game
5	Strategic Alliances and Outsourcing	Barilla
6	Product Design and Postponement	HP Deskjet
Penn State (Fall 98, Tyworth)—MBA Elective		
1	Introduction and Strategy Overview	
2	Customer Service	
3	Collaborative Forecasting	Guest speaker
4	Beer Game	
5	Bullwhip Phenomenon, VMI	Barilla
6	Inventory—Stochastic Models	
7	Inventory—TPOP Models	
8	Transportation	Burlington Northern
9	Process Management/Transportation	Saturn Corp.
10	Mass Customization and Postponement	HP Deskjet
11	Third Party Logistics	Apple Computer
12	Global Logistics	Guest speaker
13	Information Technology	Guest speaker
14	Performance Measurement	
15	Future Perspectives	
Dartmouth College (Spring 99, Pyke)—A supply chain module as part of a 18-session MBA elective on Manufacturing Strategy		
1	Supply Chain Structure	National Bicycle Industrial Co.
2	Facilities Location; European country differences	Alden Products, Inc.
3	Manufacturing in Asia; Currency Fluctuations	Mattel—Asia Manufacturing
4	Distribution Strategy	Bradco/Taylor
5	Third party logistics	Apple Supplier Hub
6	Postponement and Inventory	Hewlett Packard Universal
7	Supply Relationships	Intercon Japan
8	Supply Chain Restructuring	Massimo Menichetti
9	Lecture on Supply Relationships	

TABLE 3 (cont'd)

Session	Topic	Case
Wharton (Spring 99, Cohen and Ellison)—Supply chain treatment in a 12-session core MBA class on Operations Strategy		
1	Introduction	
2	Matching Capacity to Demand	General Appliance
3	Supply Chain Simulation	Beer Game
4	Beer Game Debrief	
5	Vendor-Managed Inventory	Barilla Pasta
6	Inventory Management: Lecture	
7	Applications of Inventory Management & Postponement	Hewlett Packard Deskjet
8	Mass Customization	National Bicycle
9	Accurate Response	Sport Obermeyer
10	Yield Management	Piedmont Airlines
11	Product Development	Cyclone Grinder
12	Concurrent Design Lecture	

case or to highlight emerging business trends. Table 2 provides a list of such news stories, again categorized within our framework. Another common supplement to lectures and cases is guest industry speakers, particularly for rapidly changing, technology-based content.

Beyond the lecture and case format, many instructors use at least one game/simulation or interactive exercise. By far the most popular simulation is the Beer Game (Sterman 1989, 1992). This game has a rich history, growing out of the industrial dynamics work of Forrester and others at MIT (Forrester 1961; Jarmain 1963). The game is so widely used, that in some cases, it is not used in supply chain electives simply because students have already played the game in an earlier class. There are many variants of the game including computer-based versions (Simchi-Levi, Kaminsky, and Simchi-Levi 1998; Chen and Samroengraja 1997) and Web-based versions (Jacobs 2000; Porteus 1998).

The Siemens Briefcase game is another supply chain game designed to be played by small groups (12–18 people) over an extended period of 1 to 3 days. The game illustrates many details of an order-based system with significant customization (Siemens 1996; Mehring, Kotler, and Kiesel 1997). The Llenroc Plastics game (Jackson 1995) is another more detailed simulation that can be played over several class periods. The Poster game is a simple game to illustrate the difficulties of forecasting and inventory planning for perishable goods (Johnson 1998b). Finally, class projects are an important part of many courses.

Table 3 contains abbreviated class syllabi for several different supply chain classes and modules. All of these classes have been successfully conducted for 4 to 5 years, garnering high teaching ratings. These classes were chosen to show a range of treatments from both graduate business programs and engineering. As one would expect, engineering classes tend to be more technical with less reliance on cases. The last two examples show supply chain modules within other courses. In general, we can see most of the 12 key components of supply chain management in each of these courses. However, there is divergence in the treatment of the topics and their relative importance within the course. Least represented is material on reverse logistics and green issues, possibly because of the dearth of teaching material.

Conclusion

As we have shown, there is a wide and growing body of materials for teaching supply chain management. As with many areas in management education, however, very current cases on hot topics are always in short supply. Since supply chain concepts are so closely integrated with other functional areas, there is a vast set of topics to cover, and specific classes often concentrate on specific areas such as logistics, manufacturing, or marketing. Likewise, supply chain concepts are often taught by instructors in several functional areas including marketing, operations, and logistics. In the future, we expect supply chain issues to become increasingly important as eBusiness and globalization drive the need for closer functional integration. This will only serve to fuel the demand for supply chain education.[1]

---

[1] The authors thank the participants of the Stanford Supply Chain Thought Leaders Conference; all those who shared their syllabi with us; and Gerard Cachon, Kyle Cattani, Edward Davis, Hau Lee, Ed Silver, David Simchi-Levi, Andy Tsay, Gene Tyworth, and Jin Whang for helpful comments.

References

ANDERSON, E., G. DAY, AND V. RANGAN (1997), "Strategic Channel Design," *Sloan Management Review*, Summer, 59–69.
ARNTZEN, B. C., G. G. BROWN, T. P. HARRISON, AND L. L. TRAFTON (1995), "Global Supply Chain Management at Digital Equipment Corporation," *Interfaces*, 25, 1, 69–93.
BALLOU, R. H. (1998), *Business Logistics Management: Planning, Organizing, and Controlling the Supply Chain*, 4th ed., Prentice Hall, New York.
BENJAMIN, R. AND R. WIGAND (1997), "Electronic Markets and Virtual Value Chain on the Info Super Highway," *Sloan Management Review*, Winter, 62–72.
BILLINGTON, C., H. L. LEE, AND C. S. TANG (1998), "Successful Strategies for Product Rollovers," *Sloan Management Review*, Spring, 23–30.
BOWERSOX, D. J. (1990), "The Strategic Benefits of Logistics Alliances," Harvard Business Review, July/August, 36–45.
BUZZELL, R., J. QUELCH, AND W. SALMON (1990), "The Costly Bargain of Trade Promotions," *Harvard Business Review,* March-April, 141–149.
CARROLL, P. (1993), *Big Blues*, Crown Publishers, New York.
CAVINATO, J. L. AND R. R. YOUNG (1996), "Logistics Casebook," Smeal College of Business Administration, Penn State University, State College.
CHEN, F. AND R. SAMROENGRAJA (1997), "Supply Chain Simulations," Columbia Business School, New York.
CHRISTENSEN, C. M. (1994), *The Drivers of Vertical Disintegration*, Harvard Business School, Cambridge, Mass.
CLENDENIN, J. A. (1997), "Closing the Supply Chain Loop: Reengineering the Returns Channel Process," *International Journal of Logistics Management*, 8, 1, 75–85.
CLM (1994), "Integrated-Supply-Chain Performance Measurement," *Council of Logistics Management Consortium*, October.
COHEN, M. A. AND N. AGRAWAL (1996), "An Empirical Investigation of Supplier Management Practices," The Wharton School, Operations and Information Management Department, University of Pennsylvania, Philadelphia.
COHEN, M. AND H. LEE (1990), "Out of Touch with Customer Needs? Spare Parts and After Sales Service," *Sloan Management Review*, 31, 2, 55–66.
COHEN, M. A., Y. ZHENG, AND V. AGRAWAL (1997), "Service Parts Logistics: A Benchmark Analysis," *IIE Transactions*, 29, 8, 627–639.
COOPER, M. C., D. M. LAMBERT, AND J. D. PAGH (1997a), "Supply Chain Management: More Than a New Name for Logistics," *International Journal of Logistics Management*, 8, 1, 1–14.
———, L. M. ELLRAM, J. T. GARDNER, AND A. M. HANKS (1997b), "Meshing Multiple Alliances," *Journal of Business of Logistics*, 18, 1, 67–89.
COPACINO, W.C. (1997), *Supply Chain Management: The Basics and Beyond*, St. Lucie Press/APICS Series on Resource Management, Falls Creek, VA.
CORBETT, C. AND L. VAN WASSENHOVE (1993), "The Green Fee: Internalizing and Operationalizing Environmental Issues," California Management Review 36, Fall, 116–135.
CUSUMANO, M. A. AND A. TAKEISHI (1991), "Supplier Relations and Management: A Survey of Japanese, Japanese-Transplants, and U.S. Auto Plants," *Strategic Management Journal*, 12 (Nov–Dec).
DAVIS, T. (1993), "Effective Supply Chain Management," *Sloan Management Review*, 34, 4, 35–46.
DORNIER, P-P., R. ERNST, M. FENDER, AND P. KOUVELIS (1998), *Global Operations and Logistics: Text and Cases*, John Wiley & Sons, New York.
DREZNER, Z. (1996), *Facility Location: A Survey of Applications and Methods*, Springer Series in Operations Research, Springer–Verlag, New York.
DYER, J. H. (1996), "How Chrysler Created an American Keiretsu," *Harvard Business Review* July–August, 42–56.
FEITZINGER, E. AND H. L. LEE (1997), "Mass Customization at Hewlett-Packard: The Power of Postponement," *Harvard Business Review*, Jan–Feb, 116–121.

FINE, C. H. (1998), *Clock Speed: Winning Industry Control in the Age of Temporary Advantage*, Perseus Books, Reading, Mass.

FISHER, M. (1997), "What is the Right Supply Chain for your Product?" *Harvard Business Review*, March–April, 105–116.

———, J. HAMMOND, W. OBERMEYER, AND A. RAMAN (1994), "Making Supply Meet Demand in an Uncertain World," *Harvard Business Review*, May/June, 83–93.

FITES, D. V. (1996), "Make Your Dealers Your Partners," *Harvard Business Review*, March–April, 84–95.

FLAHERTY, M. T. (1996), *Global Operations Management*, McGraw-Hill Company, New York.

FLEISCHMANN, M., J. M. BLOEMHOF-RUWAARD, R. DEKKER, E. VAN DER LAAN, J. A. E. E. VAN NUNEN, AND L. N. VAN WASSENHOVE (1997), "Quantitative Models for Reverse Logistics: A Review," *European Journal of Operational Research*, 103, 1, 1–17.

FORRESTER, J. W. (1958), "Industrial Dynamics: A Major Breakthrough for Decision Makers," *Harvard Business Review*, July/August, 37–66.

——— (1961), *Industrial Dynamics*, Productively Press, Cambridge Mass.

FULLER, J. B., J. O'CONOR, AND R. RAWLINSON (1993), "Tailored Logistics: The Next Advantage," *Harvard Business Review*, May/June, 87–93.

GILMORE, J. H. AND B. J. PINE (1997), "The Four Faces of Mass Customization," *Harvard Business Review*, Jan–Feb, 1997, 91–101.

GRAVES, S., A. RINNOOY KAN, P. H. ZIPKIN (1993), *Logistics of Production and Inventory*, North-Holland, New York.

GREIS, N. P. AND J. D. KASARDA (1997), "Enterprise Logistics in the Information Era," *California Management Review*, 39, 4, 55–78.

——— AND M. KELLY (1990), *Note on Facility Location,* Harvard Business School Note 689-059.

——— AND J. E. P. MORRISON (1995), "A Note on the U.S. Transportation Industry," Harvard Note 9-688-080.

HANDFIELD, R. B. AND E. Z. NICHOLS (1998), *Introduction to Supply Chain Management,* Prentice Hall Press, New York.

HELPER, S. AND M. SAKO (1995), "Supplier Relations in Japan and the United States: Are They Converging?" *Sloan Management Review,* Spring, 77–84.

HERZLINGER, R. (1994), "The Challenges of Going Green," *Harvard Business Review,* July–August, 37–50.

JACKSON, P. J (1995), "Llenroc Plastics Corporation," Cornell University, Department of Operations Research and Industrial Engineering.

JACOBS, R. (2000) "Playing the Beer Distribution Game Over the Internet," *Production and Operations Management,* to appear.

JARMAIN, W. E. (1963), *Problems in Industrial Dynamics,* MIT Press, Cambridge, Mass.

JOHNSON, M. E. (1998a), "Give Them What They Want," *Management Review,* November, 62–67.

——— (1998b), "A Note on the Poster Game," Owen Graduate School of Management, Vanderbilt University.

——— AND T. DAVIS (1998), "Improving Supply Chain Performance Using Order Fulfillment Metrics," *National Productivity Review,* Summer, 3–16.

KELLEY, B. (1995), "Outsourcing Marches On," *Journal of Business Strategy,* July–Aug, 39–42.

KOPCZAK, L., H. L. LEE, AND S. WHANG (1995), "Note on Logistics," Stanford University.

LAMBERT, D. M., J. R. STOCK, L. M. ELLRAM, AND J. STOCKDALE (1997), *Fundamentals of Logistics Management,* McGraw Hill Text, New York.

LEE, H. AND C. BILLINGTON (1992), "Managing Supply Chain Inventories: Pitfalls and Opportunities," *Sloan Management Review*, 33, 3, 65–73.

——— AND S. WHANG (1999), "Information Sharing in a Supply Chain," *International Journal of Technology Management,* to appear.

LEE, H. L., C. BILLINGTON, AND B. CARTER (1993), "Hewlett-Packard Gains Control of Inventories and Service Through Design for Localization," *Interfaces,* 23, 4, 1–11.

——— AND L. KOPCZAK (1997), "Responding to the Asia-Pacific Challenge," *Supply Chain Management Review,* Spring, 8–9.

——— AND S. NAHMIAS (1993), "Single-Product, Single-Location Models," in *Logistics of Production and Inventory*, S. Graves, A. Rinnooy Kan, and P. H. Zipkin, eds., North-Holland, New York.

———, V. PADMANDBHAN, AND S. WHANG (1997), "The Bullwhip Effect in Supply Chains," *Sloan Management Review,* Spring, 93–102.

LITTLE, A. D. (1995), *An Exchange of Knowledge Among Leading Practitioners in Supply Chain Management,* A.D. Little and Associates, Boston, Mass.

MAGRETTA, J. (1998), "The Power of Virtual Integration: An Interview with Dell Computer's Michael Dell," *Harvard Business Review,* March–April, 72.

MARIEN, E. J. (1998), "Reverse Logistics as Competitive Strategy," *Supply Chain Management Review,* Spring, 43–52.

MCCUTCHEON, D. M., A. S. RATURI, AND J. R. MEREDITH (1994), "The Customization-Responsiveness Squeeze," *Sloan Management Review,* Winter, 89–99.

MCMILLAN, J. (1990), "Managing Suppliers: Incentive systems in Japanese and U.S. Industry," *California Management Review,* Summer, 38–55.

MEHRING, J. S., M. KOTLER, AND J. KIESEL (1997), *Improving Supply Chain Performance at BCG Company: Learning with Lego Blocks,* University of Massachusetts, Lowell.

MEYER, M. (1997), *The Performance Imperative,* Wharton School Working Paper, University of Pennsylvania.

NARUS, J. A. AND J. C. ANDERSON (1996), "Rethinking Distribution: Adaptive Channels," *Harvard Business Review,* July/August, 112–120.

O'LAUGHLIN, K. A. (1997), "Five Steps to Improved Performance Measurement," *Supply Chain Management Review,* Fall, 52–58.

PADMANABHAN, V. AND I. P. L. PNG (1995), "Return Policies: Make Money by Making Good," *Sloan Management Review,* Fall, 65–72.

PORTEUS, E. L. (1998), "Web-Based Beer Game," Stanford University Executive Seminar, August.

PRTM (1997), "The Keys to Unlocking Your Supply Chains Competitive Advantage," Pittiglio Rabin Todd & McGrath, Waltham, Mass.

PYKE, D. F. (1994), "Global Sourcing at Second Glance," *Global Competitor,* 1, 3, 70–74.

——— (1998), "Strategies for Global Sourcing," *Financial Times,* February 20, (part 4 of 10 on "Mastering Global Business"), 2–4.

ROBERTSON, P. L. AND R. N. LANGLOIS (1995), "Innovation, Networks, and Vertical Integration," *Research Policy,* 24, 4, 543–562.

RUDI, N. AND D. F. PYKE (1998), "Product Recovery at the Norwegian Health Insurance Administration," *Interfaces,* to appear.

QUINN, J. B. AND F. HILMER (1994), "Strategic Outsourcing," *Sloan Management Review,* Summer, 43–55.

SCHONFELD, E. (1998), "The Customized, Digitized, Have-it-your-way Economy," *Fortune,* September 28, 115–124.

SCMR (1998), "What is the future for Third-Party Logistics?" *Supply Chain Management Review,* 2, 1.

SENGE, P. (1990), *The Fifth Discipline,* Doubleday, New York.

SHARMAN, G. J. (1997), "Supply Chain Lesson From Europe," *Supply Chain Management Review,* Fall, 11–13.

SIEMENS (1996), "Supply Chain Workshop: Briefcase Game," Siemens Corporation, Corporate Logistics North America, Newark, N.J.

SILVER, E. A., D. F. PYKE, AND R. PETERSON (1998), *Inventory Management and Production Planning and Scheduling,* 3rd ed., John Wiley & Sons, New York.

SIMCHI-LEVI, D., P. KAMINSKY, AND E. SIMCHI-LEVI (1998), *Designing and Managing the Supply Chain,* Irwin/McGraw-Hill, New York.

STERMAN, J. D. (1989), "Modeling Managerial Behavior: Misperceptions of Feedback in a Dynamic Decision Making Experiment," *Management Science,* 35, 3, 321–339.

——— (1992), "Teaching Takes Off: Flight Simulators for Management Education," *OR/MS Today,* October, 40–43.

TAYLOR, D. (1997), *Global Cases in Logistics and Supply Chain Management,* International Thomson Business Press, New York.

TRAIN, J. (1998), *Legal Issues Affecting Distribution and Supply,* Fuqua School of Business Working Paper.

VAN WASSENHOVE, L. AND M. CORBEYZ, (1998), *Production and Operations Management Core Course Teaching at the Top 20 MBA Programmes in the USA,* INSEAD Working Paper, Fontainebleau Cedex, France.

VENKATESAN, R. (1992), "Strategic sourcing: To make or not to make," *Harvard Business Review,* Nov–Dec, 98–107.

WALLER, M., M. E. JOHNSON, AND T. DAVIS (1999), "Vendor Managed Inventory in the Retail Supply Chain," *Journal of Business Logistics,* 20, 1, 183–203.

WHANG, S., W. GILLAND, AND H. L. LEE (1995), *Information Flows in Manufacturing under SAP R/3,* Stanford University Working Paper.

WOMACK, J. P., D. T. JONES, AND D. ROOS (1991), *The Machine that Changed the World: The Story of Lean Production.* Harper Perennial, New York, New York.

WOOLLEY, S. (1997), "Replacing Inventory with Information," *Forbes,* March 24, 54–58.

M. Eric Johnson is Associate Professor at the Tuck Graduate School of Business, Dartmouth College. Previously he was Associate Professor at the Owen Graduate School of Management, Vanderbilt University. He teaches courses on supply chain management, operations management, and simulation. He was previously employed by Hewlett-Packard Co. as a manufacturing engineering specialist and Systems Modeling Corp. as a consulting engineer. Through grants from the National Science Foundation, Hewlett-Packard Co., and Pepsi-Cola, Eric is conducting research in supply chain logistics, including manufacturing capacity planning, transportation system design, and inventory measurement and control. His articles have appeared in such journals as *Management Science, Operations Research, Naval Research Logistics, IIE Transactions,* and *Transportation Science.* He is currently serving on the editorial boards of *Operations Research, Management Science, Production and Operations Management, International Journal of Logistics Management,* and *Manufacturing and*

Service Operations Management. He is a research fellow of the Stanford Global Supply Chain Forum and a vice president of INFORMS. He holds a B.S. in Industrial Engineering, B.S. in Economics, an M.S. in Industrial Engineering and Operations Research from Penn State University, and a Ph.D. in Industrial Engineering from Stanford University.

David Pyke is Professor of Operations Management at the Amos Tuck School of Business Administration at Dartmouth College, where he has been on the faculty since (1987). His research interests include supply chain management, inventory systems, product recovery systems, logistics, and manufacturing in China. He has published papers in such journals as *Management Science, Decision Sciences, Naval Research Logistics, International Journal of Production Research,* and *Journal of Operations Management.* He serves on the editorial boards of *Management Science, Naval Research Logistics, Manufacturing & Service Operations Management,* and *Journal of Outsourcing.* He is a member of the Institute for Operations Research and Management Sciences, the American Production and Inventory Control Society, and the International Society for Inventory Research. He is also a Fellow of the Center for Asia and the Emerging Economies, at the Tuck School of Business.

LEVERAGING SERVICE QUALITY THROUGH SUPPLY CHAIN MANAGEMENT*

MICHAEL T. SWEENEY AND ROBIN LANE

Cranfield School of Management, Cranfield, Bedford, United Kingdom MK43 0AL
Cranfield School of Management, Cranfield, Bedford, United Kingdom MK43 0AL

Recent research into the teaching of Operations Management highlighted a consensus on the need for better balances between service and manufacturing, strategy and tools/techniques. In response to this a new Supply Chain Management case study has been written with healthcare as its subject. Key issues described in the case study are the strategy and tactics used by a nonprofit-oriented business in response to the political imperative of improving customer service and reducing operating costs. The case also enables consideration of the costs and benefits of customer and supplier colocation and their impact on supply chain management.
(TEACHING, SUPPLY CHAIN MANAGEMENT, CASE STUDY)

1. Introduction

This paper presents some initial experiences in using a new case study to teach MBA students about Supply Chain Management (SCM) within a core course on Operations Management (OM). Previous teaching experience suggested that most SCM case studies were concerned with two important issues: (1) the improvement of customer/supplier relationships and (2) the use of information systems to improve the speed and value of communication along the supply chain (e.g., through point-of-sale systems). A new case study and complementary educational material were needed to facilitate coverage of a broader range of issues within SCM, including the deployment of a supplier's personnel within customers' organizations, novel approaches using manufacturing SCM techniques within a service context, and gaining competitive advantage by moving key value-adding activities along the chain.

2. Background

The new case study has been developed against a background of research into OM teaching that highlighted a consensus on the need for better balances between service and manufacturing, strategy and tools/techniques (Goffin 1998). Consequently, the supply chain for the National Health Service (NHS) in Britain was chosen as the subject because it combines a unique set of OM challenges with a very complex supply management task in a service organization that is not profit-oriented. The case does not contain large amounts of detailed data to support teaching of tools or techniques; instead, it contains descriptive information

---

* Received December 1998; revision received May 1999; accepted September 1999.

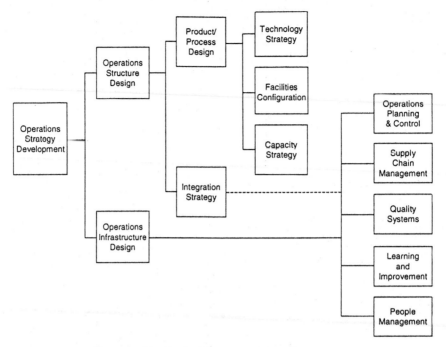

FIGURE 1. The Key Decision Areas of Operations Strategy.

that portrays an overall picture of the complex business issues that exist at both strategic and tactical levels (Lane, Sweeney and Lincoln 1998).

The OM Content Imperatives

Previous research into OM teaching also identified a critical need for an overarching framework that shows the interdependencies of the many operations design options to be discussed on an OM core course. (Goffin 1998). Figure 1 shows a top level conceptual framework developed to meet this need. It links the key decision areas of operations strategy to the range of process and resource management activities performed to build and maintain a competitive operational performance.

At the beginning of the course this framework is used to establish the importance of OM to a business, fulfilling the need described by Leschke (1998). The framework is also used as a precursor to a discussion of SCM, to highlight the importance of this topic in developing a competitive capability (Christopher 1997).

3. Educational Objectives of the Case Study

The NHS case study was designed to achieve two educational objectives:

1. To enable students to discover the planning and control procedures used for the management of an international supply chain. A feature of this case study is that its focus is a nonprofit-oriented service organization supplied by profit-oriented manufacturers.

2. To contextualize the dilemma of managing both the risk of failure of supply and the need to minimize inventory costs. This case provides an opportunity for a discussion of how to balance these two conflicting operations management problems, knowing that supply shortages may prove to be life threatening.

Thus the following study questions are set for students:

1. Prepare two diagrams that model, or map, the supply chain described in the case study and that can be used to facilitate its management.

2. What are the consequences of the current supply chain arrangements for stock management in the hospital in terms of:
   a. costs?
   b. timeliness?
3. How could the supply of stock and nonstock items be better managed for the operating theater staff and their cost of inventories further reduced?

4. Precursors to Use of the Case Study

The NHS case study enables the greatest learning when used after the operations planning and control topic (including inventory management) has been covered. Students should also be familiar with Richard Lamming's lean supply concept, which extends the simple customer-supplier relationship to one of equal partnership status (Lamming 1993).

The introduction to the case study should be a discussion of some of the well-established tools and concepts of SCM. To date the authors have found the following are most appropriate:
1. A definition of the objectives of supply chain management and how mapping can facilitate this process. Two methods of mapping are covered:
   a. The tier relationship diagram, which shows the interdependencies throughout the supply chain, as detailed in Slack and associates (1998).
   b. The map that shows each stage of the supply chain, complete with its throughput time and the level of inventory held (Scott and Westbrook 1991).
2. A simulation exercise to demonstrate the supply chain dynamics that create volatility upstream (Forrester 1961) and the need along the supply chain for up-to-date information about market demand.
3. Use of the variety funnel to show how management of variety along the supply chain can enhance flexibility and reduce stockholding costs, as applied by Benetton (Heskett and Signorelli 1985) and illustrated in Figure 2.

5. The NHS Case Study

Within the NHS supply chain, the focus of the case study is medical and surgical supplies for hospitals. In 1994–1995 the total expenditure on supplies for the NHS in England and Wales was £4.5 billion (Audit Commission 1996). With acute hospital trusts accounting for 80% of this expenditure and medical/surgical supplies representing the largest single element, this focus relates to a significant annual expenditure of around £1 billion.

Ordering Supplies for One NHS Trust

Initial sections of the case describe the situation in one particular NHS Trust, which is responsible for four different hospitals containing about 50 different areas such as wards and operating theaters. Each of these areas holds its own stock of medical consumables and orders replenishments through the Supplies Department. Personnel in the Supplies Department are not employed by the Trust, but are a customer service team employed by the Customer Services Division of a special health authority called NHS Supplies. One of the other two divisions of NHS Supplies is the major wholesaler to NHS Trusts (see Figure 3).

As the central character of the case study, the manager of the customer service team has the task of reducing expenditure on medical consumables sufficiently to enable a 2.5% reduction in the Trust's non–pay expenditure in the current financial year. Some of the difficulties the manager faces are portrayed in descriptions of two very different approaches to ordering replenishment stock. The "traditional" approach is to complete requisition forms by hand and pass them to the Supplies Department. Medical staff in some of the wards and a group of operating theaters use this approach. In contrast, other wards have adopted a new system, in which Supplies Department staff reorder stock for them with the aid of bar codes and handheld data-capture terminals.

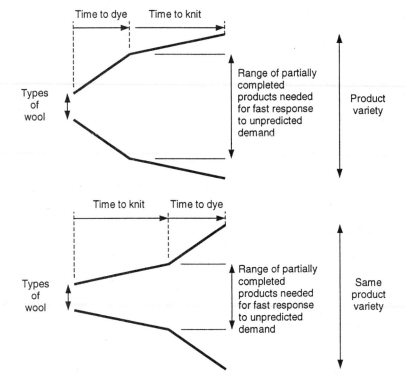

FIGURE 2. Managing Product Variety and Inventories.

This new Ward Stock Management (WSM) system has proved to be very successful in each of the 12 wards that have adopted it, reducing the annual expenditure on replenishment stock. Detailed reviews in each of the areas led to an overall reduction in the number of items stocked (see Table 1) and reduced the total value of stock held by £15,700 (57% of the previous total). It has also prompted favorable reactions from the medical staff on these wards, like the quote from a Head Charge Nurse: "Anything that takes us away from the patients is bad. . . . This new system is saving us about 5 to 6 hours a week of ordering and putting items away."

The case study then focuses on the more complex task of supplying a group of operating theaters that have two stockrooms and also hold small quantities of some items in each theater. Night staff collect the items required for each operation planned for the following day, referring to a Kardex filing system that lists items by surgeon and type of operation. Stock turns are low and the task differs from supplying the wards in three respects: (1) a more complex range of 1,336 items, which includes costly low-usage items such as surgical tools and implants; (2) some predictability of item usage through planned operations; and (3) reluctance of staff to relinquish control of the ordering task.

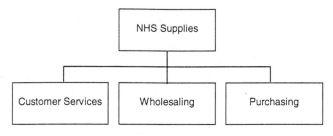

FIGURE 3. The Three Main Divisions of NHS Supplies.

TABLE 1

Range of Items Stocked in Areas Using the WSM System

	Number of Items		
Area	Pre-WSM	Post-WSM	+/−
Macmillan unit[a]	83	100	+17
Ward 1	140	127	−13
Ward 2	140	104	−36
MAU/CCU	261	150	−111
Dermatology	132	86	−46
Ward 4[a]	76	122	+46
Ward 5	160	118	−42
Ward 20	86	100	+14
Outpatients[a]	50	61	+11
Delivery suite	67	81	+14
Q6 Ward	80	68	−12
Q7 Ward	64	50	−14
Totals	1,339	1,156	−172

[a] After implementation of WSM these three areas underwent significant changes.

This reluctance is summarized in a quote from a Head Clinical Nurse of Theaters who pointed out that if one vital item was missing and an operation had to be cancelled, "You're the one who's going to take the flak, not whoever it was that did the order." In the operating theaters making good use of the surgeon's time is so important that theater staff consider surgeons to be their customers, as well as the patients.

The Wholesaler's Operation

The next major section of the case study describes the local NHS Supplies distribution center, which is part of its Wholesaling Division. The center supplies a range of 5,758 different items from stock, processing about 91,000 order lines each week and marshaling the items into about 6,250 wheeled cages ready for delivery. Over a period of several years, this center has taken on the work of three smaller centers in addition to its own, thus reducing facilities and administration costs. This necessitated changing to a 24-hour work pattern to cope with an annual throughput valued at £80 million without expanding the warehouse.

Orders are received by Electronic Data Interchange (EDI) and then stock is allocated, picked, and marshaled separately for each individual area in the hospital trust. Typically, the orders will be marshaled into wheeled cages so that one or more cages contain the order for just one area, thus simplifying handling when delivered to the hospital. The cages are then lined up next to the loading bays in the correct sequence for loading onto the delivery vehicles.

Deliveries conform mostly to routine schedules agreed between the distribution center and all of the NHS Trusts in its area. Descriptions portray the wheeled cages, the fleet of delivery vehicles, and some of the difficulties involved in delivering to certain locations, particularly community clinics that are much smaller than the hospitals. Details of the inward flow of supplies are also presented along with the main performance measures used at the distribution center (see Table 2).

Distributors and Manufacturers

The last section of the case study briefly describes two of the companies that provide medical consumables to NHS Supplies. These companies manufacture most or all of their products outside of the United Kingdom and ship them to their own U.K. distribution centers. Both supply directly to NHS Trusts as well as to wholesalers like NHS Supplies.

TABLE 2
Distribution Center Performance Levels for Mid-1998

Order lines supplied complete	98.9%
Discrepancies (errors)	0.6%
Deliveries made on time	99.5%
Average stock turns	15.6%

However, the two companies follow quite different approaches to organizing the flow of product into their distribution centers. One uses a large information system to generate sales forecasts automatically for each item in each national market around the world. These forecasts are manually reviewed to take account of forthcoming promotions or other special circumstances and are then fed back to the manufacturing plants in and around the United States, as input to their master production schedules. Manufactured product is distributed to large regions, such as Europe, where inventory managers decide exactly how much to send to each individual distribution center.

The second company uses sales forecasts to set up "standing orders" from the distribution center on manufacturing plants in Europe, Australia, and the United States. Forecast accuracy is such that between 70 and 80% of incoming product is covered by these standing orders and the rest is managed by exception.

6. Initial Case Discussion

Discussion of the case commences with the issue of mapping the supply chain for management purposes. Most students produce a map showing a five-tier chain with different supply routes, like the one shown in Figure 4.

What becomes clear from this map is the vulnerability of the wholesalers, who can be bypassed by the hospital ordering items directly from manufacturers (whose own supply networks cover many countries). This provides an excellent opportunity to discuss the real costs of different supply options. Purchasing directly from manufacturers at a lower price than from wholesalers is attractive to many NHS supply managers (Fernie and Rees 1995). However, administration costs increase rapidly with larger numbers of separate orders,

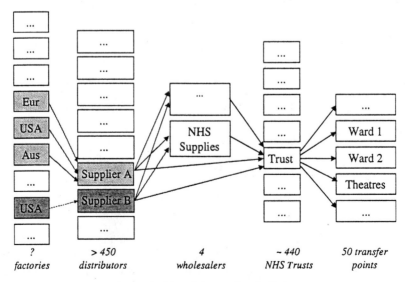

FIGURE 4. Map of the NHS Supply Chain.

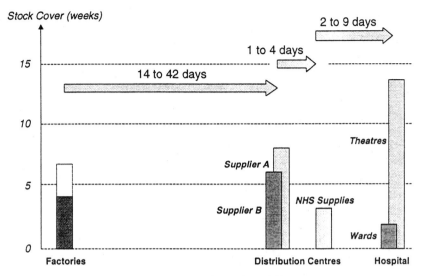

FIGURE 5. Stock Profiles and Lead Times.

communications, deliveries, and invoices; thus, an initial saving can easily be outweighed by additional costs.

The vulnerability of NHS Supplies is the stimulus for discussion of how to reduce the threat through development and provision of increased value to the customer. The constituents of its service concept through colocation can be explored here.

For the second map, most students show the stock profiles along the supply chain and the delivery lead times at each stage, as shown in Figure 5.

From this it is clear that the hospital's operating theaters hold significantly greater stocks than wards using the WSM system. This indicates that improved stock turns could be achieved. However, the question of how this could be done is to be addressed when the answers to study question 3 are discussed.

This mapping also indicates the timeliness of supply. How this is accomplished can be derived by reference to the information technologies described and provides an opportunity to discuss the "periodic review" and "continuous review" approaches to inventory control. Periodic review is ideally suited to the hospital situation, enabling medical staff to focus on caring for patients and not worry about booking individual items out of stock. However, if they are also required to perform the reordering, time pressures sometimes prompt them simply to duplicate the previous week's requisition, leading to excess demand for low-usage items. Even in the NHS Supplies distribution center, which does monitor stock levels continually, reordering is dominated by making the best possible use of the regularly scheduled deliveries from the main suppliers.

7. Leveraging Service Quality through SCM

The answer to study question 3 should be approached by first examining the issue of security of supply. The consequences of failure to supply are so great to those who work in the operating theaters that handing over full responsibility for reordering would be totally unacceptable until it became clear that shortages would not result.

Thus, a first step in the discussion of how to improve SCM for the operating theaters is an examination of the strategic benefits of the preferred customer-supplier relationships, as defined by Lamming (1993). This type of relationship leverages competitive advantage through strategic and tactical actions such as the deployment of a supplier's personnel within the customer's organization, novel approaches to using manufacturing SCM techniques within a service context, and customer-focused partnerships established along the supply chain.

Suppliers in the Customer's Organization

A supplier working within the customer's premises is a novel approach in this type of service industry, but similar to "in-plant representatives" within manufacturing (Vollmann, Cordon, and Raabe 1996). It supports full partnership between customer and supplier, with the latter able to observe firsthand the requirements and changes in demand patterns. In this case the NHS Supplies customer service team endeavor to reduce the costs of supply to the trust as part of a general drive to reduce overhead costs within the NHS.

One cost-reduction measure was implementation of the WSM system. This requires a close working relationship with the customer to decide the range of items that should be held and the stock levels that should be set up. NHS Supplies' wholesaling division is even prepared to take back any excess stock identified. In addition the customer needs help with design and installation of suitable storage. This equipment required capital investment for each ward taking on the WSM system, but yielded significant reductions in the amount of storage space required.

Manufacturing Techniques used in Service Sector

The predictable nature of item usage for planned surgical operations means that procurement can be likened to that of obtaining materials to support a master production schedule (MPS) in a manufacturing company. In this case the MPS is the schedule of operations planned for the future and the bills of materials are the lists of items required for the different operations to be performed. Two elements of customization occur: (1) some of the items may need to be a particular size to suit the patient and (2) some items may be selected to match the preferences of the surgeon.

The likeness to a manufacturing situation is a limited one. First, the significant degree of flexibility required in the surgical MPS for hospitals that deal with emergency surgery in addition to routine surgery necessitates larger buffer stocks. Second, the authority of the surgeons, which arises from the critical nature of their role, results in their personal preferences frequently overriding moves to reduce ranges of items held in stock. However, this is an element of controversy in the case that facilitates a good class discussion (Abell 1997).

Customer-Focused Supplier Partnerships

Once the potential benefits of using a materials requirements planning approach have been discussed, the question of how a supplier can provide additional customer value can be considered.

To use the analogy of modular production, students can be encouraged to visualize such an approach in a service context. Modules are combinations of surgical instruments or medical consumables listed on the hospital Kardex system associated with each operation and surgeon.

Through transfer of information on planned operations and the relevant items, a manufacturer of medical instruments and NHS Supplies are forewarned of several hospitals' future requirements. They pick the necessary sets of items and place them in a wheeled container, first at the manufacturer's site and then at NHS Supplies' distribution center, delivering them to the hospital ready to be wheeled into the operating theater at the scheduled time.

8. Reflections on the Educational Value of the Case Study

To date this case study has enabled MBA students to consider the problems of SCM from both a manufacturing and a service context. It offers an opportunity for a tutor to examine both the processes and the technologies used for SCM. Moreover, there is sufficient information included in the case to produce supply chain mappings that can be used to improve SCM.

Perhaps the unique feature of the case study is that it is focused on service SCM in a nonprofit-oriented organization. Culturally, service quality is awarded the highest priority by healthcare service providers. However, the objectives of management are to provide quality healthcare and to reduce costs. This case enables the tutor and students to contemplate on how both of these objectives can be met or whether such a goal is unattainable.

The solution may lie in the technology transfer of SCM techniques recently developed by manufacturing organizations that are striving for the same performance objectives. MBA students will not immediately link the application of materials requirements planning (MRP) methods and modular production approaches to medical supplies management and, thus, it will usually be left to the tutor to lead the discussion until this issue is reached.

Should a tutor not wish to draw students to consider such approaches, there is sufficient information in the case for it to be used purely as a primer for service SCM. In this context experience has shown that students are keen to debate the controversial issues of why surgeons are allowed to specify individual preferences rather than using a standard range of medical supplies, and the perceived value of the existing NHS Supplies' wholesale operation compared to direct delivery by manufacturers.

9. Conclusion

A new SCM case study has been used as part of a core OM course for MBA students. It has been developed as part of a teaching strategy that aims to facilitate coverage of a broad range of issues within SCM. The contents of this case study and the associated teaching note are well suited to reinforcing basic SCM concepts with an example of a nonprofit-making service industry, in which the management focus is cost control; reviewing information on many parts of a supply chain, ranging from customer through to third-tier suppliers; analyzing an extended partnership including customer, supplier, and manufacturer; and illustrating the use of manufacturing planning and control techniques in a service context.

References

ABELL, D. (1997), "What Makes a Good Case?" ECCHO Newsletter, Autumn/Fall, 4–7.
Audit Commission (1996), *Goods for Your Health: Improving Supplies Management in NHS Trusts*, Audit Commission Publications, Abingdon, Oxon, UK.
CHRISTOPHER, M. (1997), *Marketing Logistics*, Butterworth-Heinemann, Oxford, UK.
FERNIE, J. AND C. REES (1995), "Supply Chain Management in the National Health Service," *The International Journal of Logistics Management*, 6, 2, 83–92.
FORRESTER, J. W. (1961), *Industrial Dynamics*, MIT Press, Cambridge, MA, USA.
GOFFIN, K. (1998), "Operations Management Teaching on European MBA Programmes," *International Journal of Operations and Production Management*, 18, 5, 424–445.
HESKETT, J. L. AND S. SIGNORELLI (1985), *Benetton (A)*, case study ref. 9-685-014, Harvard Business School, Boston, MA, USA.
KUMAR, K. R. AND O. EL SAWY (1998), "Extending the Boundaries of Operations Management: An International Field-Studies Approach Integrating Information Systems," *Production and Operations Management*, 7, 2, 228–236.
LAMMING, R. (1993), *Beyond Partnership: Strategies for Innovation and Lean Supply*, Prentice-Hall, New York.
LANE, R., M. T. SWEENEY, AND B. LINCOLN (1998), *Supply Chain Management in the NHS*, to be lodged with the European Case Clearing House.
LESCHKE, J. P. (1998), "A New Paradigm for Teaching Introductory Production/Operations Management," *Production and Operations Management*, 7, 2, 146–159.
SCOTT, C. AND R. WESTBROOK (1991), "New Strategic Tools for Supply Chain Management," *International Journal of Physical Distribution & Logistics Management*, 21, 1, 23–33.
SLACK, N., S. CHAMBERS, C. HARLAND, A. HARRISON, AND R. JOHNSTON (1998), *Operations Management*, 2nd. ed., Pitman Publishing, London, UK.
VOLLMANN, T., C. CORDON, AND H. RAABE (1995), "Supply Chain Management (Mastering Management, part 8)," *The Financial Times*, December 15, 1995, FTS 13–14.

Michael T. Sweeney is Professor of Operations Management and Head of the Operations and Project Management Group at Cranfield School of Management. He was previously the Director of the School of Defence Management at the Royal Military College of Science, Shrivenham, UK, from February 1995 to September 1997. He joined Cranfield as a Senior Research Fellow in 1979, to study the causes of the poor delivery performance of the UK engineering industry. His current research interests are the strategic management of manufacturing and service operations. Before joining Cranfield, he worked initially as a production engineer for 10 years in the British Motor Industry. After studying for a master degree at Bath University, he was appointed to senior management positions in research and software development organizations and held both line and project management responsibilities. During this time he was responsible for leading the development of systems for design, manufacturing, and management purposes.

Robin Lane is a lecturer in Operations Management at Cranfield School of Management. His current research interests center around the effective use of information systems to support Production Planning and Control. He started work in the food industry before graduating in Mechanical Engineering from Brunel University in 1979. He then worked in Production Engineering for a short time before moving into Production Planning and Control, first with Edwards High Vacuum and then with Esselte Letraset. He moved to Cranfield University in 1988, completing a master degree in 1989. He spent six years with The CIM Institute, researching improved systems architectures to support production scheduling in an MRP II environment and was awarded a Ph.D. in 1994. Following this period of research Robin worked as an independent consultant and then as a senior lecturer at the University of Hertfordshire before joining Cranfield School of Management in 1998.

COORDINATING AND MANAGING SUPPLY CHAINS: THE GENERAL MANAGER'S ROLE*

ANANTH RAMAN

Graduate School of Business, Harvard University, Boston, Massachusetts 02163, USA

We describe the design and content of the supply chain elective course, "Coordinating and Managing Supply Chains" (CMSC), offered in the MBA program at Harvard Business School. In the tradition of the School, the course focuses on the role of the general manager as opposed to the functional specialist. This paper details the logic of the course design and outlines the teaching objectives, modules, and teaching material used in the course.

Introduction

Coordinating and Managing Supply Chains (CMSC) builds on the Technology and Operations Management (TOM) course offered in the first year of the MBA program. Whereas first-year TOM focuses primarily on product transformation and development (in other words, on manufacturing and design), CMSC emphasizes product supply, storage, and availability. Hence, inventory management, distribution economics, and retailing operations, topics not addressed in the first-year TOM, are explored in-depth in CMSC. CMSC also differs from first-year TOM in that the latter treats primarily material and information flows within an organization, whereas CMSC explores material and information flows across organization boundaries as well.

Topics

The course begins by introducing students to the concept of supply chain coordination and management by exploring how companies match supply with demand and presenting cases pertaining to transportation. Subsequently, the course considers interdisciplinary topics in supply chain management such as incentive alignment, imperfections in labor and capital markets, and the linkage between operational performance and stock market valuation. Toward the end of the course, students are permitted either to attend seven sessions related to analytical techniques in supply chain management or write a paper on a topic related to the course theme.

The CMSC course has been successful along three dimensions. One, it has received high evaluations and has consistently been one of the most popular electives offered at Harvard Business School (HBS). Many students, in anonymous surveys, have identified the course as the "best" and "most useful" at HBS. Two, course enrollment, less than 60 in Fall 1996, presently exceeds the class capacity of roughly 200 students over two sections. During the

---

* Received July 1999; revision received August 1999; accepted September 1999.

Fall 1999 semester, for example, roughly 100 students had to be "waitlisted" for the class because of the high demand we encountered. Three, and most important, CMSC has had a profound impact on a few students who have chosen to pursue careers related to the materials covered in the course. Operations management departments at most business schools face a dilemma in that few, if any, students seem to "major" in Operations Management, despite high student ratings of Operations Management courses at many schools. CMSC students at HBS have pursued careers in supply chain management in manufacturing and retailing companies, supply chain software providers, and in the supply chain practices of consulting companies. Quite a few have developed business plans based on the course themes.

The General Manager's Role in Supply Chain Management

The success of CMSC among MBA students can be traced in large part to its focus on interdisciplinary issues (i.e., the general manager's role in supply chain management). It is this emphasis on the role of the general manager that, to the best of our knowledge, differentiates CMSC from supply chain and logistics courses offered at other schools. Because they are typically expensive to employ, companies need to enlist HBS graduates in functions in which they have a comparative advantage. Hence, the course focuses on supply chain issues that an HBS MBA (or, more broadly, an MBA) would perform better than a graduate of a functional specialty course in, for example, industrial engineering, operations research, computer science, or accounting.

CMSC emphasizes topics that are at the interface of different functional disciplines. Because they tend to have knowledge of multiple functional areas relative to functional specialists such as industrial engineers or accountants, MBAs have a comparative advantage in problems and issues that span multiple areas. Consider, for example, the problem of setting target inventory levels. It would be hard for an MBA (especially an HBS MBA) to compete with a Ph.D. in operations research in optimizing specific cost or profit functions. But HBS MBAs, although they have almost no exposure to formal optimization techniques, can nevertheless make vital contributions in areas such as estimating stockout cost, a vital input to computing safety stock. How customers respond to a stockout determines the magnitude of stockout cost. It will be high if a stockout leads to lost sales and margins, relatively low if customers backorder demand. Hence, accurate estimation of stockout cost requires knowledge of both operations and marketing issues. Similarly, inventory-holding cost often needs to be estimated based on a company's debt and equity levels and the relative costs of each, considerations with which an MBA with knowledge of finance and supply chains is well equipped to deal. Firms also often need to separate fixed and variable costs in estimating inventory-holding cost, a topic that requires knowledge of accounting principles.

Time constraints prevent CMSC from addressing in depth some topics that are addressed in other supply chain courses. CMSC is, for example, relatively light on analytical techniques. Inventory models are covered during a single session, even though students who take the course have not previously been exposed to concepts such as economic order quantity (EOQ) or the Newsvendor model. Planning techniques (such as MRP and aggregate production planning) are covered during only a few optional sessions for students, even though students have not been exposed to these topics or to concepts such as linear programming in the first-year curriculum. The course instead focuses attention on topics related to general managers' primarily responsibilities in supply chain operations, namely, incentive alignment; imperfections in labor and capital markets; and organizational changes needed to achieve well-coordinated supply chains. We believe it is important to identify explicitly topics not central to a course to enable it to focus on those that are.

Intellectual Content and Learning Objectives

CMSC focuses on product storage and availability and cross-functional and cross-organizational process (i.e., material and information) flows. Solving supply chain management problems that span multiple functions and firms often, though not always, requires the knowledge of multiple functional disciplines. Consequently, CMSC, while maintaining operations management at its core, draws on and augments students' knowledge of incentives (e.g., Barilla and Campbell Soup cases), organizational structure (e.g., Nine West case), marketing (e.g., Sport Obermeyer case), finance (e.g., Northco case), sales and implementation (e.g., i2 Technologies case), and analytical techniques (e.g., Hewlett-Packard case).

Supply chain coordination and management are clearly important to business. Most HBS students, like most executives, are convinced that process flows and decisions need to be coordinated across the entire supply chain. Those not fully convinced of the benefits of supply chain coordination are convinced very early in the course. Courses in supply chain management taught at other business schools are also reasonably effective at convincing students about the importance of supply chain management.

Other business schools' courses on supply chain management do not, however, in my opinion, adequately explain the general manager's role in improving supply chain operations. To sell the course to HBS MBA students requires us to convince them that supply chain management represents a worthwhile career path. To achieve this goal, it important not only to convey that supply chain management is important, but also to emphasize that some supply chain problems require the involvement of a general manager with knowledge of multiple business functions. It is in these general management positions that the additional cost of hiring an MBA (an MBA from Harvard Business School can cost substantially more than a reasonably skilled operations researcher) can be justified by a company.

Along with considering current supply chain "best practice," CMSC considers, in situations in which existing practice does not coincide with best-possible practice, how supply chains should be managed. That is to say, the course does not hesitate to take current "best practice" to task when it lags behind the "best that can be achieved." In this respect, the course points out the "low-hanging fruit" in supply chains. Energy during the class sessions is high because cases are current and class discussion often builds on real-world experience of students, instructor, and guests.

Course Learning Objectives

Seven learning objectives have been articulated for the course.
- To impart an understanding of inventory-related costs—overstocking, understocking, inventory holding, ordering—and the trade-offs among them, and to promote and explore the appropriateness of flexibility, speed, production planning, forecasting, transportation costs, and additional capacity as levers for controlling these costs.
- To explore how matching supply with demand differs for short life cycle (e.g., fashion apparel) and long life cycle (e.g., pasta, canned soup) products.
- To impart a basic understanding of transportation issues and the trade-offs embedded in transportation choices.
- To emphasize the importance of exercising control over supply chains, to introduce principal-agent theory and the notions of moral hazard and private information into students' thinking about control issues in supply chains, and to train students to identify and remedy sources of goal incongruence in the supply chain.
- To explore imperfections in labor and working capital markets and their impact on supply chain performance, and to identify mechanisms that reduce the cost associated with these factors of production.
- To examine the value added by multiple supply-chain intermediaries, focusing on how they add value by exploiting market imperfections, and briefly focusing on the role of intermediaries in "breaking bulk" and holding safety stock.
- To expose students to the challenges and opportunities in managing retail operations. This serves two purposes by studying (1) an industry in which supply chain issues such as product availability and storage are central to firm operations, and (2) how ideas from

operations management can be applied to an industry not traditionally considered in operations management.

Top Ten Lessons

CMSC's teaching objectives can be understood in terms of a set of ten "lessons" that summarizes the central ideas conveyed in the course. I use this "Top 10 List" to review course concepts on the last day of class.

- #10. *Inventory and the lack thereof are extremely expensive and symptomatic of many problems.*

Students come to recognize that in many businesses inventory incurs substantial financial and nonfinancial costs, among them, stockout, obsolescence, and inventory carrying costs. In numerous examples throughout the course students see how inventory management affects company performance and that their stock market valuation is tied closely to retailers' ability to manage return on assets. Students encounter many case studies that demonstrate that inventory management practice is often not very sophisticated.

In addition, students recognize that excessive or inadequate inventory can be symptomatic of multiple underlying problems. During various cases in the course, the problem can be traced to operations (e.g., lack of operational flexibility), planning (e.g., suboptimal production and inventory planning), inadequate production capacity, misaligned incentives, and labor and capital market imperfections.

- #9. *For many products demand is difficult to forecast.*

A number of case studies bear out the observation that demand forecasts, which are often based on experts' judgment, tend to be extremely inaccurate. This is especially true for, but not restricted to, new or short-life-cycle products for which historical demand is scarce. Error rates (i.e., the expected absolute difference between forecast and actual demand) of 50–60% of forecast demand is not unusual in many industries.

- #8. *Responsiveness matters to (innovative) supply chains.*

This very important lesson is delivered fairly early in the course. Once students realize that judgmental forecasts are prone to substantial error, especially for new and short-life-cycle products, they are eager to find ways to match supply with demand for products with unreliable forecasts. Case analyses reveal that forecasts tend to improve significantly as more sales data are observed. Consequently, companies are advised to develop the capability to respond to sales data rather than try to plan supply based on (typically inaccurate) forecasts.

- #7. *"Perfect response" (i.e., manufacturing all product in response to market signals) and "perfect forecasts" (i.e., no forecast error) are unrealistic in most supply chains, but there are ways to improve a supply chain's ability to respond to market signal.*

Students learn that companies in most supply chains, because of the dictates of display inventory, demand seasonality, capacity constraints, and so forth, must produce a portion of projected demand before observing any sales. The course identifies a number of levers that, properly manipulated, can improve a supply chain's ability to respond to market signals; among them: lead time and setup time reduction (e.g., National Bike); delayed differentiation (e.g., Hewlett Packard); improved production planning (e.g., Sport Obermeyer); transportation choices (e.g., Burlington Northern).

- #6. *Data quality management (point-of-sale data are notoriously poor and inventory errors, even for scanned products, high) cannot be taken for granted, but must be managed.*

Detailed audits of a well-run and healthy retailer's computer records at the store-SKU (stock-keeping unit) level revealed that inventory levels were inaccurate for more than 70% of the items in a particular store. Moreover, the magnitude of the error was high; the expected gross data error (i.e., expected value of |system-physical|) was roughly 35% of the system inventory level at the store-SKU level. Students are often surprised to learn that data quality can be poor even when point-of-sale (POS) scanners are employed. The course emphasizes that good data are essential to effective supply chain management and, through an analogy with product quality, identifies numerous approaches for improving data quality.

- #5. *Software is only a small part of supply chain management.*

Before taking a course incorrectly many students conclude that sound analytical techniques embedded in appropriate software are the basis of efficient supply chains. Such students are surprised to discover that analytical techniques explain only a small portion of the success even of "supply chain software companies" such as i2 Technologies. Cases such as i2 Technologies emphasize the MBA's role in applying software to solve supply chain problems.

- #4. *Good supply chain design relies on effective incentives.*

Supply chain management refers to the coordination and control of the activities of the firms and decision-makers in a supply chain. That firms in a supply chain are often working toward different goals raises the concern that myopic, self-interested decisions might lead to suboptimal decision making (as demonstrated in the Hamptonshire Express, Campbell Soup, and Barilla case studies). The course provides students with a framework for designing supply chain control mechanisms.

- #3. *Cost differences in supply chains affect operational performance.*

Working capital and labor costs differ substantially from one firm to another. The course exposes students to market imperfections that cause working capital and labor cost to differ and identifies ways in which a supply chain can exploit these differences. Some supply chains, for example, have combined inexpensive working capital and inexpensive labor (e.g., see the Bennetton case).

- #2. *People make it happen—in supply chains as well!*

Courses in supply chain management tend to emphasize systems rather than people, even though managing people appropriately is central to good operational performance. A number of authors have portrayed quite effectively the vital role people play in operations management (see, for example, Chapter 9 of Dynamic Manufacturing). The theme is reviewed at multiple points in the course, but is central to the discussion of the CompUSA case.

- #1. *Intermediaries, thought by some to be dead and obsolete, are vital in many supply chains.*

Intermediaries continue to play a vital role in many supply chains in aligning incentives and helping to secure the lowest factor costs (see, for example, the Tale of Two Electronic Component Distributors and Massimo Menichetti cases and also the discussion of Victor Fung's interview in the Harvard Business Review).

The "low-hanging fruit" exposed by these lessons is that current practice is far from optimal in many supply chains. Many students are surprised to learn that principles of operations management apply in many areas not traditionally associated with supply chain management (e.g., retail).

Course Modules

CMSC is divided into six modules that, collectively, run 29 or 30 sessions depending on the Harvard Business School's MBA calendar. The first five modules are mandatory. The last, on analytical techniques, is optional; students can attend the classes for this module and take a comprehensive exam that covers the entire course or write a paper based on topics that are related to the course. The five modules and the key insights related in each are explained below.

Module 1: Supply Chain Fundamentals—Matching Supply with Demand

This module introduces students to the basics of inventory management and the cost associated with excessive or insufficient inventory. In going through the module, students recognize that excessive or insufficient inventory can often be a symptom of many underlying problems. The module ends by exposing students to various levers that can be used to match supply with demand such as transportation, production flexibility, production planning, lead-time reduction, demand forecasting, and delayed differentiation.

Cases and Class Sessions

Session 1: *ChemBright, Inc.* (Harvard Business School case No. 9-693-026). ChemBright, a small start-up company that manufactures private-label household chemicals, sells its products to grocery chains in the New England area. Its strategy is based on a significant logistics-based advantage. The primary case decisions are (1) how the company should respond to a price war initiated by a strong competitor, and (2) how the company can continue to exploit its logistics advantages as it pursues different growth alternatives. Students are forced to consider from a supermarket's perspective, whether to buy a commodity product ("private-label bleach") from a high-priced vendor to which it has loaned money. An effective introduction to supply chains, the case explains why even commodity products cannot be purchased on the "spot market" based on price alone.

Session 2: *Inventory Models* (Chapter 8 of *Operations Management: Production of Goods and Services*, John O. McClain, L. Joseph Thomas, Joseph B. Mazzola, Prentice Hall Publishers). This session introduces students to basic inventory models, namely, the EOQ, Newsvendor, and "Q,R" (i.e., reorder-point, reorder-quantity policies) models. The EOQ model emphasizes the trade-off between setup cost and inventory carrying cost; the Newsvendor model, the impact of demand uncertainty on inventory level. The two ideas come together in the consideration of (Q,R) models. The session ends with a discussion of how setup costs, inventory holding costs, demand uncertainty, lead time, and lead-time uncertainty affect various inventory components. The lecture emphasizes that although inventory level is optimized by holding various parameters (such as holding and setup cost) fixed, these parameters can be affected by the manager and, hence, should not be assumed to be fixed.

Session 3: *Hewlett-Packard Inkjet Printers* (Stanford University case). This case details Hewlett-Packard's supply chain for Inkjet Printers (including versions produced and sold in Europe and the assembly process for each). It emphasizes the difficulty the company is having meeting customer demand even though it carries substantial inventory of many products. Numerous possible solutions are advanced and data provided for analyzing the impact of innovations. The session follows up the discussion on inventory models and clarifies notions of safety stock. The case also introduces the idea of risk pooling in inventory management.

Session 4: *National Bicycle Industrial Company* (Wharton School of the University of Pennsylvania case). This case describes a struggling Japanese bicycle manufacturer unable to compete on cost with a product that had become a commodity. The company's solution was to provide almost unlimited variety, such that the case serves as a valuable introduction to the notion of "mass customization" and the issues that attend producing to customer orders rather than sales forecasts. Students can identify from the substantial detail provided about the production process and the company's distribution channel the changes that need to be made to execute mass customization.

Session 5: *Frito-Lay, Inc.: The Backhaul Decision* (Harvard Business School case No. 9-688-104). Prior to the Motor Carrier Act of 1980 companies with private trucking fleets were generally prohibited from selling transportation services to other companies. Deregulation of the trucking industry in 1980 permitted private carriers to offer for-hire transportation services. In 1983, as part of an effort to offset rising distribution costs, Frito-Lay considered selling miles on its backhaul lanes to other companies. Frito-Lay management had to consider whether the potential revenues from these services warranted possible degradation of service to Frito-Lay's sales force. Approval of the backhaul proposal would entail the development of a marketing plan for the transportation services. In debating the merits of the backhaul proposal, students come to recognize differences among truck types and the situations in which each might be appropriate.

Additional reading for Session 5: *Note on the U.S. Transportation Industry* (Harvard

Business School case No. 9-688-080) provides background information for the transportation cases used in the Business Logistics course. It describes the major modes of domestic freight transportation (motor carrier, rail, air, water, and pipelines), examines the characteristics of the transportation service that each mode provides, and discusses changes in the industry that have resulted from recent regulatory reform. Instructors who would spend more time on the relationship between supply chain and transportation issues might consider using the Burlington Northern (Harvard Business School Case No. 9-689-081) case.

Session 6: *Sport Obermeyer, Ltd.* (Harvard Business School case No. 9-695-022). This case describes operations at a skiwear design and merchandising company and its supply partner. It introduces production planning for short-life-cycle products with uncertain demand and affords students an opportunity to analyze a reduced version of the company's production planning problem. Details about information and material flows, including comparisons of sourcing products in Hong Kong and China, enable students to formulate recommendations for operational improvements. The case teaches students how to match supply with demand for products with high demand uncertainty in a globally dispersed supply chain.

Session 7: *Lecture—Matching Supply with Demand.* This session ties the lessons of the first module together. Suitable slides for the lecture can be found in "Module Overview: Coordinating and Managing Supply Chains—Matching Supply with Demand" (Harvard Business School note No. 5-697-126).

Recommended readings for this session include: "Matching Supply with Demand in an Uncertain World," *Harvard Business Review* (May–June 1994); "Configuring a Supply Chain to Match Supply with Demand, *Journal of Production and Operations Management Society* (Vol. 1, 1998); "What is the Right Supply Chain for Your Product?" *Harvard Business Review* (March 1997).

Module 2: *Information Flow and Incentives*

This module explores information flow and the importance of incentives in supply chains. It examines first the bullwhip effect, a topic covered in the first-year course, and revisits the causes of information distortion in supply chains. Ways to overcome information distortion are proposed and incentives identified as a barrier to overcoming the bullwhip effect. Students are introduced through a spreadsheet simulation to the basics of principal-agency theory and how the insights derived therefrom apply to supply chain operations. The module ends with a lecture on designing supply chain incentives and a case that illustrates the process by which Campbell Soup, a company cognizant of implementation difficulties and incentive misalignment, restructured its supply chain to overcome the bullwhip effect.

Cases and Class Sessions

Session 1: *Barilla SpA (A), (B), (C), and (D)* (Harvard Business School cases Nos. 9-694-046, 9-695-064, 9-695-065, and 9-695-066, respectively). Barilla SpA, an Italian manufacturer that sells to retailers largely through third-party distributors, experienced widely fluctuating demand during the late 1980s. The (A) case describes a proposal to address the problem by implementing a continuous replenishment program that would shift responsibility for determining shipment quantities from distributors to Barilla. Support and resistance within Barilla's functional areas and within the distributors approached by Barilla are considered. The session affords students an opportunity to analyze how a company can effectively implement a continuous replenishment system to reduce channel costs and improve service levels. The (B), (C), and (D) cases highlight implementation problems; the (D) case, in particular, emphasizes the importance of attending to incentive issues while reengineering the supply chain.

Session 2: *Campbell Soup Co.—A Leader in Continuous Replenishment Innovations* (Harvard Business School case No. 9-195-124).Grocery chain and wholesale demand for Campbell Soup's goods, like that for most food manufacturers' products, was driven by

Campbell's own promotional pricing structure rather than retail consumer demand. Campbell introduced continuous product replenishment (CPR) whereby it would manage its customers' inventories by linking supply to actual demand via electronic data interchange. Implementing this channel shift required a restructuring of relationships with its customers and a radical restructuring of its promotional policies.

Session 3: *Hamptonshire Express* (Harvard Business School case No. 9-698-053). This case explores the linkage between channel incentives, allocation of decision rights, and channel performance. Students are required to make various operational decisions on behalf of a newspaper publisher. A series of problems incorporates decisions related to inventory and effort level, subsidy for unsold inventory, sales commission, and so forth. Each problem is accompanied by one or more spreadsheets to enable the class to focus on the insights derived from principal-agent theory without spending an inordinate amount of time on the analytics.

Session 4: *Lecture*: *Controlling Your Supply Chain Operations* (V. G. Narayanan and Ananth Raman; Harvard Business School Working Paper).

Although most managers acknowledge the importance of designing appropriate supply chain incentives, they frequently lack adequate frameworks or techniques for doing so. This paper provides a framework for designing supply chain control mechanisms. We identify sources and examine the impact on operational performance of goal incongruence in supply chains. We then explain how to overcome, and identify some companies that have benefited from an understanding of goal incongruence in the channel.

Module 3: Retail Operations and Merchandising

This module examines an industry (i.e., retailing) in which supply chain issues such as forecasting, inventory management, and supplier relationships are crucial. Understandably, most students who take the course are unlikely to work in retailing; yet, I believe for a number of reasons that the module serves a useful pedagogical purpose. One, the problems retailers face (e.g., making data accessible, interpreting large amounts of data, reducing lead times, and so forth) are shared by firms in many other industries. Two, because retailers are dominant players in many supply chains today, it is important that the processes they follow be understood by manufacturers and distributors. Three, students typically find it easy to relate to case studies in retailing because most have experienced the industry as consumers and can readily relate to chronic problems such as stockouts and markdowns. New materials being developed for this module will be available later this year.

Session 1: *Linking Retail Financial and Operational Performance* (Chapter 7 of *Retailing Management*, 3rd Edition, by Michael Levy and Barton Weitz. Irwin-McGraw Hill). This chapter introduces students to the basics of retail financial performance and the different ways retailers earn profit. It explains, for example, the difference between the "profit path" and "turnover path." Whereas retailers that follow the "profit path" (e.g., Tiffany & Co.) earn a substantial margin each time they sell a product to a customer, "turnover path" retailers (e.g., Wal-Mart), although they earn substantially lower margins on each sale, turn their assets over at a much faster rate. The session presents recent evidence for the relationship between "operational performance" (measured through return-on-assets or inventory productivity measures such as gross-margin-return-on inventory) and a company's long-term stock market value. Similar empirical data are used to point out the trade-offs between certain operational measures (e.g., sales growth and risk of bankruptcy).

Session 2: *Towards Scientific Merchandising*: *Blending Left- and Right-brained Approaches in Retail Supply Chains* (Marshall Fisher, Ananth Raman, Anna S. McClelland, Harvard Business School Working Paper). Retailers today have the potential to track through POS scanners and store in large computerized databases sales data from which they can draw conclusions about customer preferences and supply their stores with suitable merchandise based on their understanding of these preferences. Contrary to its potential, merchandising is not particularly scientific today. Intuition dominates decision making in retailing generally, and in merchandising in particular, with little emphasis on the use of data and evaluation of trade-offs. Although numerous retailers have taken steps to capture more detailed and accurate operational and sales data, most fail to exploit these data adequately. Moreover, available data are often inaccurate and even were they accurate most retailers lack the tools to extract useful information from them. Even those able to extract information about customer preferences from sales data have seldom built into their supply chains the speed and flexibility needed to be able to respond to this information. Neither do they possess the decision tools that would enable them to incorporate this information into production and inventory planning decisions. Finally, few companies have incentive systems that encourage managers to strive for the adoption of responsive techniques. This session introduces students to "state-of-the-art" practice in retailing.

Session 3: *Merchandising at Nine West Retail Stores* (Harvard Business School case No. 9-698-098). This case describes the merchandising decision process (organization, structure, and incentives) at Nine West retail stores, a large U.S. footwear retailer. A description of changes currently occurring at Nine West provides a context in which students can recommend adjustments to the process and structure of the merchandising organization. The case explains how a fashion retailer makes merchandising decisions and explores the impact of changes in the environment on the merchandising organization.

Session 4: *CompUSA—The Computer Superstore* (Harvard Business School case No. 9-699-026). This case describes organization of computer retailer CompUSA, with particular attention to operations and company culture. It examines first the economics of, and importance of a responsive supply chain for, the PC product category. The description of company culture emphasizes the role of people-management and incentives in achieving responsiveness.

Module 4: Factor Markets and the Role of Supply Chain Intermediaries

Coordination is complicated by different labor and capital costs among the constituent firms in a supply chain. Students come to recognize that their labor and capital costs influence firms' decisions regarding capacity and inventory levels. Moreover, in light of the lessons drawn from Module 2, students discover that incentive misalignment is present in many supply chains. The combination of factor market imperfections and incentive misalignment leads to an exploration of the role of intermediaries in supply chains. Students are exposed to a number of intermediaries that, contrary to popular expectations, have grown their businesses substantially despite the growth of information technology. Most have had to redefine their businesses in response to changes in the environment.

Session 1: *Massimo Menichetti* (Harvard Business School case No. 9-686-135). This case describes a classic supply chain intermediary (termed in the trade an *impannatore*) in the Italian textile industry. It follows the integration and subsequent fragmentation of the industry and examines the extent of cooperation necessitated among the surviving firms. The case explores the impact of technology on the nature of cooperation and considers how the *impannatore*'s role might change with the introduction of new technology. The case dates from the late 1980s, thus technological details are not current, but the issues and insights attendant on the introduction of new technology remain relevant.

Session 2: *Northco (A)* (Harvard Business School case No. 9-697-017). This case considers the plight of a small school-uniform manufacturer wrestling with seasonal demand that is saddled with excess inventory when it is bought by a leveraged buyout firm. Students are required to identify ways to analyze and solve the company's problem. The case demonstrates the linkage between inventory management and operational as well as working capital finance issues. A significant portion of the class is devoted to explaining how the cost of working capital can differ from one firm to another. Class discussion revolves around whether Northco is caught in a "death spiral," in which the cost of working capital and its impact on inventory management plays a crucial role.

Session 3: *Apparel Exports and the Indian Economy* (Harvard Business School case No. 9-696-065). Indian apparel exports are enjoying considerable success in international markets, but their future is uncertain as a result of impending technological, regulatory, and market changes. This case explores the long lead times to source apparel from India and provides a situational context that enables students to explain this phenomenon. The case links supply chain coordination to macroeconomic factors such as the availability of working capital and industry fragmentation. By contrasting the case with the Sport Obermeyer and Menichetti cases covered earlier in the course, we can also gain insights into why the Indian economy failed to develop a skilled intermediary to overcome some of its supply chain problems.

Session 4: *A Tale of Two Electronic Components Distributors* (Harvard Business School case No. 9-697-064). This case discusses the role of distribution intermediaries in the electronic components industry and describes operations at two of these distributors. It serves as a vehicle for discussing the functions of distributors in the channel and for understanding the differences between two distributors and how each is likely to deal with issues such as consolidation and the rapid growth of the Internet. The case also introduces students to the complexity of managing operations at a small distributor, provides an opportunity to explore the changing role of intermediaries in a distribution channel, and stresses the importance of operations and the role of information technology and scale economies.

Session 5: *Fast, Global and Entrepreneurial—Supply Chain Management, Hong Kong Style—An Interview with Victor Fung* (*Harvard Business Review*, 98507). In this interview Li & Fung Chairman Victor Fung explains both the philosophy behind supply-chain management and the specific practices Li & Fung has developed to reduce costs and lead times, thereby enabling its customers to buy "closer to the market," Hong Kong's largest export trading company. Li & Fung has been an innovator in supply-chain management, a topic of increasing importance to many senior executives. It has also been a pioneer in "dispersed manufacturing." It performs higher-value-added tasks such as design and quality control in Hong Kong and outsources lower-value-added tasks to the best possible locations around the world. The result is something new: a truly global product. To produce a garment, for example, the company might purchase yarn from Korea, have it woven and dyed in Taiwan, and ship it to Thailand for final assembly and matching with zippers manufactured by a Japanese company. For every order the goal is to customize the value chain to meet the customer's specific needs. To be run effectively, Fung maintains, trading companies must be small and entrepreneurial. He describes the organizational approaches that help to keep Li & Fung that way despite its growing size and geographic scope: its organization around small, customer-focused units; its incentives and compensation structure; and its use of venture capital as a vehicle for business development.

During the past year Fung attended the class via videoconferencing from Hong Kong. The class brings together many lessons from the course and sets up the subsequent module on integrating supply chains.

Module 5: *Designing Integrated Supply Chains*

Picking up where the interview with Victor Fung left off, applying concepts developed in the course at one company, this module demonstrates how these course concepts can be employed to alter a supply chain. The module includes a set of cases about make-to-order manufacturer Norwalk Furniture. The (A) and (B) cases, each of which is posted on the Web with appropriate video-clips, describe the entire supply chain. The (A) case summarizes marketing and retailing elements; students are presented with a store layout and can observe the interaction between a potential customer and a salesperson. In the (B) case students are exposed to marketing and transportation issues, including various aspects of furniture manufacturing. Students are called on to develop an integrated approach to the entire supply chain set forth in the cases. The Benetton (A) case can also be used for this purpose, although the considerably greater detail provided in the Norwalk Furniture cases supports more in-depth discussion.

Norwalk Furniture (A) (Harvard Business School case No. 2-698-040).Norwalk Furniture manufactures and retails make-to-order, custom-upholstered furniture. The company's products cost approximately 10% more than comparable mass-produced furniture and are delivered 35 days after a customer places an order. This case provides the background for exploring opportunities and challenges for mass-customized, upholstered furniture. Students are made to examine closely the economics of furniture retailing and challenged to identify changes in retailing strategy and evaluate the relative merits of franchises, company-owned stores, and independent retailers. The case should be used in conjunction with Norwalk Furniture (B).

Norwalk Furniture (B) (Harvard Business School case No. 2-698-041). This case provides operational information about Norwalk Furniture's factory and transportation. Students are required to identify operational improvements, including a proposal for a cellular plant and group-incentive scheme. The case should be used in conjunction with Norwalk Furniture (A).

Benetton (A) (Harvard Business School case No. 9-685-014). Benetton, the world's largest manufacturer of woolen outerwear garments, seeks to extend its retailing network to the United States from its base in Europe. This case considers a variety of issues related to the company's marketing, manufacturing, and logistics strategies raised by the proposed move, together with specific questions about how the move should be managed. It describes a well-thought-out, functionally integrated strategy for Europe in a way that supports assessment of its applicability for a proposed U.S. effort.

Module 6 (Optional): Analytical Techniques for Supply Chain Management

Knowledge of analytical techniques such as linear programming, forecasting, yield management, and MRP is valuable for a supply chain manager. A general manager needs to be an "intelligent consumer" of these techniques, that is, be aware of the capabilities, assumptions, and limitations of each technique. For example, the general manager should be capable of understanding the assumptions implicit in the use of a particular technique and whether the technique is appropriate in a specific business context. The module also explores the organizational changes that need to accompany the adoption of analytical techniques. It does not, however, create experts in analytical techniques: students interested in becoming experts in these analytical techniques are advised to extend their knowledge beyond that imparted by this module.

Session 1: *Forecasting* (Chapter 2 from *Production and Operations Analysis*, 3rd Edition, Steven Nahmias, Irwin Publishers*)*. This session introduces students to the basics of forecasting techniques such as moving averages, exponential smoothing, and causal models such as regression analysis. It ends with a discussion of forecasts based on expert judgment and of the biases typically present in these techniques. Students quickly recognize the limitations of forecasting techniques and many are clearly dismayed that the techniques described in the chapter are fairly rudimentary. Students are surprised to learn later in the course that even modern decision support software uses many of these techniques.

Session 2: *Aggregate Production Planning* (Chapter 3 from *Production and Operations Analysis*, 3rd Edition, Steven Nahmias, Irwin Publishers). The discussion of aggregate production planning introduces students to analytical techniques used in production planning. This session introduces students to the difference between following a "level production strategy" and a "chase production strategy" to deal with predictable fluctuations in demand levels. It also introduces students to a linear programming formulation of the aggregate production planning problem (students in the course have typically never seen a level production strategy prior to this class).

Session 3: *Basics of Linear Programming* (Supplement 1 to Chapter 3 in *Production and Operations Analysis*, 3rd Edition, Steven Nahmias, Irwin Publishers). This session introduces students to techniques for solving level production strategies. Both the graphical technique and the "LP-Solver" in Microsoft Excel are covered. Considerable emphasis is placed on interpreting the output of LP-Solver, in particular, its interpretation of "shadow prices."

Session 4: *Materials Requirement Planning* (Chapter 6 in *Production and Operations Analysis*, 3rd Edition, Steven Nahmias, Irwin Publishers). The logic of MRP systems is presented even though the session tends to be tedious, because most large companies still depend substantially on such systems for production and inventory planning. Industry speaker Jim Shepherd, vice president of research, AMR Research, describes the current state of the ERP industry, typically in the latter half of the class.

Session 5: *Yield Management* ["Yield Management at American Airlines," Barry C. Smith, John F. Leimkuhler, and Ross M. Darrow, *Interfaces* 22:1 January–February 1992 (8–31)]. The last two sessions in this module deal with applications. The first application session focuses on airline yield management. "Yield Management at American Airlines" documents the dramatic savings American Airlines realized through the application of analytical techniques. Students are struck by the parallel between yield management and the Newsvendor technique studied earlier in the course. They also recognize the modifications needed to adapt the optimization approach to nuances in the airline industry (e.g., the hub-and-spoke system).

Session 6: *i2 Technologies, Inc.* (Harvard Business School case No. 9-699-042). This case describes the emergence and growth of i2 Technologies and the supply chain planning software industry. In December 1998 i2's market capitalization exceeded $2 billion. The supply chain planning software industry's annual sales were approximately $1 billion and expected to grow at 57% annually. In describing i2's products and the process by which it sold and implemented its software, the case provides students with the background needed to understand why the company has been successful, what it should do in the future, and whether new competition from companies such as SAP poses a significant threat to its future success.

Planned Future Course Development

CMSC continues to evolve as a number of other researchers at Harvard Business School and elsewhere continue to make progress in research and course development. In conclusion, I would like to describe briefly some course development I am currently pursuing, namely, the development of cases that deal with issues related to incentives and information technology in supply chains. These cases will add to the insights provided by the CompUSA, Hamptonshire Express, and i2 Technologies cases.

A substantial portion of my current course development is concerned with the quality of retail data. Contrary to what most people, including supply chain researchers, believe, it is tremendously difficult for retailers to ensure the quality of the data in their computers. At the store-item level, retail data are notoriously inaccurate: few retailers, for example, can accurately identify the amount of inventory they have for a particular stock-keeping unit at a particular store. Similarly, consumers often have difficulty finding a particular item that is in stock at a store. Although vital to understanding and managing product availability in supply chains and, hence, vital to a supply chain course, these issues have been neither adequately studied nor adequately taught. Material I am currently developing, based on research being conducted by my doctoral students, will hopefully mitigate this deficiency in the near term.

Ananth Raman, associate professor in the Technology and Operations Management area, has been on the Harvard Business Faculty faculty since 1993 and specializes in supply chain management. He teaches an MBA elective course (Coordinating and Managing Supply Chains), and in multiple executive education courses at Harvard. His research focuses on supply chain management for short-life-cycle products with unpredictable demand, and emphasizes production and inventory planning and the role of incentives. He is codirector of a Sloan Foundation–funded research project to study retail operations and merchandising practices that includes over 30 leading retailers.

AN INTEGRATED CURRICULUM FOR TEACHING SUPPLY CHAIN MANAGEMENT AT MICHIGAN STATE UNIVERSITY*

DAVID J. CLOSS, STEVEN A. MELNYK, THEODORE P. STANK, AND MORGAN SWINK

Department of Marketing and Supply Chain Management, Broad College of Business, Michigan State University, East Lansing, Michigan 48824-1122, USA

> The demand for professionals who think in terms of integrated supply chain processes has grown. The supply of graduates with such skills, however, is limited, because many business schools still operate within the constraints of "functional silos." Nevertheless, we argue that purchasing, production, and logistics faculty are uniquely positioned to lead the way in integrating supply chain management (SCM). This paper discusses the integration of these three functions as a prelude to the development of an integrated SCM curriculum. The paper then describes the undergraduate and MBA level SCM curricula at Michigan State University, which focus on horizontal line management of marketing, procurement, production, and logistics processes. The discussion identifies the challenges confronted in developing the SCM program as well as the benefits accrued.
> (INTEGRATION, SUPPLY CHAIN MANAGEMENT, EDUCATION)

Introduction

A growing concern among academics is the increasing need to augment the traditional functional perspective used in business higher education with a view that instills knowledge of the horizontal processes through which functions are connected. Changing economic forces, well-documented in research publications, have mandated that industry abandon the vertical, functional organizational structure characteristic of traditional procurement, manufacturing, and physical distribution operations in favor of a more horizontal, cross-functional structure that emphasizes process management. Integration of these activities to achieve coordinated planning, implementation, and control of goods, services, and information flows through a firm is recognized today as logistics.

The term *supply chain management* (SCM) extends logistical integration to include management of logistics networks both within and across company boundaries. SCM is the systematic coordination of activities/processes that procure, produce, and deliver products and/or services in a manner that maximizes value to end customers (Global Logistics Team 1995; Sheffi and Klaus 1998). The objective is to generate cost savings and/or better customer service over the total chain of organizations involved in supply, production, and delivery of final goods for consumption (Bowersox and Closs 1996). Clinton and associates (1997) provide evidence of the managerial shift toward SCM. They report strong agreement

---

* Received December 1998; revisions received June 1999 and September 1999; accepted October 1999.

(mean of 4.4 on a 1-to-5 scale) with the following statement: "My firm has increased its organizational commitment to a more comprehensive integrated supply chain during the past two years." In a related question, more than 34% of the sample firms reported that they now have an executive position with the words *supply chain* in the title.

Supply chain organizations require individuals who can effectively comprehend and manage integrated operations both within enterprises and between supply chain partners. According to several studies, a major concern of senior logistics managers is the limited supply of individuals trained in integrated SCM. A recent article in *Traffic World* puts it bluntly: "It's been very, very clear that demand has been chasing a short supply of supply-chain people. It's one thing to understand one mode. It's another to understand how those modes relate to each other" (Saccomano 1998).

Although the industrial trend toward an integrated supply chain perspective is strongly apparent, most of academia still operates within the constraints of "functional silos." Figure 1 illustrates the organizational predicament. Historically, the management areas of procurement, operations, and logistics have grown into highly specialized academic groups. With a few exceptions, business schools typically attach the first two groups to the POM domain, whereas logistics is firmly lodged in the marketing domain. Each group consists of faculty members who received specialized training in their respective disciplines and then pass on similar training to their students and future faculty. In typical settings, these faculty groups operate independently, often duplicating teaching, research, and outreach efforts.

Functional silos are supported and even encouraged by a combination of departmental structure and performance measures (e.g., student credit hours), which in turn drive faculty lines. As a result, separated programs prohibit students from understanding critical elements of SCM in favor of in-depth knowledge in one area. Suggestions for an integrated program are often met by faculty complaints that there are too few credit hours to permit adequate coverage of current topics in their majors, much less integrated topics. In addition, faculty members are uncomfortable about teaching in areas beyond their expertise, and integrated classroom materials are not available. The result is a strong impetus for curricula to remain functionally focused, even as industry is looking for individuals with a broad supply chain perspective.

Functional silos notwithstanding, purchasing, operations management, and logistics faculty are uniquely positioned to lead the way in integrating SCM. These functions have a history of close ties to industry that has produced a fundamental understanding of cross-functional business activities. This paper illustrates how an understanding of cross-functional activities

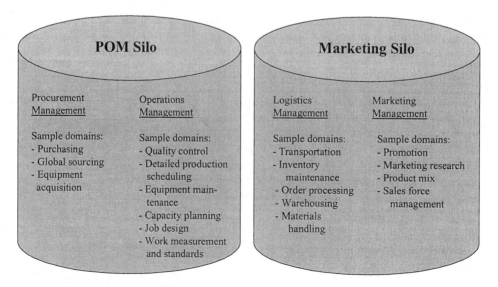

FIGURE 1. Traditional Functional Silos.

can be put to work in the development of an integrated program in SCM. As an example, the SCM curriculum at MSU is described. The program emphasizes horizontal line management processes to optimize teaching, research, and outreach efficiency while combining effectiveness in purchasing, production, and logistics. This paper updates and extends an earlier report on the SCM program at MSU (Closs and Stank 1999) by giving a detailed description of the SCM courses and by providing an update on revisions made to the program as it has matured.

Background

The concept of SCM has developed over many years as companies and industries have come to realize that great opportunities for cost and service improvements rest in the coordination of activities and processes between supply chain firms (Global Logistics Team 1995). To capitalize on these opportunities, firms are looking for those rare business school graduates who can effectively manage cross-functional processes and who can create and maintain partnerships with vendors, customers, and service providers (Sheffi and Klaus 1998). Academic programs have been slow to adapt to these needs because of barriers to change, including historical faculty lines associated with departments, entrenched courses and programs, limited availability of integrated teaching material, and traditional performance measures related to credit hours taught.

This dilemma has been well documented. Increasingly, logistics managers and educators are calling for programs that educate future cross-functional supply chain managers who are knowledgeable in both the depth and breadth of the integrated discipline (Flanagan 1994; Gentry, Keller, Ozment, and Waller 1996). Similar calls have emerged from the ranks of operations management. For years academics have lamented the fact that POM programs continue to relegate purchasing and logistics to "specialization modules" that are kept well outside the "core body of knowledge" in their curriculum designs (Bandyopadhyay 1994). The recent special issue of *Production and Operations Management* is rife with cries for a more integrated curriculum. For example, Miller and Arnold (1998) call for a move from plant-oriented conceptualizations of POM to a more expanded view that includes all stages of the value chain. Other descriptions of progressive POM curricula emphasize "systems" thinking and cross-functional integration (Morris 1997; Lovejoy 1998).

Some business programs have begun to respond. The literature tracks curricular changes that reflect integration of course materials across marketing and logistics; across logistics, procurement, and production; and across business operational processes and engineering (Rinehart et al. 1990; Rinehart and Novak 1991; Rinehart et al. 1992; Flanagan 1994). To date, however, most of the integration of SCM topics has occurred only in introductory courses or, at best, through some type of "integrative case experience" (Julien, Doutriaux, and Couillard 1998). Few business programs have consolidated course materials from different disciplines into an integrated SCM major. Moreover, many business schools continue to labor under the heavy constraints of functional separation and territorial behaviors.

One rather obvious solution is to reorganize purchasing, operations, and logistics faculty in a way that reduces some of these barriers and tensions. The next section discusses the rationale for an integrated academic unit that incorporates all aspects of the value chain, and specifically an SCM curriculum, within that department. The following section describes the integrated curriculum.

A Focus on Value Chain Management

The first step toward supply chain curricular integration at MSU was the creation in 1978 of the materials and logistics management program. The program offered common courses as the foundation for undergraduate majors and MBA concentrations in procurement, production, and logistics. The program was an improvement over a strictly functional perspective, but it still did not achieve a high level of integration. SCM disciplines were still housed in separate departments, and the material covered in each introductory course was still heavily biased toward the discipline of the instructor who delivered the course.

In early 1997, the business school at MSU created the Department of Marketing and Supply Chain Management comprised of marketing, procurement, production, and logistics disciplines. Four specific goals guide the activities of departmental faculty: (1) contribute to societal well being through enhancing the economic value-creation process; (2) enhance the national and international standing of the department through excellence in the core areas as well as overall integration in business process management; (3) gain recognition in business and academic communities through a commitment to integrative research programs and curriculum development; (4) develop and disseminate knowledge through research and learning environments pertaining to integrated marketing and SCM.

Specific measurement processes and performance metrics address two key stakeholder groups: students and employers. Nearly one-half of MSU business students at both the MBA and undergraduate levels are supply chain majors. Many students select MSU because of its supply chain programs, and therefore have strong expectations and opinions. Most student assessment processes are in the experimental stage. In addition to standard course evaluations, SCM professors often administer their own surveys, asking students' opinions regarding course content and level of integration achieved. This information is supplemented by many informal discussions between faculty and students. Curriculum review committees for various programs interview student focus groups periodically. Other measures under consideration include administering a certification-like examination for graduating students, and surveying alumni 4 to 5 years after graduation.

SCM faculty place a great deal of importance on developing and maintaining relationships with recruiters because they represent the primary customers in the system. The program maintains a faculty-directed office with at least one full-time staff person dedicated to developing industry contacts, answering requests, etc. To support this effort, about 40 employers are invited members of a supply chain advisory council. The council meets with faculty once a year to discuss curriculum issues and employer needs. In addition to faculty-led topical and roundtable discussions, students make presentations at these full-day meetings to demonstrate the material coverage and types of learning experiences they gain in SCM courses. Numerous informal contacts with employers occur during campus visits. Additionally, a dedicated business school student placement office with added capabilities for gathering and evaluating employer feedback opened in November 1999.

The Supply Chain Management Curriculum

The MSU undergraduate and MBA programs in SCM were designed to provide students with a broad foundation in marketing and customer-oriented strategies as well as depth and experience in key functional areas, including procurement, manufacturing planning and operations, inventory planning, distribution operations, and customer service. One difficult choice in creating a new curriculum involved choosing which topic areas in traditional functional areas to sacrifice to provide sufficient breadth across integrated activities. Another challenge was to make room within the limitations on credit hours for more detailed coverage of state-of-the-art solutions and approaches as well as more experience in problem solving.

A significant portion of the new time requirements was realized by eliminating topic overlap in various courses. For example, it was discovered that forecasting, inventory management and control, and facility location analysis were taught in several disciplinary areas. Similar duplication was found for customer service, quality, requirements planning, and performance measurement. It also became clear that existing academic programs, which were integrated in concept but still exhibited strong functional characteristics, had to be substantially redesigned to emphasize supply chain integration, reduce duplication, and allow for more coverage of key topics, such as information technology applications.

A cross-functional team of faculty was assigned to design the integrated curriculum. Initially, the group sought to subdivide the existing courses into five or six major modules and then form the modules into coherent classes. This would minimize changes in presentation material and facilitate teaching, because each module could be assigned to an individual faculty member. After numerous attempts at this approach proved unsatisfactory, the team realized it had to design a truly integrative sequence of courses.

The method chosen might be termed "decomposition," in that each existing course was decomposed into individual topics. The definition of each topic included the learning objectives, key points, functional perspective (procurement, production, or logistics), and the depth of coverage necessary. The functional perspective was included to identify the course from which the topic had come as well as to indicate the focus of the detailed content.

Before rearranging the material, a decision was made regarding the overall philosophy of the supply chain major within the business curriculum. Building on the Earth-to-Earth idea, topics were organized into courses at the four levels: basic awareness, core knowledge, detailed application, and process integration. The first level, required of all undergraduate business majors and MBA students, develops a basic awareness of supply chain objectives, processes, activities, and careers. The purpose is to describe the role of supply chains in business and everyday life, addressing issues and topics that all business professionals should know about. The course also meets AACSB requirements for a production or operations course.

The second level, required as the first course for all undergraduate SCM majors and MBA students concentrating in SCM, covers core knowledge regarding supply chain operations, dynamics, and strategy. It answers questions regarding why and how, providing a common base for further detailed investigations into the functional areas of procurement, production, and logistics. This core knowledge has to be of sufficient depth to allow students to obtain internships and to support detailed work in application courses. The challenge in designing this course was to replace two functionally oriented courses (one each in purchasing/production and logistics/transportation) with one integrated course in SCM (MSU is on a semester system).

The third level of courses provides detailed application of procurement, production, and logistics. Students are exposed to functional problem situations, decision making, and solution approaches. The fourth level of instruction provides an integrated supply chain management approach to strategy development and operations by emphasizing hands-on decision making via cases and simulations.

The topical material was sequenced throughout the four levels of courses to provide a consumer-focused perspective of supply chain activities, operations, and strategies. It was structured into the program depicted in Figure 2, and initiated in Spring 1998. The Appendix lists specific course topics dedicated to each area.

The Basic Awareness courses (MSC 303 and MSC 820) examine SCM in terms of firm competitiveness and a broad understanding of the activities involved. Topics include the role of supply chain processes in determining competitive advantage with respect to quality, flexibility, lead-time, and cost. The goal of instruction is simply to introduce all business students to topics relevant to Supply Chain Management. One instructor is assigned to each section of the undergraduate course. The MBA course differs in that significantly more time is spent on developing the strategic marketing elements of supply chain operations. Additionally, a team of faculty members who have expertise in marketing and supply chain management teaches MBA sections.

The Core Knowledge courses (MSC 305 and MSC 844) provide foundational knowledge required for majors pursuing a career in the field. There is some repetition in topic areas with the Basic Awareness courses, but these topics are covered in greater depth and specificity. Special emphasis is given to relating the activities to functional management and decision making under a new paradigm of integrated SCM. Core Knowledge courses show students how the components introduced in the Basic Awareness courses may be used together to manage a Supply Chain. Underscoring all instruction is the notion that the primary strategic goal of SCM is to provide the firm with an efficient and effective means of creating value for customers and consumers. New, integrative topic areas were designed to introduce the idea of value development and to position the structure of supply chain operations as part of the

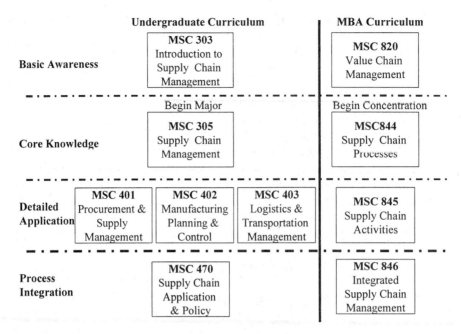

FIGURE 2. SCM Course Requirements.

basic fabric of a firm's strategy. Addressed are such issues as supply chain information systems, relationship management, and performance measurement.

Both the undergraduate and MBA Core Knowledge courses are team taught by faculty with expertise in procurement, manufacturing, and logistics. Approximately one-half of the sessions cover strategic and integrative topic areas. All instructors teach these topics in their individually assigned sections. The remaining topic areas are functional and/or process oriented. The faculty members with specific expertise in the area teach these topics across all sections. For example, each faculty member would teach the class on Supply Chain Performance Measurement in his or her individual sections. Production planning, however, would be taught to all sections by Operations Management faculty. Figure 3 presents the sequence of topics covered in the Core Knowledge courses. Similar to the sequencing of the courses

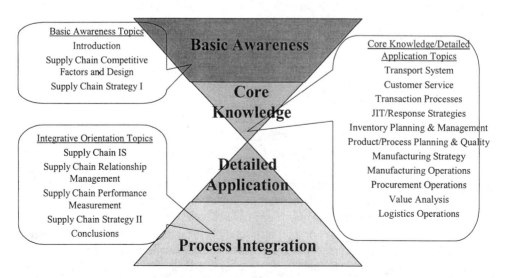

FIGURE 3. Topic Sequencing for SCM Core Knowledge Courses (MSC 305 and MSC 844).

in the curriculum, the topics presented in the course proceed from a focus on basic awareness of supply chain strategy and consumer-oriented value creation to an increasing level of knowledge and detailed application in core areas. It then reverts to a more general level to address process integration issues such as supply chain information systems and performance measurement that cross function and company boundaries.

Detailed Application courses (MSC 401, 402, 442, and MSC 845) develop functional problem-solving experience in traditional supply chain areas. The Procurement and Supply Management course provides an understanding of the purchasing function's role in fulfilling the firm's operations and competitive strategies; supplier evaluation and development; relationships with suppliers; purchasing research; negotiation; commodity planning; and cost, price, and value analysis. The Manufacturing Planning and Control course deals with theory and practice in production planning, demand management, master scheduling, materials requirements and capacity planning, shop floor control, computer-integrated manufacturing, and just-in-time systems. Finally, Logistics and Transportation Management provides a microanalysis of customer service, order management, distribution operations, facility design, and purchasing and operation of transportation services. At the MBA level, these three courses are delivered jointly under one course administration. This arrangement allows greater flexibility in sequencing and interconnecting the various topics.

The Detailed Application courses focus on in-depth understanding of analytical tools needed to make decisions in entry-level operational positions, including decision frameworks, processes, and software. Whereas MSC 305 and MSC 844 present a blueprint of how supply chain components fit together, Detailed Application courses provide a functional manager's view of the tools used to make and implement decisions affecting the firm's ability to reach strategic goals and create value for customers. Specific topic areas for these courses are also included in the Appendix.

The Process Integration courses (MSC 470 and MSC 846) cover analysis and problem solving of SCM cases, integrating knowledge obtained in previous courses. These courses give students the opportunity to apply this knowledge in a real-world, case-oriented setting. The courses also require student teams to compete in simulations that exhibit supply chain dynamics, emphasizing job skills such as teamwork and communications. Two simulations are employed. The first is a computer simulation that replicates an interactive competitive environment of a four-firm industry (Closs 1998). The simulation requires simultaneous coordination of finished goods and materials inventory management, transportation, procurement, production scheduling, warehousing, and marketing. The supply chain must be planned and managed in a time-sensitive and competitive environment. The primary emphasis throughout the simulation is timely and integrated decision implementation.

The Integrative Courses also use a Value-Chain Game that represents a retail value or supply chain (Stank 1997). Participants in the game act as managers and employees engaged in source, make, and deliver activities for three products to satisfy retail customer demand. Specific enterprises represented include suppliers, a manufacturing firm, retail customers, and the transportation providers necessary to move product between suppliers and manufacturing, between manufacturing and regional distribution centers (DCs), and between DCs and retail customers. Whereas the focus of the computer simulation is on cost and service tradeoffs among different supply chain strategies, the Value-Chain Game emphasizes the integration and coordination of internal and external activities that result from effective communications and information flows across functional areas.

The progression of knowledge, combined with significant internship opportunities, produces graduates who can excel in entry-level management positions by understanding how functional roles integrate with other activities within and external to the firm. The overall goal is to produce graduates who can think systematically about the supply chain and make functional decisions with an understanding of systemwide implications.

Benefits and Challenges

The revised SCM program was introduced during spring semester 1998. The perceived benefits and ongoing challenges of the program are reviewed in the following narrative.

Benefits

Several benefits of the SCM program have emerged. First, the curriculum process has increased faculty exposure to cross-functional teaching and research. Although faculty members are never asked to teach outside their area of expertise in advanced courses, cross-functional teaching is sometimes used for the Basic Awareness course. This helps minimize the number of faculty required to teach each course, cutting down the amount of coordination effort required. To avoid extensive "retooling" for the Core Knowledge courses, team teaching is used, which itself promotes faculty understanding of cross-functional issues, operations, and strategies. A significant number of cross-functional research initiatives have resulted from the strengthened relationship among procurement, manufacturing, and logistics faculty.

Second, students seem to recognize the benefits of a broader understanding of integrated supply chain processes combined with sufficient functional depth to perform in any supply chain position. Student comments regarding the integrated curriculum have been positive. In addition we have noted an increase in the number of students who cite the supply chain management program as their primary motivation for coming to Michigan State, particularly at the MBA level.

Third, recruiter interest has increased. Their response has been even more positive than expected. They believe the program provides a solid foundation for their specific management development and training, while allowing substantial flexibility in both initial and future job assignments. As expected, recruiting for planning-oriented jobs such as buyer/planners and logistics network analysts has increased.

Finally, the considerable reduction in duplicated efforts has made class time available for additional detail. Previously, there were student complaints about redundancy; the revised program introduces the topic (e.g., inventory management) once, discusses the basics, and contrasts the functional perspectives. This minimizes student confusion, as it encourages them to differentiate between differences in concepts rather than terminology. Students also appreciate having more time to cover state-of-the-art decision making and tools for each functional area.

Challenges and Success Factors

Achieving an integrated SCM curriculum requires that many challenges be addressed and resolved. First among these is managing resistance to change among faculty, students, and recruiters. A rather mundane yet very important contributor to faculty support for an integrated SCM program at MSU was the recognition that a combined purchasing-operations-logistics faculty would enjoy greater influence and political clout than the separate faculties individually possessed. This was an appealing prospect for faculty who had historically been relegated to "specialty areas" within larger management and marketing departments.

Team-teaching integrated SCM courses has presented quite a challenge and has produced mixed results. Several models of team teaching have been tried. The most successful approach seems to be to identify and emphasize points of integration across course contents, while also allowing for concentrated individual teaching time. For example, instructor A might teach for 1 week, then instructor B teaches for 1 week, followed by a series of "integration classes" that highlight relationships between the content from the prior 2 weeks. A serious challenge to the team-teaching approach is maintaining consistency of teaching resources. Course preparation time is increased dramatically each time a faculty team is reshuffled.

Because a SCM major is a relatively new idea, some stakeholders were uncomfortable about the inability to easily delineate expertise in purchasing, production, or logistics. They feared that the program and students would be perceived as "jack of all trades, master of none." The result might be difficulty in retaining and recruiting faculty and students, as well as in placing students. Fortunately, MSU has a long history of excellence in multiple supply chain disciplines. The business school maintains close relationships with recruiting firms, and the SCM program still allows students to position themselves by course electives and work experiences. However, business schools that are well known for education in a single discipline (e.g., operations management) might run the risk of "diluting their product image" by implementing an integrated SCM program.

At MSU we continue to wrestle with the competing aims of providing an integrated body of supply chain knowledge while maintaining deep reservoirs of functional excellence. One step we have taken is to attempt to delineate those content areas that are shared across supply chain disciplines from those that are unique to particular disciplines. Figure 4 presents a conceptual map of supply chain content areas as they have traditionally related to the three primary supply chain functions. The figure suggests that content areas such as inventory management and quality management are central and traditionally common to all three major disciplines in supply chain management, whereas areas such as negotiation, packaging, and production planning have been associated with specialized training. The goal as we see it is to seek ways to continually incorporate more and more of the content areas into the core body of knowledge without sacrificing too much depth in any single area, in effect squeezing the three circles in Figure 4 closer and closer together. The progress so far has come mostly as a result of eliminating redundancies in material across the disciplines. To progress further we recognize that we must learn to separate the core principles in a content area from their traditional context. For example, core principles of negotiation should be identifiable and equally applicable in settings of transportation management, supplier management, or manufacturing plant management.

Another challenge associated with the continuing development of the SCM program is keeping up with technology-based changes in the ways business is conducted. As the e-commerce curriculum grows, the department is seeking ways to integrate the currently

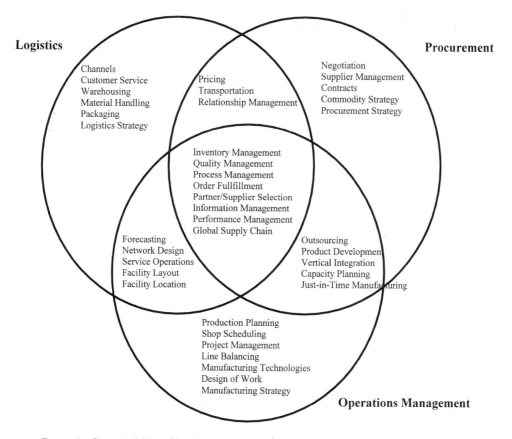

FIGURE 4. Conceptual Map of Logistics, Procurement, and Operations Management Content Areas.

separate information systems and SCM faculty bases. We have come to recognize that information technology and management is integral to all business processes. As such, the school has sponsored the creation of a "virtual information technologies group" made up of faculty from marketing and supply chain, accounting, and management departments. This group is responsible for planning, developing, and integrating information systems curricula across specific courses and departmental programs.

Many administrative issues have arisen during implementation of the new SCM curriculum. Developing integrated lesson plans requires considerable time and effort. Faculty must be willing to do the work, which may include learning more about other SCM areas. They also must be comfortable with team teaching and flexible about variable teaching schedules. Success in these areas is largely dependent on incentives and resources provided by administrators, and on the skills and capabilities of the individual faculty members. Some educators have better collaboration skills than others. It is important to identify these faculty members and to secure their participation, especially in teaching courses that contain a high degree of cross-functional content.

Other challenges include test design, grade administration, and student counseling on areas outside a faculty member's expertise. A significant concern is consistent testing and grading across faculty, especially when multiple faculty teach a single course section. As the program progresses into its third year, alternative approaches to achieving grading consistency are being evaluated. Assessing faculty teaching performance is also difficult. Initially, no mechanism existed for students to evaluate individual faculty in a team-taught course. As a result, each faculty member was assigned the average evaluation score for the team. Changes in the evaluation system enable students to assess each individual faculty separately. Beyond student evaluations, faculty performance is less formally evaluated by curriculum committees and by peers. But clear measures of faculty contributions and the value of those contributions remain elusive. Department chairs are the primary evaluators of faculty performance. However, a given chairperson may not attach the same priority to integrative teaching as curriculum designers do.

A final challenge involves assessing whether the integrated SCM program leads to better research. Presently there is a strong perceived conflict between the resources required to support an integrated SCM curriculum and those required to generate high-quality research. This conflict is poignant because it applies to untenured, assistant professors. The existing system of research-based rewards is not well equipped to incorporate rewards for assistant professors who might be asked to contribute significant amounts of time to integrative teaching and course development. Other performance issues, such as determining the number of student credit hours to assign to each faculty member, also remain complex. Administrative personnel must be instructed as to how to partition out the total student credit hours to faculty for evaluation purposes.

Conclusions

Students educated in integrated supply chain management are clearly in high demand, and business schools are struggling to respond. Although substantial organizational and historical barriers exist, the early experiences at MSU suggest that a cross-functionally delivered SCM program can be successful. Our experience suggests that restructuring the departmental organization is an important step toward real integration. Also important are a well-defined guiding philosophy, extra resources to support program development and start-up, and visible commitment from top-level administrators. At the core is the crucial importance of faculty recognition of the need for and potential benefits of an integrated program.

Early indicators suggest that the new SCM program is doing well. Students and recruiters have responded positively. Faculty members have expressed a new understanding of other functional areas and have identified areas for integrative research and teaching. Even though the start-up costs of developing new classes and courses are high, the prospective value gained by students, recruiters, and faculty appears thus far to justify the effort. In the words of John J. Coyle, a well-recognized logistics scholar, "It's an exciting time to be an educator. But we have to practice what we preach" (Saccomano 1998).

APPENDIX.
Topical Coverage for Supply Chain Courses

Level of Knowledge	Undergraduate	MBA
Basic Awareness	*Course:* Introduction to SCM (3 credits) *Description:* Integrative survey of procurement, operations, and logistics management topics. Marketing concepts covered in a separate course. *Topics:* Role of supply chains in business strategy Customer service and satisfaction Product and service design—concurrent engineering, QFD Supply chain process design—process types, choices Quality management—definitions of quality, TQM Forecasting, Operations planning and control Procurement—tools, supplier valuation Operations—detailed scheduling, staffing Logistics—transportation, warehouse management Response strategies—JIT, mass customization Performance measurement—total cost analysis Careers in SCM, Environmental issues in SCM International issues in SCM	*Course:* Value Chain Management (5 credits) *Description:* Integrative survey of marketing, supply chain, and business law topics that traces the flow of products from concept development to delivery to the final user. *Topics:* Elements of value and the value chain Marketing information and environments Supply chain processes—process types, design, and analysis Legal environment, Consumer protection Quality management—TQM, tools, improvement programs Services design and management, Product lines/brand management Supply chain flexibility—mass customization Integrated marketing communications Supply Chain strategies, Inventory management Pricing strategies, JIT—integrated supply chain Global business law, Sales force management Direct and on-line marketing, After sales support
Core Knowledge	*Course:* Supply Chain Management (4 credits) *Description:* Extends concepts introduced in prior course with greater emphasis on strategy, customers, and performance measurement. *Topics:* Supply chain competitive factors Transport system infrastructure and design Customer service, Transaction processes—order management Response-based strategies—JIT, postponement Inventory planning and management—inventory types, functions Product/process planning and quality—TQM, factory focus Supply chain strategy development, Manufacturing strategy Operations planning and control—layout, MRP Procurement, Value analysis/value engineering Logistics operations—warehousing, carrier evaluation Supply chain information systems, Relationship management Supply chain performance measurement	*Course:* Supply Chain Processes (5 credits) *Description:* Extends concepts introduced in prior course with greater emphasis on strategy, customers, and performance measurement. *Topics:* Supply chain management factors Customer focusing—customer types, perspectives Supply chain service levels/metrics, Cycle structure and dynamics Process flow analysis, capacity, and management of constraints Human resource management Insourcing and outsourcing—economies, make versus buy Time-based strategies—JIT, postponement, etc. Collaborative strategies and new product considerations Planning and forecasting techniques Inventory management—independent demand, dependent demand Information technologies—ERP Commodity strategy development—supplier evaluation Price/cost management, Advanced technology sourcing Negotiation and contracts, Manufacturing planning and control Manufacturing strategies—process design, factory focus Logistical integration, Logistical strategies, Network integration

Detailed Application	Traditional, in-depth coverage of respective topics. Courses delivered independently by functional specialists.

Course: Procurement Management (3 credits)
Description: Strategic issues in procurement and supply management. The purchasing function's role in fulfilling the firm's operations and competitive strategies.
Topics: Supplier evaluation and development
Relationships with suppliers
Purchasing research
Negotiation
Commodity planning
Cost, price, and value analysis

Course: Manufacturing Planning and Control (3 credits)
Description: Theory and practice for planning and controlling manufacturing operations
Topics: Production planning
Demand management
Inventory management
Master scheduling
Materials requirements planning
Capacity planning
Shop floor control
Computer integrated manufacturing
Just-in-Time systems

Course: Logistics and Transportation Management (3 credits)
Description: Microanalysis of logistics and transportation services including customer service, distribution operations, purchasing and operation of transportation services.
Topics: Customer service operations
Order processing
Network design
Facility design
Warehouse operations
Carrier selection
Transportation costing and negotiation
Transportation management | Coverage of procurement, operations, and logistics topics, respectively. Single course format enables a mix of jointly and individually delivered teaching

Course: Supply Chain Activities (6 credits)
Description: Analysis and problem solving of supply chain activities involving detailed study of functional areas of SCM including purchasing/sourcing, manufacturing operations, and logistics distribution. The course provides focused and detailed "drilling down" functional knowledge and skills. Attention is directed to tools, procedures, and metrics required to work in SCM.
Topics: Customer focusing
Supply Chain service levels and metrics
Cycle structure and dynamics
Process flow analysis
Capacity and management constraints
Insourcing and outsourcing
Time-based strategies
Collaborative demand/supply management
New product considerations
Planning and forecasting
Inventory—independent demand
Inventory—dependent demand
ERP
Procurement process and strategy
Building a world-class supply base
Price/Cost management and negotiation
Manufacturing planning and control systems
Manufacturing strategies
Logistics integration and strategies
SCM network integration |
| Process Integration | *Course*: Supply Chain Application and Policy (2 credits)
Description: Analysis and problem solving of SCM cases and simulations that emphasize teamwork, communication, and job skills. The course applies material to situations involving purchasing, manufacturing, logistics, and transportation as an integrated supply chain. | *Course*: Supply Chain Management (1 credit)
Description: Provides a seminar in Integrated Management. Case studies are used to develop strategic and operational insight into managing integrated supply chain engagement. A comprehensive simulated business exercise is completed during the seminar to afford student groups an opportunity to competitively interact. |

References

BANDYOPADHYAY, J. K. (1994), "Redesigning the POM Major to Prepare Manufacturing Managers of the 1990s," *Production and Inventory Management Journal*, First Quarter, 26–30.

BOWERSOX, D. J. AND D. J. CLOSS (1996), *Logistical Management: The Integrated Supply Chain Process*, McGraw-Hill, New York.

CLINTON, S. R., D. J. CLOSS, M. B. COOPER, AND T. J. GOLDSBY (1997), "World Class Logistics: A Two-Year Review," *Annual Conference Proceedings of the Council of Logistics Management*, The Council of Logistics Management, Oak Brook, IL, USA, 191–202.

CLOSS, D. J (1998), *LOGA VIII Participant's Manual*, 8th ed., Michigan State University, East Lansing, MI, USA.

———— AND T. P. STANK (1999), "A Cross-Functional Curriculum for Supply Chain Education at Michigan State University," *Journal of Business Logistics*, 20, 1, 59–72.

FLANAGAN, D. J (1994), "From Logistics Management to Integrated Supply Chain Management," in *Logistics at the Crossroads of Commerce*, J. M. Masters (ed.), *Proceedings of the 23rd Annual Council of Logistics Management Transportation and Logistics Educators Conference*, 163–181.

GENTRY, J., S. B. KELLER, J. OZMENT, AND M. A. WALLER (1996), "Themes and Issues from the 1996 Graduate Logistics Educators Symposium," in *Planning for Virtual Response*, J. M. Masters (ed.), *Proceedings of the 25th Annual Council of Logistics Management Transportation and Logistics Educators Conference*, 31–52.

Global Logistics Team at Michigan State University (1995), *World Class Logistics: The Challenge of Managing Continuous Change*, The Council of Logistics Management, Oak Brook, IL, USA.

JULIEN, F., J. DOUTRIAUX, AND J. COUILLARD (1998), "Teaching the Production/Operations Management Core Course: Integrating Logistics Planning Activities," *Production and Operations Management*, 7, 2, 160–170.

LOVEJOY, W. S (1998), "Integrated Operations: A Proposal for Operations Management Teaching and Research," *Production and Operations Management*, 7, 2, 106–124.

MILLER, J. G. AND P. ARNOLD (1998), "POM Teaching and Research in the 21st Century," *Production and Operations Management*, 7, 2, 99–105.

MORRIS, J. S (1997), "A New Approach to Teaching Production Operations Management in the Business Core Curriculum," *Production and Inventory Management Journal*, Second Quarter, 42–46.

RINEHART, L. M. AND R. A. NOVACK (1991), "Development of an Integrated Introductory Logistics Course," in *Towards the Integration of the Logistics Pipeline*, J. M. Masters (ed.), *Proceedings of the 20th Annual Council of Logistics Management Transportation and Logistics Educators Conference*, 1–19.

————, ————, D. J. CLOSS, AND J. J. COYLE (1990), "Rethinking Logistics for the 21st Century and Its Impact on Logistics Curriculum Issues," in *Logistics Management in the Year 2000*, J. M. Masters and C. L. Coykendale (eds.), *Proceedings of the 19th Annual Council of Logistics Management Transportation and Logistics Educators Conference*, 1–22.

————, ————, S. E. FAWCETT, AND G. L. RAGATZ (1992), "Logistics Operations Processes: An Approach to Teaching the Integration of Concepts Used in Manufacturing, Distribution, and Transportation Operations," in *Logistics Education for the 1990s*, J. M. Masters, (ed.), *Proceedings of the 21st Annual Council of Logistics Management Transportation and Logistics Educators Conference*, 136–163.

SACCOMANO, A (1998a), "Hard-Learned Lessons," *Traffic World*, February 9, 1998, 33–34.

———— (1998b), "School's In," *Traffic World*, October 19, 1998, 38–39.

SHEFFI, Y. AND P. KLAUS (1998), " Logistics at Large: Jumping the Barriers of the Logistics Function," in *Removing the Barriers*, J. M. Masters (ed.), *Proceedings of the 26th Annual Council of Logistics Management Transportation and Logistics Educators Conference*, 1–28.

STANK, T. P. (1997), *Logistics Value-Chain Game: Participant's Manual*, 2nd ed., Michigan State University, East Lansing, MI, USA.

David J. Closs is Broad Professor of Logistics in the Eli Broad College of Business at Michigan State University. He is coauthor of *21st Century Logistics: Making Supply Chain Integration a Reality*, *Logistical Management*, and *World Class Logistics: The Challenge of Managing Continuous Change*, and has published numerous articles in the areas of logistics strategy, systems, modeling, inventory management, and forecasting. Dr. Closs is editor of *Journal of Business Logistics*.

Steven A. Melnyk, CPIM, is Professor of Operations Management at Michigan State University. He is the lead author of numerous books in Operations Management. His research interests include shop floor control, metrics/performance measurement, time-based competition (TBC), supply chain management, process management, and environmentally responsible manufacturing (ERM). Dr. Melnyk is an active researcher whose articles have appeared in such international and national journals as *International Journal of Production Research*, *International Journal of Operations and Production Research*, *Business Horizons*, *Journal of Operations Management*, *International Journal of Purchasing and Materials Management*, and *Production and Inventory Management*. In addition Dr. Melnyk sits on the editorial review board for *Production and Inventory Management* and *International Journal of Production Research*. He is also the software editor for *APICS: The Performance Advantage* as well as the lead author on the monthly "Back to Basics" column found in that magazine.

Theodore P. Stank is Assistant Professor of Logistics and Supply Chain Management at Michigan

State University. He is coauthor of *21st Century Logistics: Making Supply Chain Integration a Reality*, *Logistical Management*, and has published numerous articles in the areas of logistics strategy, customer relevance, and internal and external integration in various journals including *Journal of Business Logistics*, *Journal of Product Innovation Management*, *Journal of Operations Management*, and *Transportation Journal*.

Morgan Swink is an Associate Professor of Operations Management in the Department of Marketing and Supply Chain Management at Michigan State University. Formerly, he worked for 10 years in manufacturing and product development at Texas Instruments Incorporated. Dr. Swink's research interests address innovation management, operations strategy, and logistics decision support systems. His current research investigates the effects of knowledge management practices on product and process innovation. He has published in various journals including *Journal of Product Innovation Management*, *Decision Sciences*, *International Journal of Operations and Production Management*, and *Journal of Operations Management*. He holds a Ph.D. in Operations Management from Indiana University.

EDUCATION INITIATIVES ON LOGISTICS AND SUPPLY CHAIN MANAGEMENT FOR SERVICE PROVIDERS IN HONG KONG*

RAYMOND K. CHEUNG, JIYIN LIU, AND YAT-WAH WAN

Department of Industrial Engineering and Engineering Management, Hong Kong University of Science and Technology, Clearwater Bay, Kowloon, Hong Kong

This paper documents the initiatives taken by the Hong Kong University of Science and Technology to upgrade the workforce of the logistics industry in Hong Kong. These initiatives are a new undergraduate program and a graduate diploma program to ease the long-term and short-term personnel shortage of the industry; a forum that provides a tripartite communication channel for government, industry, and academia; and a computational logistics laboratory that builds up the software infrastructure for the industry.
(TRANSPORTATION AND LOGISTICS, SUPPLY CHAIN MANAGEMENT, EDUCATION PROGRAMS, SERVICE PROVIDERS)

1. Introduction

As a gateway to Pearl River Delta (PRD), the light industry center of China, Hong Kong has been handling an astonishing amount of goods exported from and imported to PRD. With annual volumes of over 1.5 million tons of air-cargo and nearly 15 million twenty-foot equivalent units (TEU) of ocean containers, Hong Kong is one of the largest and most efficient international air and sea hubs in the world. Such volumes translate into more than 20% of GDP and well over 20% of total labor force (Thompson 1997).

Although Hong Kong can celebrate its past success in freight transportation, new challenges make it impossible for Hong Kong's logistics industry to limit itself to this traditional role. To remain successful, Hong Kong must transform itself into a global supply chain hub. We argue that, to take up its new role, Hong Kong needs:
- a new generation of engineers and managers for the logistics industry;
- retraining of the current middle to upper management of the industry;
- an establishment of close ties among industry, academics, and government;
- sufficient local human resources and infrastructure support for developing decision-support software.

Recognizing such needs, the Department of Industrial Engineering and Engineering Management (IEEM) of Hong Kong University of Science and Technology (HKUST) continues to regard logistics as one of its main focuses and has done so since its founding in 1993. To address the needs of the logistics industry of Hong Kong, IEEM at HKUST has started a number

---

* Received June 1999; revision received September 1999; accepted November 1999.

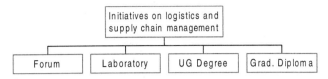

FIGURE 1. Four Initiatives on Upgrading the Workforce in Logistics and Supply Chain Management.

of initiatives to help upgrade the logistics workforce in Hong Kong. First, an undergraduate (UG) degree program on transportation logistics management was established in 1997 with its first group of students enrolled in the autumn of 1998. Second, a graduate diploma program for logistics and supply chain management professionals was developed and launched in July 1999. Third, an industry forum, called HKUST Logistics and Supply Chain Forum, was formed in late 1997. The forum has hosted a number of workshops and meetings for both academics and practitioners to exchange ideas and commission research. Finally, in December 1997, a computational logistics laboratory was established and a technical research team was formed to develop the necessary software infrastructure to support teaching and research on logistics and supply chain management (see Figure 1).

This paper documents the process that IEEM has gone through to develop the initiatives. Through the paper, readers can understand how education initiatives have been taken in one of the most important transportation logistics hubs in the world. Information such as this is essential for those who are considering a similar endeavor.

Organization of this paper is as follows: Section 2 lists the characteristics of the logistics industry in Hong Kong and discusses their implications, Section 3 describes our initiatives in detail, and Section 4 concludes our discussion and lays out the future plan.

2. Logistics in Hong Kong

Hong Kong's economy has been experiencing a great transition since China adopted the open-door policy 20 years ago. This has been reflected in the dramatic restructuring of its industries, the extensive expansion of its infrastructure, and the rapid growth of its logistics-related sectors. This transition, together with a free economic system, has formed the unique characteristics of Hong Kong's logistics industry. These characteristics dictate the needs and hence set the prescription of the logistics industry.

2.1. Achievements as an Established Transportation Hub

The open-door policy of China had a great impact on the structure of Hong Kong industries and provided golden opportunities for the logistics industry of Hong Kong. Attracted by huge supplies of cheap labor, land, and materials, factories originally based in Hong Kong gradually moved north. Today, Hong Kong–based companies own around 50,000 factories and employ more than 5 million workers in PRD. Despite the relocation of the production facilities, most companies still maintain their headquarters in Hong Kong. Consequently, Hong Kong has become a planning and marketing nerve center of the export-oriented manufacturing industry in the PRD region. A large proportion of raw materials and subassemblies of the manufacturing plants in PRD is imported and the majority of finished products are exported through Hong Kong. This has resulted in a rapid increase of freight traffic in Hong Kong. An investigation of the composition of the work force clearly shows the shift from manufacturing (35% in 1983 to 9% in 1998) to distribution-related services (20% in 1983 to over 30% in 1998), which include transport, storage, imports/exports, wholesale, and retail.

Rated as one of the world's freest economies by the U.S. Heritage Foundation, Hong Kong has been famous for its trading and reexport activities. A result of these activities is its intense freight traffic. Every week, over 800 ocean-going vessels visit the port; over 1,500 aircraft provide direct flights to nearly 100 cities all over the world; tens of thousands of containers are carried by barges between Hong Kong and PRD. To handle the increasing freight traffic, Hong Kong has invested heavily in transportation infrastructure. This includes the new $21 billion airport project that houses the world's largest air-cargo terminals, the new container terminal that adds another 2.6 million TEUs to Hong Kong's container terminal capacity, and the River Trade Terminal that has a 1.3 million TEU capacity for barge services. In addition, the establishment of a logistics park in Hong Kong is also on the government's agenda. All these developments, together with its financial might, have strengthened Hong Kong's role as a global transportation hub.

2.2. *Challenges for Further Development and the Need for Qualified Personnel*

Past success does not guarantee future success. A number of challenges have arisen recently, which include the pressure on costs, the competition from the neighboring cities, the lack of government-led efforts on logistics, the changing needs for new logistics services, and the emergence of information technology.

Hong Kong's success in the transportation logistics industry has set an example that all the nearby cities want to follow. There are four relatively new and sizable airports within 100 kilometers of Hong Kong: Macau, Zhuhai, Guangzhou, and Shenzhen. The terminal charges in these airports are 30 to 80% lower than that in Hong Kong. The deep-sea container port of Yantian, just 3 kilometers from Hong Kong, handled over 1 million TEU in 1998 and offered terminal charges 30% lower than fees in Hong Kong. The port of Yantian and two of its neighboring ports, Skekou and Chiwan, have a phenomenal annual growth rate of over 60% in the last 3 years. All these ports have already affected Hong Kong's share in handling import/export cargoes of PRD.

Whereas the Hong Kong government has tried to play merely a supportive role instead of having a direct hand on any industry, the governments in other Southeast Asia regions have set some favorable policies to increase the competitiveness of their logistics industries. Japan has adopted a new Integrated Logistics Guideline as a national policy since 1997 to foster cooperation among logistics service providers (Suzuki 1999). Taiwan has established a Warehousing Transshipment Zone and redeveloped the Export Processing Zone to attract more transshipment cargo. Singapore's government granted land at low rates to logistics operators to build their logistics centers. Major international couriers, at the same time, have developed their hubs in Singapore, Taipei, Manila, and Subic Bay. Without a clear policy on logistics, incentives for new development from logistics providers in Hong Kong can be limited.

Another challenge comes from the ever-increasing customer requirements, such as mass customization, just-in-time replenishment, and speedy delivery. A positive consequence of such requirements is the rise in the number of manufacturers outsourcing logistics functions. Most logistics providers in Hong Kong are eager to get into these new services. The question is whether they are ready. For example, to run a supplier hub for a manufacturer, the logistics service provider should know how the manufacturer's enterprise resource planning systems function so that their services can match with the manufacturer's production schedule.

Yet another challenge for Hong Kong logistics providers is the competency in using information technology that has already been widely adopted in their American and European counterparts. Currently, the levels of technology used in different sectors of the logistics industry in Hong Kong are very diverse. For example, on one end of the spectrum are the two air-cargo terminal operators and the four container terminal operators. These operators are private companies and large in size. They have invested substantially in information technology for managing their intense cargo-handling activities. At the other end are the numerous trucking companies that are small in size. The majority of them have a fleet size of less than five trucks and very few trucking companies maintain a fleet of over 100 vehicles.

There are no dominant players in this sector. The use of information or decision technology in making their dispatching decisions is rare. Between the two ends is a group of over 500 freight-forwarding companies, of which some have used information technology in their business, but mostly on documentation handling.

To remain competitive, the logistics industry needs to be upgraded by adopting new technology and concepts. Yet, until 2 years ago, none of the degree programs in Hong Kong specialized in logistics management. Retraining of the existing staff is also urgently needed for short-term solutions. Most middle to upper management personnel in the industry establish their credentials and secure their positions by starting as line operators and working diligently in the field for many years. Being in the industry for so long and getting used to the traditional operations mean that they have little chance to get exposed to advancements in supply chain management and logistics. Many need systematic refreshment of ideas and technology.

3. Education Initiatives

In spite of Hong Kong's supreme role in the global transportation network, there has been a lack of formal, comprehensive education programs for the industry. There was no degree program tailored for the industry until 1997. Students could learn only certain concepts such as supply chain management and logistics from courses scattered in different schools. At the time, the B.Sc. (Hons.) Degree in Shipping Technology and Management offered by the Department of Maritime Studies of Hong Kong Polytechnic University was the only degree program relevant to the industry. In the past, the program primarily placed emphasis on maritime transport, rather than the logistics industry.

There are certificate, diploma, higher certificate, and higher diploma programs offered in technical institutes and technical colleges, which are subdegree programs comparable to those offered in the 2-year community colleges in the United States. These programs are clearly vocational, aiming at training clerical officers and technicians. There are overseas programs enrolling students in distance-learning mode, e.g., the master programs in Integrated Logistics Management and in Logistics Management, a UG program offered by the RMIT University in Australia, and the Master of Management jointly offered by the Macquarie University in Australia and Hong Kong Management Association in Hong Kong. Most of these overseas programs are at the graduate level and are generally aimed at practitioners. These programs concentrate on management and strategic issues that may not completely address the needs specific to Hong Kong.

There are other vocational programs offered by various professional bodies: the diploma jointly offered by the Hong Kong Logistics Association and Hong Kong Productivity Council, the certificate courses by the Shippers Council, the certificate courses by the Hong Kong Management Association, and all sorts of programs offered by different trade unions and industrial organizations. Most of these programs focus on issues at the operation level and often serve only one particular function of a particular sector of the industry.

It is clear that Hong Kong needs a full-time, local degree program to train a new generation of engineers for the industry. These engineers must be equipped with up-to-date knowledge on information systems, supply chain management, logistics, and analytical decision tools. They are the workforces that will revolutionize the industry to keep up with the pace of modern development. At the same time, Hong Kong also needs an education program for the middle to upper management of the industry. This will provide immediate, although temporary, relief for the pressing demand to remain competitive in the logistics industry.

In response to this industry need, we have taken two education initiatives to address various aspects of the logistics industry: an undergraduate degree program and a graduate diploma program for middle to upper managerial personnel. In addition we have launched two supportive initiatives: a forum for tripartite (industry, academics, and government) communication and a computational logistics laboratory for software training and development. The following sections explain each of these initiatives in detail.

3.1. *The Undergraduate Degree Program*

On completion of the undergraduate program, students should understand the basics of the logistics industry and have practical insight into the needs of the industry. The formal title of the program is Bachelor of Engineering in Industrial Engineering and Engineering Management (Transportation Logistics Management). It is a 3-year program, fashioned after the dominant mode of UG degree programs in Hong Kong.

There were several major hurdles to clear in setting up the program to design a curriculum that suited the needs of Hong Kong, to convince the School of Engineering that the new program should be offered, and to merge the new program with the existing programs in the department.

The curriculum design process started with research on similar education programs in both engineering and business schools. Web sites were visited and catalogs were examined. Industrial friends who were key players of the industry were consulted. Contents of vocational courses offered by various bodies were studied and opinions of professional societies were solicited. With all these interactions, the form of the program gradually became clear.

Convincing the School of Engineering to start a Transportation Logistics Program was not as difficult as first imagined. Basically, the industry's needs and the suitability of the curriculum spoke for the program and the School of Engineering was quickly convinced. There was more effort spent on satisfying the requirements set by the Hong Kong Institution of Engineers, the statutory body authorized by the Hong Kong Special Administrative Region Government to accredit all engineering programs in Hong Kong. The statutory body specified the mix of content of engineering programs. But the content of a program in Transportation and Logistics Management was unconventional, compared with existing accredited programs. Fortunately, our program was designed primarily for technical personnel who would also be system developers on logistical, communication, decision support, and optimization systems in industry. The content is technical enough to satisfy the criteria of the statutory body.

The merge of the new program with the existing program in the department took some effort. It was impossible to double the resources for the addition of the new program and hence the two programs were not to be drastically different from each other. On the other hand, they had to be distinctively different from each other so that a new program was justified.

Because the new program and the old program shared many core and required courses, namely, mathematics, programming, and decision techniques, roughly two-thirds of the courses remained the same. These common courses significantly reduced the demand of additional resources. Adding new courses offered by other service departments further reduced the demand. Most new courses from the department were related to local (or regional) practices, which in any case we needed to develop. The addition of one faculty member on the logistics area partially relieved the merging problem.

In the following sections, we explain the curriculum, using two complementary dimensions: first the rationale and then the structure of the courses. For the rationale, we give the motivation and justification; for the structure, we show graphically in Figure 2 the relationship of different components of the curriculum.

3.1.1. RATIONALE OF CURRICULUM. We believe that students should have a clear picture of the industry right at the beginning of their study; therefore, a course describing the detailed operations of various components of the industry (IEEM 141) is offered in the first year. Most of the course materials were gathered from our on-site company visits. For example, students were hired in summers to station in companies to document the actual practices and process

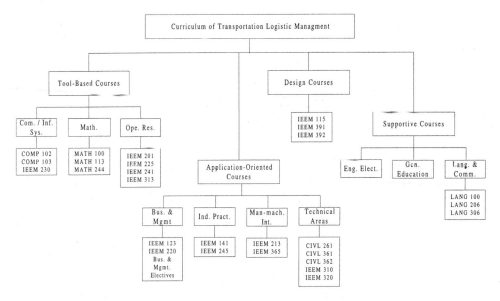

FIGURE 2. The Components of the IETM Curriculum.

flow. In the course, we had arranged 5 site visits and 8 to 10 talks from industrial professionals per semester. A follow-up course is offered in the second year describing the flows in supply chains (IEEM 245). The course design was different from those offered in business schools, which put more effort on the business aspect of the industry. We do not preclude our graduates from taking business-oriented posts in the industry, but we would like them to have the capability to start with technical, operational posts; hence, our program has a strong dose of mathematical and statistical decision techniques, including standard courses in operations research, and probability and statistics (IEEM 201, 225, 313, MATH 244).

Another course requirement in network optimization, routing, and fleet management (IEEM 241) was included, since an export-oriented economy definitely needs knowledge in distribution. Although the program concentrates on freight transportation, it seems worthwhile for students to have knowledge on urban traffic; hence, an appropriate course in that area was introduced (CIVL 261). Since computer, information systems, and programming are essential tools for decision techniques, the program includes structural training in information-related courses, covering computer fundamentals, languages, databases, and information systems (COMP 102, 103, IEEM 230).

Specific logistics functions, such as inventory control, are covered in tailor-made courses (e.g., 310). The management concept, an indispensable knowledge block of the curriculum, is covered by both the departmental and service courses (IEEM 220, business and management electives). A final-year project (IEEM 391, 392) lasting for two semesters is required for students to apply what they have learned to solve practical problems. There are other standard courses on mathematics, engineering, management, languages, and general education in the curriculum. The students are also required to take electives from other schools to broaden their knowledge.

3.1.2. STRUCTURE OF CURRICULUM. Figure 2 shows the structure of different knowledge blocks in the curriculum. The courses are classified as tool-based, application-oriented, design-based, and supportive. The tool-based courses are grouped under computer and information systems, mathematics, and operations research. The application-oriented courses are grouped under business and management, industrial practices, man-machine systems, and technical areas. The design-based courses introduce design techniques and provide real-life problem-solving experience. The supportive courses supplement students with engineering knowledge, general liberal education, languages, and communication skills. See Appendix A for the schedule of courses offered.

With additional input from industry, we may continuously need to make minor modifications to the program. In particular we are considering the addition of three required courses in the following areas: geographical information systems, transportation economics, and trades and international relations of Asia Pacific. These new requirements, however, will result in reducing the number of elective courses that students can take.

The whole curriculum requires 100 credits. Each credit corresponds to approximately one 1-hour lecture time per week for one semester. In addition, students are required to take industrial training for 10 weeks during the summer and winter breaks.

The program first enrolled students in 1998. As measured by the number of applicants, and eventually the quality of students, the program was favorably accepted. In fact the average quality of students is comparable to popular programs, although our program lacks the top students. In 1999 the initial application statistics of the program were good, although the aftermath of the economic crisis and the series of bad news in the transportation and logistics industry reduced the number of applications. Nonetheless, the quality of students has remained the same.

With the benefit of hindsight we suggest to others who want to set up similar programs that they first understand the regional needs. Without proving need, it is hard to convince the School of Engineering to allow the setup of a logistics-oriented degree program, to attract students, and to gain support from industry. The curriculum of the program must be designed carefully and it does not waste time to reiterate the curriculum-design steps. Suggestions from industry and overseas experts are indispensable. Finally, there must be thorough discussion throughout the whole department on the new program. Concerns and worries of colleagues must be voiced and resolved. The program cannot be successful without the full support of the department.

If the program is set up at a business school, we suggest trimming the technical content of the program by consolidating courses. Natural combinations of courses include the following: the four operations research courses IEEM 201, 225, 241, and 313 into two decision-analysis courses, one deterministic, one stochastic; the two programming courses COMP 102 and 103 into one; the two mathematics courses MATH 100 and 103 into a calculus course; and three Civil courses CIVL 261, 361, and 362 into an urban traffic and infrastructure course. To strengthen the business sense of the students, the following topics should be added to the program: business and company law, organizational behavior, human resource planning, micro- and macroeconomics, transportation economics, urban and regional geographic, and e-commerce.

3.2. Graduate Diploma Program

The degree program provides a long-term solution for the personnel shortage of the industry. As the logistics industry is expanding and the services provided evolving, there is a great and urgent need for personnel with modern logistics management knowledge. For an immediate solution, it is necessary to retrain the existing staff in the industry. For this purpose a graduate diploma program was developed.

The program includes a total of 10 modules and students are required to take at least 9 modules out of the 10. Each module consists of 2 full days of teaching, for a total of 14 hours. Upon successful completion of 9 modules, the School of Engineering awards a Graduate Diploma in Transportation Logistics Management. Because the program targets practitioners, the class meeting times are on Saturdays. To ensure that the participants have sufficient background to take the courses, applicants to the program are required to have a degree or at least 2 years' experience at a supervisory level in the logistics industry.

There are 10 modules in this diploma. See Appendix B for a brief description of each

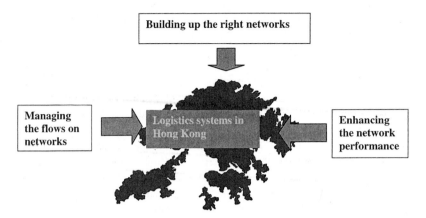

FIGURE 3. The Three Dimensions of the Graduate Diploma Program.

module. The modules are grouped into three dimensions of the operations and management of logistics systems: (1) building up global supply networks that use Hong Kong as a hub, (2) monitoring the network performance and quality, and (3) managing flow (goods, information, money) on the networks using new technologies (see Figure 3).

In the first dimension, we focus on how a distribution network is set up and operated, where Hong Kong serves as a hub and as a control center. There are four modules in this dimension:

1. Strategic Management Decision Making in Global Logistics Environment
2. Transportation Systems in China
3. Shipping Operations and Marketing
4. Shipping Finance and Legal Issues

In the second dimension, we assume that a global distribution network has been set up. To show how to align business processes with the distribution network and how to ensure the quality of the services provided, two modules are offered:

1. Design and Implement Effective Business Processes
2. Quality Management and Engineering

In the third dimension, we offer four modules on techniques in managing information and goods flow in the supply chains:

1. Global Supply Chain Management
2. Transportation Operations Management
3. Enterprise Resource Planning
4. Information Technology and Computer Applications to Logistics Service Providers

The 10 modules were designed in the incubation stage of the program. After the first year of the program, we may increase the number of modules offered. Two potential new modules under consideration are global sourcing and forecasting methods.

This program was first offered in July 1999 and the quota of 30 students was completely filled. With more than 10 years of relevant experience, most of the students hold middle-managerial to executive positions in their respective companies. Among the students, about one-third are from companies that require logistics services (such as manufacturers) and two-thirds are from companies that provide logistics services (such as freight forwarders).

3.3. *Supporting Activities*

To design an education program that is relevant to industry and in pace with changing technology, we also developed an industrial forum to cultivate academic-industry interactions and a computational logistics laboratory to support research and teaching activities and conduct projects.

The mission of the Forum is to enhance the competitiveness of Hong Kong's distributive services in the southern China region. In late 1997 the Forum formed alliances with the Stanford Global Supply Chain Management Forum and a similar forum at Eindhoven University, The Netherlands, to build a global network with other institutions with similar focuses and approaches to logistics and global supply chain management. Through the Forum, we have organized a number of workshops and seminars. Topics range from "port development" to "contingency planning for air-cargo service" to "the future direction of supply chain management." Speakers include academics from Hong Kong and overseas, government officials, and senior executives from industry. Some issues raised during the workshops and seminars have led to some project studies for both undergraduate students and the graduate diploma students.

The objectives of the laboratory are (1) to build decision support infrastructure for managing logistics activities in supply chains; (2) to study theories and techniques for design, implement, and control of logistics systems; (3) to develop local cases on supply chain management; and (4) to provide technical training for practitioners. The laboratory currently houses four full-time research staff and a number of research students. Examples of recent projects include an analysis of warehouse location because of the airport relocation, capacity requirement analysis and planning at terminals, and a study on the current status of supply chain management in Hong Kong. The laboratory has provided tools to a number of UG students in conducting their software-oriented final-year projects.

4. Conclusion

In about 2 years, the Department of Industrial Engineering and Engineering Management at the Hong Kong University of Science and Technology has designed and implemented a number of education initiatives to upgrade the workforce in Hong Kong's logistics industry. These initiatives include a Bachelor of Engineering Degree in Transportation Logistics Management, a part-time Graduate Diploma program in Transportation Logistics Management, an industry-oriented HKUST Logistics and Supply Chain Forum, and a computational laboratory on logistics. The primary focus of these initiatives is to upgrade the workforce for the transition of Hong Kong from a pure transportation hub to a value-created hub in global supply chains.

These initiatives represent only a starting point for a long-term campaign to propel the professionalism of Hong Kong's logistics industry. We expect that a number of hurdles will have to be overcome. For example, the general public's understanding of the importance of logistics and supply chain management to Hong Kong is still very low. Effort for recruiting talents who will devote their careers in logistics has been difficult. The future development requires a government-industry-academic tripartite effort.[1]

---

[1] We thank an anonymous referee and the editor for their valuable comments. Our work was supported in part by UGC Research Infrastructure Grant RI95/96.E04 and RGC Competitive Earmarked Research Grant HKUST6047/97E of Hong Kong.

Appendix A. A List of Courses for the Degree Program BEng in IEEM (Transportation Logistics Management)

First year, fall semester:
  IEEM 115 Engineering Design and Communication
  IEEM 123 Engineering Economy
  COMP 102 Computer and Programming Fundamentals I
  MATH 100 Introduction to Multivariable Calculus
  LANG 100 English for Academic Purposes
  ENGG Engineering Elective
  GEE General Education Elective
First year, spring semester:
  IEEM 141 Logistics and Freight Transportation Operations
  MATH 244 Applied Statistics

COMP 103 Computer and Programming Fundamentals II
MATH 113 Introduction to Linear Algebra
LANG 100 English for Academic Purposes
SB&M Business and Management Elective
GEE General Education Elective

Second year, fall semester:
IEEM 201 Operations Research I
IEEM 213 Ergonomics in Work Place Design
IEEM 245 Logistics Planning and Service Management
LANG 206 English for Engineering Management I
SB&M Business and Management Elective
2 GEE General Education Electives

Second year, spring semester:
IEEM 220 Engineering Management
IEEM 225 Operations Research II
IEEM 230 Industrial Database Systems
IEEM 241 Routing and Fleet Management
CIVL 261 Traffic and Transportation Engineering
LANG 206 English for Engineering Management I

Third year, fall semester:
IEEM 310 Integrated Production Systems
IEEM 313 System Simulation
IEEM 320 Facilities Layout and Material Handling
IEEM 391 Transportation Logistics Management Project I
LANG 306 English for Engineering Management II
IEEM IEEM elective
ENGG Engineering Elective

Third year, spring semester:
IEEM 365 Cognitive Engineering and Human Performance
IEEM 392 Transportation Logistics Management Project II
Any one of the following two:
   CIVL 361 Transportation Facilities Design
   CIVL 362 Transportation System Operations
LANG 306 English for Engineering Management II
IEEM IEEM elective
ENGG Engineering Elective

Appendix B. Brief Descriptions of the Modules in the Graduate Diploma Program

Strategic Management Decision Making in Global Logistics Environment

This module conveys the basic conceptual and operating background on logistics and supply chain and introduces strategic decision-making tools for global logistics professionals. It puts logistics decisions in the context of general management so that decisions can be integrated with overall corporate goals and tactics.

Transportation Systems in China

This module introduces the management system of transport in Mainland China. It covers the marketing analysis and the developments of freight transportation by rail, by road transport, by midstream and ocean transports, and by containers. It also discusses the strategies and issues related to the cross-border traffic between Mainland China and Hong Kong.

Shipping Operations and Marketing

This module presents an overview of the global maritime industry in two parts. First, it discusses management concepts as applied to terminals and container systems, vessel management, terminal management and support operations, seaport environmental concerns, and shipboard operations. Second, it covers the role of marketing in global maritime trade, marketing information systems and the marketing environment, marketing analysis and product decisions, and marketing communication.

Shipping Finance and Legal Issues

It presents cost-effective models applied to shipping finance, capital budgeting, and strategic planning in the maritime industry. It discusses problem solving and decision making, using financial information to manage a business or move cargo on ocean-going vessels. It also covers the basics of maritime law and liabilities of carriers and shippers at sea.

Design and Implement Effective Business Processes

This module, for both logistics professionals and global manufacturers, focuses on the design and implementation of effective business processes. It shows how to reduce management layers, clarify process ownership, and enhance employees' initiatives to take charge of their work. Computer-based modeling techniques are used to show how the approach is applied in real-life business processes.

Quality Management and Engineering

This module presents the fundamental concepts, ideas, tools, and techniques of quality management and quality engineering methods for service industries. Case studies and business applications are discussed for illustrating how to (1) identify the role of total quality management in business, (2) apply quality tools and techniques, (3) recognize the power of statistical process control, and (4) design experiments.

Global Supply Chain Management

This course shows how to gain market shares, reduce costs, improve customer services, and increase profits and returns to assets by using the concepts of integrated supply chain management, such as information sharing, reducing bullwhip effects, postponement, merge-in-transit, and vender-managed inventory.

Transportation Operations Management

This module focuses on the resource planning and operations management in freight transportation systems over space and over time. The course looks at the long-term planning problem of network design, the short-term resource planning problems for vehicle and crew, and the real-time decision problems on equipment deployment. Concepts, tools, performance measures, and the value of real-time information in tackling these problems are discussed through case studies.

Enterprise Resource Planning

This module presents the fundamental concepts of production planning and control with enterprise resource planning (ERP) systems. It emphasizes practical applications of information technology in enterprise resources management and provides hands-on experiences with the latest technology in ERP systems (SAP and Symix). It discusses how ERP technology can be applied to transportation-related operations.

Information Technology and Computer Applications to Logistics Service Providers

This course shows how to use information technology to coordinate activities among suppliers, producers, and distributors. It also illustrates how evolving information technology helps an enterprise to improve its business process and enables the business to incorporate new technology for electronic commerce in the future.

References

SUZUKI, S. (1999), "Trends on Logistics in Japan and the Responses," Proceedings of the 1999 *International Logistics Conference*, January 1999, Taiwan, 23–34 (written in Japanese).

THOMPSON, P. (1997), "Hong Kong's Port and Its Future," Speech on October 16, 1997, as the Chairman of the Hong Kong Port Development Board.

Raymond K. Cheung is an Associate Professor of Industrial Engineering and Engineering Management at the Hong Kong University of Science and Technology. His current research interests include network optimization, routing and scheduling, stochastic optimization, and their applications in transportation and logistics. After winning the George Dantzig dissertation prize and an NSF Career Award while at Iowa State, he returned to Hong Kong and worked with his colleagues to initiate research and educational programs in logistics.

Jiyin Liu is an Assistant Professor of Industrial Engineering and Engineering Management at the Hong Kong University of Science and Technology. His research is in the areas of operations planning and scheduling in production and logistics systems, optimization models, and heuristic methods and their applications.

Yat-wah Wan is an Assistant Professor of Industrial Engineering and Engineering Management at the Hong Kong University of Science and Technology. His research interests are applied stochastic processes, queueing theory, stochastic modeling and scheduling, and transportation logistics.

THE STATIONARY BEER GAME*

FANGRUO CHEN AND RUNGSON SAMROENGRAJA

Graduate School of Business, Columbia University, New York, New York 10027, USA

Booz, Allen & Hamilton Inc., New York, New York 10178, USA

This paper presents a variant of the popular beer game. We call the new game the *stationary beer game*, which models the material and information flows in a production-distribution channel serving a stationary market where the customer demands in different periods are independent and identically distributed. Different players, who all know the demand distribution, manage the different stages of the channel. Summarizing the initial experience with the stationary beer game, the paper provides compelling reasons why this game is an effective teaching tool.

(OPERATIONS MANAGEMENT, SUPPLY CHAIN MANAGEMENT, TEACHING, BEER GAME)

1. Introduction

The beer game is an exercise that simulates the material and information flows in a production-distribution system. It has four players: a retailer, a wholesaler, a distributor, and a factory. Customer demand (in kegs of beer) arises at the retailer, which replenishes its inventory from the wholesaler, the wholesaler from the distributor, and the distributor from the factory. In each period, the channel members must decide how much, if any, to order from their respective suppliers and the factory must decide how much, if any, to produce. There are transportation leadtimes in shipping the material from one location to another, and there is a production leadtime at the factory. While material flows from upstream to downstream, information flows in the opposite direction through order placements. There is an order processing delay, or information leadtime, between when an order is placed and when the order is received by the supplier. The players share a common objective to optimize the system-wide performance. For more details on the beer game, see, e.g., Sterman (1984, 1989).

In the beer game, the customer demand is 4 kegs per period for the first several periods and then changes to 8 kegs per period for the rest of the game. Moreover, the players have no prior knowledge about the demand process. (The numbers 4 and 8 are not important, but the demand pattern and the players' lack of information about it are.) Here in the stationary beer game, the customer demands in different periods are independent and identically distributed, and all the players a priori know the demand distribution.

There are compelling reasons why the stationary beer game is an attractive teaching tool.

---

*Reprinted from *Production and Operations Management*, Vol. 9, No. 1, Spring 2000, pp. 19–30.

First, it is quite common that companies have some knowledge about the market demand and are able to use that information for planning purposes. This feature is captured in our game since the players know the customer demand distribution. [If one uses the stationary beer game in conjunction with the Barilla SpA (A) case (1984), students can easily see the appropriateness of this assumption.] Second, there exists a theoretical benchmark for the supply chain, i.e., what rational players do and what the optimal supply chain performance is. It is useful to have this piece of information since students often ask what we, the instructors, would have done. (For the original beer game, however, there does not exist such a benchmark.) Third, students often find it an interesting exercise to formulate a replenishment strategy by using the demand distribution, and they are often eager to discuss the rationale behind their strategies. Fourth, the stationary beer game can be used as an example of a periodic-review inventory model that is often taught in Operations Management or Supply Chain Management courses (see, e.g., van Ryzin 1998). The experience with the game helps students visualize important inventory concepts. Finally, with our computer program, it is easy to run the game and to collect and display the results. It is our experience that a single instructor is sufficient for a class of 60 students.

2. The Stationary Beer Game

Consider a supply chain consisting of four stations: a factory, a distribution center, a warehouse, and a retail store. Material flows from upstream to downstream (i.e., from the factory to the distribution center, then to the warehouse, and finally to the retail store), whereas information in the form of replenishment orders flows in the opposite direction. Both the material and information flows are subject to delays. Different players manage the stations. They only have access to local inventory status and make local replenishment decisions. Customer demand arises at the retail store only. The demands in different periods are independent and identically distributed random variables. The demand distribution is known to all the players. Holding costs are incurred at each station for their on-hand inventories, and backorder costs are incurred only at the retail store for customer backorders. The goal is to minimize the *total* holding and backorder costs incurred in the entire supply chain.

Figure 1 depicts the material and information flows in the supply chain. The figure also specifies the two kinds of delays at each station. For example, suppose the retail store orders 10 kegs from the warehouse on Monday. The warehouse receives this order on Wednesday. This information delay is due to the administrative steps in processing an order. On Wednesday, however, the warehouse only has 5 kegs of beer, so it ships 5 kegs to the retail

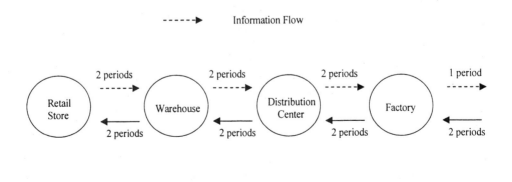

FIGURE 1. The Supply Chain and Its Leadtime Parameters.

TABLE 1
Cost Parameters

Location	Holding Cost ($/keg · period)	Penalty Cost ($/keg · period)
Factory	0.25	0
Distribution center	0.50	0
Warehouse	0.75	0
Retail store	1.00	10

store and backlogs the remaining 5. This shipment of 5 kegs arrives at the retail store on Friday. This delay is due to transportation.

The demands in different periods are independent, identically distributed, normal random variables. The normal distribution is discretized and truncated at zero to avoid negative demand values. The demand in a period has mean 50 and standard deviation 20.

Holding costs are assessed at every station for on-hand inventories. Each station must satisfy the orders from its downstream player (or the customers) as much as possible. In case of a stockout, the excess is backlogged. A penalty cost is assessed only at the retail store for customer backorders. This reflects the supply chain's desire to provide good customer service. (In contrast, the original beer game charges a penalty cost at each station. As we will see later in Section 5, when the stations are managed as cost centers, a penalty cost is charged at each station.) Table 1 summarizes the cost parameters.

A computer program is available for playing the game (see the Appendix).

3. Theoretical Benchmarks

For the stationary beer game (under the objective of minimizing the long-run average total cost in the supply chain), the optimal strategy for each station is to place orders so as to keep its installation stock at a constant target level, i.e., to follow an installation base-stock policy. The installation stock for a station is its on-hand inventory minus its backorders plus its outstanding orders (i.e., orders placed but not yet received). Notice that the installation stock at a station is local information and thus an installation base-stock policy is feasible under the game's information structure. The optimal target levels for the retail store, the warehouse, the distribution center, and the factory are 280, 225, 214, and 153, respectively. The resulting minimum long-run average total cost is $125 per period. [We refer the reader to Chen (1999) for a proof of the optimality of this policy and an algorithm for finding the optimal target levels.]

Figure 2 depicts the replenishment orders and net inventories at each station if all the players follow the optimal strategy. The average cost over the first 30 periods of the game (the default game length) is $196 per period. (This is different from the theoretical benchmark because of the initial conditions of the game. As we increase the length of the simulation, the average cost per period converges to $125.) Notice that the order stream at each station is identical to the customer demand process shifted in time (except for the first few periods due to, again, the initial conditions of the game). Therefore, the variance of replenishment orders does not increase from downstream to upstream.

If we eliminate the information delays, the theoretical minimum supply-chain cost drops to $51 per period, a 60% savings. This may result from the use of advanced information technology. Without information delays, the optimal strategy for each player is still an installation base-stock policy, but the target levels are now 157, 117, 110, and 107 for the retail store, the warehouse, the distribution center, and the factory, respectively.

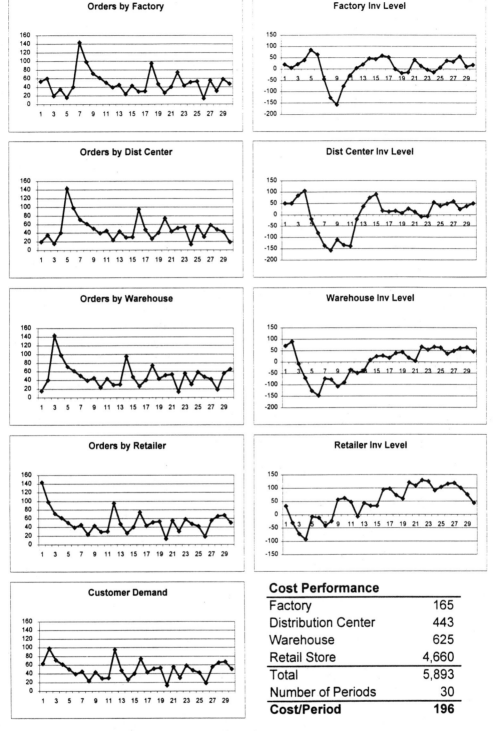

FIGURE 2. Results under the Optimal Strategy.

4. Our Experience

The stationary beer game has now been used in several master-level courses in both engineering and business schools. It has received great reviews from students. Below, we

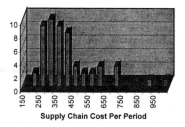

FIGURE 3. Cost Data from Spring 1999.

concentrate on our most recent experience in the core Operations Management course here at the Columbia Business School. In the spring semester of 1999, there were eight sections of Operations Management with a total of 500 students. We used the game at the beginning of the Supply Chain Management module of the course. We spent one class (80 minutes) to introduce the game with a demonstration and to let students play a training version of the game (which the computer program provides). The students then played the game "for real" outside of class and handed in a disk containing the team's results. We spent the following class to debrief the game together with a discussion of the Barilla case. Before the demo session, we asked students to download the computer program from the course's web site, to read the case that describes the game in detail, and to form groups. (We allowed more than one student at each station. Typically, two students managed a station.) The students then brought their laptop computers to the demo session. Each instructor was able to run the demo session without any help from teaching assistants.

Although the supply chain cost is $196 per period (over the first 30 periods) under the (long-run average) optimal strategy, the actual costs achieved by our students varied greatly. Figure 3 is the histogram of the cost data. (After removing those teams with incomplete results, we have 55 teams left. One team achieved a per period cost of $182, which is actually lower than the benchmark cost of $196. This is possible since the optimal strategy minimizes the long-run average cost.)

One of the key observations from the original beer game is the so-called variance amplification phenomenon, i.e., upstream orders tend to be more volatile than the down-

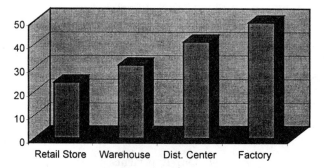

FIGURE 4. Variance Amplification in Spring 1999.

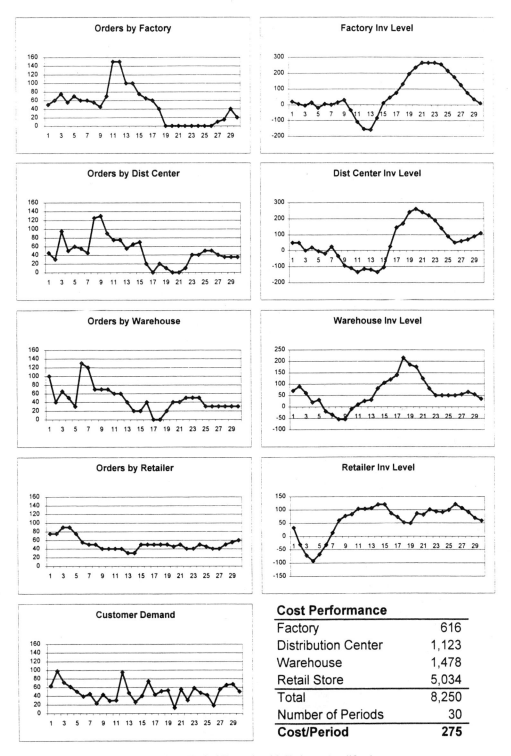

FIGURE 5. A Typical Example with Variance Amplification.

stream ones. Can the same be said for the stationary beer game? We computed the standard deviation of the order stream for each station in each team. Figure 4 plots the average

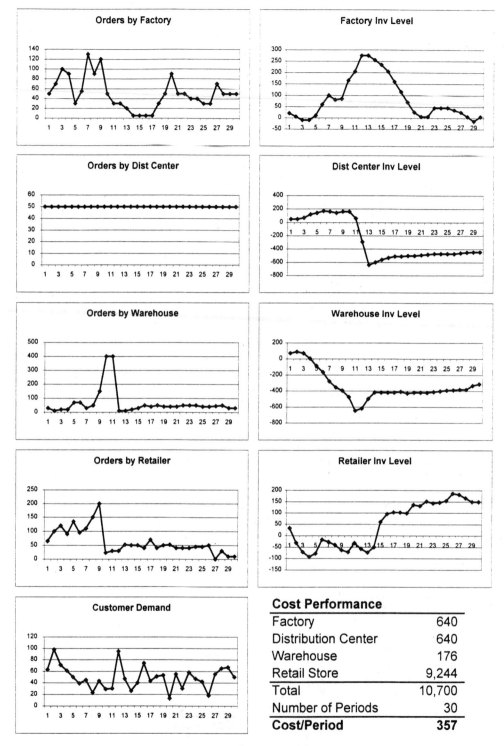

FIGURE 6. An Interesting Strategy.

standard deviation across teams by position. Interestingly, the variance-amplification phenomenon persists. Figure 5 is typical, where orders tend to become more volatile as they go upstream.

It is not surprising that the students used the demand distribution to formulate their strategies. For example, consider Figure 6. For each of periods 10 and 11, the warehouse ordered 400 kegs of beer. Apparently, these unusually large orders (relative to the mean demand in a period) did not move the distribution center, which continued to order the mean demand every period. Therefore, the information about the demand distribution helped mitigate, but not eliminate (as Figure 4 shows), the amplification of order variance. (One would wonder what the factory was doing given a steady stream of orders from the distribution center.)

Here, a natural question arises: If each station orders the mean demand (i.e., 50 kegs) every period, what will the supply chain's total cost be? This can lead to a very interesting discussion. After a while, it is not difficult for the students to see that this is a terrible strategy in the long run. The right way is to "manage" the inventory position (net on-hand inventory plus outstanding orders), i.e., placing an order every period so as to maintain a target inventory position. This is a key concept in inventory management. (A station's inventory position is also referred to as its installation stock in inventory theory.) Earlier, we mentioned that the optimal base-stock level for the retail store is $S = 280$. The total leadtime at the retail store is 4 periods (2 periods of transportation leadtime plus 2 periods of information leadtime). Therefore, the total demand during this leadtime has mean $\mu_L = 4*50 = 200$ and standard deviation $\sigma_L = \sqrt{4*20} = 40$. From the formula $S = \mu_L + z\sigma_L$, we have $z = 2$, implying a fill rate of 99% (see, e.g., van Ryzin 1998).

5. Extensions

The stationary beer game can be easily modified to simulate a supply chain with a different incentive and/or information structure. An alternative incentive structure is to manage the supply chain as cost centers, i.e., each player is charged the costs incurred in his or her own station under a predetermined accounting rule. On the other hand, an alternative information structure is to transmit the customer demand information to the upstream stations. Here is how. When the retail store places an order, it is also required to state what the most recent customer demand was. This demand information is then "tagged" to the order and travels to the warehouse; when the warehouse receives this information, it is required to tag the information to its next order to the distribution center, and so on. Therefore, each upstream player has two pieces of information coming from downstream in each period: a replenishment order and the corresponding customer demand value. The two incentive structures and the two information structures lead to four games (Table 2). Note that Game I here is the stationary beer game.

When the supply chain is managed as cost centers, the costs charged to each station are based on its accounting inventory level, which is determined by assuming that the immediate upstream supplier is perfectly reliable (i.e., it never runs out of stock). Therefore, it is likely that a station's accounting inventory level is different from its actual inventory level. For Games II and IV, each station is charged a holding cost if its accounting inventory level is positive and a penalty cost otherwise. Table 3 provides the accounting costs for each station. These cost parameters have been chosen so that if the players act rationally, the (actual) supply chain cost as measured by using the (actual) cost rates in Table 1 is minimized. (The actual supply chain cost may be different from the sum of the accounting costs.)

The incentive structure determines who the winners are. For Games I and III (with the team structure), the winning team is the one with the lowest supply chain cost. For Games II and IV (with the cost-centers structure), there are winning individuals, instead. Here, the accounting cost at, e.g., the retail store, is compared with the accounting costs of all the other retail stores. The one with the lowest accounting cost is a winner. Therefore, there will be four winners, one for each station. Of course, they may not come from the same team.

TABLE 2
Four Games

	Demand Information Not Transmitted	Demand Information Transmitted
Team	Game I	Game III
Cost centers	Game II	Game IV

TABLE 3
Accounting Costs for Games II and IV

Location	Holding Cost ($/keg · period)	Penalty Cost ($/keg · period)
Factory	0.25	0.3
Distribution center	0.25	0.4
Warehouse	0.25	0.7
Retail store	0.25	10.7

When the players are rational, the actual supply chain cost should be identical across the four games. In reality, this may not be the case and the discrepancy can be used to illustrate the impact of accurate demand information and decentralized decision-making. The computer program can be used to play all the four games. We hope that Games II, III, and IV will be used in classrooms in the near future.[1]

This paper is dedicated to the students in the MBA core course B6801 Operations Management in the spring semester of 1999 at the Columbia Business School. Their input to the development and improvement of the stationary beer game is invaluable. We are grateful to Professors Nelson Fraiman, Fred Silverman, and Garrett van Ryzin for agreeing to try the new game in the OM course and for their helpful suggestions and comments. We also thank the editors of this special issue and the referees of this paper for their suggestions and comments that have significantly improved the exposition of the paper. Financial support from the National Science Foundation, the Columbia Business School, and the Eugene Lang Foundation is gratefully acknowledged.

Appendix

A Computer Program for Playing the Game.

Supply Chain Simulations, a Visual Basic for Excel application, was developed for the sole purpose of playing the games described in this paper. (To obtain a copy of the program and related materials, please send an e-mail to the first author at fc26@columbia.edu.) With the program, the games are easy to run and fun to play. The only requirement is that each station have a computer with Excel for Office '97 (Version 8). Therefore, there are four computers in a team. These computers are stand-alone. (We are in the process of developing a web-based version.) Consequently, the passing of information between two stations is done manually. Below, we present the benefits of using the program from the standpoints of both the players and the instructor together with some screenshots of games in progress.

Benefits to Players

As anyone who has played the original beer game knows, a significant amount of time is spent executing the mechanics of material and information flows. It is not easy to handle shipments of dozens of pennies (if not hundreds) while the instructor is trying to keep all teams in sync. Supply Chain Simulations automates almost all of the game mechanics. Furthermore, since the program acts as an "instructor" guiding the players through every step of the game, confusion is minimized and teams can proceed at their own pace.

The interface was designed to help the students visualize the material and information flows. The screen may be different depending on the game played. Figure A1 and Figure A2 are screenshots from Games I and IV, respectively.

The program tracks all relevant state variables for the players, such as inventory level and outstanding orders, and presents them in both numerical and graphical formats (see Figures A3 and A4).

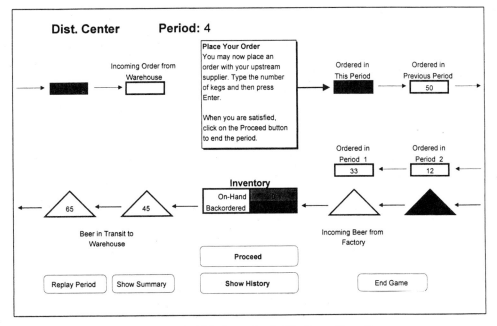

FIGURE A1. The Main Screen for the Distributor (Game I).

Players may choose to play a training version, which uses different demand values and moves at a slower pace. This allows them to learn at their own pace and practice any strategies they may have devised before playing "the real thing."

Benefits to Instructors

From the instructor's point of view, setting up the game for use is simple. Although the game comes "ready to play" as is, the instructor is free to change many of the game's parameters, including demand and cost parameters

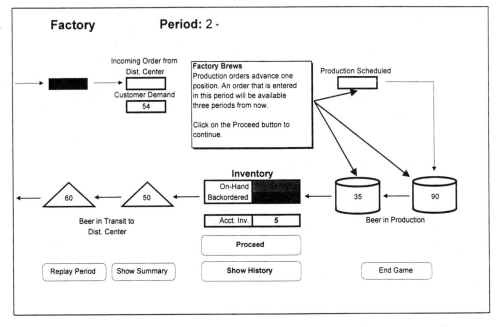

FIGURE A2. The Main Screen for the Factory (Game IV).

Beer History Sheet

Return To Main Screen | Show Graphs | Use the PgUp and PgDn keys to scroll

Position: **Dist. Center**

Period	Starting Net Inven.	Quantity Received	Warehouse Order	Quantity Shipped	Ending Net Inven.	Starting Outstanding Orders	Order to Factory	Ending Outstanding Orders	Holding & Backorder Cost	Cumulative Cost
1	50	24	33	33	41	137	33	146	21	21
2	41	55	44	44	52	146	12	103	26	47
3	52	16	65	65	3	103	50	137	2	48
4	3	42	49	45	(4)	137	60	155	0	48
5	(4)	20	42	20	(26)	155	65	200	0	48
6	(26)	15	32	15	(43)	200	65	250	0	48
7	(43)	50	40	50	(33)	250	65	265	0	48
8	(33)	65	12	45	20	265	40	240	10	58
9	20	65	30	30	55	240	30	205	28	86

FIGURE A3. The History Screen.

and the game length. Once the parameters are set, the instructor need only distribute the program to each player. Password protection ensures that the parameters won't be tampered with. No other materials are needed during play. This eliminates the need for constructing game boards, procuring stacks of index cards, and gathering mounds of change needed in the original beer game.

Since the program guides players through the steps of the game and automates the bookkeeping tasks, the need for instructor supervision is minimal. In fact, once players have been introduced to the game and shown how to use it, it is possible for them to play the game on their own, outside of class. Those familiar with the original beer game can appreciate the reduced handholding requirements.

At the end of a game, the program records the results for each team onto a floppy disk, automatically generating results ready for classroom use. This allows for rapid turnaround of results.

It is our intention that Supply Chain Simulations be used as a virtual laboratory. The structure of the games and the customizability of the parameters allow many different hypotheses to be tested under controlled conditions. The ease with which data is recorded and compiled lets instructors build a comprehensive database of experimental results after only a few semesters.

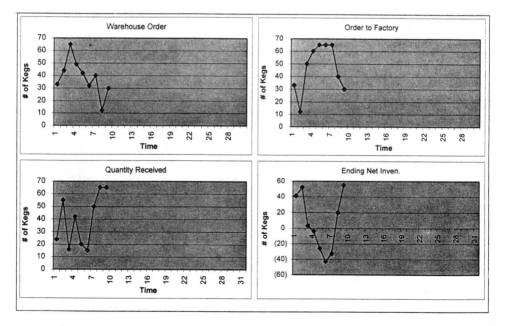

FIGURE A4. In-Game Graphics.

References

BARILLA SPA (A) (1984), Harvard Business School Case, N9-694-046.

CHEN, F. (1999), "Decentralized Supply Chains Subject to Information Delays," *Management Science,* 45, 8, 1076–1090.

STERMAN, J. (1984), "Instructions for Running the Beer Distribution Game (D-3679)," Sloan School of Management, MIT.

——— (1989), "Modeling Managerial Behavior: Misperceptions of Feedback in a Dynamic Decision Making Experiment," *Management Science*, 35, 3, 321–339.

VAN RYZIN, G. (1998), "Analyzing Inventory Cost and Service in Supply Chains," Teaching Notes, Columbia Business School.

Fangruo Chen is Associate Professor of Management Science and Operations Management at the Graduate School of Business, Columbia University. His research area is multi-echelon inventory models/supply chain management. He has published many articles in Management Science, Operations Research, Naval Research Logistics, Operations Research Letters, and European Journal of Operational Research. In 1997, he received the prestigious CAREER award from the National Science Foundation. He is an associate editor of Management Science, Operations Research, and Manufacturing & Service Operations Management.

Rungson Samroengraja is an Associate with Booz, Allen & Hamilton. He received his doctorate from Columbia University's Graduate School of Business in 1999. His research examined the effects of demand variability in multi-echelon inventory models. His current work involves restructuring value chains and improving channel performance across a broad range of industries such as life sciences, specialty chemical and publishing.

PLAYING THE BEER DISTRIBUTION GAME OVER THE INTERNET*

F. ROBERT JACOBS

Kelley School of Business, Indiana University, Bloomington, Indiana 47405, USA

This paper describes an Internet implementation of the Beer Distribution Game. Many teachers demonstrate the bullwhip effect that is often observed in supply chains by playing this game with their students. This implementation has the advantage of considerably reducing the time required to play the game.

(SUPPLY CHAIN MANAGEMENT, BEER GAME, INTERNET, GAME)

Introduction

Possibly one of the most widely used classroom exercises for demonstrating the dynamics of a supply chain is the Beer Distribution Game. The System Dynamics Group developed the exercise at the Massachusetts Institute of Technology's Sloan School of Management (Sterman 1989). Normally the game is played manually on a game board with paper demand and order cards. Pennies are used to track the movement of cases of beer. This paper describes a version of the game that can be played over the Internet that has the advantages of quicker setup, quicker game play, and quicker analysis of game results.

The Beer Distribution Game simulates a phenomenon known as the "bullwhip" effect. The classic example of the bullwhip effect was observed at Procter & Gamble (P&G) with the sales of Pampers diaper (Lee, Padmanabhan, and Whang 1997). While the consumers, in this case babies, consumed diapers at a steady rate, the variability of demand grew as it progressed up the supply chain. For instance when P&G looked at demand for raw materials to their suppliers, such as 3M, they saw large swings. Many additional examples of the phenomena have been identified in the literature.

The manual version of the game is played on a board that represents the production and distribution of beer (see Figure 1). Teams of students represent different parts of the supply chain. Players take on the following roles to simulate the supply chain echelons for each brewery:

- the retailer sells cases of beer to a consumer and orders cases of beer from the wholesaler,
- the wholesaler sells cases of beer to the retailer and orders cases of beer from the distributor, and
- the distributor sells cases of beer to the wholesaler and orders beer from the factory.

---

* Reprinted from *Production and Operations Management*, Vol. 9, No. 1, Spring 2000, pp. 31–39.

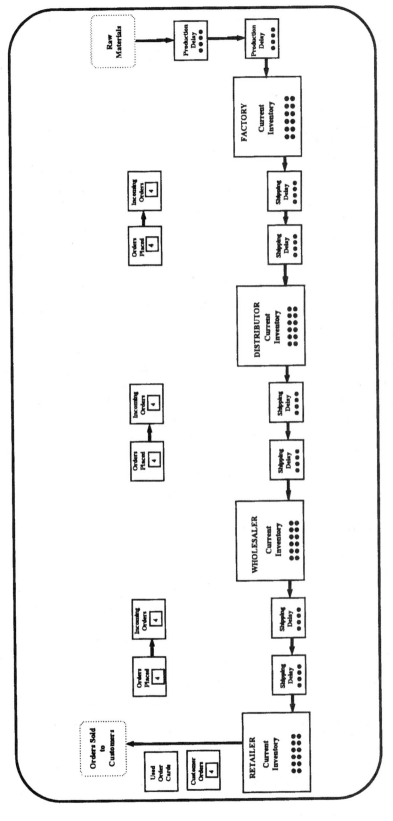

FIGURE 1. Beer Distribution Game—Manual Board Setup.

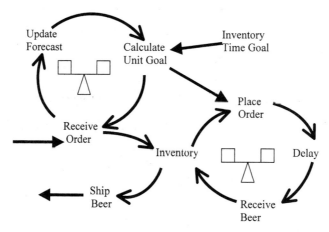

FIGURE 2. Model of the Decision Process for Players of the Beer Game.

- The factory brews the beer.

Pennies represent cases of beer and are moved between the positions on the board. The object of the game is to minimize two inventory related costs: holding cost ($0.50/case/period) and backordering cost ($1.00/case/period). Costs are assessed each period at each echelon as the game is played. During each period the players receive orders, evaluate their inventory position and decide orders and shipments for their echelon. Consumer demand for beer is simulated using a deck of cards according to a predetermined sequence and given to the retailer each period. A fixed shipping delay of two periods between each echelon simulates the time required to receive, process, ship and deliver orders. In the case of the factory, a lead time of two periods is required to produce a new beer order.

The game starts in equilibrium with 12 cases of beer in inventory at each echelon and 4 cases in each of the delay positions (see Figure 1). Normally, the simulation begins with four weeks of steady demand (4 cases per week) and all the players are directed to order and ship four cases each period, to maintain the initial equilibrium. Following the four-period startup, players are then instructed to order any quantity they wish. At this point, there is an increase in customer demand to eight cases per week. This change in demand induces disequilibrium into the system to which the students must react. A complete description of the game including the specific "rules of play" is given in Heineke and Meile (1995).

Note that the increase in demand is introduced at the retailer, who may respond with a change in the size of the order to the wholesaler. The retailer, in deciding what to order, may perceive the increase in demand in a number of ways. The wholesaler does not see the change in the order size until the next period. So the knowledge of this change in demand propagates through the system over the next four to five periods.

Sterman (1989) performed econometric tests to explain player behavior and found that an anchoring and adjustment heuristic for stock management was a good fit to the behavior. As noted by Sterman, players fall victim to several "misperceptions of feedback." Specifically, the players failed to account for control actions, which had been initiated but have not yet had their effect (i.e. they were looking at inventory on-hand rather than inventory position). In Sterman's studies, the majority of players attributed the dynamics they experienced to external events, when in fact these dynamics were internally generated by their own actions.

Professor Dan Steele of the University of South Carolina, has developed an interesting model of the process that the decision-maker uses in playing the Beer Game (see Figure 2). His model includes a forecast of the future demand. This forecast is used to calculate a stocking level goal that the player thinks is appropriate. An actual order is then placed in an attempt to bring the inventory up to this target level. When the upstream player sees this order, for example when the wholesaler sees the order from the retailer, the player reacts by ordering even more inventory. As we move up the supply chain toward the factory, the impact of the demand spike is further overstated, thus inducing the bullwhip effect.

Major causes for the bullwhip effect in practice have been proposed as: 1. Demand forecast updating, 2. Order batching, 3. Price fluctuation, and 4. Rationing and shortage gaming (see Reference 2). Although, in playing the Beer Game, we do not explicitly state what caused the change in demand at the retailer, students likely perceive that some external event has caused this change in demand. If we believe Professor Steele's model, then forecast updating and the processing of this new information relative to the current inventory position, is the major reason for the effect generated in the Beer Game simulation.

The Internet version of the game actually is driven by demand supplied in a file, so it is easy to input alternative demand streams that are representative of external factors as mentioned above. Price fluctuations could be reflected in periods of high and low demand that represent buying patterns influenced by the pricing. Placing limits on the maximum capacity of the factory could simulate rationing. There are many scenarios that could be developed to demonstrate various external factors as found in the real world. Performing experiments to study the impact of these proposed causes for the bullwhip effect could be an interesting research project.

Playing the Internet Version of the Game

Playing the manual version of the game can be a great experience, but it consumes a significant amount of time. Typically it takes about an hour to explain the game and get the game board set up. Another hour and half is spent actually playing the game. After playing the game the students must be given time to tabulate results, calculate costs, and construct graphs. A debriefing is then completed that takes another 30 to 45 minutes. In total, a minimum of three hours needs to be devoted to the game. Often the debriefing is complicated by errors in tabulating results that can lead to confusion.

With the Internet version of the game, students work at personal computers in a classroom, using a web browser to play the game. A special program resident on a web server keeps track of the game. Many teams can play the game simultaneously (to date the program has been used with eight teams playing at the same time). The program is designed to take decisions from each position in the distribution system, check that the decisions are valid, compute inventory and backorder levels, and calculate costs. At any point in the simulation, detailed graphs can be requested which show inventory, backorder, and ordering information for each position on a team.

To start the game, students are divided into teams, and then each student (or pair of students) is assigned a position on the team (retailer, wholesaler, distributor, or factory). Students log into the system from the beer game starter screen (see Figure 3) by simply clicking into their position. Keep in mind that each team plays the game totally independent of the other teams. The instructor leads the students through each period of playing the game.

Players are presented with the screen shown in Figure 4. This screen has three frames. The frame at the upper left is used to record decisions. Here the player enters the number of cases to ship downstream and the number of cases to order from the upstream position. The program will not allow a player to ship more than the combined current demand plus backlog, nor can the player ship beer that is not currently in inventory.

The instructor determines when each period has passed and manually triggers the update of the system. The server records the decisions and updates the inventory positions using a special instructor form (see Figure 5). Players may change their decisions at any point up to the time when the program is instructed to update the database. The top right panel (Figure 4) shows the current inventory position. This area shows the current demand, backorder position, shipment amount, inventory level, the amount that will be delivered next period, the amount that will be delivered two periods from now, and the current proposed order. The inventory and backorder

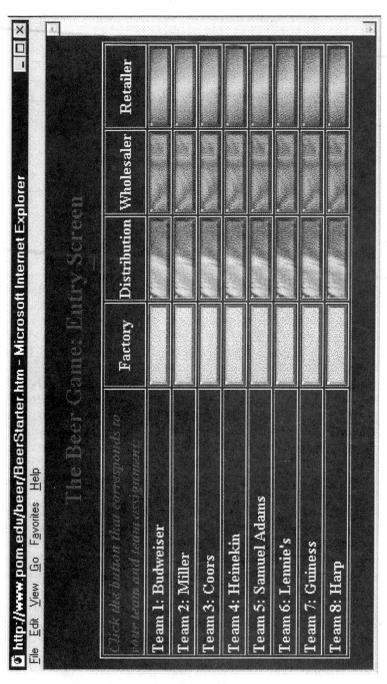

FIGURE 3. Initial Screen Selection Screen.

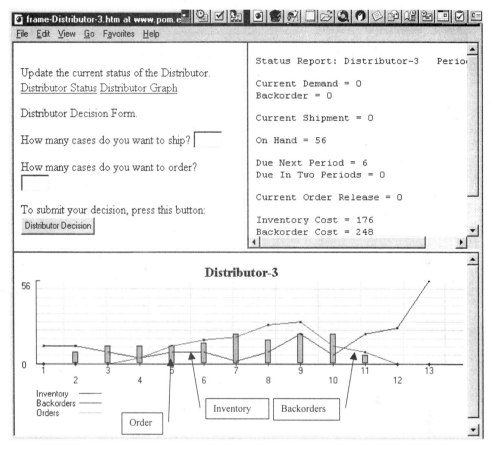

FIGURE 4. Playing Screen.

costs incurred by the player are also displayed in this panel. The player asks for this screen to be updated by clicking on a status update button in the decision panel.

A graph, in the lower panel, shows the inventory, backorders, and orders (shown with the bars) up to this point in the game. The graph is updated manually by clicking on the graph update button in the decision panel. The graph gives the player data on how the game has gone thus far (the inventory and backorder lines are different colors on the computer screen, but have been annotated for this paper). In looking at the graph, one might be surprised to see that the player has backorders and inventory during some of the periods. The data shows the status at the beginning of the period, so it is possible that a player has just received some inventory and the player is in a backorder position relative to demand. Normally students will ship exactly what was ordered plus the backlog subject to availability but some students may decide to hold back inventory thinking that the request from the downstream position does not seem reasonable.

Normally, the game is played for 35 to 40 periods to fully capture the "bullwhip" effect in the system. The Internet version can be played at a rate of approximately 45 seconds per period allowing the entire game to be played in 35 minutes. Clearly, one of the main advantages of using the Internet version is the speed in being able to complete the exercise. Valuable class time need not be spent moving poker chips, recording inventory levels, and calculating costs.

On completion of the game, the debriefing session can start immediately since statistics and graphs documenting the performance of each team are immediately available. Figure 6 shows a debrief graph for a particular team. From this figure, which for clarity only includes

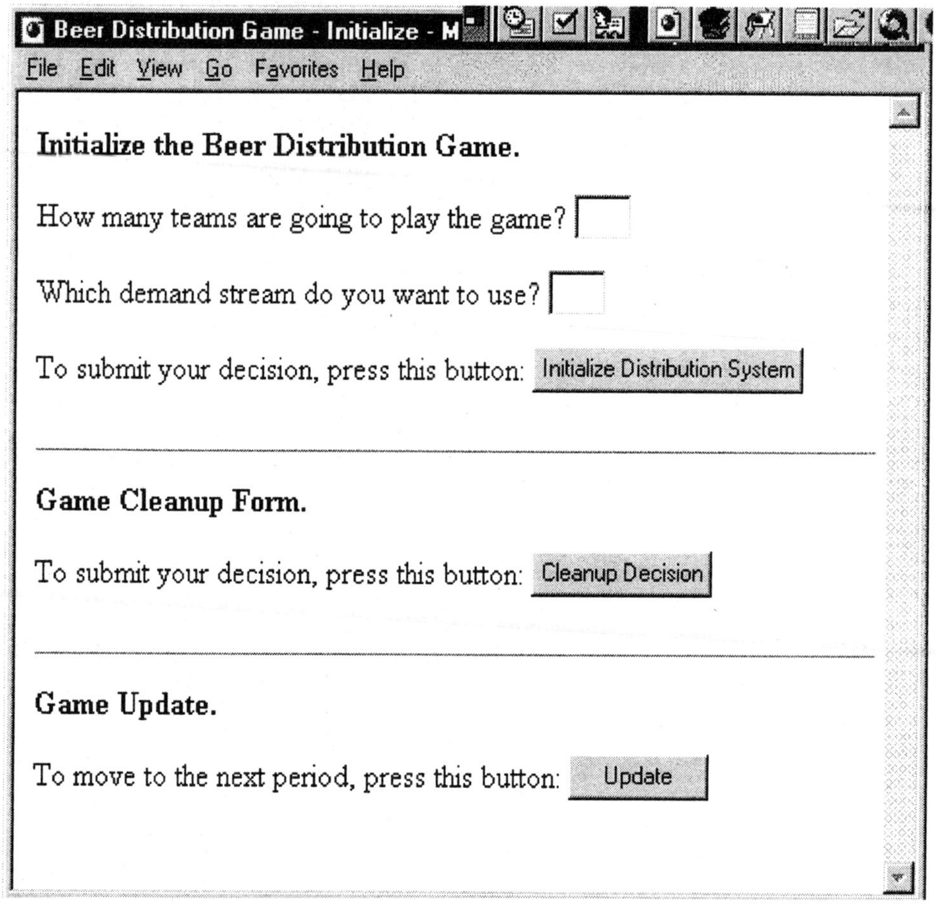

FIGURE 5. Instructor Screen.

25 simulated periods, we see how significant levels of inventory were built in reaction to the increase in demand in period four. In each panel, a graph showing one of the positions on the team is displayed. In the case of the simulation shown in Figure 6, inventory levels reached a maximum of 339 units at the wholesaler, 465 units at the distributor, and 500 units at the factory. A quick scan of the variation in the size of the orders at the retailer, wholesale, distributor and factory shows how each player reacted differently to the information. On viewing the graphs, team members can easily recall and explain what happened as they played the game. A significant benefit of the Internet version of the game is that it eliminates the confusion during the debriefing due to student errors in tabulating the results.

In addition to discussing the performance of each of the teams, the debrief session should also show examples of the bullwhip in actual settings. A few examples are given in Lee et al. (1997). A model that helps to explain the behavior such as Figure 2 can also be used. Finally, a discussion of how companies should design their supply chain and information support systems to avoid the problem, is a useful way to conclude the discussion.

Conclusions

The Internet version of the game was developed in August 1996 and has been used at Indiana University and other schools on many occasions. The program can be run off the web site at http://www.pom.edu/beer/, and need not be installed on a local server. In the future, the program may be made available for installation on a local server.

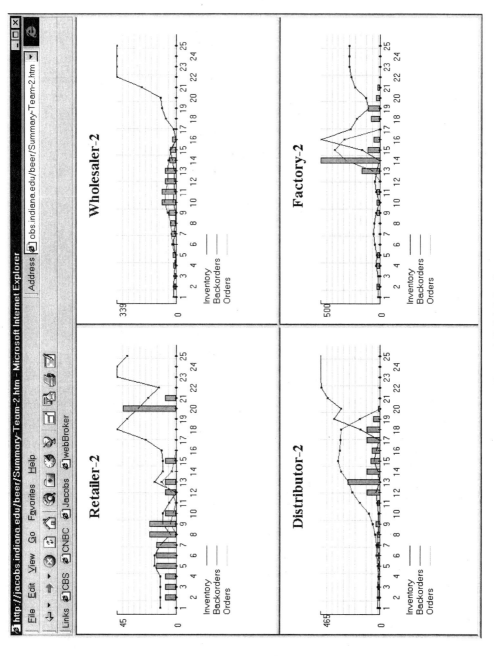

FIGURE 6. Debrief Graphs.

The Internet Beer Game represents one of the first implementations of a management game that uses the Internet. By taking the administrative burden of running the game off the shoulders of the students and instructors the Internet can improve the quality of the experience and leave more time for learning and analysis.

References

HEINEKE, J. N., AND L. C. MEILE (1995), Games and Exercises for Operations Management: Hands-On Learning Activities for Basic Concepts and Tools, Prentice Hall, 1995, 101-111.

LEE, H. L., V. PADMANABHAN, AND S. WHANG (1997), "The Bullwhip Effect in Supply Chains," *Sloan Management Review* (Spring, 1997), 93-102.

STERMAN, J. D. (1989), "Modeling Managerial Behavior: Misperceptions of Feedback in a Dynamic Decision Making Experiment," *Management Science,* Vol. 35, No. 3 (March 1989), 321-339.

F. Robert Jacobs is Professor of Operations Management at the Kelley School of Business, Indiana University. He has degrees in Industrial Engineering, Computer and Information Science, an MBA, and a Ph.D. in Operations Management. He has published 4 books and over 30 research articles on topics that include inventory control, the design of manufacturing facilities, cellular manufacturing, and the scheduling of manufacturing operations. He is the co-author of an Operations Management textbook titled, *Operation Management for Competitive Advantage* (Irwin/McGraw-Hill).

TEACHING SUPPLY CHAIN MANAGEMENT PRINCIPLES: THE OTOGEL SIMULATION EXERCISE*

KATHLEEN E. MCKONE

Department of Operations and Management Science, Carlson School of Management, University of Minnesota, Minneapolis, Minnesota 55455, USA

> This paper describes an experiential simulation that uses Lego building blocks to teach general management principles regarding supply chain management. This team-based experience requires students to work with suppliers, manufacturers, and retailers to produce and deliver products to meet demand. Teams are evaluated by their total profits, which are based on revenues from meeting demand in a timely manner and costs of labor, facilities, inventory, and raw materials. Multiple periods are played; each period involves additional complexities. Process improvements after each period lead to lessons concerning supply chain management, including designing for manufacturability, postponing customization, managing inventory, and coordinating decision making.
> (SIMULATION, SUPPLY CHAIN MANAGEMENT, MANAGEMENT EDUCATION)

Introduction

Experiential simulations and games are an effective way to provide a significant learning engagement for students while breaking up the tedium often present in courses that consist entirely of lectures and cases. As Dewey (1987) says, "We can and do supply ready made 'ideas' by the thousand; we do not usually take such pains to see that the one learning engages in significant situations where his own activities generate, support, and clinch ideas—that is perceived meaning or connections." Kolb and Lewis (1986) note that because simulations present a broader experiential learning environment than cases, simulations provide the best support for active experimentation. Other authors also emphasize the benefits of experiential and/or cooperative learning (Dev 1990; McKeachie 1994; Saunders 1997). In particular, some recent articles emphasize the important role that games and simulations can play in management education (Laforge and McNichols 1989; Keys and Wolfe 1990; Levy and Bergen 1993; Lane 1995). My goal was to create a classroom activity that allowed students to apply the methods and concepts from my course and experience the challenges of a "real-world" environment.

The Otogel simulation exercise was developed to demonstrate supply chain dynamics, primarily from the view of the manufacturer. In particular, the exercise allows students to see the impact of supply, production, and demand uncertainties on supply chain performance. The exercise allows students to experiment with process modifications, product design

---

* Received December 1998; revision received May 1999; accepted September 1999.

changes, inventory positioning, and information systems that allow them to improve the responsiveness and increase the profits of the supply chain.

The simulation allows students to experience the challenges of supply chain management implementation rather than simply reading or talking about them. By operating a scaled-down version of a real-life supply chain, students are able to experience the complexities of a supply chain; however, unlike real life, where the consequences of important decisions are often difficult to see because of their long-term nature and the distance between various parts of the organizations, students receive quick feedback on their decisions because both time and space have been compressed in this simulation. This rapid feedback allows them to see the consequences of their decisions and derive general lessons from their successes and failures.

The Otogel exercise was developed with the intention of creating an active learning environment for diverse student bodies. It has proven successful with MBA and executive students—one class of 30 second-year MBA students gave the simulation an average rating of 4.5 on a scale of 1 (very poor) to 5 (excellent). The effort required to develop and run this teaching simulation has been worthwhile in terms of student learning and the enthusiasm it has generated for the material. Responses from students have included: "The game was a great tool for learning," "Simulations are excellent in driving home the key topics for me," and "The simulations and games set your course apart."

This paper provides a brief description of the Otogel simulation exercise, discusses the key lessons from the simulation, and makes suggestions for successful execution.

Description of the Simulation

The Otogel simulation shares the concepts of two exercises that use interlocking building blocks to teach general production management principles. The first, the Gazogle Exercise, was developed by Elliott Weiss (1999) at the University of Virginia, and the second, the Lego Production Game, was developed by Robert Caraway at the University of Virginia. These exercises have provided the foundation for the production component of the Otogel exercise. The Otogel exercise considers the dynamics of the production environment but also includes additional complexities for the manufacturer in terms of the supplier and customer demand processes. Therefore, Otogel demonstrates several key issues of supply chain management.

In this section, the required materials, the scoring of the simulation, and the execution of the simulation are described.

Required Materials

The exercise requires: (1) Lego building blocks (about three 900-piece buckets for each team provide the right color and mix of blocks for the simulation); (2) an Otogel operations manual for each team, describing the student roles and operation processes (a document that is available on request from the author); (3) introduction slides (shown in Appendix 1); (4) score cards (shown in Appendix 2); and (5) a timer or bell to show the passage of weeks during the exercise.

Scoring

The goal for each team is to maximize profits. Suppliers, manufacturers, and customers receive revenue from sales of each good unit, or Otogel (a diagram of an Otogel is shown in Figure 1). The costs differ for each level of the supply chain but include such things as the costs of raw materials, inventory, defective product, facilities, and labor. See the sample scoring sheets in Appendix 2. Initially, the supplier, the manufacturer and the retailer are provided with separate performance reviews after each round. However, scores for the total supply chain are provided after two rounds of play. It is interesting to evaluate the different

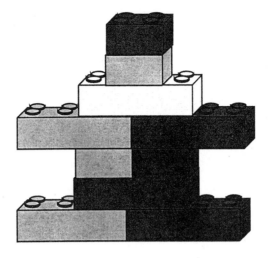

Note: There are 4 possible types of Otogels. Each has the same configuration; however, the colors of the blocks change. There are 10 different raw materials used to make the 4 Otogel types--five block colors (blue, black, white, yellow, and red) and two block sizes (2x2, and 2x4). Details of the products are provided in the operations manual.

FIGURE 1. Diagram of an Otogel.

actions taken when all players are evaluated under one overall performance measure. Typically, the change in performance metrics yields much more collaboration among supply chain partners.

Execution of the Simulation

An approximate timeline for the preparation and execution of the exercise is provided in Table 1. Before the class, the room is set up with tables that represent the production work

TABLE 1
Timeline for Preparation and Execution

Activities	Total Time (minutes)	Class time (minutes)
Set up room	0–45	
Students enter room/	45–60	
Instructor distributes assignments		
Instructor describes Simulation	60–70	0–10
Student teams prepare for simulation	70–85	10–25
Instructor answers questions		
Simulation Execution—Round 1	85–93	25–33
Student improvement session	93–107	33–47
Instructor tallies scores		
Simulation Execution—Round 2	107–115	47–55
Student improvement session	115–130	55–70
Instructor tallies scores		
Simulation Execution—Round 3	130–138	70–78
Student improvement session	138–152	78–92
Instructor tallies scores		
Simulation Execution—Round 4	152–160	92–100
Debrief	160–190	100–130

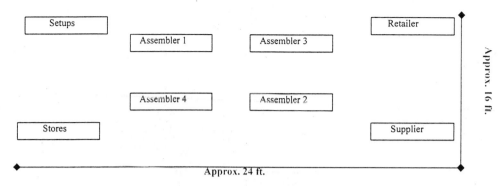

FIGURE 2. Otogel Setup for One Team.

areas, the storeroom, the setup area, the supplier, and the retailer as shown in Figure 2. As students enter the class, they are provided with a sheet that assigns them to a team and discusses their role. Team size ranges from 12 to 15 students, depending on the class size. Ten students form the production team (typically including 1 stores manager, 4 assemblers, 3 material handlers, and, if the class size permits, 1 production supervisor and 1 sales manager) and are provided with an operations manual that describes the production process and roles for the students. The retailer (1–2 students) and supplier (1–2 students) are also provided with a description of their roles. If extra students are available, it is also helpful to assign one observer to each team. These students are effective at recalling key improvements and evaluating team performance and can be instrumental in the debrief session for the exercise. In addition, they can help tally up the team scores at the end of each simulated month. The facilitator plays the role of the final customer and is responsible for communicating the actual demand for Otogels.

Before starting the simulation, the facilitator provides a brief introduction to the simulation and its goals (see Appendix 1 for sample slides). Then, the teams are given 15 minutes in which to organize and plan for the first month of operation. Although some improvements are apparent on inspection of the current supply chain, no modifications to the existing process are permitted before the first round. The first round consists of four 2-minute periods, in which each period equals a simulated production week. Each period begins with the facilitator (final customer) requesting a specific number of products, products A, B, and/or C. At the end of each week, the number of on-time, high-quality, delivered Otogels, stockouts, and defects are recorded. At the end of 4 weeks, which comprise the first round, scores are calculated (based on the delivery performance and operating costs) and announced to all teams. Each team then has 10–15 minutes to modify the supply chain. The next three rounds are run the same way as the first round with additional complexities added each round.

During the first round, the customer's demands are relatively simple. There is one customer per team and three possible products. Customers specify a standard delivery time of 1 week and always order in multiples of 5 units (the standard production batch size is 5 units). In the second round, the customer begins to also place rush orders (which require delivery within half a week or 1 minute in simulation time). In addition, not all the orders are in batches of 5 units. Students must speed up their delivery time and learn to adjust to the new order requirements. The third round is similar to the second round except that volume increases. The customer announces that its competitor has gone out of business and that they have picked up the competitor's share of the market. This round allows students to see how responsive their operation is to volume changes. The fourth and final round is much more complex. A new customer has entered the market and has gained a significant portion of the market share because they have introduced a new product. The new customer requires production of the new product D as well as the original products A and B. The teams need to decide how to communicate with two customers, adjust to the varying demand, and incorporate a new product into the supply chain.

In addition to the uncertainty in the customer-demand process, there are also sources of variability in the supply and production process. The supplier has an expected lead time of 1 week. However, because of variability in the process, the lead time ranges from one-half to 1 week (a coin toss determines the time). In addition, sometimes the wrong parts are delivered as a result of human error, or defective parts (the wrong size blocks are placed into the supply bins as defective parts) are delivered because of the supplier process quality. Also, a minimum order quantity of 50 pieces further complicates the raw material ordering process.

There are also several sources of variability within the production plant. Because there is a lot of variability in the customer demand, it is often necessary to establish a safety stock of raw materials in the storeroom. The manufacturing process, which consists of assembly of blocks by student assemblers, has some variability built into it (assemblers with large fingers often have more difficulty assembling the small blocks and those with children often are more skilled at block building). In addition, before each batch is started, a setup time must be incurred. The assembler must obtain a setup card, which illustrates the production step, from across the room, incurring time before assembly. This interruption to the manufacturing process causes disruptions in the delivery process.

After executing the Otogel simulation, it is essential that at least 30 minutes be spent debriefing the exercise. McKeachie (1994) emphasizes the need to have either a written or oral report on an experiential learning exercise to ensure that it is educational to the students. I chose to have a group discussion, which helps students to recognize the learning points from the exercise and identify general ideas that are applicable to other situations. In the debrief session, students are able to identify the uncertainties within the entire supply chain, considering sources of variability from suppliers, manufacturers, and customers, and to discuss modifications that help reduce and manage these uncertainties. Details of the debrief session are provided in the next section.

Lessons from the Exercise

This exercise allows students to have a brief hands-on experience with supply chain management. The exercise, although relatively simple, creates an environment in which students are often overwhelmed by the uncertainties within the system. The students quickly learn that issues, such as variability in the supplier lead time and quality, uncertainty in demand, inflexible production processes, and inadequate communication systems, create an environment that makes it challenging, if not impossible, to meet 100% of demand in a timely manner at the specified quality level. Typically, the discussion of the complexities of the simulation and the student improvements allows students to consider additional complexities and solution approaches for real-life supply chains. This discussion leads the class to develop general supply chain management principles.

Specific Lessons from Otogel

There are several process modifications and simplifications that enable the teams to improve the responsiveness and increase the profits in the supply chain. First, on analysis of the production process, it becomes obvious that the work areas are spread out and do not allow for a smooth flow of materials, creating the need for excess movement of materials, extra material handlers, and additional time for materials to flow through the plant. Students typically notice that rearrangement of the plant allows for a more efficient process. The primary lessons here have to do with production efficiencies; however, it is clear to the student that without these changes it is difficult for the manufacturer to respond quickly to changes in customer demands.

Second, when the product designs are analyzed, some students recognize that the production process can be simplified by making modular components and then assembling the modules to create the final products. One modular component is used in all three products and is therefore critical to have on hand at all times. The other three modules are used in two products each. By building and stocking modules, the manufacturer can respond more quickly to customer demands. Sometimes, the manufacturer requests subcomponents to be delivered from the supplier (the students negotiate the details of this supply option).

Third, when manufacturing the product according to the operation manual, the process is very inflexible: batches must always be 5 units and setup times are relatively long (associated with traveling to pick up the specification sheet at a distant location). Simple changes, such as moving assembly closer to the setup table, enable students to reduce setup times. In addition, it is possible to build large batches of the modular components and increase productive time without building too much inventory.

Fourth, changes to the raw material delivery process also must be made in order to meet orders on time. These changes include (1) reorganization of the supplier's area for easier sorting and delivery of materials, (2) modification of the ordering and delivery process (improved clarity in ordering systems, reduced minimum order-size, and refined inventory management policies accounting for uncertainty and dependence of demand), and (3) improvement of supplier quality.

Finally, the supplier, producers, and retailers are often ineffective simply because there is poor communication and coordination between partners in the supply chain. The teams make simple modifications to the supply chain that enable them to gather information, coordinate decision making, and improve responsiveness throughout the supply chain. For example, often students do not even think to ask for demand forecasts from their customer. When they do so, they get valuable information that allows them to plan for peaks in demand by ordering supplies and scheduling production appropriately. In terms of coordination, they recognize that the elements of the supply chain are closely linked—the weakest link (or bottleneck) determines the throughput of the system. In addition they recognize that planning is required from the supplier to the customer. When different components of the supply chain are not coordinated, chaos develops and orders are missed. Overall, the students recognize that simple changes to the product design, production process, and inventory policies can have a large impact on the responsiveness of the supply chain to customer demands.

General Lessons for Supply Chain Management

The framework shown in Appendix 3 is useful when debriefing this exercise because it considers the roles of suppliers, manufacturer, and retailers in improving the effectiveness of the supply chain. First, the key uncertainties in supply, production, and demand are reviewed. Then, we discuss the modifications that were made in the Otogel exercise or that can be made in real life. Finally, we proceed to discuss issues of coordination and information sharing across the entire supply chain. Many of the product- and process-related supply chain modifications are discussed in Davis (1993). Other related articles are listed in Appendix 3, indicating their relevance to each part of the debrief framework. Although these articles are not critical to the understanding of the exercise, they do provide useful examples of supply chain improvement efforts.

Effective Use of the Exercise

The exercise was initially designed to fit half way through a second-year MBA course called Production and Inventory Management at the Carlson School of Management. Before the exercise, students are exposed to traditional inventory management models and lean production techniques. They can apply these principles here but also learn that there are additional complexities in the supply chain that require more sophisticated methods and processes. The exercise, therefore, provides an excellent introduction to the materials covered later in the class that deal with supply chain management. Using the exercise early in the class, with cases and readings to follow, allows students to reflect on the Otogel experience and use the simulation's lessons to make decisions and solve problems.

The exercise can be used as a capstone to summarize learning points to date or as a justification for principles to come. The exercise takes approximately 2 hours to run, although it can be compressed to $1\frac{1}{2}$ hours with a $\frac{1}{2}$ hour debrief to follow in the next class period. Therefore, it can easily fit into various course situations. The author has used this exercise in MBA, executive, and general management training programs.

Depending on the placement of this exercise in the course, the facilitator can discuss what has been covered and/or what still needs to be covered in the course to understand how to manage the complexities of supply chains. This discussion allows the facilitator to reemphasize the learning points from the simulation and to link the lessons to the overall course. Cases that have been used in conjunction with this exercise include Sport Obermeyer (HBS 9-695-022) and Barilla Pasta (HBS 9-695-065). For an extended course, additional cases, such as H.E. Butt (HBS 9-196-061) and Merloni (HBS 9-690-003), or computer simulation exercises, such as MILS (Severence and Murray 1996) and Lenroc Plastics (Muckstadt and Jackson 1997), can also be useful learning activities.

This exercise has been very effective in operations management classes because it is (1) easy to implement, (2) a fun learning experience for students, and (3) a great tool for illustrating supply chain management methods and processes. Please feel free to contact the author for additional details regarding the Otogel simulation exercise.[1]

---

[1] The author thanks Elliott Weiss and Robert Caraway for their assistance in developing this exercise and Mark Zoia for his suggestions on this paper.

Appendix 1: Sample Introduction Slides

Otogel

An Exercise in Supply Chain Management
Developed by Kate McKone

The Procedure

- Round 1
  - Follow the production supervisors manual.
  - No changes can be made to layout or process.
  - Calculate score
  - Improvement Session
- Rounds 2-4
  - Same Procedure

The Otogel Supply Chain

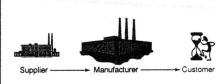

Supplier → Manufacturer → Customer

The Procedure

- Improvement Session
  - Anyone can make suggestions.
  - Changes may include the following:
    - seating arrangement
    - placement of tables
    - placement of Legos on tables
    - number of people assembling
    - design of assembly process
    - modification of supplier delivery process
    - change in communication systems
    - almost any other changes are allowed—be creative!

Otogel Simulation Goals

- Experience complexities of running a factory
- Experiment with Re-engineering and Supply Chain Management Principles.
- Identify some issues related to implementing these systems.
- Have fun while learning!

Your Score = Your Net Profit

- Revenues
  - Regular orders ($500)
  - Rush orders ($600)
- Costs
  - Tables ($750)
  - Employees ($1000)
  - Inventory ($2/unit/period)
  - Defects ($250/unit)
  - Rush orders from suppliers ($2/piece)

Object of the Game

- Satisfy your customer's needs by delivering **what** the customer orders, **when** the customer orders it, at the **quality** level the customer requires.
- The ultimate **GOAL** is to make **MONEY!**

Let's Get to Work!!

Appendix 2: Otogel Score Sheets

SUPPLIER'S RESULTS

Production Results		Wk1	Wk2	Wk3	Wk4	Total
Ordered						
Reg. Units Delivered						
Rush Units Delivered						
# Rush Orders Placed						
Units Defective						
Units Short						

Round 1

Financial Results	Revenues			
	# Reg Parts	____	* $10 =	
	# Rush Parts	____	* $12=	
	Add'l revenue	____	*	
	Total Revenues		=	
	Costs			
	# workers	____	* $1000 =	
	# tables	____	* $750 =	
	# Defective	____	* $5 =	
	# Rush orders	____	* $50 =	
	# Parts sold	____	*$5 =	
	Add'l costs	____	* =	
	Total Costs		=	
	NET PROFIT (LOSS)		=	
Service Results	Fill rate			
	1- (units short/units ordered)			

RETAILER'S RESULTS

Round 1

Production Results		Wk 1	Wk 2	Wk 3	Wk 4	Total
Units Ordered						
Units Delivered						
Units Short						

Financial Results	Revenues			
	# Total Units	____	* $625 =	
	Total Revenues		=	
	Costs			
	# workers	____	* $1000 =	
	# table	____	* $750 =	
	# Reg. Units	____	* $500 =	
	# Rush orders	____	* $600 =	
	# Inventory	____	* $5 =	
	Total Costs		=	
	NET PROFIT (LOSS)		=	
Service Results	Fill rate			
	1- (units short/units ordered)			

MANUFACTURER'S RESULTS

Round 1

Production Results		Wk 1	Wk 2	Wk 3	Wk 4	Total
Units Ordered						
Reg. Units Delivered						
Rush Units Delivered						
Units Defective						
Units Short						

Financial Results	Revenues			
	# Reg Units	____	* $500 =	
	# Rush Units	____	* $600 =	
	Other Revenues	____	* =	
	Total Revenues		=	
	Costs			
	# workers	____	* $1000 =	
	# tables	____	* $750 =	
	# Defective	____	* $250 =	
	# Reg. Parts	____	* $10 =	
	# Rush parts	____	* $12 =	
	# Inventory	____	* $1 =	
	Total Costs		=	
	NET PROFIT (LOSS)		=	
Service Results	Fill Rate			
	1-(units short/units ordered)			

SUPPLY CHAIN RESULTS

Round 1

Results	Profit	
	--Supplier	
	--Manufacturer	
	--Retailer	
	Total Profits	
	Service	
	--Fill Rate to Customer	

Appendix 3: Sample Debrief Framework

	Problems	Possible Modifications
Supplier Davis (1994) Davis (1993)	Otogel • Accuracy of order preparation • Time of order preparation • Delivery time • Quality of materials Other • Volume/mix flexibility	Otogel • Source locally to shorten lead times (move closer to supplier) • Review stock frequently • Pre-inspect quality and/or improve supplier process Other • Follow industry standards (to increase part availability) • Share information with strategic partners
Manufacturer Feitzinger and Lee (1997) Lee and Billington (1995) Davis (1993)	Otogel • Production uncertainty (setup time, production time) • Worker skill • Batch requirements Other • Equipment breakdowns • Long lead-times • Flexibility issues	Otogel • Identify bottlenecks and redesign processes to increase capacity • Create flexible environment (reduce setups, change layout & shorten cycle times) • Use standard processes • Use common components in many products or subcontract componentns • Promote DFM, DFA, etc. • Establish inventory levels for raw materials, work-in-progress, & finished goods Other • Produce generic products • Set buffer level and capacity appropriately
Retailer/Customer Cachon and Fisher (1997) Davis (1993)	Otogel • Uncertain forecasts • Uncertainty of future demand (volume, mix & timing) • Variety of products Other • Variety of products • Seasonality	Otogel • Manage delivery expectations (provide forecasts) • Build near customer • Improve forecasting techniques Other • Reduce product offering & options • Adjust FGI safety stocks • Design for localization • Customize products after production (software, not hardware)
Overall Fischer (1997) Handfield and Nichols (1999) Sengupta and Turnbull (1996) Womack and Jones (1994)	Otogel • Lots of noise • "Fat" organization (Lots of players) Other • Lack of info. system • Global supply chain (difference in time & distance) • Conflicting incentives	Otogel • Design the supply chain recognizing impact of each stage on the product/service • Integrate control and planning sys. Other • Combine databases, monitor accuracy • Do not make decision independently • Redesign organizational/system incentives • Define goals for supply chain

References

CACHON, G. AND M. FISHER (1997), "Campbell Soup's Continuous Replenishment Program: Evaluation and Enhanced Decision Rules," *Production and Operations Management*, 6, 3, 266–276.

DAVIS, D. (1994), " Partnerships Pay Off," *Manufacturing Systems*, November, 4–14.

DAVIS, T. (1993), "Effective Supply Chain Management," *Sloan Management Review*, Summer, 35–46.

DEV, C. S. (1990), "Measuring the Value of Experiential Learning," *The Cornell H.R.A. Quarterly*, August, 105–107.

DEWEY, J. (1987), "Thinking in Education," in *Teaching and the Case*, L. B. Barnes, C. R. Christensen, and A. J. Hansen (eds.), Harvard Business School Press, Boston, MA, USA, 9–14.

FEITZINGER, E. AND H. L. LEE (1997), "Mass Customization at Hewlett Packard: The Power of Postponement," *Harvard Business Review*, 75, 1, 116–122.

FISHER, M. L. (1997), "What Is the Right Supply Chain for Your Product?" *Harvard Business Review*, 75, 2, 105–116.

HANDFIELD, R. B. AND E. L. NICHOLS, JR. (1999), *Introduction to Supply Chain Management*, Prentice Hall, Upper Saddle River, NJ, USA.

KEYS, B. AND J. WOLFE (1990), "The Role of Management Games and Simulations in Education and Research," *Journal of Management*, 16, 2, 307–336.

KOLB, D. A. AND L. H. LEWIS (1986), "Facilitating Experiential Learning: Observations and Reflections" in *Experiential and Simulation Techniques for Teaching Adults*, L. H. Lewis (ed.), Jossey-Bass, San Francisco, CA, USA, 99–107.

LAFORGE, R. L. AND C. W. MCNICHOLS (1989), "An Integrative Experiential Approach to Production Management Education," *Decision Sciences*, 20, 1, 198–207.

LANE, D. C. (1995), "On a Resurgence of Management Simulations and Games," *The Journal of the Operational Research Society*, 46, 5, 604–626.

LEE, H. L. AND C. BILLINGTON (1995), "The Evolution of Supply-Chain-Management Models and Practice at Hewlett-Packard," *Interfaces*, 25, 5, 42–63.

LEVY, D. AND M. BERGEN (1993), "Simulating a Multiproduct Barter Exchange Economy," *Economic Inquiry*, XXXI, 314–321.

MCKEACHIE, W. J. (1994), "Field Work and Experiential Learning," in *Teaching Tips*, D.C. Heath and Company, Lexington, MA, USA, 139–142.

MUCKSTADT, J. A. AND P. L. JACKSON (1997), "Lenroc Plastics: Market-Driven Integration of Manufacturing and Distribution Systems," Technical Report No. 898, School of Operations Research and Industrial Engineering, College of Engineering, Cornell University, Ithaca, NY, USA.

SAUNDERS, P. M. (1997), "Experiential Learning, Cases, and Simulations in Business Communication," *Business Communication Quarterly*, 60, 1, 97–114.

SENGUPTA, S. AND J. TURNBULL (1996), "Seamless Optimization of the Entire Supply Chain," *IIE Solutions*, 28, 10, 28–32.

SEVERENCE, D. AND D. MURRAY (1996), *The Michigan Integrated Logistics System Game*, School of Business, University of Michigan, Ann Arbor, MI, USA.

WEISS, E. N. (1999), "The Gazogle Experiential Exercise: The Dynamics of High Performance," Darden School Teaching Note, University of Virginia, UVA-OM-0887.

WOMACK, J. P. AND D. T. JONES (1994), "From Lean Production to the Lean Enterprise," *Harvard Business Review*, 72, 2, 93–103.

Kathleen E. McKone is Assistant Professor of Operations and Management Science in the Carlson School of Management at the University of Minnesota. She earned her B.S. and M.Eng. degrees from Cornell University, School of Operations Research and Industrial Engineering, and her M.B.A. and Ph.D. degrees from University of Virginia, Darden Graduate School of Business. Before entering Darden, Kate worked at the Procter & Gamble Company. Her current research and teaching interests include total productive maintenance and supply chain management. She is the author of numerous articles in the areas of production and operations management. These have appeared in journals such as *Production and Operations Management* and *Journal of Operations Management*.

A PRACTICAL SETTING FOR EXPERIENTIAL LEARNING ABOUT SUPPLY CHAINS: SIEMEN'S BRIEF CASE GAME SUPPLY CHAIN SIMULATOR*

JOYCE S. MEHRING

*College of Management, University of Massachusetts Lowell,
Lowell, Massachusetts 01854, USA*

Siemens Brief Case Game Supply Chain Simulator provides a practical setting for experiential learning exercises about supply chains. The game, drawing upon an actual situation, models the jobs of nine supply chain activities required to transform an order placed by the customer into a delivered product. Using the detail and complexity of the game, instructors can develop learning exercises that focus on a wide range of supply chain management issues. This paper describes two learning exercises with different objectives and for different audiences that we successfully delivered using the Brief Case Game. One exercise provides a concrete example of typical activities in a supply chain and their interactions. The other exercise leads students to discover what creates a need for coordination, what activities in a supply chain require coordination, and what methods work well. These exercises are suited for small upper level undergraduate and graduate courses in logistics and supply chain management. While significant resources were used to develop exercises and deliver the game, students were enthusiastic about the approach and demonstrated that they learned about the complexity inherent in managing supply chains.
(SUPPLY CHAINS, EXPERIENTIAL LEARNING, SIEMENS BRIEF CASE GAME, COORDINATION)

Introduction

In this paper, we present the Siemens Brief Case Game (BCG) Supply Chain Simulator as a simplified supply chain with realistic detail upon which the instructor can build experiential learning exercises about a range of supply chain issues. The game models the activities of nine participants in a supply chain: a customer, a supplier, BCG's Sales division (sales order processing, sales traffic, and warehousing), and BCG's manufacturing division (procurement, subassembly, final assembly, plant order processing, and plant traffic and warehousing.) Participants in the game exchange 'orders,' 'purchase' Lego blocks from a supplier, ship the blocks in 'trucks,' make 'products' from the blocks, and distribute the products to the customer. BCG's objectives are to commit to orders at requested times (availability), to deliver the complete orders at the time committed (reliability), and to make a substantial contribution to profit.

The Brief Case Game's physical simulation creates an environment for experiential learning. In the experiential approach, students are given an opportunity to learn from

---

*Reprinted from *Production and Operations Management*, Vol. 9, No. 1, Spring 2000, pp. 56–65.

observation, active experimentation, concrete experience, and abstract conceptualization (Agogino and Wood 1994; Kolb 1984). This approach is well suited to study supply chains since it has been used successfully to develop a systems view, develop problem solving skills, and to practice integrating and synthesizing concepts (Jackson 1996). The instructor is a guide, who provides context, poses problems, suggests analyses, scores solutions, and summarizes lessons. Students take an active role in learning. When used in a classroom, the simulation experience will be most rewarding if the instructor, as a guide, develops a learning exercise or context for the session. Throughout the game, the facilitators can suggest analyses or pose questions that focus on the selected topic.

This paper describes two learning exercises that we successfully implemented using the game. To focus participant's attention on particular learning objectives, we gave students a case to read, discussed concepts of key importance prior to the simulation, and provided some guidelines for the simulations. One exercise, for undergraduate logistics students, provided students with a concrete example of a supply chain that they could use to explore the transportation, warehousing, inventory management, and customer service concepts covered in the course. The other exercise, for graduate logistics students, provided a setting in which students examined the need for coordination, the supply chain activities that require coordination, the methods used to coordinate activities, and the factors that cause particular coordination methods to succeed or fail. Other exercises could focus on material management methods, on information systems that provide forecast and inventory visibility, on distribution and procurement strategies, or on more general reengineering.

An experiential learning approach worked well in both these exercises. Students learned what tasks were needed to process an order and to produce and deliver the product to the customer. They learned how a decision made in one activity affected other activities. They learned how investments in infrastructure or implementation of different systems, procedures, and management approaches can affect lead times, on-time delivery, and costs. Given sufficient time, students play the game with different strategies, experience the impact of these strategies, and compare performance. Our experience with this approach was positive overall. Although it took a great deal of effort to develop and deliver the exercises, the students were enthusiastic and demonstrated an improved understanding of the supply chain issues after the exercise.

Siemens Brief Case Supply Chain Game: The Setting

The Brief Case Game Supply Chain Simulator (Siemens 1995a, 1995b) provides a practical setting for exercises about supply chains. The Simulator's supply chain consists of a customer, a supplier, sales order processing, sales traffic and warehousing, plant procurement, subassembly, final assembly, plant order processing, and plant traffic and warehousing. Figure 1 shows the flow of materials and order information among these nine activities. Participants in the simulation play the roles of employees in these activities and carry out the tasks needed to transform an order issued by the customer into a delivered product. A minimum of nine players is needed. And most activities easily accommodate an additional player who can assist with tasks and record data. The players' objective is to operate the company to achieve good supply chain performance with respect to customer service (time and quality) and profit contribution.

The game, which we purchased from Siemens Corporation, includes Lego blocks to represent materials; order forms for customer, device, and purchase orders; trucks of various capacities to transport materials; and boards with areas of limited capacity designated for production lines, inspection lines, and inventory storage space for each activity. The game also includes an instructor's manual and a participants' manual that provide job descriptions and cost and lead time information for each of the nine activities, instructions on how to setup materials and orders for the initial round of the game, and other data and forms.

Material and Information Flow
Siemens Brief Case Game Supply Chain Simulator

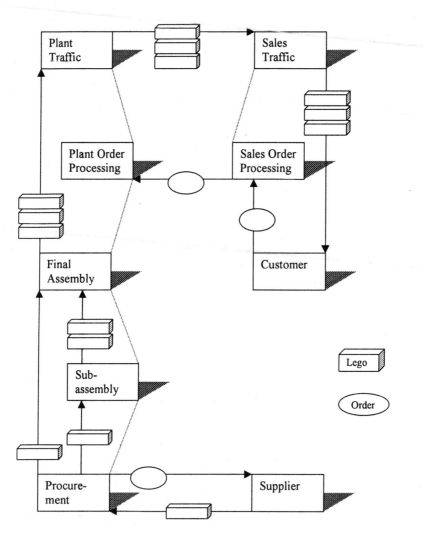

FIGURE 1. Material and Information Flow: Siemens Brief Case Game Supply Chain Simulator.

Playing an eight-turn period required about two and one-half hours. In addition, several hours are needed to prepare order forms and worksheets and to set up the game boards, orders, and Lego blocks for each run. In an academic setting, we feel that exercises with specific learning objectives are needed to focus the learning experience. However, the game can be played without additional structure. The time required developing exercises and supporting materials varies.

To convey the level of detail and complexity of the simulation, we briefly describe the way material processing, order processing, lead time, costs and capacity constraints, objectives, and time horizons are represented in the game. A more detailed description can be found in a case describing the game (Mehring, Kotler, and Kiesel 1997) or in the manuals provided with the game (Siemens 1995a, 1995b).

MATERIAL PROCESSING. BCG makes and delivers two products: a white device and a black device. The three raw materials needed to make these products are red, black, and white Lego blocks. Procurement receives these blocks by truck from the supplier, inspects the incoming goods, and moves white and black blocks to subassembly and red blocks to assembly. Subassembly makes black and white components from three black blocks and two white blocks, respectively. Final assembly combines each component with one red Lego block to produce black and white devices. These devices are moved to the plant warehouse and then are shipped by truck to the sales distribution center as requested. The sales office ships product by truck from the sales distribution center to the customer as ordered.

ORDER PROCESSING. The customer orders products, using customer orders, from BCG's sales office. The number of customer orders and order sizes placed by the customer each turn may be prespecified for the customer. Alternatively, the customer will place orders each turn subject to constraints on the total number of orders and on the average order size per period. The sales office confirms the orders placed by the customer and ships devices from the sales distribution warehouse to customers. The sales office orders product, using device orders, from the plant to replenish their stock. The plant confirms these orders, fills them from stock in the plant warehouse, ships them to the sales distribution center, and refills the plant warehouse with devices produced by final assembly. Procurement orders raw materials, using purchase orders, from the supplier.

PROCESSING AND LEAD TIMES. The processing time for each activity is specified in the job description. The orders from the customer to sales, from sales to plant, and from the plant to the supplier are transmitted only by mail. The order is prepared in one turn, sent the beginning of the following turn, and received the beginning of the next turn. Receiving a shipment also requires two turns. The truck is loaded in one turn, sent the next turn, and received the next. Within the sales department and the plant, orders for materials or materials are conveyed in one turn. Given the supplier's lead times for blocks of certain colors, the minimum lead time to fill a customer, device, or purchase order ranges between four to seven turns. The lead time may be longer due to lack of available product.

COSTS AND CAPACITY CONSTRAINTS. Each player's job description provides data about costs, lot sizes, and capacity for the activity to which they are assigned. Procurement incurs costs of ordering raw material, inspecting incoming material, and carrying inventory. Subassembly and final assembly incur costs for setting up equipment, overtime and undertime production, material handling, and inventory carrying costs. The sales department incurs ordering costs (for devices from the plant), order processing costs, transportation and material handling costs, and inventory carrying costs. The plant warehouse incurs order processing costs, transportation and material handling costs, and inventory carrying costs. The inventory carrying cost per unit reflects the increasing value of the product as it moves from raw materials to finished goods. The supplier and customer are provided with similar unit costs for their operation. Some truck capacities limit shipments each turn. The number of blocks, components and devices that inspection, subassembly, and final assembly can process in each turn are limited by inspection and production line capacities.

COMPANY OBJECTIVES AND PERFORMANCE MEASURES. The players' objectives are to manage the lead times and costs to achieve good performance with respect to: delivery (shipment) capability, delivery (shipment) reliability, profit contribution, and quality. Delivery (shipment) capability is the percentage of orders whose confirmed delivery (ship) date is less than or equal to the requested delivery (or ship) date. This measure assesses the capability to meet the desired delivery (ship) date. Delivery reliability is the percentage of orders whose actual delivery date is on or before the confirmed delivery date. This measure assesses the reliability in meeting the promised delivery date. Quality is measured by the percentage of defective items. Profit contribution is measured by calculating the revenue from items delivered and the costs incurred in production during the period.

TIME HORIZON. A simulation run or period consists of eight turns. In each turn, each player's first task is to transmit or ship the orders or materials that the player prepared in the prior turn. Mailboxes and shipping docks for national sales, the plant warehouse, plant procurement, the customer, and the supplier are located on a large wheel. Within the divisions, items are moved by hand. After sending mail or shipping material, the players take orders or materials from their incoming source. Then, they carry out their tasks (e.g., processing orders, assembling product, loading trucks, or issuing orders) and record shipment and order dates, inventory, setups, and other information. At the end of each eight-turn period, each activity measures and reports its performance using this data. These reports are rolled up into division reports and a company report on customer deliver capability, customer delivery reliability, quality, and profit contribution.

What is a Supply Chain? An Undergraduate Course Exercise

The objective of this exercise is to give undergraduate students a concrete example of a supply chain that they can use to examine the transportation, warehousing, inventory management, and customer service concepts covered in the logistics course. This exercise is designed for an elective course in logistics management, with a class size of fewer than 20, that could meet periodically in 2.5-hour sessions. The audience for this exercise is juniors or seniors majoring in industrial management or business administration who have completed courses in operations management and marketing.

THE EXERCISE. To provide students with a common view of a supply chain, we ask them to read the case 'Improving Supply Chain Performance at BCG Company: Learning with Lego Blocks' (Mehring et al. 1997), prior to the first simulation session. This case introduces students to BCG's current supply chain, its organizational structure, its supply chain performance measures, and the pressure it is under to achieve desired customer service and profit contributions. The simulation and the case present BCG as a functionally organized company. Each supply chain activity communicates and/or moves material only between itself and its immediate neighbors. Three pairs of activities (the customer and sales office, the sales office and plant order processing, and procurement and the supplier) require external mail or truck transportation to move orders or materials. The other pairs of activities convey information and materials internally.

In the simulation exercise, participants are assigned roles and provided with job descriptions for their activity, including data on lead times and costs, and guidelines for playing the game. Students are given a sales forecast for black and white devices for a period and a plan that shows how many devices, components, and raw materials would be needed in a turn if sales are the same each turn. In this exercise, we ask students to use a base stock system to manage inventory, ordering what they use each period. Given the importance of leadtime in delivering orders and products on time and in setting target inventory levels, we spend some time discussing the lead times required to move orders and materials between selected activities. Players can modify their inventory management approach if desired. Their material management approaches will need to account for changeover costs and times, limited truck capacities, and manufacturing and inspection capacity.

This simulation exercise was conducted in four 2.5-hour sessions in an undergraduate course in logistics. To introduce students to BCG's supply chain, the first simulation session was held in the second week of the course. Just after the midpoint of the course, two sessions were spent simulating the supply chain using the guidelines proposed for this exercise. In these sessions, students experienced how tasks, lead time, and costs in one activity affect other activities and ultimately performance. At the end of the course, student teams, drawing upon their experiences with the game and the concepts covered in the course, presented recommendations on changes that BCG should make to improve performance. The class then selected several of the suggested improvements and simulated the supply chain with these changes.

STUDENT LEARNING. The students viewed the BCG Supply Chain Simulator as a working case study. To them, the game presented a simplified, but realistic, distribution scheme, and incorporated enough factors to thoroughly demonstrate the complexity and concerns that are inherent in supply chains. In one student's words, 'The game showed that there were a lot more costs than just trucking expenses and warehousing costs.... The game showed the effects of having too much inventory, or too little. These costs were a lot larger than I could ever imagine. Without the game, it would have been tough to visualize all the costs.... The game also showed me all the different departments concerned with logistics, and their functions. It explained the big paper trail associated with getting the product from point A to B. Logistics is a lot more important than I thought. In a company, a lot of attention should be paid to this field. By properly setting up your routes and books, you can save a lot of money. ... The introduction of many technologies can help out a company tremendously. We learned the value of EDI, computer spreadsheets, and similar technologies.' Overall, students felt that the supply chain game made the course interesting and taught valuable lessons. Observing students engaged by the game, their assessments of the game, and the percentage of students that demonstrated excellent performance in the course, I judged this exercise to be effective.

Coordination in Supply Chains: A Graduate Course Exercise

The objective of this exercise is to convey what creates the need for coordination, what supply chain activities therefore require coordination, what methods can be used to coordinate activities, and what factors cause particular coordination methods to succeed or fail. This exercise is designed for a graduate course in logistics management, an elective course with a class size of 20 or less. The audience for this exercise is master's level students in manufacturing management or business administration who have completed courses in operations management and marketing. Most students who take the graduate logistics course have significant work experience within a manufacturing firm.

COORDINATION FRAMEWORK. To develop material for this exercise, we constructed a coordination framework that was based on the work of Malone and Crowston (1994), Thompson (1967), and Mintzberg (1979). In this framework, dependencies create a need for coordination in order to achieve desired global performance. Thus, coordination is viewed as managing the interdependencies or linkages among activities or among actors. A wide range of coordination methods is available to manage dependencies. These methods include direct supervision, standardization (rules, program, procedures), standard procedures, plans (targeting), goals, liaison or integrating managerial roles, and teams (Galbraith 1973; Mintzberg 1984; Crowston and Malone 1994). The degree of dependency and the extent of uncertainty and of conflict make some methods better suited than others to manage the dependency (Thompson 1967; Victor and Blackburn 1987).

Material and information dependencies and different methods of coordinating dependent activities are very evident in supply chains. There are sequential dependencies when outputs from one task are required before another task can begin; reciprocal dependencies when order information must be exchanged before the tasks can be completed; and simultaneous dependencies when several activities may (or may not) be performed at the same time. Supervisors can manage dependencies by giving decision-making authority for both activities to one person. Standard specifications can coordinate processes by eliminating the need for additional information about materials. Standard skills and norms, gained through training,

TABLE 1
Coordination Exercise Questionnaire

Role
   What role do you play in the supply chain game?
Material dependencies
   What activities do you depend on for materials?
   What activities depend on your activity for materials?
   What activities share resources/assets with your activity?
Information dependencies
   What activities do you depend on for information?
   What activities depend on your activity for information?
   With what activities do you share information?
Coordination methods for material dependencies
   What methods are used to coordinate the activities that you depend on for materials?
   What is the extent of conflict among the activities?
   What is the extent of uncertainty among the activities?
   How successful do you expect this coordination method to be?
   What do you see as the key strengths and weakness of the approach to managing material dependencies?
Coordination methods for information dependencies
   What methods are used to coordinate the activities that you depend on for information?
   What is the extent of conflict among the activities?
   What is the extent of uncertainty among the activities?
   How successful do you expect this coordination method to be?
   What do you see as the key strengths and weakness of the approach to managing material dependencies?

provide people with common knowledge, rules, and beliefs, which aid in coordination. Production and inventory plans and schedules can coordinate activities with sequential dependencies by providing target quantities and timing. Liaisons and teams can achieve coordination through negotiation or mediation among people in different activities.

The most effective coordination method for two activities will depend on the degree of their interdependency, the extent of conflict among participants, and the extent of uncertainty at the time an action must be taken. Thompson (1967) suggests using plans to coordinate sequential dependencies and mutual adjustment (teams) to coordinate reciprocal dependencies. Victor and Blackburn (1987) suggest using rules and standard operating procedures when interdependence and conflict are low, direct supervision (chain of command) when interdependence is low and conflict is high, and mutual adjustment when interdependence is high and conflict is low. When there is little uncertainty, Galbraith (1973) suggests using planning and when uncertainty is great, for example, because of an unexpected event, he and Beck and Fox (1994a, 1994b) suggest methods of mutual adjustment. Thus, as uncertainty and interdependency increase the suggested coordination, the method moves from standard procedures, through plans, toward lateral processes such as teams and integrating managers. As conflict increases, the suggested choice moves from lateral processes such as negotiation to mediation and then to direct supervision.

THE EXERCISE. To prepare students for this exercise, we introduce them to the coordination framework described above and to the BCG Company and its supply chain. The students are given a brief lecture about the various types of dependencies and coordination methods and are introduced to BCG's supply chain by reading the BCG case described earlier. After receiving their job assignment, we focus their attention on coordination issues by asking them questions about the dependencies that they will have to manage and the coordination methods that they will use. They are asked for their perception of what activities their assigned activity depends on for material and information, what activities depend on their activity, what methods BCG uses to coordinate their activity with other activities, and their expectation of the effectiveness of these methods (Table 1). Also, they are asked their perception of the extent of the interdependence, the extent of conflict, and the extent of uncertainty of the specific dependencies that they will manage. At the end of the simulation session, they revisit these questions taking into account their experiences playing the game.

Participants are provided with guidelines for conducting the simulation exercise. As in the previous exercise, they are given a sales forecast for the initial eight-turn period; a plan that shows how many devices, components, and raw materials each activity would need to produce in a turn if sales are constant; and some examples of lead times. However, these students, who have studied alternative material management systems, are asked to select a production planning and inventory control approach for their activity. Each participant also is given a spreadsheet to collect data needed to calculate the delivery (shipment) availability, delivery (shipment) reliability, and cost for their activity. At the end of the eight turns, players review performance for their activities, for their division, and the company. On the basis of this review, the players propose improvements and, after considering the investment cost for the improvements, select some for implementation. After simulating the supply chain with the improvements, they prepare and review the department, division, and company reports. The players, reflecting on what they learned from the simulation exercise, again answer the questions about dependencies and coordination methods. The session is wrapped up with a discussion of lessons learned.

We conducted this coordination exercise in an all day session, placed at the beginning of the last third of a graduate logistics class. At that point, students had studied tradeoffs among customer service, transportation, inventory, and warehousing using case studies; they had an understanding of material management issues from previous courses and an understanding of multiechelon inventory issues from playing the Beer Distribution Game (Sterman 1995). The students simulated three eight-turn periods. The first period was a trial run in which the participants learned the details of their job. In the second period, the game was played using the guidelines described in this section. In the third period, the game was played with their recommended changes in the organization of the activities, the layout, and management of the supply chain.

STUDENT LEARNING. As participants simulated the supply chain, they observed the dependencies that create a need for coordination and the uncertainty associated with the dependencies. Players depended upon their neighbors on the supply chain for Lego blocks and orders and their neighbors depended upon them. They observed not only sequential dependencies, but also reciprocal dependencies in order placement and confirmation. When faced with product shortages or late deliveries, they became aware of their indirect dependence on activities other than their neighbors. The division and company reports at the end of a period also helped the players recognize the tradeoffs among activities that need to be coordinated to improve company and supply chain performance.

The students' understanding of who depends on who improved as a result of playing the game. Prior to playing the game, the students did not have a good understanding of the direct and indirect dependencies. After playing the game, students more accurately identified those activities that were directly dependent on other activities. For example, the plant order processing and traffic group came to understand that the sales distribution center depended directly on them for materials and that in BCG's organization the customers depended on them indirectly. Two thirds of the class changed their assessment of the activities that depended on their activity for materials or information.

The supply chain activities were coordinated initially through formal communications and with informal liaisons. The players managed the material and orders flowing between customer and plant, between sales and the plant, and between procurement and the supplier by formal communication (orders). Within the plant, material requests initially were made orally once each turn to their immediate neighbors. Within the plant, the rudimentary material plan provided only minimal guidance to those coordinating production and purchasing. As play progressed, the students wanted to communicate directly with other participants in the chain, but given the existing coordination mechanisms, the responses still required long lead times.

The players observed the variability in material and information flow that made these dependencies a challenge to coordinate. They observed variable lead times and high inventory. Some of the variability resulted from BCG employees' choices of lot size, ordering policies, inventory policies, and shipping policies. Some of the variability resulted from the customer's variations in sales or the supplier's variation in lead time for raw materials. In the former case, the players tried to reduce the variability through changes in company operations. In the latter case, the players worked with the customer or supplier to reduce the variability.

The students' understanding of the effectiveness of different coordination methods improved after playing the game. The students' proposed improvements included an information system that would give each activity at BCG immediate access to sales order information. This reduced lead times and distortion in information (Lee, Padmanablhan, and Whang 1997), and resulted in reductions in inventory. The plant chose a base stock (pull) inventory system to manage materials in their warehouse, subassembly, and assembly operations, with target inventory sufficient to cover the expected demand and safety stock. Thus, material flow within the plant was coordinated by the requests for inventory replacements. To handle unexpected events, the purchasing agent and an on-site supplier representative worked as a team to manage supply replenishment. In this exercise, the students demonstrated an appropriate choice of plans, liaisons, and teams for coordination.

Experiential Learning Exercises with the Siemens Brief Case Game: Conclusions

Exercises using the Siemens BCG Supply Chain Simulator, a simple but detailed model of a supply chain, engaged students in learning about the many approaches to managing complex supply chains. In the exercise that introduced supply chains, undergraduate students learned what jobs were necessary to turn an order into a finished product. Through this approach, the students recognized the many costs, the challenges of managing inventory and order processing, and the role of information systems in achieving timely customer service and strong profit contributions. In the coordination exercise, graduate students with industrial experience learned about activities other than ones they had performed. By carrying out detailed tasks in the game, they experienced the need to coordinate with other activities in the chain to accomplish their goals. After the exercise, students had an improved understanding of who depends on whom in the chain and were better able to recommend appropriate coordination methods for particular activities. These exercises worked well in small classes that could be scheduled periodically in 2.5-hour periods. The exercises successfully conveyed the detail and complexity of supply chains for manufactured products. And, students identified causes for long lead times, high inventory, and costs and learned approaches for improving the supply chain performance.

References

AGOGINO, A. M. AND W. H. WOOD III (1994), 'The Synthesis Coalition: Information Technologies Enabling a Paradigm Shift in Engineering Education,' Keynote talk, in Hyper-Media in Vaasa '94: *Proceedings of the Conference on Computers and Hypermedia in Engineering Education,* M. Linna and P. Routsala (eds.), 3-10.

BECK, J. C. AND M. S. FOX (1994), 'Supply Chain Coordination via Mediated Constraint Relaxation.' *Proceedings of the First Canadian Workshop on Distributed Artificial Intelligence,* Banff, Alberta. May 15, 1994.

———— AND ———— (1994b), 'Mediated Conflict Recovery by Constraint Relaxation,' *Proceedings of AAAI-94 Workshop on Models of Conflict Management in Cooperative Problem Solving,* Seattle, Wash., August 6, 1994.

GALBRAITH, J. R. (1973), *Designing Complex Organizations,* Boston, Mass.: Addison Wesley.

JACKSON, P. L. (1996), 'Lessons Learned from the Lenroc Plastics Experience,' Cornell University, www.orie.cornell.edu/~jackson.

KOLB, D. A (1984), *Experiential Learning: Experience as the Source of Learning and Development,* Englewood Cliffs, N.J.: Prentice Hall.

LEE, H. L., V. PADMANABLHAN, AND S. WHANG (1997), 'Information Distortion in a Supply Chain: The Bullwhip Effect,' *Management Science,* 43, 4, 546-558.

MALONE, T. W. AND K. CROWSTON (1994), 'The Interdisciplinary Study of Coordination.' *ACM Computing Surveys,* 26, 1, 87-11.

MEHRING, J. S., M. KOTLER, AND J. KIESEL (1997), *Improving Supply Chain Performance at BCG Company: Learning with Lego Blocks,* College of Management Working Paper 97-10-1, University of Massachusetts Lowell, Lowell, Mass.

MINTZBERG, H. (1979), The Structuring of Organizations. Prentice Hall, Englewood Cliffs, NJ.

MINTZBERG, H. (1984), "A Typology of Organizational Structures," In Organizations a Quantum View, Miller, D. and P. H. Friesen (Ed.), Prentice Hall, Englewood Cliffs, N.J.

SIEMENS CORPORATION (1995a), *Brief Case Game Participant's Binder,* Iselin, N.J.

——— (1995b), *Brief Case Game Instructor's Manual,* Iselin, N.J.

STERMAN, J. D. (1995), 'The Beer Distribution Game,' in *Games and Exercises for Operations Management,* J. N. Heineke and L. C. Meile (eds.), 101-112.

THOMPSON, J. D. (1967), *Organizations in Action: Social Science Bases of Administrative Theory,* McGraw Hill, New York.

VICTOR, B., AND R. S. BLACKBURN (1987), 'Interdependence: An Alternative Conceptualization.' *Academy of Management Review,* 12, 3, 486-498.

Joyce S. Mehring is an Associate Professor in the College of Management at the University of Massachusetts Lowell. She holds a B.A. from Bucknell University, a M.S. in Mathematics from the University of Michigan and a Ph.D. in Transportation Systems from the Massachusetts Institute of Technology. Dr. Mehring's research interests are supply chain management, decision support for production and logistics activities, and resource allocation planning. Her earlier work appears in journals such as *Interfaces, The Logistics and Transportation Review, Production and Inventory Management Journal,* and *Transportation Research.* At UMass Lowell, she teaches operations and logistics management and chairs the Manufacturing and MIS Department. Dr. Mehring has extensive business experience. She held senior positions at Amoco Corporation in the information systems department and at Charles River Associates Inc. in the transportation and energy consulting groups. She began her consulting career at Arthur D. Little, Inc. focusing on production, inventory and distribution issues for manufacturing firms. Dr. Mehring has presented her work at Decision Sciences Institute, INFORMS (Institute for Operations Research and Management Science) and the Production and Operations Management Society. She has served as an officer of professional groups, most recently, the New England Roundtable of the Council of Logistics Management.

THE PC-BASED SIMULATION GAME, *LEAN PRODUCTION*, FOR CONTROLLING THE SUPPLY CHAIN OF A VIRTUAL BICYCLE FACTORY*

GUENTHER ZAEPFEL AND BARTOSZ PIEKARZ

Department of Industry and Production Management, University of Linz, Linz, Austria
Department of Industry and Production Management, University of Linz, Linz, Austria

Lean Production is an interactive simulation game modeling a bicycle factory and its supply chain. The game includes a logistics planning and control system based on the manufacturing resources planning (MRP II) concept and an integrated controlling information system including business planning, performance indicator systems, and more. The player's decisions about logistic and financial issues are simulated and reported with a variety of graphical-analysis tools. The game should provide the player with a general idea of how to control the supply chain, using an integrated supply chain–controlling tool, and how to act in complex and dynamic situations to meet business objectives.
(SUPPLY CHAIN CONTROLLING, SIMULATION GAME, CONTROLLING INFORMATION SYSTEM, LOGISTICS)

1. Controlling the Supply Chain: An Overview

Controlling the supply chain requires a variety of individual but interrelated operative decisions, which have to be made continuously, about the following:
- Material supply logistics (order quantities, delivery dates, terms of payment, replenishment when shortages occur, etc.)
- Production logistics (aggregate and master production scheduling, material requirements planning, order release dates, batch sizing, release of partial batches, splitting and overlapping of batches, priority rules for the workstations and machine centers, etc.)
- Distribution logistics (distribution requirements planning, express deliveries, distributed stock keeping, internal deliveries between distribution centers, distribution control in case of shortages, etc.)

Each decision interacts with other ones in different ways. These decisions and the goals behind them are in part contradictory, which means that the degree of realization of one goal can have a negative effect on the realization of another. The best example is the classical conflict between mean lead time and capacity utilization in a shop-floor environment. Supply chain managers, therefore, have to take into account the effects and impact of their decisions and actions (although these are not always visible) to successfully control the supply chain.

---

* Received December 1998; revision received June 1999; accepted July 1999.

Version	Decisions for Material Supply	Decisions for Production	Decisions for Distribution
Basic-Version	- order quantities - economic order quantities - replenishment of shortages	- aggregate planning - master production scheduling - capacity planning - lot sizing	- number of trucks - loading quantity - express deliveries - inventory deployment - resolution in the case of delivery conflicts
	as above plus	*as above plus*	*as above plus*
Advanced-Version	- determination of safety stocks - terms of payment.	- material requirements planning - overlapping/splitting - priority rules - maintenance levels - lot sizing methods	- marketing activities - payment conditions

FIGURE 1. Necessary Decisions in the Simulation Game.

Another difficulty is the fact that, in many cases, decisions only take effect later, making direct impact impossible to determine. This phenomenon is called *time lag*.

All in all, the characteristics of such decisions can be described as complex because of the variety of individual decisions to be made and the interaction between them. The complexity of a system increases with the number of decisions to be made and the interactions between them when specific goals must be achieved (see Simon 1977; Doerner 1997). The PC-based simulation game, *Lean Production*, offers two options concerning complexity (see Figure 1).

1. *Basic Version.* In this mode the number of decision variables is limited to the most important actions of material, production, and distribution logistics. Decisions concerning the material requirements planning, the shop-floor control, and the financial transactions are automatically set by the simulation program.

2. *Advanced Version.* In addition to the decisions of the Basic Version, further actions must be made (see Figure 1). The *Lean Production* game is much more complex than the well-known *Beer Game* because a lot of interrelated decisions must be taken by the decision maker (Sterman 1989; Kaminsky and Simchi-Levi 1997).

In both versions the supply chain manager is concerned with a network of interrelated decisions that can cause different system states along the supply chain. The decision quality that a supply chain manager delivers depends on the following two factors: the knowledge of the cause-and-effect relationships and efficient planning methods and tools.

The *knowledge of the cause-and-effect relationships* encompasses what the decision maker knows about the influence of the decisions on the system states, especially how the decisions impact on revenues, costs, short term profits, cash payments, and the return on investment as a whole. In the form of a cause-and-effect chart, Figure 2 describes a network of decisions that forms the basis of the simulation game.

The rounded components in Figure 2 represent the independent variables, which can be divided into two groups, as follows:

1. *Direct controllable* independent variables, which stand for management action parameters and depend on decisions very often taken by various people with different goals.

2. *Noncontrollable* independent variables, which stand for external effects on the system that cannot be controlled by management; they are simply assumed as the "sales scenario" (trade cycle, specific markets, competitive situation, etc.).

The boxes stand for the dependent variables, the system states, or the degrees of realization that are determined by the independent variables. The type of determination is shown by the arrows between the variables combined with the symbols "+" and "−," where respectively "+" stands for a positive relationship of the type "the more, the more" (e.g., the higher the order quantity, the higher the material stock on hand), and "−" stands for "the higher, the

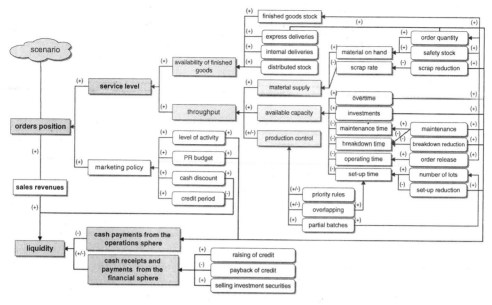

FIGURE 2. Cause-and-Effect Chart.

lower" and vice versa (e.g., the lower the scrap rate, the higher the material supply). They make no statement, however, about the quantitative dimension and the time lag between cause and effect. In a networked system a variable can also affect itself; this is called a *feedback circuit*.

The availability and use of efficient planning methods and tools help to handle the complexity of managing the supply chain. For this purpose the game *Lean Production* offers a logistics planning system (LPS) and a controlling information system (CIS); these are presented in detail in Sections 2.2 and 2.3. Summarizing, the process of managing the supply chain can be interpreted as a control circuit as pictured in Figure 3. The supply chain manager controls the state of the physical supply chain by changing the state of the manipulated variables (e.g., order release quantities) in the LPS; the general objectives specify the goals to be achieved. The state of the physical supply chain (the dependent variables) can be described by the controlled variables (using key performance indicators such as system utilization, throughput, delivery service level, and mean lead time) in the CIS. Disturbance

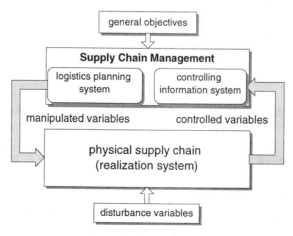

FIGURE 3. Control Circuit.

variables (material shortages, machine breakdowns, scrap, etc.) also take effect on the realization system; in some cases the supply chain manager will have to take countermeasures to "get the system under control."

The *Lean Production* game offers a simplified physical supply chain of a virtual bicycle factory and a logistics planning (based on the MRP II concept) and controlling system. With the aid of the planning and controlling system, the player can make decisions for every period. The game simulates the effects on the physical supply chain and the goal achievement of the decisions and presents the results to the player. After analysis of the system status for the current period, a new planning run can start. Therefore the *Lean Production* game can be used for:

- teaching logistics management and supply chain controlling
- teaching production management (because it is based on the MRP II concept)
- analyzing case studies (generated by playing the game) in a broad context (from logistics to accounting and finance)
- analyzing trends and values of specific performance indicators (over 250 are available)
- analyzing different strategies in connection with simulation results

In the following section we describe the elements of the PC-based simulation game in more detail.

2. The Simulation Game *Lean Production*

The *Lean Production* game portrays the basic logistic processes of sales, distribution, commission/collection, production, material supply, and purchasing in a simulated bicycle factory. Service processes such as marketing activities (ensuring and increasing sales), the realization of projects (gradually improving the production system), and financial transactions (ensuring liquidity, increasing profitability) are considered as well. The supply chain consists of the following areas: Material Supply and Purchasing, Sales and Marketing, Production, and Distribution. The information flow proceeds from top to bottom, beginning at the customer (order placement, sales plan) past the production planning to the material order. The material flow, however, proceeds from the supplier to the distribution center and its customers, in exactly the opposite direction (see Figure 4).

The bicycle factory offers three product lines (mountain bikes, trekking bikes, city bikes) consisting of three to four models each, from the expensive professional model with the best equipment to the cheap amateur model with standard parts. The models are available in up to eight variants, differing in frame size and design (women's or men's bicycle, etc.). Altogether, three types, 10 models and 48 variants are planned, produced, and delivered.

The object structure of the simulation model includes:

- 48 bicycle variants grouped in 10 models and 3 product lines
- 82 in-house components (frames, wheels, rims, spokes)
- 50 workstations
- 5 production sites
- 38 purchased parts (forks, drive units, accessories, etc.)

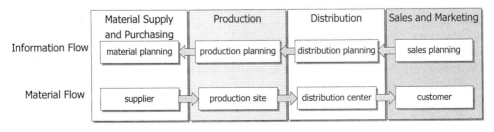

FIGURE 4. Information and Material Flow in the Supply Chain.

- 10 suppliers
- 4 sales areas, each with its own distribution center supplied by a transportation capacity of up to 30 trucks

Corresponding to the control circuit of the supply chain of Figure 3, the basic elements of the simulation model of *Lean Production* are the physical supply chain, the Logistics Planning System, and the Controlling Information System.

2.1. The Physical Supply Chain

The material flow of the supply chain begins with ordering and shipment of the material by the supplier. The purchasing department coordinates material requirements for production with deliveries by suppliers. On the one hand, the required material parts per supplier are determined according to type, quantity, and time of delivery; on the other hand, the goods are accepted at the materials receiving department, are then inspected as to their correspondence with the purchase orders (e.g., regarding the quantity and quality), and, if they are not to be directed into the (just-in-time) production process, are transferred to the material store.

The production system consists of five production sites located in five different states of the United States (see Figure 5)—final assembly, frame production, wheel production, rim production, and spoke production—with a total of 50 workstations. The material flow between the production sites plays an important role in production planning. The assembled bicycles are transferred to the finished goods store, i.e., combined by means of pick lists to deliveries to the distribution centers in the goods outward office and distributed by the company's own fleet of trucks or by a logistic service partner. The distribution centers sell the bicycles to customers or regional wholesalers and additionally manage marketing activities.

The United States was chosen as the general sales market. It was separated into four sales areas: Pacific, Central, South, and Atlantic. A distribution center that supplies the local wholesalers and retailers was set up in each of the four sales areas. Because of the varying geographic and demographic characteristics, the mix in the product lines differs. For example, in the Pacific area more mountain bikes and in the Atlantic area more city bikes are sold. In addition, the sales areas differ as to their distance to the final assembly site (in Dallas, TX), their average amount of trade discounts, their marketing policy, and their number of

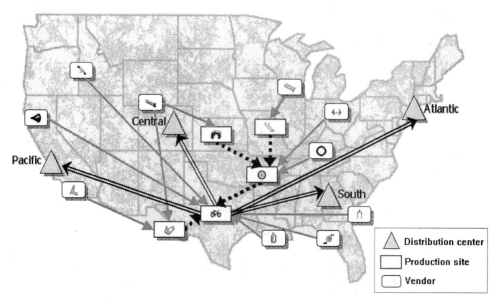

FIGURE 5. View of the Supply Chain of the Virtual Bicycle Factory.

traveling salesmen charged on commission. However, the discount rates and the credit period are the same for all sales areas in terms of payment.

2.2. *Logistics Planning System*

The logistics planning system (LPS) has the objective to plan and control activities through the whole supply chain and to quantify quantitative and temporal effects on the enterprise's resources. The LPS is based on the MRP II planning concept; its functionality is based largely on commercial enterprise resources planning (ERP) software (e.g., SAP R/3).

2.2.1. SALES PLANNING. At the beginning of the business year a sales plan is drawn up for each of the sales areas based on the three general product lines. On the basis of integrated business planning, this plan is the starting point for the enterprise's budget and the parameter "orders position percentage" (starting at 100%). The goal of marketing activities is high market attractiveness of the company, to keep present customers and to attract potential ones. Depending on the market attractiveness, the orders position varies during the business year. Unlike the market attractiveness, this percentage can be easily operationalized. The critical factors of market attractiveness are the terms of payment for the customer (cash discount, credit period), the quality (the degree of meeting the requirements of customers), the public relations image of the enterprise, and the delivery service (the throughput of a period as a percentage of the amount released). The conditions of payment, the public relations budget, and the level of the marketing activities per sales area may be determined individually and have different effects on the profit and the liquidity (e.g., high discounts cause more customers to pay in cash, thereby on the one hand increasing the liquidity, while on the other reducing the profit).

2.2.2. DISTRIBUTION PLANNING. The task of the distribution department is to compile orders and deliver the finished goods (bicycles) to the individual distribution centers. The two major goals of the sales area are high delivery service on the one hand and low transportation costs and penalties (prearranged penalties for exceeding delivery deadlines) on the other.

Decisions in the following areas must be made within the limits of the goal conflict between maximal delivery service and minimal costs: the number of trucks employed, the minimum load of bicycles per truck, deliveries by an express delivery service (e.g. when punctual delivery by truck is not possible), and internal deliveries (deliveries of required bicycles between distribution centers). Such internal deliveries assume that there is distributed a finished goods stock, which means that available stock is distributed from the plant to the local distribution centers. The effects of keeping distributed stock on the delivery service depend on whether the stock can meet the demand; e.g., this demand cannot be met when the required bicycles of one distribution area are kept in another and internal deliveries are not allowed. Internal and express deliveries improve the overall delivery service; however, they involve higher transportation costs (resulting from low utilization in the first case and express fees in the second).

Supposing that the demand for bicycles exceeds the supply of finished bicycles, a decision must be made as to which sales area will be preferred in receiving the shipment. Sales planning must decide how to solve this sort of delivery conflict (e.g., fair-share allocation or preference of distribution centers with the lowest transportation costs). Planned sales figures are regarded as given by the sales department and must be reached. If the enterprise cannot meet the requirements, penalties must be paid for exceeding deadlines.

2.2.3. PRODUCTION PLANNING. The goal of production is to meet the distribution requirements at the lowest cost possible. The central tool for production planning is certainly the manufacturing resources planning (MRP II) concept. The supply chain manager schedules the work orders in conformity with the available capacities; therefore, each production site is a

planning level / attributes	planning period	planning object	capacity unit
aggregated planning /monthly	12 months	product lines (3)	production site
aggregated planning /weekly	8 weeks	models (10)	production site
Master Production Scheduling	8 weeks	variants (48)	work station

FIGURE 6. Levels of Production Planning.

single capacity unit on an aggregated level (see Figure 6). The capacity load profile shows the utilization of each production site based on its bottleneck workstation.

In the aggregated planning on a weekly basis, the product lines are divided into models according to the aggregated bill of materials. In addition, the weekly fluctuations in the demand of each model (the sales plan is determined on a weekly basis) are taken into consideration. The planned capacity utilization of each resource can be determined more accurately, and the dynamic structure of the utilization of each production site is also taken into account. One prerequisite of this procedure must be emphasized: the profile of capacities of each production site is to be harmonized with the workload (which has to be highly predictable). Investing in new workstations and scheduling overtime or a second shift can increase the total capacity (available capacity). This also affects the profit and liquidity.

The production quantity for each bicycle variant, regarding workstation and week, must be determined on the basis of the master production schedule (MPS; see Figure 7). Every workstation is charged with the setup and operating times according to the routing file. This

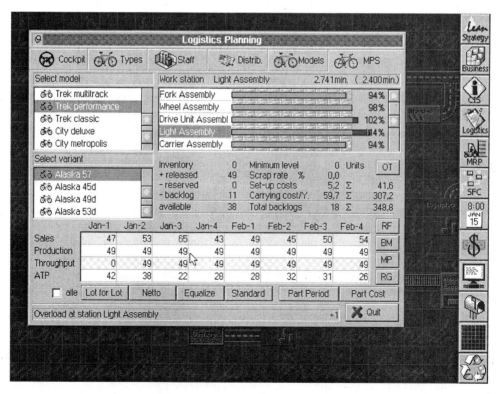

FIGURE 7. Master Production Scheduling.

reveals possible bottlenecks at an early stage. If the available capacity is exceeded, the MPS must be modified in amount and/or in release date by the planner. The actual control tool is the input/output plan, which is a table of cumulated figures of production release and stock increase for a time horizon of 8 weeks. The Available To Promise (ATP) stock is the ATP stock of the previous week minus the sales plus the production throughput, excluding reserved parts for current orders and including the work-in-process inventories. Input/output plans are used at all three levels of production planning.

The input/output plans are calculated for each production component on the basis of the master production schedule and the material requirements plan. Of course, the order release has to be coordinated by type, release time, and amount with the production sites because one area is a supplier of another (e.g., rims and spokes are needed to assemble a wheel). Because the planned mean lead time of 1 week is identical for all production sites, a quite simple kind of farsighted recursive coordination can be employed (see Figure 8). The components for the MPS of week 4 have to be finished and delivered by the end of week 3, and to enable production of the frames and wheels in week 3, rims, spokes, and purchased parts have to be available by the end of week 2. The net material demand is calculated using bills of materials and the current stock available. In the basic version of the game, material requirements planning is automatically handled by the software.

In the planning process, capacity utilization charts for every workstation as well as production flowcharts for the subsequent inspection serve as visual tools. In addition there are various lot-sizing methods to choose from (e.g., lot-for-lot, least–unit cost batch size, part period, etc.). A production database with BOMs and routing files for every part produced in the bicycle factory is also available.

2.2.4. MATERIAL SUPPLY AND PURCHASING (ADVANCED VERSION). The two basic goals of the material supply are the rival objectives of ensuring the supply of purchased parts and components but also of low inventory costs. Material requirements planning has to be adapted to the master production schedule and the plans of the precursory production sites. Purchasing ensures economical prices and reliable supplies. Besides the purchase price per part, every delivery of a purchased part causes various fixed-ordering and carrying costs, quantity and cash discounts, and credit periods, depending on the supplier. From time to time material shortages may occur. These shortages depend on the individual supplier as well as on the quantity ordered and the terms of payment (usually a supplier prefers cash payment). When a material shortage occurs, an automatic replenishment can be adjusted for the next period. The following options are also available: lot-sizing methods (part-period, cost-per-part), an ABC analysis of the material value per part and of the purchase volume per supplier, and delivery service level ratios for each supplier.

Period 1	Period 2	Period 3	Period 4
MPS	MPS	MPS	MPS
frames	frames	frames	frames
wheels	wheels	wheels	wheels
spokes	spokes	spokes	spokes
rims	rims	rims	rims
purchased parts-2	purchased parts-3	purchased parts-4	purchased parts

FIGURE 8. Dynamic Structure of the Production Plan in Each Production Site.

2.2.5. SHOP FLOOR CONTROL (ADVANCED VERSION). For all five production sites, basic parameters can be specified by which the production process simulation is performed on the shop-floor–control level. The same variants of a bicycle are pooled to a single batch to reduce setup operations. The order release is carried out at the beginning of each week; however, if required material for a specific batch is not available, this batch can be delayed or split. The number of released batches and the splitting/overlapping factors per batch result in more setup operations. The quantity of production and the level of maintenance cause various and, in part, contrary effects on lead times and capacity utilization. Other important action parameters are the priority rules at every workstation that determine the order of batch processing. A standard batch size can be set for every production batch. When material backlogs occur, parts of the original batch size (partial batches) can be released into the production process. Investments can be made in the fixed assets (increasing the number of machine centers of a specific workstation) as well as in staff training.

2.2.6. FINANCIAL SERVICES (ADVANCED VERSION). With its goals of ensuring liquidity (short-term), profit control (midterm), and profitability as the Return On Investment (long-term) in the simulation model, financial management has only a limited range of action that relates to assuming and repaying a loan or selling long-term investment securities; however, it is closely connected to the decisions of the whole supply chain. The toolbox of financial services includes the balance sheet, profit and loss statements, financial ratio systems, cost unit accounting, liquidity forecasts, and weekly financial reports. The complexity of achieving the goals is not solely the result of the limited range of action in the financial sphere but rather depends on all the decisions made along the supply chain and their effects on the financial goals of liquidity, profit, and profitability.

2.3. *Controlling Information System*

The controlling information system complements the logistics planning system by visualizing the cost, performance, and financial effects of decisions taken along the supply chain. The CIS is based on the principles of visual controlling. Key performance indicators are visualized on a map and are color-coded to reflect their values; therefore, it is also possible to visually determine the system bottleneck.

2.3.1. SUPPLY CHAIN ANALYSIS. Supply chain analysis starts with a bottleneck analysis. One element of the supply chain becomes a bottleneck when it restricts compliance with objectives in the utmost way. Because logistic bottlenecks occur along the whole supply chain, an adequate set of key performance indicators is needed to display the current states and the development over time of the system elements during the controlling process. This is addressed in the simulation game by using a supply-chain key performance indicator (SCI) system. To provide a quick overview of the whole supply chain, for every element in the chain there is a corresponding performance indicator (e.g., delivery service as a percentage) and the current bottleneck (sales area, production site, supplier group) is shown. In addition one can see the trend so far of the selected key performance indicator.

2.3.2. DISTRIBUTION, PRODUCTION, AND STOCK INFORMATION SYSTEMS. The *distribution information system* (see Figure 9) informs about the four distribution centers, the trucks employed, and the delivered bicycles. In addition the stock information system presents the quantities and delivery deadline status of bicycles in the finished goods stock and the four distribution centers, including an overview of the current transport loads on the trucks and their locations. For every truck the current position and its load are shown in a separate overview. The delivery service indicator, coded by bicycle model, is shown for every distribution area and its warehouse as well. Other key performance indicators such as truck utilization, the use of different means of transport, and the average distribution costs per bicycle are computed as well. The *production information system* employs a variety of performance indicators such

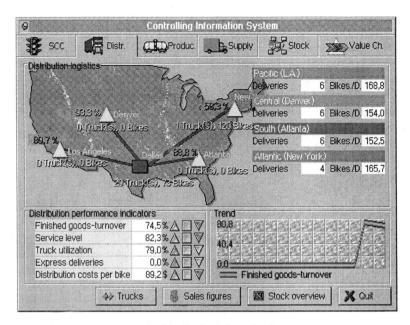

FIGURE 9. Distribution Information System.

as capacity utilization, mean lead time, throughput rate, material coverage, and scrap rate. Separate indicators are available for each of the five production sites. The *stock information system* offers a visual and monetary overview of the distribution of finished goods, components, and parts throughout all distribution warehouses and production sites. In addition system quality indicators for the company as a whole are computed.

2.3.3. DATA WAREHOUSE The Lean DataWarehouse program, which runs under MS-Excel, offers some of the features of a professional data warehouse solution. Its database consists of over 250 performance indicators and values taken from the simulation game, where they are recorded by the system automatically. The data can be read into the Excel program and are then available for a variety of reports and analysis tools. The built-in drill-down functionality allows reducing selected key performance indicators to their components. Graphical reports visualize up to six different trends for the whole simulation period. Furthermore, the correlation analysis supports examination of the trend of two different indicators to test a logical connection (a possible time lag between the two values has to be considered as well).

Lean DataWarehouse includes the following reports and analysis tools:
- the supply-chain key performance indicator system (with drill-down functionality)
- value chain analysis
- financial ratio system (with drill-down functionality)
- competitive advances profile (with drill-down functionality)
- graphical reports and correlation analysis

3. Supply Chain Case Study

This section focuses on the concrete process of supply chain controlling. It contains a small case study, in which logistic bottlenecks are identified and proper countermeasures are developed. The case study is illustrated with screen shots from the simulation game.

3.1. *Identification of a Logistic Bottleneck*

The starting point for logistic bottleneck identification is supply chain–indicator (SCI) analysis (see right panel of Figure 10). The analysis shows that the current bottleneck element

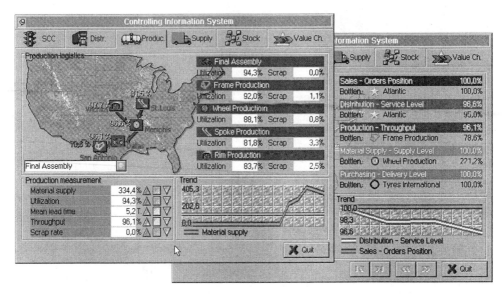

FIGURE 10. Controlling Information System.

is production. The throughput of final assembly with a value of 96.1% can be described as rather good, but might serve as a signal for a possible stable bottleneck in one of the production sites. To find this out we examine the production information system (see Figure 10, left panel). Here we have an overview of the key performance indicators from all five production sites.

Although the throughput of final assembly is not critical, we notice a rather weak value in the frame production (78.6%). Unless adequate stocks are available, this might greatly restrict the material supply for the subsequent area, final assembly, and so limit its output in the future. Thus we examine in detail the production segment frame production, where we are looking for the workstation that most constricts system throughput. We switch to the Production Data Analysis, which creates a material flowchart for all workstations and lists all relevant throughput time operations (total work time, setup time, maintenance time, breakdown time; see Figure 11, left panel). Because of the total capacity utilization rate of 100% and a work-in-queue of another 806 minutes (see Figure 11), the workstation Sandblasting is determined as the current production site bottleneck. The input/output process in the flowchart further indicates an increasing queue volume, because the input rate is higher than the output rate. This statement is validated by a visual analysis of the system queue over the last 5 planning weeks (see Figure 11, right panel). Through the arrangement and color of the queue indicator lights (turning from green to red and rising), the bottleneck of the frame production is easy to identify.

If we compare the percentages of the operation times, two operations stand out quite significantly. The 43.6% share of setup time and 14.5% of breakdown time are much higher than comparable mean values of the production site as a whole (19.2% setup operations and 4.4% breakdown time).

Possible reasons for the high percentage share of setup time because of the simulation model and decisions that were made (system parameters) include the following (compare the cause-and-effect diagram in Figure 2):

- the relative high number of different variants—and therefore different lots—in the frame production
- the long setup time at the workstation Sandblasting
- several setup operations for each partial lot because of overlapping/splitting lots

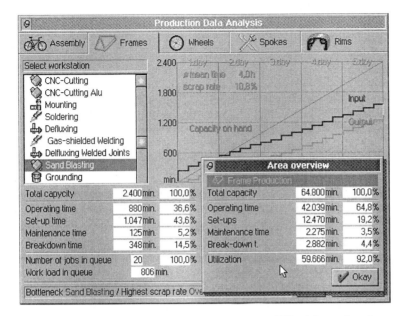

FIGURE 11. Production Report and Visual Queue Overview.

- a high breakdown rate and a long maintenance period at the respective workstation, causing more frequent failures

3.2. *Countermeasures*

Some essential starting points for countermeasures thus become apparent. The general objective is not only to relieve the bottleneck but also to remove it in the medium or long run. These measures should not be seen as a haphazard bunch of measures, but rather as producing a concerted group of measures to increase the system throughput and decrease the work-in-queue. This particular case indicates implementing all of the following:
- plan overtime at the workstation Sandblasting
- change the priority rule to "longest operational time" to merge partial batches and save setup operations
- increase maintenance time to prevent failures
- initialize a setup reduction project to reduce setup time as a long-term effect

After the measures have been put into practice, their impact on the total system should be observed carefully because side effects (e.g., higher maintenance costs) could arise.

4. Practical Use in Teaching

The computer-based simulation game *Lean Production* has been in use at the Department of Industry and Production Management at the University of Linz for more than 3 years. In this period it has been tested by more than 100 students in several courses of Logistics Management. The simulation software was also improved in many ways to meet new requirements and accommodate many helpful suggestions of its users. Meanwhile, the game is also in use for logistics education at other universities in Germany and Austria.

4.1. *Course Outline*

The *Lean Production* game can be used as an extension to existing courses or in a stand-alone course dedicated to a logistic issue (e.g., Production or Supply Chain

Management, MRP II, Logistics Controlling). Basically a step-by-step introduction to the subject is recommended to avoid confusing the students with the large variety of tools and reports within the program. We recommend the following procedure consisting of a minimum of five meetings (each about 4 hours) and four homework assignments between them:

1. *Introduction.* The introduction should be dedicated to the key issues of logistics management. The students can be divided into groups of three or four, with any distribution of tasks within a group being possible (e.g., one is responsible for distribution, another for production or supply or finances). Each group is graded separately and should get a copy of the simulation software. Homework for the next meeting: examination of the controlling tools used in the simulation game.

2. *Controlling tools.* To gain a deeper understanding of the controlling tools implemented in the software, the theory behind each tool should be discussed first (applicability, objectives, meaning, restrictions). The functionality and its implications can be demonstrated using the simulation game. Homework: analysis of a case study.

3. *Case study.* Based on any saved game generated with the simulation game (whereby any specific case study can be prepared by the course instructor), the systematic approach to analysis of the logistic chain can be practiced. Each group presents its results and conclusions based on the case study. Identifying bottlenecks, including trend and value analysis of key performance indicators, is very important in controlling the supply chain. System bottlenecks should be identified using the drill-down functionality of the data warehouse. Finally, proper countermeasures should be proposed to relieve and eliminate bottlenecks. Homework: logistics planning.

4. *Logistics planning.* Before the actual simulation game, aggregate planning should be performed for the supply chain. The key parameters are the aggregate production quantities on the level of product groups and the capacity planning for distribution and production. The conflict between the objectives of high system utilization, adequate inventory levels, and minimum costs should particularly be treated in subsequent discussion. Homework: simulation of the supply chain (which means to play the simulation game at last).

5. *Simulation study.* Following the planning phase, a complete simulation study is to be done, which means that all the groups should play the game through the whole simulation year using their aggregate plans. The goal is to achieve as many points as possible, resulting primarily from a high return on investment rate. The final group presentation should cover the basic strategy, measures taken, and the achieved results. The presentation can be complemented by using the trend reports from the data warehouse, because not only the results but also the order of events that led to them are important. It is also possible to play the game for a second time (arranging another meeting) and to compare both results. In this case we recommend using the basic version of the game for the first run, and the advanced version (coupled with a more difficult sales scenario) for the second run.

4.2. *Experiences*

In general our experiences with this simulation game were very encouraging and promising. Each semester the general satisfaction of the students with the simulation game was queried in a detailed questionnaire. A majority of about 60% found the game very interesting and another 30 to 40%, interesting. The difficulty of the game was rated by 50 to 70% as very high, but almost all students (90%) profited from playing the game for their studies. Stated as particular benefits were the high degree of reality of the simulation model and the ensuing recognition of the complexity and dynamics. Likewise, the understanding of interconnections of the whole system, the practical use of management techniques, and the game itself all had a positive effect on the students' opinions. The spectrum of students' reactions ranged from holistic system understanding to the complete confusion of those who did not understand the cause-and-effect relationships (see Figure 2). Finally, the time investment for the whole course was rated high.

4.3. *Summary*

The simulation software permits the user interactive and dynamic control of materials and cash flow in the virtual supply chain. The user learns about the coordination of the planning and controlling activities of a supply chain. In the context of the whole enterprise, this is a very complex task, given that individual activities and their planned results entail side effects on other objectives and that positive and negative feedback occur. The simulation technique is a suitable tool for learning how to think and how to solve problems in complex decision situations. In reality, critical and complicated situations rarely occur and the time lags are long. It takes a while to notice the implications of one's decisions; sometimes it is even impossible to clarify them. A computer-simulated scenario might be simpler than reality, but it serves as a quickly moving tool that immediately allows us to realize the mistakes we have made and gives us a chance to improve (see Doerner 1997). Computer-simulated models are therefore excellent for teaching how to handle difficult situations of high complexity and dynamic structure (see Biethahn et al. 1994, Section 1).

All in all, the interactive simulation game, *Lean Production*, should
- give the player a general idea about how to control the whole supply chain and manage the support processes of finance and R&D
- provide a tool for testing different strategies and operative plans
- give some hints as how to design and improve a controlling information system
- train students in the interpretation and use of logistics and financial performance indicators
- encourage thinking in a general perspective and in processes rather than in details and functions

4.4. *Note*

The system requirements include a personal computer with the MS-DOS operating system or MS-Windows 95/98 or NT in DOS-mode. The simulation software was developed at the Department of Industry and Production Management at the University of Linz, Austria. Further information and a free download of the game can be found on our home page at http://www.ifw.uni-linz.ac.at/lean.html

References

BIETHAHN, J. ET AL. (1994), *Simulation als betriebliche Entscheidungshilfe—Fortschritte in der Simulationstechnik*, Band 8, Vieweg Verlag, Braunschweig/Wiesbaden, Germany.
DOERNER, D. (1997), *The Logic of Failure: Recognizing and Avoiding Error in Complex Situations*, Perseus Press.
KAMINSKY, P. AND D. S. SIMCHI-LEVI (1997), "A New Computerized Beer Game: A Tool for Teaching the Value of Integrated Supply Chain Management," http://iems.nwu.edu/~levi/prolog/at the Northwestern University Production and Logistics Laboratory, Evanston, IL, USA.
SIMON, H. A. (1977), "How Complex Are Complex Systems?" F. Suppe and P. D. Asquith (eds.), *Proceedings of the 1976 Biennial Meeting of the Philosophy of Science Association*, Vol. 2, Edwards Brothers, Ann Arbor, MI, USA, 507–522.
STERMAN (1989), "Modeling Managerial Behavior: Misperceptions of Feedback in a Dynamic Decision Making Experiment," *Management Science*, 35, 3, .
ZAEPFEL, G. AND B. PIEKARZ (1996), *Supply Chain Controlling—Interaktive und dynamische Regelung der Material- und Warenfluesse*, Ueberreuter Verlag, Vienna, Austria.
——— AND ——— (1998), "Regelkreisbasiertes Supply Chain Controlling—Ein heuristisches Konzept zur Beherrschung von Logistikketten, demonstriert an dem computergestuetzten Planspiel Lean Produc-

tion," in *Innovationen in der Produktionswirtschaft*, H. Wildemann (ed.), TCW-Verlag, Munich, Germany.

Guenther Zaepfel is Full Professor for Business Administration and the head of the Institute of Industry and Production Management at the University of Linz, Austria. The Institute maintains close ties with industry. Since 1998 he has been the Vice Dean of Studies at the Faculty of Social Sciences, Economics, and Business at the University of Linz. He is the author and coauthor of 14 books and over 65 papers in journals such as *European Journal of Operational Research* and *International Journal of Production Economics*. His research fields are supply chain management, production logistics, production planning and control systems, strategic production, and logistics management.

Bartosz Piekarz is currently an assistant at the Institute of Industry and Production Management, University of Linz, Austria. He holds his master degree in Business Informatics and has worked in consulting for several years. Mr. Piekarz is also coauthor of some publications concerning supply chain management. His current research thrust involves supply chain–controlling tools, process-oriented performance measurement, and the development of logistics management games.

A SIMULATION GAME FOR TEACHING SERVICE-ORIENTED SUPPLY CHAIN MANAGEMENT: DOES INFORMATION SHARING HELP MANAGERS WITH SERVICE CAPACITY DECISIONS?*

EDWARD G. ANDERSON JR.

Management Department, CBA 4.202, The University of Texas at Austin, Austin, Texas 78712-1175, USA

DOUGLAS J. MORRICE

MSIS Department, CBA 5.202, The University of Texas at Austin, Austin, Texas 78712-1175, USA

For decades, the Beer Game has taught complex principles of supply chain management in a finished good inventory supply chain. However, services typically cannot hold inventory and can only manage backlogs through capacity adjustments. We propose a simulation game designed to teach service-oriented supply chain management principles and to test whether managers use them effectively. For example, using a sample of typical student results, we determine that student managers can effectively use end-user demand information to reduce backlog and capacity adjustment costs. The game can also demonstrate the impact of demand variability and reduced capacity adjustment time and lead times.
(SUPPLY CHAIN MANAGEMENT, TEACHING POM, SYSTEM DYNAMIC, BUSINESS GAMES)

1. Introduction

In response to growing demand from our corporate partners, the authors have recently completed development of a Supply Chain Management course for our Executive Education Program. In developing the course, the authors drew from many materials that have been developed to support teaching this topic. For example, several new textbooks are either entirely or partially devoted to this topic (Copacino 1997; Gattorna 1998; Handfield and Nichols 1998; Ross 1998; Simchi-Levi, Kaminsky, and Simchi-Levi 1999). Additionally, in order to give the clients a better 'hands-on' feel for many supply chain management problems and how they might be mitigated, the course includes a module featuring the famous Beer Distribution Game developed at MIT almost 30 years ago (Sterman 1989b; Senge 1990). The Beer Game allows teams of players to simulate the workings of a single product distribution supply chain in which each player manages the inventory of a retailer, wholesaler, distributor,

---

* Names of the authors in this paper appear in alphabetical order. Reprinted from *Production and Operations Management*, Vol. 9, No. 1, Spring 2000, pp. 40–55.

or manufacturer. In its original form, the game is set up as a physical simulation, but it is also available as a computer simulation (e.g., Simchi-Levi, Kaminsky, and Simchi-Levi 1999). Sterman (1989b) extols the value of using simulated exercises to help the students gain first hand knowledge of such things as the "bullwhip effect" (Forrester 1958; Lee, Padmanabhan, and Whang 1997a, 1997b) and the benefits of lead-time reduction and information sharing. However, many of our corporate partners operate inside of service supply chains, which behave differently from finished goods inventory distribution chains. Although these clients might find the Beer Game interesting and we might be able to extrapolate some principles to fit their business environment, the game is not ideal. In particular, service supply chains typically do not have inventory stocks that are replenished directly through order placements, but rather only backlogs that are managed indirectly through service capacity adjustments. The Beer Game models the former sort of supply chain quite well, but is not as representative of the latter. For example, the Beer Game assumes for reasons of pedagogical simplicity an infinite manufacturing capacity. While this assumption is reasonable when simulating a distribution supply chain, it is problematic in a service supply chain. Consequently, the authors have developed a game that more closely resembles service supply chains and the types of decisions made within these contexts.

In this paper, we develop a supply chain game with three main features:

1. The supply chain has multiple, potentially autonomous, players performing a sequence of operations.
2. Finished goods inventory is not an option because the product or service is essentially make-to-order.
3. Each player manages order backlog by adjusting capacity.

The game we developed is called the *Mortgage Service Game*. Like the Beer Game, we chose to model a specific application as opposed to using a generic model. A specific application has much greater pedagogical value because participants are more likely to assume the roles within the game and make the simulation more closely mimic reality. Additionally, the mortgage service supply chain provides a realistic application that encompasses all the features listed above. The principles learned from this game can be easily generalized to other industries that have supply chains with similar features (e.g., Wheelwright 1992).

Aside from being an integral part of a service supply chain course, a second major use of the game is for research and assessment purposes. In particular, how well do the students apply the supply chain principles that they are taught in class? For instance, can the students effectively use end-user demand information to improve their performance? And if they can, how much will they benefit? The Mortgage Service Game can help researchers answer these sorts of research questions. To demonstrate this use, we present in this paper a sample of typical student results from classroom experience in playing the Mortage Service Game. We analyze the results to determine how effectively student managers can use end-user demand information to reduce backlog and capacity adjustment costs, thus ameliorating the "bullwhip effect." From the analysis, we determine that indeed students do improve their performance significantly by using end-user demand information, both in a statistical sense and relative to an "optimal" benchmark. This is an encouraging result, given the demonstrated difficulty with which managers cope with dynamically complex environments (Sterman 1989b).

The remainder of the paper is organized in the following manner. Section 2 contains a description of the Mortgage Service Game simulation model. Section 3 briefly describes the behavior of the Mortgage Service supply chain. Section 4 outlines various teaching strategies that can be used to describe principles in capacity management with and without end-user demand information. Additionally, this section also presents the results from classroom use of the simulation game. Section 5 discusses extensions to the service game and contains other concluding remarks.

2. The Mortgage Service Game

To make the service supply chain game concrete, we will use it to represent a simplified mortgage approval process from application submission through approval. The model's purpose is to capture the essential elements of reality common to most service supply chains rather than perfectly simulate the mortgage industry. As such, some supply-chain complexities idiosyncratic to the mortgage industry are not modeled in the interest of pedagogical simplicity. The model is currently implemented in the Vensim© Simulation Package (Ventana Systems Inc. 1998) and iThink Simulation Package (Richmond and Peterson 1996). Figure 1a depicts the basic logic of the model in the form of a Vensim block diagram. An equivalent iThink model is used to conduct the game in a classroom setting (see Section 3.1 for more details).The graphical user interface of an iThink model is given in Figure 1b.

Each mortgage application passes through four stages: initial processing (i.e., filling out the application with a loan officer), credit checking (confirmation of employment and review of credit history), surveying (a survey of the proposed property to check for its value, as well as any infringements upon zoning laws or neighboring properties), and title checking (ensuring that the title to the property is uncontested and without liens). Mechanically, all the stages operate in an identical manner, so we will describe here only the survey section of the model as an example of each stage's processing. As each application is checked for the credit worthiness of its applicant (*credit checking* in the diagram), the application flows from the backlog of credit checks (*Credit Check Backlog*) to join the backlog of surveys (*Survey Backlog*). Each week, based on the backlog of surveys—which is the only information available to the player controlling the survey stage of the system when using a decentralized strategy—the player sets the target capacity of the system by deciding to hire or fire employees: in this case, surveyors. However, it takes time to actually find, interview, and hire or, conversely, to give notice and fire employees; so the actual *Survey Capacity* will lag the *Target Survey Capacity* by an average of 1 month. Those surveyors currently in the employ of the survey company will then carry out as many surveys as they can over the next week. Finally, as each application's survey is completed (*surveying*), the application will then leave the *Survey Backlog* to join the next backlog downstream—in this case, the *Title Check Backlog*. Each of the other four stages functions analogously.

In real life, of course, the purpose of each of these checks is to eliminate those applications that are too risky. However, again for reasons of pedagogical simplicity, we will assume that each application is ultimately approved. This is reasonable because, despite the fact that a random survival rate for each stage does indeed complicate real-life management of the chain, the primary dynamic control problems derive from other sources. In particular, the largest problem results from each stage of the process generally being managed by a separate company. Each of these companies controls its own individual capacity; however, it typically only sees its own backlog when making the decision, not the global new application rate or other stages' backlogs. This creates something akin to the bullwhip effect (Lee et al. 1997b) seen in the Beer Game (Sterman 1989b), albeit here the inventories controlled are strictly backlogs. Also, as in many real life services, there is no way for a player to stockpile finished goods inventory in advance as a buffer against fluctuating demand. Rather, each stage must manage its backlog strictly by managing its capacity size, that is the number of workers it employs.

Mathematically, the structure for each stage of the process is as follows (Let stages 1, 2, 3, and 4 refer, respectively, to the application processing, credit checking, surveying, and title checking stages):

$$B_{i,t+1} = B_{i,t} + r_{i-1,t} - r_{i,t} \tag{1}$$

$$r_{i,t} = \min(C_{i,t}, B_{i,t} + r_{i-1,t}) \tag{2}$$

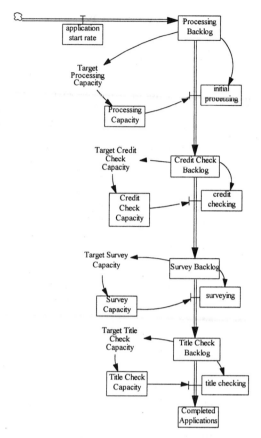
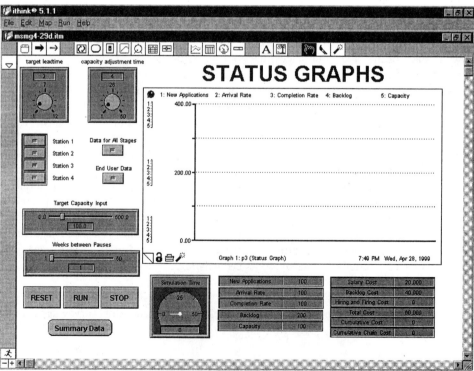

FIGURE 1. (a) Block Diagram of Mortgage Service Game. (b) Graphical User Interface of The Mortgage Service Game.

where $B(i,t)$, $C(i,t)$, and $r(i,t)$ refer, respectively, to the backlog, the capacity, and the completion rate at stage i on day t. Note that $r(0,t)$ represents the new application start rate, which is determined exogenously, for example, by the instructor. In the game, this variable remains at a constant level over an initial period of time. At a certain point in time $r(0,t)$ steps up to a higher level where it remains constant for the remainder of the game. For simplicity, we will assume that each employee has a productivity of one application per day. Because of this simplifying assumption, the completion rate of applications at any stage is constrained to the minimum of the backlog plus any inflow from the previous stage (if material is constraining processing) or the capacity (the more typical case). Each stage's backlog is initialized at the beginning of the game to $\lambda[r(i,0)]$, where λ is a constant representing the average nominal delay required to complete a backlogged application. Each stage's capacity is initialized at $r(i,0)$ so that the backlogging and completion rates at each stage are in balance (see Equations 3 and 4 below). Hence, if there were no change in the application start rate, there would never be a change in any backlog, capacities, or completion rates throughout the service chain.

At the beginning of each week (i.e., every 5 business days), each company can change its target capacity by deciding to hire or lay off employees. However, it takes time to advertise, interview, and hire employees, so the rate of capacity change is given in Equation 3.

$$C_{i,t+1} = C_{i,t} + \frac{1}{\tau}(C^*_{i,t} - C_{i,t}). \qquad (3)$$

The target capacity $C^*(i,t)$ set by the player is restricted to be nonnegative. For purposes of this game, τ, the capacity adjustment time, is set to 1 month, that is 20 business days (which is, in reality, a bit optimistic if large hiring rates are required). In essence, each stage's capacity will move one twentieth of the gap from its current value toward its target each day. Thus, the capacity adjustment occurs not in a lump on any particular day but rather stretches out over many days. For example, if the target capacity suddenly increases by a one-time fixed amount, 5% of the increase will arrive the next day; 5% of the remaining 95% gap will arrive on the second day, and so on in an exponentially decreasing manner. This translates into an average lag for hiring (or firing employees) of 20 business days. If for some reason, however, the player makes another capacity change before the original adjustment is complete, the old target will be thrown out, and the next day capacity will begin to adjust from its current value toward the new target.

If for some reason a player cannot be found for each stage, the target capacity decision will be made as follows:

$$C^*_{i,t} = \frac{B_{i,t}}{\lambda} \qquad \text{if } (t \text{ modulo } 5) = 0$$

$$C^*_{i,t} = C^*_{i,t-1} \qquad \text{otherwise}. \qquad (4)$$

Thus, each week the target capacity for each stage will be set directly proportional to the stage's current backlog $B(i,t)$ and inversely proportional to the nominal service delay time λ. This is not meant to be an optimal policy in any sense; however, it seems to reflect reasonably well how real players make decisions in capacity management games (Sterman 1989a). Thus, if the application start rate is unvarying, the long-run average application will take λ weeks to complete per stage. One can of course vary λ either by stage or over time to make the game more complex.

The goal of each team of four players (or each individual depending on the scenario) is to minimize the total cost for the entire supply chain resulting from employee salaries and service delays. Each employee will cost $2000 to hire or lay off and $1000 per week to

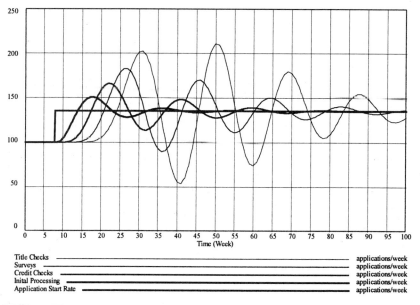

FIGURE 2. Applications Processing for All Stages Over Time (i.e., $r_{i,t}$).

employ (or $200 per application when fully utilized). Each backlogged application costs $200 per week in potential customer alienation.

Although the management of capacity at each stage in the mortgage service supply chain may be well understood (e.g., Equations 3 and 4), backlog (and other performance measures) may exhibit very complex behavior, because the stages do not function independently but are linked in a supply chain. Therefore, we devote the next section to describing the system behavior and the output generated by the simulation model in Figure 1.

3. System Behavior

To illustrate system behavior, let us examine the response of the initial applications processing rate to a step increase of 35% in application starts (Figure 2). More specifically, $r(0,t)$ remains at 20 starts per day until after 8 weeks, when it jumps to 27 starts per day. The number of starts per day then remains constant at 27 until the end of the game in week 100. Note that in this section, the capacity adjustment time τ is set to 4 weeks, and the target backlog delay λ is set to 2 weeks. Also, note that we are using here the nonoptimal—but often realistic—capacity adjustment heuristic described in Equation 4. We chose this scenario because it provides a good illustration of the complexities that arise even in this relatively simple supply chain.

Immediately after the increase in starts after 8 weeks, the processing backlog increases because processing capacity lags behind the increase in application starts (Figure 3). After a week's delay, the processing capacity will begin to adjust to the increase in the backlog. However, the backlog will still increase until week 13.

In week 13, the processing capacity, and hence the application processing rate, catches up with the application starts. However, the capacity must actually overshoot its final settling point at 135 applications per week (Figures 2 and 4) because, during the time that processing capacity lagged application starts, the backlog has increased by more than 65% (Figure 3). Thus, the capacity overshoot is necessary in order to reduce the backlog back to its new equilibrium value. In fact, the capacity will continue to increase as long as the backlog exceeds the target delay of two week's processing, which will continue until week 17. From this point on, the capacity begins to reduce, but it still exceeds the new start rate; hence, the

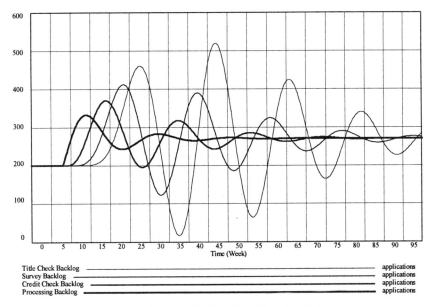

FIGURE 3. Stage Backlogs Over Time (i.e., $B_{i,t}$).

backlog will itself drop below its final equilibrium and keep dropping until week 23. At this time, the amount of capacity required to process the backlog in 2 weeks is less than the application start rate. Thus, despite the fact that the backlog is growing, the capacity will continue to drop until week 27, when the backlog once again exceeds its final equilibrium value. From this point, the application capacity and processing will increase to begin another, albeit less pronounced, cycle.

Because the credit check stage in this scenario has no access to end-user information, it only sees the output from the initial processing stage. As described, there is a lag between when end-user information increases and capacity arrives at the initial processing stage.

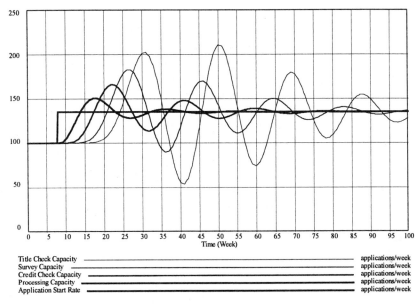

FIGURE 4. Stage Capacities Over Time (i.e., $C_{i,t}$).

Thus, the peak in backlogged applications from initial processing will arrive at credit check delayed even beyond the target backlog delay of 10 business days. This delay prevents timely reaction from the credit check player. Because of the bullwhip effect in initial applications processing, the applications will also arrive at credit checking with a peak quantity greater than that which arrived at initial processing (see the initial applications processing output week 17 in Figure 2). Thus, the bullwhip process described in the initial application stage will repeat itself with greater force at the credit check stage. Further, when the downturn in initial processing arrives in weeks 23 through 31, the credit check stage does not know that this is result of the first stage's overcapacitization. Hence, credit checking will mistakenly believe that end-user demand has dropped and adjust its capacity downward more vigorously than it might otherwise. Credit checking capacity reductions will continue even after the backlog begins to rebuild at initial processing beyond its new equilibrium (week 27). Since the output from initial processing has a greater maximum amplitude than the application start rate followed by a series of ever-dampening cycles, credit checking's behavior will continue to repeat, albeit with ever-lessening force.

The same basic repeating cycles of backlog, capacity, and processing will occur for the same reasons at the survey and title check stages, though the cycles are increasingly more lagged and forceful at each stage.

4. Teaching Strategies

The Mortgage Service Game is played under two main strategies: decentralized and new application starts information strategy. Sections 2 and 3 describe the game in terms of the decentralized strategy. Each stage operates autonomously and makes its capacity decisions based on its own backlog. In the new application starts information strategy, each stage makes capacity decisions based on its own backlog and the new applications rate. In other words, each stage gains more visibility by being able to observe end-user demand in each time period. For those stages at which the computer makes the target capacity decision, Equation 4 changes to:

$$C_{i,t}^* = \alpha r_{0,t} + (1 - \alpha) \frac{B_{i,t}}{\lambda} \quad \text{if } (t \text{ modulo } 5) = 0$$

$$C_{i,t}^* = C_{i,t-1}^* \quad \text{otherwise.} \quad (5)$$

where $0 \leq \alpha \leq 1$. The degree to which each stage in the chain bases its target capacity on the new application rate is determined by the magnitude of α. In this case, the same value for α is used for all stages that set target capacity using Equation 5. A more complicated version of the game could be designed to permit a different α for each stage.

4.1. Classroom Use

We conducted mortgage service simulation exercises in two courses. One course contained 17 masters' level students (MBA and Master of Science in Engineering) studying operations simulation modeling. These students were technically oriented and the Mortgage Service Game exercise was used to teach concepts in supply chain management and operations modeling in the service sector. The other course had 23 students, mostly MBAs, studying supply chain management. Although these students were less technically oriented, they were familiar with several supply chain concepts, including the beer game (both physical and computerized) and the bullwhip effect in the management of supply chain inventories.

4.1.1. SET-UP. Both classes played a stand-alone PC version of the Mortgage Service Game. In this version of the game, each team of students managed only the survey stage in the chain, leaving the computer to manage the remaining stages. Teams were assigned to an intermediate stage in the supply chain in order to illustrate the dynamics resulting from information and capacity adjustment lags. In order to mitigate the perception of the computer performing "black box" functions, we provided students with complete details about the operations of the game at all stages (i.e., Equations 1 through 5). In fact, the only information the students were not given was how and when the demand stream changed. For all of the exercises described below, we used the following demand stream: $r(0,t)$ remains at 20 starts per day until after 8 weeks, when it jumps to 27 starts per day. The number of starts per day then remains constant at 27 until the end of the game in week 50. Most teams consisted of two students. However, a few teams had three members, and in one case, we had a single-student team.

We used the Mortgage Service Game to demonstrate two main points. The first point was to illustrate the supply chain dynamics resulting from information and capacity adjustment lags. The second point was to illustrate the impact of end-user demand information. Therefore, during the class each team performed two exercises with the Game: one was to manage capacity and backlogs at the survey stage without new applications information and the other was to manage the stage with that information. The following instructions were given at the beginning of class: "We will play the game twice: once with no new applications information provided to the property survey stage and once with new applications information provided to the property survey stage. Some of the groups will start with new applications information in the first round. The remaining groups will start with no new applications information. New applications information availability is reversed in the second round. The target lead-time equals 2 weeks (or 10 days) and capacity adjustment time equals 4 weeks (or 20 days). For the computer-controlled stages, the weight (i.e., the α value) on the new application rate will be set equal to zero when no new applications information is provided and 0.5 when new applications information is provided. New applications will begin at 20 per day (or 100 per week) but then will change by an unspecified amount at an unspecified point in time. Hence, there is no use trying to anticipate the change and the timing of the change from the previous run. Each stage (including the survey of property stage) will begin with a backlog of 200, capacity of 20 per day (or 100 per week), and target capacity of 20 applications per day (or 100 per week), i.e., each stage (and hence the entire supply chain) will begin in equilibrium. Each game will be conducted for 50 rounds, where each round corresponds to 1 week." Hence the students were given complete information on what they were to do and what the computer would be doing with respect to each exercise. We chose these parameters for the classroom exercises based on simulation results similar to those found in Anderson and Morrice (1999). These results show that with the parameters used, rational decision making behavior will lead to improved performance with new applications information. Additionally, since we conducted both exercises in one 75-minute period, each exercise was limited to 50 weeks.

Prior to conducting the exercises, we gave a complete description of all information displayed on the graphical user interface of the iThink model in Figure 1b. "Target Leadtime" and "Capacity Adjustment Time" are displayed in the top left-hand corner of the screen. The players cannot change these parameters. Just below these parameters, one can select the station managed by the student team. This was set to "Station 3" for both exercises. "The Data for All Stages" allows the administrator of the game to change the demand stream. The players cannot change this setting after the game starts. If the "End User" data button is selected, then new applications rate data is displayed during the game. Again, the players cannot change this setting after the first round of the game is played. The "Target Capacity Input" lever allows the players to control the target capacity. "Weeks between Pauses" determines the duration of each round of the game. We set this to one, and it cannot be changed by the players. The "Reset" button resets the game, the "Run" button advances each round, and the "Stop" button stops the game. The "Summary Data" button opens a window that provides summary data at the end of each game. The "Simulation Time" dial displays the current time of the simulation. The graph and a table directly below the graph display the

TABLE 1

Paired T-Test for the Cumulative Cost Differences

	No New Applications Information	New Applications Information
Mean cumulative cost (in millions of dollars)	$6,885,197.88	$6,379,592.35
Standard deviation	$754,037.20	$571,651.90
Observations	17	17
Hypothesized mean difference	0	
Degrees of freedom	16	
t-Statistic	-2.76	
$P(T \leq t)$ one-tail (P value)	0.007	

New Applications rate (in the exercise in which new applications information is provided). Additionally, they provide Arrival Rate, Completion Rate, Capacity, and Backlog for the current stage being managed by the players (in both our exercises, the survey stage). The final table contains the costs results based on the cost structure described in Section 2.

4.1.2. ANALYSIS. We collected data from 7 teams in the operations simulation class and 10 teams in the supply chain management class. Since each team played the game twice, a total of 34 data records were generated. Each record contains data on the mean backlog, standard deviation of the backlog, and cumulative cost at each stage. The standard deviation of the backlog can be used to illustrate supply chain dynamics and a bullwhip effect. The cumulative costs can be used to demonstrate the impact of new applications information. The players recorded these data after each game from the "Summary Data" window. Therefore, they received direct feedback on supply chain dynamics and the impact of new applications information.

In what follows, we performed several statistical tests that rely on the data being normally distributed. In all cases, the hypothesis of normality was not rejected, on the basis of the Chi-square, Kolmogorov-Smirnov, and Anderson-Darling in BestFit software (Palisade 1996). We must point out that since these data sets are quite small, the power of the test for rejecting the null hypothesis of normality is small.

Since the exercises in both classes were run under the same experimental conditions (i.e., using the same lab and the same instructions), we decided to pool the results. Further support for pooling the data resulted from statistical tests on the difference between cumulative costs for the last two stages with and without new applications information (from now on these data will be referred to as the cumulative cost differences). We consider these data the best indicators of performance because the teams managed the survey stage and therefore only impacted the performance of the last two stages in the supply chain. Neither an F-test on the equality of variances, nor a two-sample t-test on the equality of means on these data detected significant differences at the 5% level.

On the pooled data we conducted a paired t-test on these data to determine whether or not the players' performances were significantly better when new applications information was available. Table 1 contains highly significant results: the paired t-test shows that, on average, players had a significantly lower mean cumulative cost when new applications information was available.

Another way to assess the players' performance with and without information is to compare the difference between the mean cumulative costs in Table 1 with the difference between cumulative costs that could be obtained using an optimal strategy. The optimal strategy uses Equation 5 with an optimally selected value for α to manage survey stage target capacity (and $\alpha = 0.5$ for all other stages) when new information is available and Equation 4 to manage target capacity at all stages without information. It is important to note that this comparison is not perfect, since the players were not limited to selecting α but could set the actual target capacity. However, many players indicated that they were following a policy closely related to Equations 5 and 4 with and without information, respectively (please see the discussion of player strategies below). To select α optimally for the survey stage, we constructed a nonlinear program to minimize total cumulative cost over all stages. A grid search and the GRG2 solver in Microsoft Excel was used to select the α optimally for the survey stage. The cumulative cost difference using the aforementioned strategies with and without information is roughly $900,251. Given the difference between the mean cumulative costs in Table 1 of roughly $505,606, it is evident that, on average, the players performed quite well relative to this optimal strategy.

In order to understand how the students managed the survey stage with and without new applications information, we asked them to record their management strategies under both scenarios. Without new applications information, some teams used the local arrival rate to set target capacity, some teams used local backlog, and others used a combination of the two. With new applications information, several teams used a combination of either new applications rate and local arrival rate or new applications rate and local backlog. For these teams, the weight on the new applications information varied from 0.5 to 1. Anderson and Morrice (1999) show that using Equations 5 to manage target capacity at all stages with an α in the range of 0.5 to 1 for the scenarios used in this paper will result in lower cumulative costs than using an α value of zero. This would explain some of the performance improvement noted in Table 1.

Two other strategies mentioned by several teams were used under both scenarios often in conjunction with the above strategies. These two strategies are illustrated by the target survey capacity decisions of a "typical" team that are shown in Figure 5a. First, it was common for teams to reduce backlog and hold excess capacity in order to, as one team put it "handle any waves of arrival." Interestingly, however, the team presented in Figure 5a primarily did this when they had end-user demand information. Without it, they resorted much more strictly to what they termed a "reactive" strategy, hedging only slightly beginning in week 11. Additionally, a number of teams resorted to changing target capacity periodically, if necessary, but not too often. This was done in order to reduce hiring and firing activity. For example, the team presented in Figure 5a stated that they tried to change their target capacity at most every 5 weeks. Both of these strategies are to be expected because they are common in practice. Backlog is considered negative as is adjusting work force levels too frequently. Anderson and Fine (1998) point out that when lags in the hiring and firing process exist, adjusting work force levels less frequently is a rational management approach.

Interestingly, the end-result of all these player strategies was often to create capacity and backlog behaviors similar to those created by the heuristic presented in Section 3. As shown in Figure 5b, the simulated heuristic has behavior qualitatively similar to the typical team's, in that both of their capacity behaviors are basically sinusoidal, with a period of 20 weeks. However, the team appears to have begun to hedge a bit in week 11, which the heuristic cannot do. This initial hedging gives the team more time than the heuristic before the survey backlog begins to rise (Figure 5c). Thus, the team can react more smoothly to the changes in incoming applications over the remainder of the simulation. The team's backlog variation is also accordingly somewhat less through week 30. At this point, however, the typical team appears to reduce its target backlog goal from its initial position at 200 applications, thus making comparison with the heuristic problematic. In summary, the heuristic does seem to capture much, though not all, of the typical team's behavior, at least for the case without end-user information.

At a more macro level of analysis, Figure 6, a and b, contain plots of standard deviation of backlog at all stages for the 17 teams with and without new applications information, respectively. The x-axis for each plot lists the four stages in the supply chain denoted by S1 (initial processing) through S4 (title checking). Each plot contains a line graph for each team

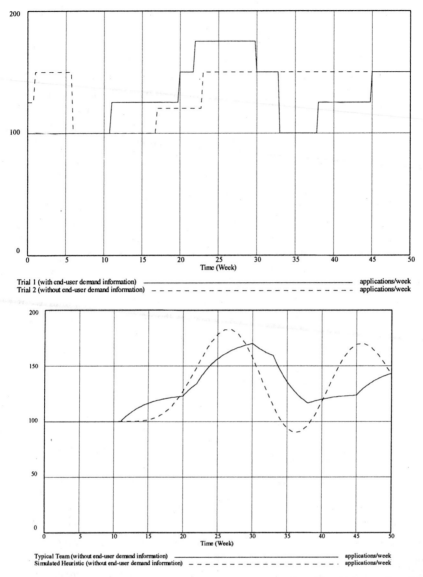

FIGURE 5. (a) Target Survey Capacity over Time for a Typical Team (i.e., $C^*_{3,t}$). (b) Survey Capacities for the Typical Team versus the Simulated Heuristic (i.e., $C^*_{3,t}$). (c) Survey Backlogs for the Typical Team versus the Simulated Heuristic (i.e., $B^*_{3,t}$).

that shows their standard deviation of backlog across all stages. Table 2 contains the average (over the 17 teams) mean and standard deviation of the backlog for the survey and title checking stages with and without new applications information.

A couple of observations can be made from these data. First, the bullwhip effect is evident from the increasing average standard deviation of the backlog as one moves down the supply chain under both scenarios. Note that the average standard deviation of the backlog drops at the title stage because, in general, players manage the survey stage with excess capacity or with lower than average backlog (compare average mean backlog at the surveying stage with this statistic at other stages in Table 2). This result is consistent with the strategy that several teams stated they were using. Second, we observe that the bullwhip effect is somewhat mitigated by having new applications information (compare the average standard deviation of the backlogs for both scenarios in Table 2). Note that due to the size of the data set, we

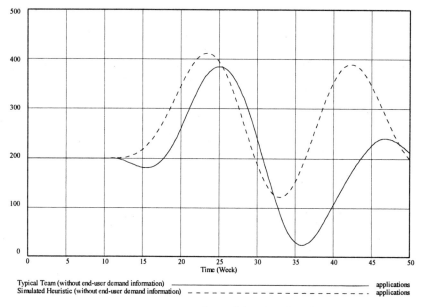

FIGURE 5 (*continued*).

were not able to establish statistical significance on our observations about the data in Table 2 and Figure 6, a and b. Our comments are based on trends observed in these data.

We designed the lab sessions to account for a learning effect by having half the teams (8 of the 17) start with new applications information first. We strongly suggest that the game be conducted in this manner because the data appear to contain a learning effect. We will refer to the data set containing cumulative cost differences of the teams who played the new applications information game first as DS1; the data set containing the cumulative cost differences of the remaining teams will be called DS2. DS1 contains all four teams with positive cumulative cost differences, i.e., DS1 contains all the teams that performed worse with new applications information. An F-test did not detect a significant difference between the variances of DS1 and DS2. However, a two-sample t-test did detect a significant difference between the means of these two data sets at the 5% level (the p value was 0.011).

It is possible that the above learning effect is due, at least in part, to an *anticipation effect*. In both games, the players faced the same demand. Hence, after the first game, the players could just anticipate the same demand pattern for the second game. We argue that this did not happen in our game for two reasons. First, we explicitly told the students not to anticipate the demand change and its timing from the previous run, since these amounts were randomly selected on each run (see Section 4.1.1). Second, an anticipation effect was not apparent in the data. To test this, we compared the results for the without information games played first with results from the without information games played second and found no significant difference. If an anticipation effect were present one would expect to observe better second round results, since players have already seen the demand stream from the first round in the game with information.

Incidentally, the learning effect mentioned above was completely due to the difference in the results for the games with information (i.e., results for the games with information played in the second round were significantly better than results for the games with information played in the first round). These results are less likely due the anticipation effect, since a second round game with information is proceeded by a first round game without information that does not explicitly provide the new applications information. We argue that the results are more likely to be due to a learning effect because managing with more information choices requires experience.

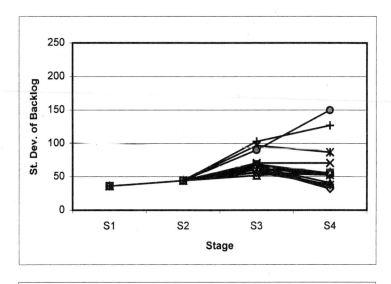

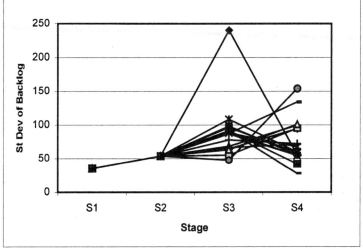

FIGURE 6. (a) Standard Deviation of Backlog with New Applications Information. (b) Standard Deviation of Backlog Without New Applications Information.

Further analysis and control of both learning and anticipation effects can be performed using more comprehensive experimental designs (generally requiring larger data sets) than we have considered in this analysis. This will be part of our future research.

TABLE 2

Average Mean and Standard Deviation of Backlog for All Stages

Statistic	No New Applications Information	New Applications Information
Average mean backlog at applications processing	262.1	265.1
Average mean backlog at credit checking	258.4	258.7
Average mean backlog at surveying	149.1	97.4
Average mean backlog at title checking	261.0	266.2
Average st. dev. backlog at applications processing	35.3	36.1
Average st. dev. backlog at credit checking	53.9	44.1
Average st. dev. backlog at surveying	89.4	67.9
Average st. dev. backlog at title checking	76.2	61.6

4.1.3. FEEDBACK. We suggest that a feedback session be conducted after the Mortgage Service Game exercises. We found that providing results similar to those given in Section 4.1.2 is of great pedagogical value. Game participants learn from their own results as well of the results of others. Additionally, they get the opportunity to observe trends in the data, which is especially important for those who had worse performance with new applications information.

4.1.4. OTHER EXERCISES. If time permits (or there are a large number of participants who can be subdivided into smaller groups), other exercises can be conducted with the current version of the Mortgage Service Game. In particular, one can look at different capacity adjustment times (i.e., different values for τ) and different values for average nominal delay (i.e., different values for λ).

5. Discussion and Conclusions

In this paper, we have introduced a simulation game to teach service-oriented supply chain management principles. The Mortgage Service Game provides a realistic application with results that can be generalized. We envision using this game instead of the Beer Game with participants who have supply chains without finished goods inventory. However, it could be used to complement the Beer Game in a supply chain management course that covers both finished goods inventory management and service management. Furthermore, the Mortgage Service Game can be used to illustrate supply chain management principles in a make-to-order environment.

As future research and development, we plan to embellish this game in a number of ways. First, we plan to develop a web-based version of the game. As we have demonstrated, the PC version of the game can be an effective tool for teaching management strategies in a service supply chain. However, the PC version limits the game to one team playing with the computer. An initial web version of the game would be the same as the PC version except that the former would permit up to four teams to play with each other in the same game. The computer using Equation 4 (or Equation 5) to set target capacity would only play stages not covered by a team. Subsequent versions of the PC and web-based games will be extended to include a global information strategy in which all backlog and capacity information is shared across all stages, a collaborative strategy in which global information is available and capacity can be shared across all stages, and a centralized management strategy in which global information is available and a single team manages capacity for all stages. Ultimately, the web-based version will permit us to develop a virtual environment for constructing supply chain exercises that will closely mimic reality.

We also plan to embellish the demand stream (i.e., the new application starts) so that it can be both nonstationary and random. Adding randomness would enhance playing multiple rounds because the demand stream would not be exactly the same each time the game is restarted. However, we must point out that randomness in demand can and should be carefully controlled in such games since noisy demand could mask variance propagation by the system. One major advantage of a simulation environment is the ability to select common random number streams for the demand so that all participants would face exactly the same noisy demand conditions.

Finally, this paper provides an introduction to players' behavior during the Mortgage Service Game. We plan to conduct further experiments and a statistical analysis similar to Sterman (1989a, 1989b). These efforts should provide significant pedagogical insights beyond those reported in this paper.[1]

---

[1] Professor Vishwanathan Krishnan of the Management Department at the University of Texas at Austin also contributed to the development of the Supply Chain Management course for the Executive Education Program. We also acknowledge the contributions of Dr. David Pyke and of two anonymous referees, whose suggestions improved this paper immeasurably.

References

ANDERSON, E.G. AND C. H. FINE (1998), "Business Cycles and Productivity in Capital Equipment Supply Chains" in *Quantitative Models for Supply Chain Management,* S. Tayur, M. Magazine, and R. Ganeshan (eds.), Kluwer Press, Boston, 381-415.

—— AND D. J. MORRICE (1999), "A Simulation Model to Study the Dynamics in a Service-Oriented Supply Chain," in Proceedings of the 1999 Winter Simulation Conference, to appear.

COPACINO, W. C. (1997), *Supply Chain Management: The Basics and Beyond,* St Lucie Press, Boca Raton, Florida/APICS, Falls Church, Virginia.

FORRESTER, J. W. (1958), "Industrial Dynamics: A Major Breakthrough for Decision Makers," *Harvard Business Review*, 36, 4, 37-66.

GATTORNA, J. (1998), *Strategic Supply Chain Alignment: Best Practice in Supply Chain Management,* Gower Publishing Limited, Hampshire England.

HANFIELD, R. B. AND E. L. NICHOLS (1998), *Introduction to Supply Chain Management,* Prentice-Hall, Englewood Cliffs, NJ.

LEE, H.L., V. PADMANABHAN, AND S. WHANG (1997a), "Information Distortion in a Supply Chain: The Bullwhip Effect," *Management Science,* 43, 4, 516-558.

——, ——, AND —— (1997b), "The Bullwhip Effect In Supply Chains," *Sloan Management Review*, 38,3, 93-102.

RICHMOND, B. AND S. PETERSON (1996), Introduction to Systems Thinking, High Performance Systems, Inc., Hanover, NH.

ROSS, D. F (1998), *Competing Through Supply Chain Management: Creating Market-Winning Strategies Through Supply Chain Partnerships,* Chapman & Hall, New York.

SENGE, P. M. (1990), *The Fifth Discipline,* Doubleday, New York.

SIMCHI-LEVI, D., P. KAMINSKY, AND E. SIMCHI-LEVI (1999), *Designing and Managing the Supply Chain: Concepts, Strategies, and Case Studies,* Irwin/McGraw-Hill, Burr Ridge, IL.

STERMAN, JOHN D. (1989a), "Misperceptions of Feedback in Dynamic Decision Making," *Organizational Behavior and Human Decision Processes,*, 43, 3, 301-335.

—— (1989b), "Modeling Managerial Behavior: Misperceptions of Feedback in a Dynamic Decision Making Experiment," *Management Science*, 35, 3, 321-339.

VENTANA SYSTEMS, INC. (1998), Vensim Version 3.0., 60 Jacob Gates Road, Harvard, MA 01451.

WHEELWRIGHT, S. C. (1992), "Manzana Insurance—Fruitvale Branch (Abridged)," Harvard Business School Case Study 9-692-015, Harvard Business School Publishing, Boston, MA.

Edward Anderson is an Assistant Professor of Operations Management in the Management Department at the University of Texas at Austin. Professor Anderson's research and teaching interests include system dynamics in operations management, operational models of core competencies and knowledge management in supply chains, technology and innovation models of manufacturing firms, computer simulation, dynamic programming, and optimal control. Professor Anderson received his B.A.S. majoring in Electrical Engineering and History from Stanford University. He received his Ph.D. in Operations Management from the Massachusetts Institute of Technology. Previously, he was an engineer at the Ford Motor Company Electronics Division where his work led to three patents. Professor Anderson currently researches with Ford Motor Company and Hewlett-Packard on strategic supply chain design and operations strategy.

Douglas Morrice is an Associate Professor in the Management Science and Information Systems Department at the University of Texas at Austin. He received a Bachelor's degree in Operations Research from Carleton University in Ottawa, Canada. He holds an M.S. and a Ph.D. in Operations Research and Industrial Engineering from Cornell University. Professor Morrice has extensive consulting, teaching, and research experience in the areas of Management Science and Supply Chain Management. Dr. Morrice has worked with Schlumberger analyzing and improving their operations and logistics using optimization and simulation techniques. Additionally, he has taught executive education courses to consultants at Price Waterhouse Coopers in the area of Supply Chain Management. His current research interests focus on optimization and risk management in the supply chain. At the University of Texas at Austin, Professor Morrice teaches Supply Chain Management, Management Science, and Operations Simulation.

THE INTEGRATION ASPECT OF SUPPLY CHAIN MANAGEMENT: A FRAMEWORK AND A SIMULATION*

RAM GANESHAN, TONYA BOONE, AND ALAN J. STENGER

QAOM Department, The University of Cincinnati, Cincinnati, Ohio 45221-0130, USA
The Fisher College of Business, The Ohio State University,
Columbus, Ohio 43210-1399, USA
The Smeal College of Business Administration, Penn State University,
University Park, Pennsylvania 16802, USA

The concept of supply chain management seems to be an essential element in many of today's operations and logistics management programs. Yet, there is still a lack of integrative frameworks and teaching tools that specifically tie together different supply chain concepts. This paper has two specific objectives. First, we describe an intuitive hierarchical framework that instructors can use as a convenient "road map" to classify and categorize supply chain concepts. Second, and also the focal point of this paper, we describe in detail a tool, the Supply Chain Simulator (SCS), which helps the student appreciate the scope of decisions that need to be made and their impact on managing today's complex supply chains. The supply chain simulator is based on the hierarchical approach, and has been successfully used to teach supply chain management to students at the undergraduate, MBA, and executive levels.

(SUPPLY CHAINS, PEDAGOGICAL SIMULATION)

1. Introduction

Since the term "supply chain management" (SCM) was coined by Houlihan in 1985 (Houlihan 1985), it seems to have taken a life of its own. Those of us who research and teach SCM agree that the concept refers to a set of networked organizations that work together to source, produce, and ultimately distribute products and services to the customer. However, the nature of cooperation between firms has been widely discussed, from a variety of angles, by different members in the supply chain under different names. "Efficient Consumer Response," "Quick Response," "Integrated Logistics," "Channel Management," "Just-In-Time Retailing," and "Value Chain Management" seem to be some of the popular terms that attempt to describe the concept of integrating some or all of the constituent links in the supply chain. Bowersox, Closs, and Helferich (1988) put forward the concept of SCM that is perhaps most relevant to our discussion:

> . . . a single logic to guide the process of planning, allocating, and controlling the financial and human resources committed to physical distribution, manufacturing support, and purchasing operations.

---

* Received November 1998; revision received August 1999; accepted September 1999.

We will interpret this to mean greater coordination of activities—both planning and control functions—across the entire chain, and just between a few of the chain members. Additionally, we view supply chain management as a compromise between full vertical integration in the channel, where the material, information, and cash flows are entirely owned by a single firm; and total independence of the several firms operating in series in a channel. The central premise in SCM is that strategic and tactical coordination between the various players in the chain is the key to providing effective customer service, and often leads to substantial improvements in logistical performance and shareholder wealth.

The increased importance of SCM/logistics has led *US News and World Report* (October 27, 1997, p. 104) and *Working Woman* (February 1999, pp. 42–51) magazines to cite it as the hottest career track for business majors. Jobs such as "Customer Supply Chain Manager," "Logistics Engineer," "Vendor Managed Inventory Coordinator," "Business Process Consultant," etc. require the interested student to be trained explicitly in concepts that integrate the various firms, functions, and technologies in the supply chain [see, for example, the career guide of the Council of Logistics Management (CLM)]. Although several schools have well-developed integrative courses, there is still a lack of integrative frameworks and tools that specially tie together different supply chain concepts. There are several textbooks available today, specifically at the undergraduate level of instruction, that have many of the essential elements, but are weak in explaining some of the links in the supply chain, or do not show how the various elements in the chain are linked together. Still several other schools have successfully implemented "tool-based" courses in SCM. These train the students on a variety of aspects in SCM, but sometimes fail on the integration aspect.

This paper has two specific objectives. First, we describe an intuitive, hierarchical approach that in our experience is well suited to teach both the strategic and operational issues in supply chain management. The hierarchical approach is comprehensive yet loosely structured, making it easy for the interested instructor to easily adapt it to suit his or her needs. Second, and also the focal point of this paper, we describe in detail a tool, the *Supply Chain Simulator* (SCS), which helps the student appreciate the scope of decisions that need to be made and their impact on managing today's complex supply chains. The supply chain simulator is based on the hierarchical approach and has been used successfully to teach supply chain management to students at the undergraduate, MBA, and executive levels.

The remainder of the paper is organized as follows. The second section gives an overview of the hierarchical approach around which we structure our SCM course and the SCS. The third section describes the general nature of our course and gives a brief narrative of the environment in which we run the SCS. The fourth section describes the logic behind the simulator and how we implement it in our classes. The fifth section presents some thoughts we have about extending the usefulness of the simulator. We conclude with a summary of the paper.

2. A Hierarchical Approach to Achieving Supply Chain Integration

Clearly the idea of supply chain management is to view the chain as a total system, and to fine-tune the decisions about how to operate the various components (firms, functions, technologies, and activities) in ways that produce the most desirable overall system performance in the long run. Doing so is extremely difficult because of the number and complexity of the decisions to be made, as well as the inter- and intraorganizational issues that must be addressed.

After working with many companies dealing with these issues over the years, we believe that a four-step hierarchical approach is best suited to teach the seemingly endless set of decisions and initiatives that apparently seem to be classified under the umbrella of supply chain management. Our intent here is not to provide a rigid framework but more to illustrate a loose and flexible "road map" that instructors can use to classify and categorize supply

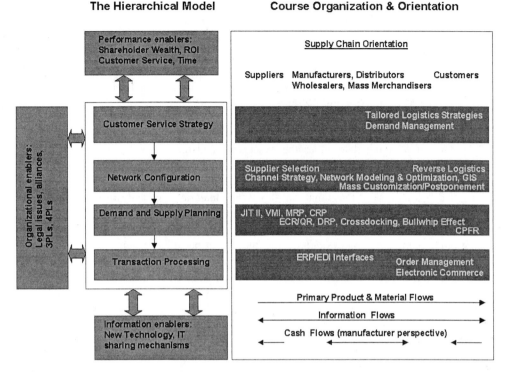

FIGURE 1. Sample Course Design.

chain concepts. The simulation tool we describe later in the paper is also based on the following hierarchical model.

The origins of the hierarchical approach go back to Anthony (1965) and Hax and Meal (1975). The fundamental idea behind the approach is to first do high-level, or strategic, planning on an aggregate basis, and then develop lower-level (and more detailed) plans within the constraints laid out by the higher-level planning (Stenger 1987).

Figure 1 summarizes the hierarchical model. Additionally, it also shows how the model is related to the general organization of our supply chain management course.

Step 1: Customer Service Strategy

It is our premise here that the firm has already gone through the process of establishing a corporate-wide business strategy, i.e., has well-determined lines of business, core competencies, growth objectives, and stakeholder commitments. From a supply chain strategy perspective, the execution of the business strategy will involve understanding and setting customer service requirements of each product-market segment, identifying opportunities for differentiation (Shapiro 1984), and deciding on strategic responses to customer requirements to maximize revenue with the most efficient use of capital resources. Students appreciate that with a well-defined supply chain strategy, it is possible to substantially improve the seemingly conflicting goals of shareholder wealth and customer service.

Step 2: Network Configuration

This step primarily involves the determination of the supply chain network, i.e., choosing the channels of supply and distribution (Fisher 1997), and defining the best supply chain network options and associated costs of offering varying levels of service. This includes choosing the optimal number, location, role, associated linkages, and aggregate plans of each channel partner. Once the supply chain network is defined and put into place, it very much determines the levels of service it can provide to customers.

When we teach network configuration, we identify the different product, information, cash, and process flows in the supply chain, and analyze how we can position resources to optimize these flows. For example, if the customer service strategy is growth oriented with a premium on mass-customization, the product flows can be altered by several means—such as postponement or process reversal—to optimize for this strategy.

Step 3: Demand and Supply Planning

This stage of planning determines the exact flow and timing of materials such as raw material release to manufacturing facilities, or finished goods to the distribution centers or customer markets. The network configuration phase has already determined the locations, origins, and destinations of these material flows. The material flow and timing decisions are typically arrived at by using time-phased, or requirements planning, techniques, working from the forecasted demand back through the supply chain to the raw material sources. Additionally, examples abound (and we use them as a backdrop when teaching) of firms using specialized demand and supply planning procedures: Collaborative Planning, Forecasting, and Replenishment (CPFR), Efficient Consumer Response (ECR), and Quick Response (QR) on the outbound side; and Vendor Managed Inventory (VMI), Continuous Replenishment (CRP), and JIT II on the inbound side.

Step 4: Transaction Processing and Short Term Scheduling

Customer orders arrive at random, and they are assigned to a predetermined (by supply chain configuration methods) location and carrier. The flow of this order (timing and quantity) through the supply chain is already determined by the demand and supply planning process. Transaction processing is therefore more like a day-to-day accounting system, tracking and scheduling every order to meet customer demand. Sample transactions include order entry at the retail markets, physical replenishment and order fulfillment of the goods at the distribution centers, and material releases and purchase orders at the manufacturing facility.

As Figure 1 indicates, supply chain integration is facilitated by three key factors. First, the emergence of new technology and the ability to share information between channel partners has greatly enhanced existing operational efficiency of participating firms. For example, the emergence of the Internet has spawned a genre of direct-to-customer distribution channels. Additionally, initiatives such as CPFR, made possible by recent advances in Web-based communication, make even the traditional channels of distribution extremely efficient, resulting from the improved ability to share accurate information between channel partners in "real time."

Second, in the face of globalization and technological change, firms are increasingly experimenting with different organizational options. Examples abound of "strategic alliances" (like GE Appliances and Ryder Logistics) that match up core competencies; or innovative outsourcing arrangements such as Andersen Consulting's Fourth Party Logistics (4PL) concept. In many cases, an overabundance of core-competencies or the emergence of a new distribution channel have led to spin-offs that allow the establishment of smaller and more manageable supply chains (see Giles and Hancy 1998).

Third, firms are increasingly realizing that partnering with channel members—either at a strategic level, like setting up dedicated alliances or at an operational level such as information sharing—improves cash flows and consequently shareholder value. Benetton (quick response), Wal-Mart (everyday low prices), and Hewlett-Packard (product postponement) are outstanding examples of companies who have increased shareholder wealth by effective supply chain management. For example, in the PC industry, the postponement of assembly to the distributor from the manufacturer increased the Economic Value Added (EVA) from 0.4 to 1.6% of sales for the distributor (Evans and Danks 1998)!

In our experience, a good number of firms, either explicitly or implicitly, have been evolving toward the hierarchical approach over the years. Examples include Alcan Aluminium, Citgo Petroleum, Dow Chemical, Millennium, and Digital Equipment Corporation. Some of the firms, DEC for example, do not necessarily follow a strict hierarchy; rather they attempt to solve all or at least a majority of the levels simultaneously. Furthermore, several of the supply chain software vendors provide a suite of software options, each addressing a level or a group of levels in the hierarchy. For example, CAPS Logistics has the Supply Chain Designer that addresses the first two levels of the hierarchy and the RoutePro, which is primarily a short-term scheduling utility (references to the software taken from CAPS Logistics' marketing literature).

3. Course Design and Simulation Narrative

The use of hierarchical models to teach operations classes is not new (see the framework in Vollman, Berry, and Whybark 1992). Our perspective on the hierarchical approach is broader in the sense that it explicitly considers supply chain strategy, customer, and shareholder issues. Additionally, we cut across firm boundaries to include all the relevant firms, activities, organizations, and technologies that make up the supply chain. We know at least five business schools that explicitly use or plan to use the hierarchical model we have presented—Penn State, Ohio State, University of Tennessee, College of William and Mary, and the University of Cincinnati—all of whom traditionally have had strong logistics and supply chain programs at the undergraduate, MBA, and executive levels of education.

At the MBA level, the course is taught as a case-oriented one, supplemented with readings (typically from business magazines and trade journals), in-class exercises, and minilectures that relate to specific topics shown in Figure 1 (details are available from the authors). The Appendix shows a sample MAB course schedule developed around the hierarchical model. A similar outline is used for our undergraduate classes, except that the readings are replaced by chapters from popular logistics textbooks (e.g., Ballou 1999). We use the hierarchical approach in our executive programs, but because of time constraints, not in the detail described in Figure 1. Rather, we typically limit ourselves to any one level of the hierarchy or a specific topic (say Electronic Commerce) in supply chain management. At all levels of instruction, however, we make a deliberate effort to show how each topic cuts across firm boundaries and, in many cases, across different levels of the hierarchy.

In our experience, the hierarchical approach gives students an integrative framework around which they can build their understanding of SCM. The primary purpose of the hierarchical approach, as we see it, clarifies how the various elements and concepts in supply chain management are linked to each other.

In addition to an integrative framework, however, the student also needs hands-on experience where he/she can actually experience realistic situations in which such a framework is used. To meet that objective we have authored a comprehensive tool, the Supply Chain Simulator (SCS), programmed in Visual Basic (a programming system for the Windows platform), that uses the hierarchical approach in simulating the operation of a supply chain under a number of alternate environments.

Our specific goals in developing and using the SCS were:

1. To provide the student a tool to analyze supply chains that is comprehensive (i.e., that includes most of the relevant costs and constraints), and that captures the essential elements of product, information, and cash flows in the supply chain.

2. To provide a set of supply chain metrics—including those of cost, customer service, time, and shareholder wealth generation—that the student can use to evaluate alternative supply chain configurations.

The SCS simulates the long-term operations of a supply chain under a number of environments and configurations. As the ensuing discussion shows, the simulator allows the student to alter:

(1) strategic elements of the supply chain network, i.e., the constituent customer markets, distribution centers, plants, supplier locations, and transport modes; (2) tactical elements such as forecasting options, demand and supply planning options; and (3) the more operational elements such as the safety stocks and planning horizons at every constituent facility. Based on student decisions, the SCS generates a detailed report, giving performance at each facility and, more importantly, key supply chain metrics that the student will use to evaluate the efficacy of the chosen supply chain plan.

We use an unpublished case "MAS Manufacturing" (for details see Ganeshan and Stenger 1999) as a companion to the SCS. The case is a result of a long-term project that one of the authors of this article was involved with. The case is about the design and operation of a supply chain for a firm, called "MAS" for the purposes of this discussion.

The case describes a company operating in a typical supply chain for fast-moving consumer goods. The simulation focuses on the individual firm within a supply chain context, because the unit of analysis will continue to be the firm for most students once they are in the workplace. If the individual firm cannot make itself viable within the supply chain, then it puts itself in danger of going out of business. In the simulation, the firm in question can alter its relationships with its customers and suppliers, as well as its internal operations, so that both it and the supply chain can improve their joint performance.

We give a brief narrative of the case so the reader can appreciate the scope and the depth of the decisions the SCS helps students make.

Abridged Simulation Scenario Narrative

MAS produces a line of household cleaners, chemicals, and associated accessories in Denver, Colorado. These products are currently sold in the West and Midwest, but not on the East Coast. Founded in the early 1950s, the company has had its ups and downs as it has struggled toward stable, profitable growth. The president and CEO recently asked her top managers to consider the best way for the company to "bring our growth under control so we can increase profits and return on investment." We provide the students with Figure 2, which shows the background conversations in the case.

PRODUCTS AND MARKETS. The MAS line of household cleaners and chemicals is sold primarily at the retail level through grocery and discount channels. We provide the student with the current supply chain for MAS (see Figure 3). The company has no direct sales force, but rather uses food brokers to sell to customers on a commission basis. Ten district sales managers are located around the market, each supervising several brokers. Although the company promotes sales in a variety of ways, its primary promotional expenditures are devoted to television, with spot ads on afternoon soap operas and late night news programs.

We also provide the students with the price of the product (which is constant across markets), FOB terms, and the annual demand and associated seasonalities in each of these markets.

THE DISTRIBUTION SYSTEM. Because of the large number of Less than Truckload (LTL) shipments to customers and the long distances to be covered, MAS has several distribution centers (DCs), which are located in Los Angeles, CA; Denver, CO; Dallas, TX; Chicago, IL; and Detroit, MI.

The distribution centers are resupplied primarily by rail to reduce transportation costs. The students are given the option of choosing between rail Boxcar loads or Trailer on Flat Car (TOFC, also known as "Piggy-back"), each with different costs of shipping. The students are also given the option of shipping by truck at LTL or the Truckload (TL) levels. In addition to the operating economies of the DCs (investment, and fixed and variable costs for several levels of throughput), the transportation rates and lead-time statistics for each of the transport modes are provided to the student. These obviously differ for each origin and destination pair (lane).

The inventories at the distribution centers are controlled in the "base case" by means of reorder points. Whenever an item's inventory level at a DC reaches its reorder point, a

Exhibit 2: Background Conversations in the Case

Helen Clark (CEO): You've all had a few days to think about my challenge–and it's something you should have been wrestling with anyway–so what have you come up with?

Dick Strickland (V.P. Production): There is no question that we can produce more than we are selling. Projections for sales next year are 18.5 million pounds of product, and I could squeeze almost 27 million pounds out of the plant if we needed it. I think we should start selling in the East. The incremental production cost would only be around $.43 per pound. And we can sell it for two dollars a pound.

Beth Rankin (Director of Distribution): That may be true, but the freight costs are going to eat us up. I think we should stay in our market territory and use the excess production capacity in Denver for meeting peak period demands. That would reduce inventories substantially compared to what we have now with all your production smoothing–and we all know what it costs to carry inventory these days. We're manufacturing a lot of product before we need it.

Linda Cole (V.P. Marketing): I'm all for expanding sales, Dick, you know that. But I think we're going to have to have an East Coast plant if we expect to penetrate that territory. Not only will that cut Beth's freight and reduce inventories; it will also give our customers a second source, reducing the likelihood that something will disrupt their supplies. Anyway, that market is bigger than our Denver plant alone can handle.

Strickland: Yes, but you're talking about a lot of money for an entirely new plant, and we would still be stuck with excess capacity in Denver. Maybe we should try to penetrate only part of that market.

Stan Penzotti (Director of Purchasing): I know a new plant in the East would be expensive, Dick, but it would sure make our raw material sourcing a lot easier and cheaper. We would be near many of those water-supplied terminals. It would probably reduce our raw material costs by 5 to 10 percent. And we could design out some of those bottlenecks we have in the current plant.

Clark: Those are some interesting ideas, but I'm not so sure we are currently operating as efficiently as we should. What about the way we are currently servicing our customers? Is that holding back sales? Or how about those inventories? Do we really need a plant warehouse in addition to the distribution centers? Maybe we should expand; but before we go any farther, I think we need a serious study of the alternatives.

FIGURE 2. Background Conversations in the Case.

resupply is requested from the factory warehouse located in Denver, CO. The factory warehouse, meanwhile, forecasts DC requirements in the future. However, students are given an option to invest in a collaborative forecasting and planning (CFPR) system. This system

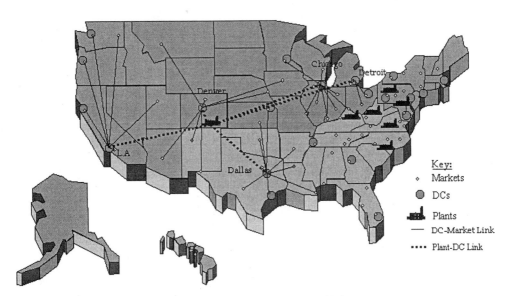

FIGURE 3. The Current MAS Supply Chain.

allows cooperation with customers to improve forecasts and replenishments through greater downstream visibility of demand and inventory positions. Furthermore, the approach uses distribution requirements planning (DRP) techniques to do the time-phased plan. The forecast errors, both at the DCs and the factory warehouse (when students do not choose to use the CPFR system), are used in computing safety stocks and reorder points. We provide the student with historical data on forecasting accuracy.

PRODUCTION. MAS currently uses one plant located in Denver to satisfy all its distribution needs. The capacity at the Denver location is close to 27 million pounds of product per year. This assumes 7 days a week, 24 hours a day operation (21 eight-hour "turns" per week). In general, the plant can turn out 25,000 pounds of product in an 8-hour work turn, allowing for standard preventive maintenance procedures. Adding afternoon, midnight, and weekend turns increases many of fixed and variable costs of production. This is the result of wage premiums required for extra shifts and weekends, as well as the increased wear on the equipment. We provide the student with operating economies—fixed and variable costs at various capacities—to run the plant.

It is also possible to purchase some adjoining land and expand production operations in Denver. The expansion would involve not only new facilities but also some revamping of the old facilities. The overall result would be to reduce variable costs. The students are provided with detailed expansion economies also.

After a good deal of study, six sites have been selected as potential locations for a new plant in the East. These are: Covington, KY; Parkersburg, WV; New Kensington, PA; Allentown, PA; Richmond, VA; and Raleigh, NC. Any new plant will use a new technology, so that even though Eastern labor costs may be higher than those in Denver, less manpower will be used. The operating economies (investment, fixed, and variable costs for varying levels of production) are also available to the student.

Also located at the Denver plant is a warehouse for holding raw materials and finished goods. The finished goods stored there consist of stocks used for replenishing the distribution centers, and stocks resulting from production smoothing. There is a possibility to eliminate the Denver plant warehouse to save on investment and operating costs. In this case, product would be allocated to the distribution centers as it comes off the production line. It is undecided at this time whether to include a plant warehouse in any new Eastern plant. The costs of operating the Denver plant warehouse (and the associated sunk investment allocated to it) are also available as are the ones at the six new locations.

PURCHASING AND SUPPLY. The case also allows the students to plan the procurement of three raw materials, Cans/Bottles, Chemicals, and Corrugated. We give the students the locations of the suppliers; they are typically located on the Gulf Coast, but they also operate water-supplied terminals on the East Coast and in major cities along the Mississippi and Ohio Rivers.

The prices, FOB terms, and the cost and performance statistics of the transportation modes (rail boxcars, TOFC, TL, and LTL) from each of the suppliers to Denver and the six potentially new ones are available to the student.

4. Simulation Logic and Implementation

A Brief Explanation of How the Simulator Works

Figure 4 illustrates the basic hierarchical logic that is used to program the SCS. We give only a brief explanation of the logic. The SCS first reads all the data required by the simulation. This includes the products, markets, and sales data; detailed data on the operating economics of each facility in the supply chain; the freight options, cost structure, and delivery performance of each of the transportation modes. The student then completes the network design phase of the hierarchical model through a graphical user interface (GUI; see Figure 5). The

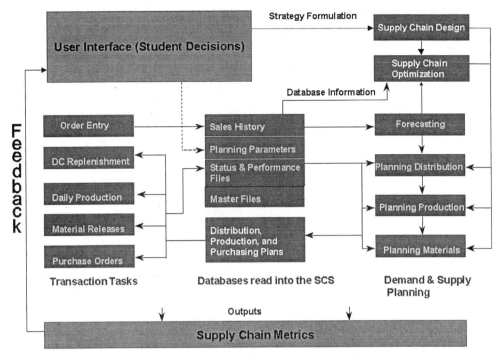

FIGURE 4. The SCS Logic and Simulation Program Flow.

data, together with the design and planning parameters input by the student (as the ensuing discussion shows, they are forecasting methodologies, safety stocks, time fences, etc.), define the nodes and operating procedures of the supply chain. We have written a simple network optimization routine that determines how the resources are allocated in the supply chain, i.e., allocation of customer markets to DCs, DCs to plants, and plants to suppliers (i.e., we help the student fill the "arcs" in the supply chain network). At the end of this stage, the physical supply chain is completely defined, i.e., nodes and the corresponding arcs between them are determined.

Our planning horizon is 13 periods (1 year), each period consisting of 20 days. At the beginning of the planning period, demand is forecast at each of the DCs, safety stocks are updated to match the desired service level, and distribution plans are generated at every DC. The result of the DRP is the determination of the DC needs in each time period of the planning horizon (13 time periods). The needs are then appropriately aggregated at the supplying plant warehouse and a feasible warehouse-shipping schedule is generated. In turn, this schedule generates a need for finished goods in every time period, and thus a production plan is produced that satisfies the needs over the planning horizon. The plan is smoothed, if necessary, to satisfy any capacity constraints. The production plan serves as the starting point for the supply planning process, which results in the determination of raw material needs and supplier-shipping plans.

Once the plans are computed for the entire time horizon, the SCS begins daily simulation until the end of the current planning period (1, 2, or 3 months, depending on the time fence), collecting supply chain performance data every day of the simulation. Once the next planning period is reached, the planning cycle is performed again, i.e., the DC forecasts are updated, distribution and supply plans are generated, and so on. In our simulation model, after an initial warm-up period (to allow for initial conditions), statistics are collected for 3 years to average random effects.

At the end of the simulation the SCS furnishes the student with detailed financial (fixed, variable, and investment costs) and logistical (service levels, inventories, and capacity

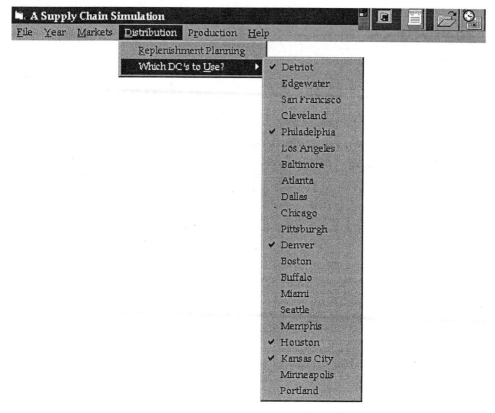

FIGURE 5. The Simulation Visual Interface.

utilization) performance at every facility in the network. In addition we provide detailed supply chain metrics, categorized by activity (see, for example, Figure 6). The metrics include both time and cost factors that relate to how responsive and cost effective the current supply chain plan is. The SCS report also includes what have come to be known as "Boardroom Metrics" (see Tyndall, Gopal, Partsch, and Kamauff 1998), such as return on investment (ROI), EVATM, profit contribution, customer service levels, and overall supply chain cycle time. In our experience such an activity-based metric system helps the student quickly identify potential areas for improvement in the supply chain.

Implementing the Simulation and Student Decisions

As the Appendix suggests, we typically structure the course so that the student, after an introduction to supply chain strategies, is introduced to the lower levels of the hierarchy. This prepares the student well for the first exercise using the simulator: making the current supply chain or the "base case" run more effectively. The student can alter the following parameters in the simulation:

1. *Retail or market-level forecasting methodology.* Students have a choice between two methods: one that simulates a DC-retail collaborative forecast that, although relatively expensive, produces lower forecast errors; and the other that simulates an independent DC forecast of the retail demand (of course, this is cheaper and produces higher forecast errors).

2. *Demand and supply planning method.* The students have the choice of using a collaborative planning and forecasting method (CPFR), in which the plants have visibility of DC requirements versus the order point method, in which the plant manager independently forecasts the DC needs. The CPFR initiative, of course, is the more expensive option as a result

Activity Based Costs and Performance

	Total Costs	Unit Costs	Time (days)
In-bound Activities			
Purchase Costs	$30,527,566.00	$.8417	
Freight Costs	$ 672,913.33	$.0186	
In Transit to Plant	$ 189,509.38	$.0052	5.34
In bound Holding	$ 1,015,862.00	$.0280	28.30
Production Related			
Plant Fixed Cost	$7,700,000.00	$.2123	
Plant Var. Cost	$6,893,466.50	$.1901	
WIP Holding	$1,120,963.48	$.0309	10.00
Out-bound Activities			
Plant Warehouse Fix Cost	$255,600.00	$.0070	
Plant Warehouse Var Cost	$849,342.00	$.0234	
Plant Warehouse Inv Cost	$977,162.31	$.0269	22.25
In Transit Holding to DC	$356,730.84	$.0098	8.12
Distribution			
DC Freight In	$ 591,688.78	$.0163	
DC Fixed	$ 124,420.00	$.0034	
DC Var	$ 528,421.21	$.0146	
DC Holding	$ 328,449.13	$.0091	7.36
Freight to Customer	$8,635,699.02	$.2381	
In Transit to Customer	$ 198,799.92	$.0055	4.30
Administrative	$100,000.00	$.0028	
Totals	$61,066,592.00	$1.6838	85.65

Boardroom Metrics

	Total Annual Costs	Cost / Unit
Total Sales	$72,534,534.12	$2.0000
Total Fixed	$ 8,180,020.00	$0.2255
Total Variable	$48,699,096.84	$1.3428
Total Inventory	$ 4,187,477.00	$0.1155
Profit Contribution	$11,467,942.12	$0.3162

Investment

Plants	$20,000,000.00
Plant Warehouse	$ 900,000.00
Distribution Centers	$ 1,244,200.00
Inventory	$ 1,094,830.38

Supply Chain Customer Service and Utilization Measures

Supply Chain Service Level:	97.86%
Order Cycle Time to Customer	4.30 days
Average Time through Supply Chain	85.65 days
Average Production Capacity Utilization	82.26%

Financial Performance

Profit Margin:	15.81%
Return on Investment:	49.35%
Projected EVA:	$8,115,748.12

FIGURE 6. Supply Chain Metrics (a Portion of the Simulation Output).

of the special information technology requirements. In effect the student trades off cost against the negative effects of the bullwhip phenomenon.

3. *Customer service levels.* The student sets the target "fill-rate" at every DC. The fill-rate is the fraction of the total retail (market) demand that is shipped from the DC inventory.

4. *Safety inventories of finished goods at plant warehouses, and raw material safety stocks at the inbound locations.* This gives the student an opportunity to examine the effect of inventory at various points in the supply chain.

5. *Time fences.* The student gets an opportunity to choose how often the material plans in the supply chain get updated. Of course, choosing a more frequent update policy is more expensive.

The students do the assignments in groups of three or four. The first assignment gives the student insight into the effects of the more operational elements on the performance of the supply chain. In our experience, the following are the key outcomes of the learning process. The participants:

- gain insights into the costs and benefits of collaborative forecasting and planning, both at the retail and the manufacturing level.
- understand the impact of holding inventory at various points in the supply chain. For example, holding relatively more finished goods inventory at the DCs (as opposed to the plant) is a more expensive option, but also has the highest impact on market or retail fill-rates.
- better understand the impact on fill-rates of more frequently updating demand and supply plans. Although updating the plans daily or weekly is more expensive than a monthly update, the students recognize that it produces a higher fill-rate on average.
- realize that even operational elements in the supply chain can have a significant impact on boardroom metrics. Most student groups show significant improvements in financial, time, and cost metrics as a result of operating the supply chain more effectively.

The second assignment asks the students to formulate a customer service strategy and configure the supply chain for the next 5 to 10 years. In addition to altering any of the five parameters discussed earlier, they have the option to:

1. Change market configurations: start selling in new markets and close certain markets down, if needed, to balance supply and demand.

2. Change DC configurations: close down some or all of the existing DCs and open new ones from the 21 potential sites available to them.

3. Open a new plant in the East, if needed, and set its capacity.

4. Change modes of transport in every constituent link in the supply chain.

Students learn during the course of this second exercise that it is possible to succeed with different customer service strategies. For example, a high-growth strategy would be to open new markets all over the United States in the next 5 years, build and operate a plant in the East, and establish several DCs to serve the increased demand. However, this is also capital-intensive, possibly resulting in low ROI and EVATM. A medium-growth and a high customer service strategy, on the other hand, would be to expand Denver's production, open select markets, and replenish them through nearby DCs with LTL shipments. Such a strategy, however, will produce lower profit margins resulting from controlled growth. The point is that students learn the delicate balance between costs, customer service, time, and shareholder wealth when they are formulating their strategies.

Second, students learn to appreciate the impact of production capacity on distribution operations, specifically inventory levels and fill-rates. Because of the highly seasonal nature of demand, the students need to plan enough capacity to build up inventory in time for the spring cleaning season.

Finally, this part of the assignment makes the students appreciate the impact of network configuration elements such as market, DC, and plant locations, and transport modes on supply chain performance. For example, although more expensive, a faster mode of transport decreases response time and cycle-inventories.

We use the two-assignment sequence at all levels of instruction. For both undergraduates and MBAs, we extend the process over several weeks. Because of the typical time compression in executive programs, we use a simplified version of the user interface with fewer degrees of freedom at the executive level. This allows us to complete the entire process in half a day. Unfortunately, this leaves little time to cover all the theory and techniques surrounding the case.

The feedback from students (at the undergraduate, MBA, and executive levels) has been very positive. Over the last 2 years we have had comments such as ". . . gives the big picture . . . ," ". . . great exposure to realistic situations . . . ," ". . . hands-on supply chain experience was wonderful . . . ," and the like. Additionally, such comments were also accompanied by high course evaluations! Executives find it eye-opening, to say the least. Most do not realize how much slack and waste might exist in their supply chains under the traditional functional approach to such operations. Furthermore, they have never really looked at the impact of supply chain initiatives on the "boardroom measures." Their usual response is, "How can I get a tool like this for my business?"

5. Discussion and Future Directions

The Supply Chain Simulator is a work in progress. Plans are underway to include the next version as part of a textbook on supply chain management to be published by Prentice-Hall. One of the important issues is for the students not only to see the results of their decisions, but also to understand why those results occurred. Right now the SCS is pretty much a "black box." Students set the input parameters and then view the final results. Obviously there is some temptation to revert to trial-and-error techniques. We caution students against this because, given the number of degrees of freedom, the trial-and-error approach is not a good use of their time. At the undergraduate and MBA levels, we are able to extend the process and cover the theory as we go through the various case assignments and subassignments. In fact we are adding to the number of assignments to further enhance the learning. At the executive level, given the short time frames of such courses, we are able to do less. Executives do tend to focus more on trial-and-error approaches because they seek quick results.

We are in the process of developing much more extensive graphical output of time series data so that students can see how the supply chain acts over time. In particular, they can view how various initiatives, especially cycle time reduction, tend to mitigate the negative effects of the bullwhip effect.

We are debating whether we should allow students to change parameters interactively as a run progresses. Then they could make corrections if they saw performance was not progressing as they had hoped. The disadvantage of this, however, is that it becomes even more difficult to explain why the results came out like they did. Another approach would be to provide some intermediate diagnostics that would let the student quickly abort a run in which, for example, she/he has not provided sufficient production capacity, or has made some other poor choice. In such a case the diagnostic needs to explain why the choice caused the problem (as instructors we are often called on to act in this diagnostic role, explaining why some results look illogical, but are in fact a natural consequence of the set of decisions made).

In any case the SCS is just one tool we use to try to explain and demonstrate the dynamics of supply chains. No one approach is sufficient, given the broad scope of supply chain management.

6. Summary and Conclusions

In this paper we have discussed an approach to teaching and demonstrating supply chain management concepts to students. The task is challenging because of the systems nature of the supply chain approach and the interrelationships between the various activities in the chain. The hierarchical methodology helps to simplify and structure the decisions that must be made in supply chains. In addition it provides an excellent "road map" throughout the course. Although it is true that synchronous planning techniques and advanced planning and scheduling tools are blurring the distinctions between the levels in the hierarchy, these approaches are made more apparent through the use of the hierarchical model.

The Supply Chain Simulator is particularly valuable in providing students with a way to see the impact on overall performance of the various decisions that might be made in designing and operating a supply chain. In addition they see the interrelationships between the various activities under different operating parameters. Students come away with a new appreciation for the need to do two things well in supply chain management. First, the right supply chain needs to be designed for the specific products and firm strategies in question. Second, they see the large impact on supply chain and firm performance when the resulting supply chain is operated effectively.

Our conclusion from this is that neither students, nor managers, can effectively design and operate supply chains without taking a total systems approach. And they cannot do this without decision support tools that can quantify the trade-offs between all the activities in the supply chain.[1]

[1] We thank Professor David F. Pyke of Dartmouth College and two anonymous referees for insightful comments on earlier versions of this paper.

Appendix. Sample MBA Class Schedule (Details Available from Authors)

I. Customer Service Strategy

Ganeshan, "Four Steps to Effective Supply Chain Management," *Inbound Logistics*, February 1999, 16.
Fuller, O'Connor, and Rawlinson, "Tailored Logistics: The Next Advantage." (HBR Article: 93305)
Shapiro, "Get Leverage from Logistics." (HBR Article: 84313)
Case: Benetton (A) (HBS Case: 9-685-014)

II. Order Management

Shapiro, Rangan, and Svioka, "Staple Yourself to an Order." (HBR Article: 92411)
Kumar and Shraman, "We Love Your Product, but Where Is It?" *The McKinsey Quarterly*, 1992, 1, 24–44.
Case: Digital Equipment Corporation: Complex Order Management (HBS Case 9-690-081)

III. Demand and Supply Planning: *Customers, Products, and Distribution*

Jain, "Forecasting at Colgate-Palmolive Company," *The Journal of Business Forecasting*, Spring 1992, 16–20
Tyndall, Gopal, Partsch, and Kanauff, *Supercharging Supply Chains*, Wiley: New York, 1998, 173–208.
Sharp and Hill, "ECR: From Harmful Competition to Winning Collaboration," in *Strategic Supply Chain Alignment*, Gower: Hampshire GU11 3HR, UK, 1998, 104–122.
Case: Procter & Gamble: Improving Consumer Value Through Process Redesign (HBS Case: 9-195-126)

IV. Pinacor/Tote double tour of the distribution Centers (*CLM local roundtable event*)

V and VI. Demand and Supply Planning: *Manufacturing and Purchasing* (2 *sessions*)

Fisher, Obermeyer, Hammond, and Raman, "Accurate Response: The Key to Profiting from QR," *Bobbin*, February 1994, 48–62.
MacDuffie and Helper, "Creating Lean Suppliers: Diffusing Lean Production Throughout the Supply Chain." (CMR Article: CMR090)
Case: Sara Lee: QR at Hanes (HBS Case 9-191-021)
Case: Campbell Soup: A Leader in Continuous Replenishment (HBS Case: 9-195-124)
Supply Chain Simulator Exercise I *Presentations: Improving the Base Case*

VII. Network Configuration: *Product Flow Management for Mass Customization*

Feitzinger and Lee, "Mass Customization at Hewlett-Packard: The Power of Postponement." (HBR Article: 97101)
Case: HP Deskjet Supply Chain (Stanford Business School Case)

VIII. Network Configuration: Transportation Choice and Planning Reverse Logistics Flows

Crum and Holcomb, "Transportation Outlook and Evaluation," in *The Logistics Handbook*, Robeson and Copacino (editors-in-chief); Howe (associate editor), The Free Press, 465–479.
Case: Frito-Lay: The Backhaul Decision (HBS Case: 9-688-104)

IX and X. Network Configuration: Network Modeling and GIS (2 sessions)

Bender, "How to Design an Optimum Worldwide Supply Chain," *Supply Chain Management Review*, Spring 1997.
Fisher, "What Is the Right Supply Chain for Your Product?" (HBR Article: 97205)
Camm, Chorman, Dill, Evans, Sweeney, and Wegryn, "Blending OR/MS Judgement, and GIS: Restructuring P & G's Supply Chain," *Interfaces*, January–February 1997.
Case: Kodak Business Imaging Systems Division (HBS Case: 9-693-043)
Supply Chain Simulator Design Exercise II: *Strategy Formulation and Network Configuration*

XI. Supply Chain Enablers: Information Systems (Enterprise Solutions)

Gries and Kasarda, "Enterprise Logistics in the Information Era." (CMR Article: CMR088)
Grackin and Dobrin, "Make Better Schedules," *Information Week*, April 21, 1997, 18–24.
Case: Vandelay Industries (HBS case, 9-697-037)

XII. Supply Chain Enablers: Information Systems (Electronic Commerce)

Rayport and Sviokla, "Exploiting the Virtual Value Chain." (HBR Article: 95610)
Rayport and Sviokla, "Managing the Marketspace" (HBR Article: 94608)
Case: Dell Online (HBS Case: 9-598-116)

XIII. Supply Chain Enablers: Organizational Structures

Gattorna, "Fourth Party Logistics: En route to Breakthrough Performance in the Supply Chain," in *Strategic Supply Chain Alignment*, Gower: Hampshire GU11 3HR, UK, 425–445.
Case: Laura Ashley and FedEx Strategic Alliance (HBS Case: 693-050)

XIV. Supply Chain Enablers: Performance and Course Wrap-up

Lambert, "Logistics Cost, Productivity, and Performance Analysis," in *The Logistics Handbook*, Robeson and Copacino (editors-in-chief); Howe (associate editor), The Free Press, 260–302.
Scott and Westbrook, "New Strategic Tools for Supply Chain Management," *International Journal of Physical Distribution and Logistics Management*, 1991, 21, 1, 23–33.

References

ANTHONY, R. N. (1965), *Planning and Control Systems: A Framework and Analysis*, Harvard University Graduate School of Business Administration, Cambridge, MA, USA.
BALLOU, R. H. (1999), *Business Logistics Management: Planning Organizing, and Controlling the Supply Chain*, 4th Ed., Prentice Hall, Upper Saddle River, NJ, USA.
BOWERSOX, D. J., D. CLOSS, AND O. K. HELFERICH (1988), *Logistical Management*, Macmillan, New York.
EVANS, R. AND A. DANKS (1998), "Strategic Supply Chain Management" in *Strategic Supply Chain Alignment*, Gower, Hampshire, UK, 425–445.
FISHER, M. L. (1997), "What Is the Right Supply Chain for Your Product?" *Harvard Business Review*, 75, 105–116.
GANESHAN, R. AND A. J. STENGER (1999), *MAS Manufacturing*, Unpublished teaching case, ML #0130, The University of Cincinnati, Cincinnati, OH, USA.
GILES, P. AND A. HANCY (1998), "Alternative Organization Options" in *Strategic Supply Chain Alignment*, Gower, Hampshire, UK, 410–424.
HAX, A. AND H. MEAL (1975), "Hierarchical Integration of Production Planning and Scheduling" in *Studies in Management Sciences: Logistics*, Vol. 1, M. A. Geisler (ed.), Elsevier, New York, 63–69.
HOULIHAN, J. B. (1985), "International Supply Chain Management," *International Journal of Physical Distribution and Materials Management*,15, 22–38.
SHAPIRO, R. D (1984), "Get Leverage from Logistics," *Harvard Business Review* 62, 119–126.
STENGER, A. J. (1987), "Electronic Information Systems—Key to Managing Integrated Logistics Management" in *Proceedings of the* 17th *Annual Transportation and Logistics Educators Conference*, Atlanta, GA, USA, 12–26.
TYNDALL, G., C. GOPAL, W. PARTSCH, AND J. KAMAUFF (1998), *Supercharging Supply Chains*, John Wiley & Sons, New York.
VOLLMAN, T. E., W. L. BERRY, AND D. C. WHYBARK (1992), *Manufacturing Planning and Control Systems*, Irwin, Homewood, IL, USA.

Ram Ganeshan's expertise is in the areas of supply chain management and information technology management, primarily in the chemical, hi-tech, and retail contexts. In addition to his academic appointment, he serves on the Board of Directors of two companies: American Pallet Management Systems, a reverse-supply chain management company based in Deer Park, NY, and WinVision, a supply chain-IT provider based in Santa Clara, CA. His education includes graduate degrees in operations and logistics management from Penn State University, and The University of North Carolina at Chapel Hill. Ram is also coeditor of the recent book *Quantitative Models for Supply Chain Management*.

Tonya Boone's teaching, research, and consulting expertise are in the areas of knowledge management, design and implementation of IT, and technology transfer primarily in service firms. Tonya's current research focuses on studying the impact of IT on knowledge acquisition in service firms; and investigating the extent to which information technology has impacted supply chain operations. Tonya has a doctorate in Operations Management from the University of North Carolina at Chapel Hill and an MBA from the College of William and Mary. Before joining the Fisher School faculty, Tonya has been an electrical and electronics engineer and eventually project manager, leading several engineering and technology projects for a large East-coast service organization.

Alan J. Stenger's teaching and research interests focus primarily on the organization and management of supply chain and logistical activities in manufacturing and merchandising firms. Before joining the Smeal College faculty, Dr. Stenger gained applied professional experience at the Dow Chemical Company, where he was manager of distribution planning for consumer products. Since then he has engaged in a wide range of consulting and management programs with many Fortune 500 firms, including AT&T, Dow Chemical, EDS, GE, GTE, IBM, Johnson & Johnson, Merck, Procter & Gamble, and Shell Chemical. Active in executive education, Dr. Stenger is the Faculty Director for Penn State's 10-day Program for Logistics and Supply Managers. As Associate Director of the Center for Logistics Research, he also serves as a faculty leader for several public and company-specific supply chain programs.

AN ACTIVE LEARNING EXERCISE: SUPPLYING HOOP DREAMS*

BURAK KAZAZ AND HERBERT MOSKOWITZ

School of Business, Loyola University Chicago, Chicago, Illinois 60611, USA
Krannert Graduate School of Management, Purdue University,
West Lafayette, Indiana 47907-1310, USA

We describe a board game in which students assume the roles of supply chain enterprises and move game pieces (e.g., Legos, Velcro, etc.) that represent the parts of a basketball hoop. They then assemble these parts and form the final product and sell it to the customers. The game is the first of its kind to illustrate the concepts of shortage gaming, synchronization of the flow of parts, demand uncertainty and its impact on location selection, competition and cooperation, and customer service. Students playing this game build skills in both decision making and the execution of operations plans. The game also provides professionals an opportunity to visualize the new role of the operations function, and thus prepares them for the needs of today's supply chain management principles.

1. Introduction

In this paper, we describe a learning tool, a game called "Supplying Hoop Dreams" (SHD). The game can be freely downloaded from the following Web address: http://www.luc.edu/schools/business/academics/kazaz.htm. It is used to prepare students and professionals for the newest trend in supply chain management. The prevailing idea in supply chain management is to focus on a team-based competition in which companies see themselves as part of an integrated supply chain. Traditionally, companies focused on manipulating their costs by constantly negotiating with the suppliers. This technique may have allowed operations departments the immediate benefit of lower acquisition costs, yet the overall supply chain costs remain the same as the supplier commits to lower quality standards, etc. As a result, the cost to the consumer is not decreased.

The latest notion, an integrated approach, requires that enterprises make a conceptual shift with regard to other members of the supply chain. Nicholas (1998) writes that this calls for a change in the culture of an organization from the traditional approach of "negotiating" parties to the new role: "collaborating" with the suppliers. This involves including suppliers in the concurrent engineering and design of the product, in team-based quality improvements, and in an integrated supply chain perspective. Our exercise responds to the classroom need of aiding professionals in understanding what this new role requires.

One of the important contributions of the SHD Game is the illustration of all the factors that contribute to the bullwhip effect, which is defined as the inefficient management of product

---

* Received December 1998; revision received September 1999; accepted October 1999.

flows and inventory in the supply chain (Lee, Padmanabhan, and Whang 1997b). Concerning other games, such as the Beer Distribution Game (BDG) (see Sterman 1989), Goodwin and Franklin (1994), for example, set the foundation for understanding, but do not provide students with the opportunity to witness *all* of the factors behind this effect. Our exercise, on the other hand, illustrates all of the four primary reasons for the bullwhip effect. According to Lee, Padmanabhan, and Whang (1997b), the four contributing factors are the following:

1. *Information distortion:* As enterprises place orders, the upstream players use it as demand for its products rather than the actual sales occurring at the downstream.

2. *Order batching:* Companies engage in forward buying (i.e., acquiring more than what they need for the next time period) and allocate the fixed costs (e.g., ordering costs) to a higher number of products to obtain lower unit costs through economies of scale. Examples of this include ordering a full-truck load rather than a less-than-truck load to distribute the fixed transportation cost to a higher number of products.

3. *Price fluctuations:* Enterprises offer discounts on their products to push more products out of the inventory. However, this comes at a price: increased uncertainty in customer demand.

4. *Shortage gaming:* When retailers recognize that a distributor does not have sufficient inventory to fill the demand for all retailers, they inflate their order sizes beyond what they need. They take this conservative action, hoping that the distributor will allocate the insufficient supply in proportion to the order sizes.

Extensive discussion on the bullwhip effect can be found in Davis (1993), Lee and Billington (1992), Lee, Padmanabhan, and Whang (1997a, 1997b), and Metters (1997).

In addition to teaching all four reasons for the bullwhip effect, the SHD Game highlights several other issues related to competition among enterprises. For example, in our game there are two suppliers who provide raw materials to the manufacturer and there is a common part that can be purchased from either of these suppliers. Students role-playing these suppliers, decide on the price of the raw materials every week. This enables a "price competition" among enterprises within the supply chain. This setting motivates a postgame discussion over the subject of "competition versus cooperation." Thus, students in SHD actually have the opportunity to observe the impact of competition while recognizing the benefits of cooperation.

1.1. Comparison of the SHD Game and the Beer Distribution Game

In the downstream portion of the supply chain there are two retailers who compete for products from the same distributor. The demand for these retailers is not constant as in the Beer Distribution Game, and fluctuates over weeks, introducing *demand uncertainty*. Although the bullwhip effect still appears in this setting, the game motivates another discussion—the implications of the *location selection* of the distributor. We intentionally provide the retailers with negatively correlated demand to discuss the implications of correlated demand patterns on the location selection of the distributor. We use negative correlation here because of the insights it affords the distributor with regard to inventory management.

The setting of multiple retailers enables us to introduce another important issue behind the bullwhip effect—*shortage gaming*. When students role-playing the retailers recognize that the distributor has an insufficient inventory of products to satisfy the demand of each retailer, they inflate their order sizes. The rationale behind this increase in order sizes is that retailers hope the distributor will allocate the available inventory according to the percentage of the total order sizes. Students experience this phenomenon in SHD when the distributor falls short of the supply. When this is the case, students find themselves in an argument over a short supply of Legos (products), and complain about the distributor's allocation policy. This experience motivates a strong postgame discussion on how the limited supply of inventory should be allocated among retailers.

SHD teaches the importance of the *synchronization of parts flow* under the presence of unbalanced lead times. In the upstream of the supply chain, there are two suppliers (see Figure 1) that feed the manufacturer. The first supplier provides the backboard and the rim and has a 2-week lead time, whereas the second supplier is in charge of the net and the rim and has a 3-week lead time. The students assuming the role of the manufacturer in the supply chain are challenged with synchronizing the flow of parts into their facilities. The manufacturer then assembles these three parts and ships the final product to the distributor.

In the upstream portion of the supply chain, it should be noted that both suppliers provide a common raw material (the rim) and set prices every week. Therefore, the game enables students to see the impact of *price fluctuations* while creating a *price competition* among enterprises. Because suppliers do not see each other's price, they feel the pressure to decrease their prices to attract the manufacturer. Although the manufacturer is not allowed to negotiate prices during the game, this setting enables the instructor to motivate a postgame discussion about competition versus cooperation. During the game, students role-playing these suppliers view each other competitively, and continuously decrease their prices. This gives tremendous power to the manufacturer. At the end of the postgame discussion, however, both suppliers agree that, had they been cooperating, they could have made higher profits instead of leaving all the profits to the manufacturer. A detailed discussion over the subject of competition versus cooperation can be found in Fine (1998).

Each team in this exercise has the following objectives: maximize the total supply chain profit while maximizing the order fill rates. The total supply chain profit is determined by total revenue minus the sum of the costs of ordering, holding inventory, and backorders of each enterprise in the chain. The second objective relates to the customer service level, where order fill rates are the basis for performance evaluation.

The network structure of SHD is notably different from that of the BDG, in which there are four enterprises that form the supply chain: a retailer, a wholesaler, a distributor, and a factory. In SHD, however, there are two retailers who are supplied by the distributor; the

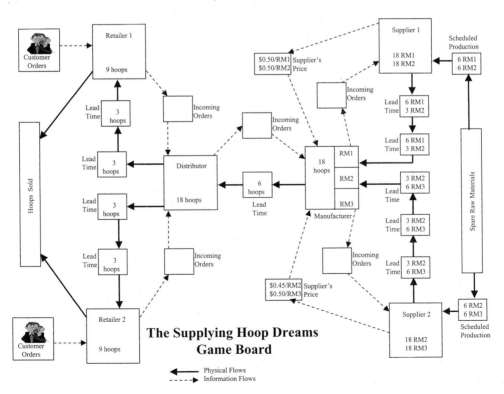

FIGURE 1. The Board of the Supplying Hoop Dreams Game.

distributor orders from the manufacturer and the manufacturer receives raw materials from two different suppliers. In total there are six enterprises each played by at least one student. Whereas the transportation lead time is a constant 2 weeks between enterprises in the Beer Distribution Game, it varies for each player in SHD. For example, the manufacturer has a 2-week lead time with the first supplier and 3-week lead time with the second supplier. Furthermore, there is 1 week of order processing lead time in the Beer Distribution Game; however, in SHD information regarding order quantities is immediately passed on to the upstream players.

Several universities in Executive MBA, MBA, and advanced undergraduate courses, as well as seminars and certificate programs for professionals, use SHD. Student comments on the game are overwhelmingly positive. Among the many benefits, they appreciate the opportunity to build decision-making skills through active participation based on real-world practice. Professors who implement the game have provided similar feedback as well. They use the exercise as a tool to motivate the pitfalls of supply chain management and to teach how these operations can be managed effectively. A Chief Information Officer (CIO) in an Executive MBA class had played the Beer Distribution Game before and, although the Beer Distribution Game taught the value of sharing demand information, he liked the fact that the Supplying Hoop Dreams Game gave a clear example of "shortage gaming."

The paper is organized in the following manner: Section 2 describes how SHD is played. Section 3 contains the details of the lessons learned from the exercise. Section 4 provides potential variations that can be used to implement the game. Conclusions are presented in Section 5.

2. The Dynamics of the Game

In this section, we explain how SHD is played. As can be seen in Figure 1, there are six positions in the supply chain: two retailers, one distributor, one manufacturer, and two suppliers. Each of these positions can be played with preferably one (or at most two) player(s). Students are asked to form teams of six. The objective of each team is to maximize the total supply chain profit (the total of revenue minus the sum of ordering, inventory holding, backordering, purchasing, and transportation costs of all six enterprises) while maximizing their fill rates as a measure of their service quality.

The materials used in SHD include a game board (a large print of Figure 1), Legos (Velcro pieces or pipe cleaners may be substituted) with three different colors for each team, a position worksheet (see Table 1) for each player, and blank order sheets. Each color of Legos (or Velcro) represents a different raw material. When three different colors are attached at the manufacturer, the final product is produced. To eliminate repetitive setups, it is recommended that instructors laminate game boards and blank order cards. Students are asked to use nonpermanent overhead pens so that the order cards can be used again in the future. Furthermore, empty inventory and order graphs are provided for each position if the game is not played in a computer lab.

The inventory in each position is initialized as follows: 9 hoops for each retailer, 18 hoops at the distributor and 18 hoops (or 18 of each raw material) at the manufacturer. There is also an initial inventory in the pipeline: 3 hoops in each "Lead Time" square between retailers and the distributor, and 6 hoops in the "Lead Time" square between the distributor and the manufacturer. In between the manufacturer and Supplier 1, there are 6 units of Raw Material 1 and 3 units of Raw Material 2 in each "Lead Time" square. Similarly, there are 3 units of Raw Material 2 and 6 units of Raw Material 3 in each "Lead Time" square between the manufacturer and Supplier 2.

The sequence of the game requires each player to follow a four-step cycle once in every game-week. This involves receiving incoming inventory, filling orders by shipping hoops (or raw materials in the case of suppliers), recording the status of inventory and backlog, and

TABLE 1
Example Position Worksheets

Retailer 1

Week	Quantity Received	Incoming Order R1	Customer Demand	Quantity Delivered	Inventory	Backlog	Order Size	Weekly Revenue	Weekly Cost	Weekly Profit	Weekly Fill Rate
1											
2											

Retailer 2

Week	Quantity Received	Incoming Order R2	Customer Demand	Quantity Delivered	Inventory	Backlog	Order Size	Weekly Revenue	Weekly Cost	Weekly Profit	Weekly Fill Rate
1											
2											

Distributor

Week	Quantity Received S1/RM1	Quantity Received S1/RM2	Quantity Received S2/RM2	Quantity Received S2/RM3	Incoming Order R1	Incoming Order R2	Quantity Delivered to R1	Quantity Delivered to R2	Inventory	Backlog	Backlog (R1)	Backlog (R2)	Order Quantity	Weekly Revenue	Weekly Cost	Weekly Profit	Weekly Fill Rate (R1)	Weekly Fill Rate (R2)
1																		
2																		

Manufacturer

Week	Quantity Received S1/RM1	Quantity Received S2/RM2	Quantity Received S2/RM3	Incoming Order	Quantity Sent to Distributor	Inventory Hoops	Backlog Hoops	Extra Inventory RM1	Extra Inventory RM2	Extra Inventory RM3	Sup. 1 Ordered RM1	Sup. 1 Price RM2	Sup. 1 Ordered RM2	Sup. 2 Price RM2	Sup. 2 Ordered RM2	Sup. 2 Ordered RM3	Weekly Revenue	Weekly Cost	Weekly Profit	Weekly Fill Rate
1																				
2																				

Supplier 1

Week	Quantity Received RM2	Incoming Order (RM1)	Incoming Order (RM2)	Quantity Shipped (RM1)	Quantity Shipped (RM2)	Inventory (RM1)	Inventory (RM2)	Backlog (RM1)	Backlog (RM2)	Production Scheduled (RM1)	Production Scheduled (RM2)	Asked Price for Next Week (RM2)	Weekly Revenue	Weekly Cost	Weekly Profit	Weekly Fill Rate (RM1)	Weekly Fill Rate (RM2)
1																	
2																	

Supplier 2

Week	Quantity Received RM3	Incoming Order (RM2)	Incoming Order (RM3)	Quantity Shipped (RM2)	Quantity Shipped (RM3)	Inventory (RM2)	Inventory (RM3)	Backlog (RM2)	Backlog (RM3)	Production Scheduled (RM2)	Production Scheduled (RM3)	Asked Price for Next Week (RM2)	Weekly Revenue	Weekly Cost	Weekly Profit	Weekly Fill Rate (RM2)	Weekly Fill Rate (RM3)
1																	
2																	

placing new orders. In the case of the suppliers, they also submit the price of the raw materials for the next week to the manufacturer. At the beginning, the game is initialized with prices from Supplier 1 as $0.50 for each raw material 1 and 2, and as $0.45 for each raw material 2 and 3 from Supplier 2. It is recommended that the two retailers start the game. When the retailers finish their four-step cycle, the distributor starts his/her four-step cycle. Next, the manufacturer starts playing when the distributor completes his/her cycle. Finally, the two suppliers play their turn. On completion of the cycle by the suppliers, the game repeats the same procedure for the next game-week. This sequential play should be followed until students become familiar with the four-step cycle. Each player can then play simultaneously every week without waiting for the previous enterprise to complete his/her four-step cycle. The details of the four-step cycles for each position can be found in the description of the game.

It takes approximately 1.5 hours to complete 20 to 25 weeks. This should be sufficient to experience all possible outcomes of the game, and there is no need to complete all 52 weeks. However, informing the students that the game will end in 52 weeks will eliminate end-game effects (e.g., cases such as students not ordering to decrease their final inventory, etc.). The instructor should announce the termination of the game at the end of 1.5 hours (or earlier if all teams reach week 25).

The instructors provide the retailers with random demand. The demand is nonstationary because there is a change in the process at the end of the sixth week. During the rest of the game, it follows a stationary process. Next, the procedure that can be used to generate random demand with negative correlation is explained.

2.1. *The Procedure for Generating Random Demand with Negative Correlation*

The demand for each retailer is first generated using a discrete distribution, then a dispersion term is added (or subtracted) to create negative correlation. In the first 6 weeks, a discrete distribution for the values of (2, 3, 4) is used with the probabilities (0.3, 0.4, 0.3), whereas in the rest of the game a discrete distribution for the values of (5, 6, 7) is used with probabilities (0.2, 0.6, 0.2). The mean for these distributions, μ, is 3 and 6, respectively. Denoting the random variables generated by these processes as d_1 and d_2 for each retailer, we then check whether d_1 is greater or less than the mean. If d_1 is less than μ, then a dispersion term of $u \times 2$ is further subtracted from d_1, where u is generated using a uniform distribution between 0 and 1. The maximum dispersion is limited to 2 units and this is equal to the difference between the highest and lowest values for the discrete random variables. When d_1 is less than μ, d_2 is increased by a complementary dispersion term $(1 - u) \times 2$. However, if d_1 is greater than μ, then a dispersion term of $u \times 2$ is further added to d_1, and d_2 is decreased by $(1 - u) \times 2$. Finally, these values are rounded to the closest integer to provide integral values for the demand. It should be noted that these dispersion terms guarantee that the demand for each retailer follows negative correlation. D_1 and D_2, the demand of each retailer, can then be expressed as follows:

$$D_1 = \begin{cases} d_1 - u \times 2 & \text{if } d_1 < \mu \\ d_1 + u \times 2 & \text{if } d_1 \geq \mu \end{cases}$$

$$D_2 = \begin{cases} d_2 + (1 - u) \times 2 & \text{if } d_1 < \mu \\ d_2 - (1 - u) \times 2 & \text{if } d_1 \geq \mu \end{cases}$$

It should be noted that the means of D_1 and D_2 are still equal to μ. This process usually generates demand for retailers with 15 to 40% of negative correlation.

The implication of the negatively correlated demand on the location selection of the distributor is presented in Section 3.

3. Lessons of the Game

In this section, we present the lessons that SHD highlights. The game is designed to provide hands-on experience with the many challenges that one faces in managing the supply chain. It responds to the need students have to engage in the execution of inventory planning. Alternatives to improving the management decisions are provided for each of these problems. Students see the dangers of suboptimization on the total supply chain profits at the end of the game. They appreciate the value of team play and, in the end, find that organizations of supply chains should carry an integrated enterprise perspective rather than the traditional functional perspective.

We begin this section with a discussion on demand uncertainty and its implications on the location selection of the distributor. This is followed by an explanation of shortage gaming and the bullwhip effect. Then, the importance of the synchronization of parts flow in the upstream portion of the supply chain is described by using the unbalanced lead times of the suppliers. Later, we show the inventory, backlogging, and financial performance implications of price competition between two suppliers. Finally, we present an explanation of order-fill rate and its use as a means of performance evaluation.

The downstream portion of the supply chain, as presented in Figure 1, contains two retailers who are provided with a random demand every week. These two retailers do not communicate with each other, and thus do not know the demand of the other player. Furthermore, the demand is negatively correlated between the two retailers as described in Section 2.1. The impact of demand uncertainty combined with the distributor's location on inventory levels is explained later.

3.1. *The Location of the Distributor and its Impact on Inventory Levels*

Using the random nature of retailers' demand, the game stimulates a strong discussion regarding the alternatives for distributor's location. Inventory management principles are used to show the impact of these location choices. It should be noted that the game involves periodic review; therefore, order-up-to policies should be followed. We initiate the conversation by asking those students who played the role of the factory about their preferences with regard to the location of the distributor. We then repeat the same question to those who role-played the retailers. Students almost always prefer the distributor to be closer to their own site. In the end, students find themselves arguing on where the distributor should be located.

The nature of the demand pattern provides students with both insightful and practical solutions for the location decision by using inventory levels. We first present students the demand that occurred at each retailer. An example of a demand pattern used in one of the games is shown in Figure 2. Students recognize that, because of negative correlation, demand at each retailer shows opposite dispersion from the mean. More important, students learn that the total demand shows a variance that is smaller than the sum of each retailer's variance.

$$var\,[D_1 + D_2] = var\,[D_1] + var\,[D_2] + 2\,cov\,[D_1, D_2]$$

Because of the negative correlation, the covariance term, $cov\,[D_1, D_2]$ is negative, so:

$$var\,[D_1 + D_2] \leq var\,[D_1] + var\,[D_2]$$

When demand information is shared among enterprises of the supply chain, students see that this property can decrease the required safety stock level of the distributor. They understand that the further the distributor is located from the retailers (the higher the lead time), the higher the safety-stock commitment at the distributor and retailers. We discuss how moving the distributor closer to the retailers results in savings through the reduction in safety stocks and total inventory levels.

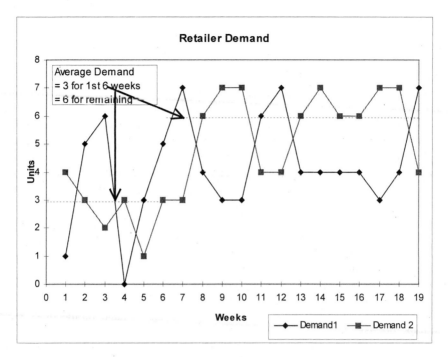

FIGURE 2. Example Graph for Retailer Demand.

The implications of the distributor's location combined with sharing demand information on inventory levels are a result of the "risk pooling effect." [A detailed discussion of inventory policies in supply chain management can be found in Silver, Pyke, and Peterson (1998, Chapter 12).] We discuss with students the case when the distributor can be located next to the retailers with no lead time in between. In this case, the distributor can deliver products instantly to the retailers in the quantity ordered while receiving an almost constant flow of products from the manufacturer. Although the distributor's safety stock increases because of increased lead time, retailers' safety stock decreases because of the immediate deliveries made from the distributor (zero lead time). The decrease in retailers' safety stock justifies the increase in that of the distributor because of negatively correlated demand. In the current setup of the game, however, the distributor is 2 weeks away from the retailers. Consequently, the amount shipped to each retailer is received in 2 weeks and usually is not equal to that week's demand because of the demand fluctuations. Students realize that such a structure causes excess inventory or backorders (when insufficient safety stock is carried at the retailers). On the other hand, they usually show a reaction to the effect of location proximity between retailers and distributor, in particular to no lead time. We then provide examples of such practices, such as Wal-Mart and Sam's Club in the same shopping mall area in the Midwest, and Jewel and Osco retail stores located next door or across the street from each other. We also describe how their warehouse (similar to the function of the distributor in SHD) is situated behind these retail stores. Students appreciate the fact that the distributor is now more flexible to alter the allocation of its inventory between these retailers.

Obviously, relocating the distributor closer to the retailers is not the only solution that improves the system performance. However, this discussion over the location also motivates the study of other solutions such as vendor-managed inventory, channel alignment, etc.

3.2. *Shortage Gaming*

The game also illustrates the concept of shortage gaming. The network structure of the supply chain with two retailers and one distributor feeding them creates a clear scenario for this phenomenon. During the game, when the distributor receives orders from retailers exceeding its total inventory of hoops, the distributor has to make a decision as to how to allocate the insufficient supply between the two retailers. In general, students playing the role of the distributor follow an allocation policy based on the percentage of order sizes received from each retailer. When retailers recognize that the distributor does not have a sufficient supply to satisfy both retailers simultaneously, they increase their order sizes tremendously to a quantity much higher than they actually need. They respond this way to influence the distributor and thus receive a higher share of the insufficient supply. In certain instances, aggressive students increase their order sizes by more than 10 times what they would order normally. We also discuss with the students how such behavior can be observed in actual practice. As stated in Lee, Padmanabhan, and Whang (1997b), Motorola experienced an increase in orders it received for its cellular phones before Christmas in 1994 because of an anticipation of shortages. Similarly, IBM experienced an unexpected increase in orders for its Aptiva PCs before Christmas of 1994. In both instances, the orders from retailers were cancelled after the Christmas holiday.

At this point in the discussion, students can learn about alternative solutions. One of the solutions recommended in Lee, Padmanabhan, and Whang (1997b) is that distributors allocate the insufficient supply according to historical sales information. General Motors practiced this solution in the past with its allocation of cars to dealers.

3.3. Information Distortion

The information distortion in the supply chain causes students to manage their inventories inefficiently. A common behavior is that when students are not provided with the same quantity they ordered from the upstream players, they inflate their order sizes. Upstream players, however, recognize this as a sign of an increase in demand, and thus, increase their order sizes. As a result, students experience a shortage of inventories, and incur unnecessary backorder costs. This behavior continues for 8 to 10 weeks followed by a glut of inventory in the supply chain. At this time, they incur unnecessary inventory holding costs. This is

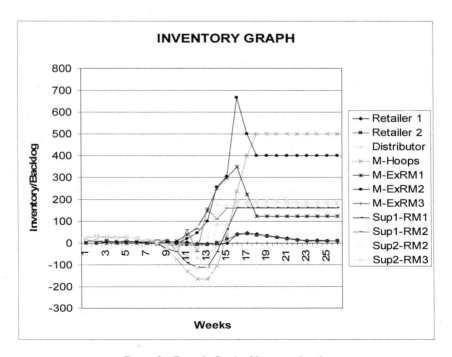

FIGURE 3. Example Graph of Inventory Levels.

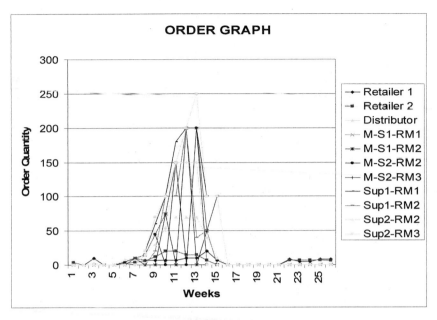

FIGURE 4. Example Graph of Order Sizes.

caused by the distortion of information in the supply chain. An example of inventory and order graphs from classroom experimentation is provided in Figures 3 and 4, respectively.

This discussion helps students understand the value of sharing demand information with upstream players. Although some students who play the role of the retailers show some resistance to such an idea at first, later they unanimously agree that communicating about demand would reduce the bullwhip effect. They learn that information sharing would benefit all as the upstream players recognize the changes earlier and respond more quickly to the downstream players.

3.4. *Synchronization of Flow of Parts into the Manufacturer*

SHD teaches the importance of the synchronization of parts flow. Given that the two suppliers have unbalanced lead times, the manufacturer needs to synchronize the inflow of raw materials. In the game, the first supplier has a 2-week lead time, and the second supplier has a three-week lead time. In most experiments, students playing the role of the manufacturer experience backorders for hoops while having inventory of (at least) one raw material. When this is the case, the manufacturer incurs both backorder and inventory holding costs simultaneously. This is usually sufficient for them to appreciate the importance of synchronization.

We then discuss how synchronization can be accomplished. We motivate the discussion as follows: suppose that a quantity of q is ordered from the 3-week lead time supplier. In the following week, the same order quantity, q, should be placed with the 2-week lead time supplier so that an equal number of parts arrive at the factory at the same time. Although the solution for the synchronization of parts flow is relatively simple, it takes many rounds of play before most of the students recognize this solution.

3.5. *Competition versus Cooperation*

SHD creates an environment where the two suppliers compete via prices to win the order of the manufacturer for the common raw material. At the beginning of the game, the manufacturer usually prefers Supplier 2 for this raw material (the rim) because of its lower price. Later in the game, when the manufacturer falls in backlog, the role-player starts ordering from Supplier 1 because of its shorter lead time. Students see the trade-off between the cost (purchasing price) and the lead times through this experience. Although Supplier 2 is the winner of the orders at the beginning because of its lower price, Supplier 1 starts decreasing its price as well, and initiates a price war. As a result, the manufacturer switches the orders from Suppler 2 to Supplier 1, and increases its order size beyond actual need. This is an example of what is known as "forward buying." At the beginning, suppliers cannot provide them with the quantity requested and fall into backlog. Furthermore, suppliers take the increased order size as a signal for increased demand. They plan their production and inventory with these numbers ending up with high levels of unwanted inventory. On the supplier end, it creates more fluctuations in demand and thus results in higher levels of unwanted inventory and backlog, and safety stock. From the manufacturer's perspective suppliers cannot provide them with the material on time in the quantity they want. These all negatively impact the performance of the chain.

3.6. Customer Service

SHD also emphasizes the issue of customer service. The position worksheets provided for each player in Figure 4 have a column for the weekly fill rate. Before the start of the game, fill rate is defined:

$$\text{Fill rate} = (\text{amount delivered}/\text{amount necessary to be shipped}) \times 100\%$$

The term "amount necessary to be shipped" is equal to the sum of backorders from the previous week and the demand of the current week. The distributor is specifically asked to keep track of the performance of the fill rate, separately for each retailer.

As a result of the bullwhip effect, students usually find their fill rates unsatisfying at the end of the game. This instills an appreciation for better management of customer service. More importantly, after the postgame discussion, students uniformly respond that demand information must be shared with other members of the supply chain. Furthermore, they recognize that sharing information will lead to better planning of inventory, improving fill rates, and increased customer satisfaction.

3.7. Total Profit

At the end of the game, students are asked to find the profit of the position they played. They first sum the costs of inventory holding, ordering, transportation, purchasing, and backordering. They then subtract this sum from the revenue they generated from sales. A good exercise is to ask students to calculate their average weekly profit of the entire supply chain. Students notice that the results vary quite drastically, and several teams post losses rather than profits. It also gives an estimate for gains from streamlining operations in the supply chain. Here, students recognize that individual performance is not as important as the overall profitability of the supply chain. This is particularly important for the professionals who play this game as it motivates the necessary changes in corporate culture. Firms such as Ford are currently trying to change the culture of their purchasing people to recognize the importance of an integrated enterprise perspective. Assessing the total profit of the supply chain, rather than that of the manufacturer, allows players to witness this impact.

4. Potential Variations and Future Revisions

This section suggests several variations of the game. The first one deals with forecasting. Students can be asked to forecast demand for the upcoming weeks and use it in their plans. Another variation includes extending the price competition to the downstream of the supply chain. However, to implement such a variation at the retailers, we need to introduce a new demand pattern that is varying by different price levels. This can be accomplished in a computerized version. Another variation can be the addition of direct transportation from the manufacturer to the retailers, with a shorter lead time at an extra cost. Such a revision would provide a springboard to understanding the impact of transportation costs on safety-stock levels and their corresponding costs. Furthermore, an addition of random exchange rates for one of the suppliers would increase the value of the game as it illustrates the issues in a global supply chain. Such an addition would enable students to see how macroeconomic factors influence the ordering/purchasing decisions and what can be done to mitigate the risks. The downside of this alternative is that it would complicate the calculations of the manufacturer and slow down the pace of the game.

Another option is to use computers to play the game rather than a game board. Although we have developed Excel spreadsheets to play SHD, we find that such an implementation does not allow students to visualize the physical dynamics of the entire supply chain. In the computer version students focus so much on their spreadsheet that they lose sight of the "big picture." The physical play of the game facilitates interaction, and students respond quickly to changes in the environment.

We are currently developing an Internet version of SHD that will illustrate a holistic view of the events and animate the flow of parts and products on the computer screen. The Internet version of the game will have several benefits: the ability to test the performance of different ordering policies, and the ability to play the game with students on different campuses, thus providing experience in managing a "global" supply chain, etc. However, this version is likely to preclude the physical interaction benefit just mentioned.

5. Conclusions

SHD has proven to be a teaching tool that is as useful as it is fun. Students enjoy the ability to visualize the supply chain, particularly the cases where they can observe the concepts learned in the classroom. These include demand uncertainty, location selection, the bullwhip effect, shortage gaming, the impact of competition and collaboration, and customer service levels.

We have received extremely positive results in all institutions in which the game is used. One Loyola MBA student wrote: "I found this (SHD) a lot of fun and useful. Active participation allowed us to see each step and the effects of each action. Very good!" Participants find the exercise to be a good simulation of real-world practices, and appreciate it as it builds skills for decision making and the execution of operations plans. Comments from written evaluations include:

"Fun, hands on learning!"

"Helped to visualize the difficulties of lead times in an unpredictable environment; showed the effects of carrying and not having significant inventory."

"Excellent hands-on tool!"

"Great—Do more with it. Most people do not understand these concepts in Supply Chain."

"Good activity to prove the point of supply chain problems."

"Excellent! It truly helps you understand the 'bullwhip effect' and the challenge of running a business with your goal of maximizing profit."

SHD can also be a useful research platform for studying managerial/purchasing behavior, an opportunity we are currently also considering.[1]

---

[1] The authors are grateful to all of the students who participated in SHD at Loyola University Chicago, Purdue University, Elmhurst, and Carthage College—their insight has been invaluable. Our thanks go to Purdue University MBA alumni Jim Kunsman, Harish Lakshman, and John Porco for their contributions during the development of the exercise. Our appreciation also goes to Dr. James Ward of Purdue University for several discussions that were held during the earlier stages of the exercise, to Dr. Gary Wilson of Elmhurst College, and to Dr. James Zydiak of Loyola University Chicago for their continuous feedback on the implementation of the game.

References

DAVIS, T. (1993), "Effective Supply Chain Management," *Sloan Management Review*, Summer, 35–46.

FINE, C. (1998), *Clock Speed*, Perseus Books, Reading, MA, USA.

GOODWIN, J. AND S. FRANKLIN (1994), "The Beer Distribution Game: Using Simulation to Teach Systems Thinking," *Journal of Management Development*, 13, 8, 7–15.

LEE, H. AND C. BILLINGTON (1992), "Managing Supply Chain Inventory: Pitfalls and Opportunities," *Sloan Management Review*, Spring, 65–73.

———, V. PADMANABHAN, AND S. WHANG (1997a), "Information Distortion in a Supply Chain: The Bullwhip Effect," *Management Science*, 43, 4, 546–558.

———, ———, AND ——— (1997b), "The Bullwhip Effect in Supply Chains," *Sloan Management Review*, Spring, 93–102.

METTERS, R. (1997), "Quantifying the Bullwhip Effect in Supply Chains," *Journal of Operations Management*, 15, 89–100.

NICHOLAS, J. (1998), *Competitive Manufacturing Management*, Irwin McGraw-Hill, Burr Ridge, IL, USA.

SILVER, E. A., D. F. PYKE, AND R. PETERSON (1998), *Inventory Management and Production Planning and Scheduling*, John Wiley & Sons, New York.

STERMAN, J. D. (1989), "Modeling Managerial Behavior: Misperceptions of Feedback in a Dynamic Decision-Making Experiment," *Management Science*, 35, 3, 321–339.

Burak Kazaz is an Assistant Professor in the Information Systems and Operations Management Department in the School of Business in Loyola University Chicago. His primary research is in the area of global supply chain management with particular interest in the influence of fluctuating exchange rates. His work in this subject has been rewarded with awards and grants by institutions like IBM, APICS, and Loyola University Chicago. Dr. Kazaz conducts research in other areas as well, including project management, pricing, and optimization in manufacturing environments. His teaching responsibilities at Loyola include global supply chain management, logistics, and operations management in the Executive MBA, MBA, and undergraduate programs. Dr. Kazaz teaches the global supply chain management class in a dynamic environment in which he and his students implement consulting practices in BP Amoco. Recently, Dr. Kazaz was awarded by BP Amoco for his excellence in teaching and his contributions to the company.

Herbert Moskowitz is the Lewis B. Cullman Distinguished Professor of Manufacturing Management and is Director of the Dauch Center for the Management of Manufacturing Enterprises at the Krannert Graduate School of Management, Purdue University. His area of specialization is management science and quantitative methods, with emphasis on manufacturing and technology, total quality management, quality improvement tools, and judgment and decision making. He has been at Purdue since 1970 and has had visiting appointments at the University of Mannheim, West Germany, the University of British Columbia, the London Business School, and the Wharton School. He holds a BS degree in mechanical engineering, an MBA and a Ph.D. in management from UCLA. Dr. Moskowitz is the coauthor of five texts and has published about 140 articles in the areas of decision making, optimization, management science, and quality control in academic journals. He has obtained various grants for the National Science Foundation, the Office of Water Resources Technology, and other governmental agencies.

TEACHING SUPPLY CHAIN CONCEPTS WITH THE NEWSBOY MODEL*

NILS RUDI AND DAVID F. PYKE

The Simon School, University of Rochester, Rochester, New York 14627, USA
The Tuck School, Dartmouth College, Hanover, New Hampshire 03755, USA

This paper presents an alternative method of teaching the standard Newsboy model. In addition to a retailer, who orders using the Newsboy quantity, we also examine the profit of a manufacturer who supplies the retailer. We provide the reader with several solved homework problems that can generate significant student interest. The first addresses the effect of different wholesale prices and illustrates double marginalization. The second applies the model to a problem of postponing differentiation, the third deals with market structure, and the fourth involves a supply contracting problem using the theory of real options. We found that this method of teaching, and the supply chain exercises, generated significant student interest in an MBA elective.
(INVENTORY MODELS, NEWSBOY MODEL, REAL OPTIONS, SUPPLY CHAIN MANAGEMENT)

1. Introduction

The Newsboy model is a *single-period* inventory model often used for short-life-cycle products like fashion apparel, shoes, sporting goods, furniture, and toys. Certain popular case studies, such as Sport Obermeyer (Hammond and Raman 1994) and Mattel: Vendor Operations in Asia (Johnson 1998), address the supply chain issues of short-life-cycle products. Many instructors use these cases in conjunction with the Newsboy model to provide students with both strategic concepts and tactical tools (Johnson and Pyke 2000). Researchers have also employed the Newsboy model to investigate supply chain problems (e.g., Rudi and Zheng 1997; Corbett and Tang 1999). This model has been taught in Inventory electives and, more recently, in core Operations Management courses at both business schools and in industrial engineering programs. Most textbooks do not provide a formal derivation of the solution because of the assumed lack of capability of the students, or they apply Leibnitz's rule and place it in an appendix. See, for instance, Krajewski and Ritzman (1999), Nahmias (1997), and Silver, Pyke, and Peterson (1998).

In this paper, we present an alternative method of teaching the standard Newsboy model that does not rely on Leibnitz's rule and therefore is much more intuitive and accessible for many students. We begin by developing a technical note that can be used directly by students. It is contained in Sections 2 and 3 of this paper and is intended as stand-alone materials. In the first part of the note, Section 2 of this paper, we develop an intuitive expression for the

---

* Received September 1999; revision received October 1999; accepted November 1999.

expected profit function, transforming it to a form in which underage and overage costs are isolated. This form allows students to understand important managerial insights. We derive the retailer's optimal order quantity and discuss its impact on the retailer's and manufacturer's profit. We demonstrate how these values can be computed in Excel. Finally, we demonstrate interesting applications of the Newsboy model using solved problems. These illustrate concepts of double marginalization, postponement, and different market structure. Some of the problems are intended as student homework exercises, so answers are provided in the Appendix.

In the second part of the note, Section 3 of this paper, we introduce a supply contracting problem that uses some concepts from real options theory as a method to share risk between the retailer and the manufacturer. The results are identical to Pasternack (1985), but we found the concept of options to have higher appeal to finance-oriented MBA students than return prices. We show how the choice of the option price and the exercise price can replicate the optimal solution of an integrated firm as well as creating any allocation of the system profit.

Finally, in the Appendix, we provide a teaching note for conducting a class using the technical note. The teaching note expands on the solutions to the problems and provides insights from our experience with the material in a supply chain elective at Tuck.

Porteus (1990) presents the Newsboy model and several extensions for a more research-oriented audience. The approach presented here was used in Rudi and Zheng (1997) and in Rudi, Kapur, and Pyke (1999). Lau (1997) presents formulas for computing the expected cost for several probability distributions. Rudi and Zheng (1997) characterize the optimality conditions of the postponement problem addressed later in Homework Problem #2, and Zemel (1998) has developed a spreadsheet for computing the corresponding expected profit. Finally, see Pasternack (1985), Cachon (1999), Lariviere (1999), Tsay, Nahmias, and Agrawal (1999), Corbett and Tang (1999), and Anupindi and Bassok (1999) for other types of supply contracts. The next two sections can be handed out as a reading for students to use in preparation for class discussion.

2. The Newsboy Model

The Newsboy problem derives its name from a common problem faced by a person selling newspapers on the street. The merchant must decide, before observing demand, how many papers to buy; and once the day is over, the newspapers have little value. These decisions appear in a wide array of industries and they are notoriously difficult. Every Christmas, for instance, news reports focus on the inability to find certain extremely popular toys. At the same time, retailers are left with piles of toys that turned out to be less popular than expected.

In general, the Newsboy problem has the following characteristics. Before the season, the buyer must decide how many units of each item to purchase. The procurement lead time tends to be quite long relative to the selling season, so the buyer cannot observe demand before placing the order. Because of the long lead time, there is no opportunity to replenish inventory once the season has begun. Unfortunately, demand for these items tends to be highly uncertain, often because they are fashion goods whose styles change from season to season. Demand occurs during the selling season. If supply exceeds demand, the excess must be sold at a loss (salvaged), and if demand exceeds supply, the unmet demand is lost. The costs associated with these events are called overage and underage costs. *Overage costs* capture markdowns or inventory holding costs, if it is possible to carry stock over to the next year. *Underage costs* include lost profit margin, and perhaps the costs of expediting; buying stock from a competitor to meet the demand; and customer ill will.

2.1. Expected Profit

Consider a retailer who sells a short-life-cycle or single-period product. The retailer orders Q units (the decision variable) before the season at unit wholesale price W. Then demand D

is observed, and the retailer sells units (limited by the supply Q and the demand D) at unit revenue R (where $R > W$). Any excess units can be salvaged at unit salvage value S. For example, excess units can be sold on sale at a reduced price where $S < W$; they are sold at a loss. Before the selling season, demand is uncertain. However, the retailer knows the probability distribution of demand. Most of our analysis allows for a general, continuous demand distribution, but in computations we employ the normal distribution, which is commonly used in practice.

To facilitate the modeling we will introduce an important definition:

$$y^+ = \begin{cases} y & \text{if } y \geq 0 \\ 0 & \text{otherwise.} \end{cases}$$

We often call y^+ *the positive part of* y. For example, $3.4^+ = 3.4$ and $(-2)^+ = 0$.

Let us examine each term of the retailer's profit function. The retailer earns revenue from the units sold and she can recover some of the value of excess units through sale at the salvage value, but she must acquire each unit at the unit acquisition cost.

The number of units sold is limited by the demand D and by the supply Q. If $Q < D$, the retailer can sell Q units, and if $Q > D$ she can sell D units. So the revenues obtained by ordinary sales are the unit revenue R times the number of units sold, and can be expressed as:

$$R \min(D, Q).$$

If $Q > D$ then there are $Q - D$ units left over; and if Q is not larger than D, then there are no leftovers. Therefore, the number of units left over can be written as $(Q - D)^+$. The salvage value of the extra units is given by the unit salvage value times the number of units left over, yielding the following expression:

$$S(Q - D)^+.$$

Finally, the acquisition cost is simply the unit wholesale price W times the number of units bought Q. Because it is a cost, it is negative in the profit expression:

$$-WQ.$$

Because demand is unknown at the time of decision (i.e., when Q is determined), we are interested in the *expected profit as a function of* Q, which we denote by $\Pi_r(Q)$. From the previous discussion, we have that:

$$\Pi_r(Q) = E[R \min(D, Q) + S(Q - D)^+ - WQ]. \tag{1}$$

2.2. From Profit to Opportunity Cost

We will now manipulate $\Pi(Q)$ to rewrite it in a different form. For the first term, we use the rule:

$$\textit{Rule 1:} \quad \min(D, Q) = D - (D - Q)^+. \tag{2}$$

Let us verify this equation. If $Q < D$, then $D - (D - Q)^+ = D - (D - Q) = Q$, which is the same as the minimum of the two when Q is smaller than D. If $Q \geq D$, then $D - (D - Q)^+ = D - 0 = D$, which again reproduces the minimum of the two for the case that Q is greater than or equal to D. We can conclude that the rule is correct.

We do not rewrite the term reflecting the salvage value, but for the acquisition cost term, we use the following rule:

$$\textit{Rule 2:} \quad Q = D - (D - Q)^+ + (Q - D)^+. \tag{3}$$

Let us also verify this equation. If $Q < D$ then $D - (D - Q)^+ + (Q - D)^+ = D - (D$

$-Q) + 0 = Q$, which reproduces Q. If $Q \geq D$ we get $D - (D - Q)^+ + (Q - D)^+ = D - 0 + (Q - D) = Q$. Therefore, we see that this rule also is correct.

Using these two rules, we can rewrite $\Pi_r(Q)$ as the following expression:

$$\Pi_r(Q) = E[R(D - (D - Q)^+) + S(Q - D)^+ - W(D - (D - Q)^+ + (Q - D)^+)]. \quad (4)$$

By collecting similar terms, we get:

$$\Pi_r(Q) = (R - W)ED - \overbrace{E[(R - W)(D - Q)^+ + (W - S)(Q - D)^+]}^{G_r(Q)}. \quad (5)$$

The first term of this expression for the expected profit $(R - W)ED$ is the *unit margin* times the expected demand (i.e., the forecast). This term is the *expected profit with no demand uncertainty* (i.e., *perfect information*). The rest of the expression, defined as $G_r(Q)$, is then *the cost of demand uncertainty*. The first term of $G_r(Q)$ is the expected number of units short $(D - Q)^+$ times the unit opportunity cost per unit short $R - W$ (the lost margin). This unit opportunity cost is the *unit underage cost*:

$$C_u = R - W.$$

Similarly, the second term of $G_r(Q)$ consists of the expected number of leftover units $(Q - D)^+$ times the unit opportunity cost per unit left over, which is $W - S$. This unit opportunity cost is the *unit overage cost*:

$$C_o = W - S.$$

The expected cost of demand uncertainty can then be rewritten as:

$$G_r(Q) = E[C_u(D - Q)^+ + C_o(Q - D)^+]. \quad (6)$$

2.3. *Optimal Order Quantity*

The retailer must determine *the order quantity that will give the highest expected profit*. If we examine expression (5) we see that the first term does not have a Q in it. Therefore, the first term is not affected by the order quantity. Because of this, setting Q to maximize $\Pi_r(Q)$ gives the same result as setting Q to minimize $G_r(Q)$. This minimization is performed by taking the derivative of $G_r(Q)$ and then finding the value of Q that makes the derivative equal to zero.

By looking at expression (6) we see that the change in $(D - Q)^+$ when we increase Q by one unit (i.e., the derivative) is -1, with the probability that $D > Q$. That is, if D is not greater than Q, an increase in Q of one unit has no impact on $(D - Q)^+$ because the expression equals zero. If $D > Q$ an increase in Q by one unit causes $(D - Q)^+$ to decrease by one unit. It follows that the derivative of the first term of (6) is:

$$-C_u \Pr(D > Q).$$

By the same reasoning the change in $(Q - D)^+$ when we increase Q by one unit is 1, with the probability $\Pr(Q > D)$. Thus, the derivative of the second term of (6) is:

$$C_o \Pr(Q > D).$$

The derivative of $G(Q)$ is then:

$$G_r'(Q) = -C_u \Pr(D > Q) + C_o \Pr(Q > D). \quad (7)$$

Because $\Pr(D > Q) = 1 - \Pr(D < Q)$, we can rewrite the derivative as:

$$G_r'(Q) = -C_u[1 - \Pr(D < Q)] + C_o \Pr(D < Q). \quad (8)$$

By equating this derivative to zero and rearranging terms, we get the following *Newsboy optimality condition*:

$$\Pr(D < Q) = \frac{C_u}{C_u + C_o}. \tag{9}$$

If we can find the value of Q that satisfies expression (9), then this is the optimal value of Q, which we denote by Q^*.

NORMAL DISTRIBUTION. In this subsection assume that demand is normally distributed with expected value μ and standard deviation σ. We can then easily find the optimal order quantity using Microsoft's Excel spreadsheet:

$$Q^* = NORMINV(C_u/(C_u + C_o), \mu, \sigma).$$

EXAMPLE. Let $R = 100$, $W = 50$, and $S = 20$. Then

$$C_u = 100 - 50 = 50,$$

and

$$C_o = 50 - 20 = 30.$$

The right-hand side of the optimality condition then becomes:

$$\frac{50}{50 + 30} = 0.625.$$

Let the demand be normally distributed with mean $\mu = 1{,}000$ and standard deviation $\sigma = 300$. Then the optimal order quantity can be found by entering the following expression in a cell in Excel:

$$= NORMINV(0.625, 1{,}000, 300).$$

The result is $Q^* = 1{,}096$. This means that the optimal decision is to order 96 units more than the forecast.

2.4. *The Opportunity Cost and Expected Profit*

The opportunity cost expression is more difficult to calculate. For the normal distribution, we have the following formula in Excel:

$$G_r(Q^*) = \sigma \times (C_u + C_o) \times NORMDIST(NORMSINV(C_u/(C_u + C_o)), 0, 1, FALSE). \tag{10}$$

In our example, we can calculate $G(Q^*)$ by writing the following statement in an Excel cell:

$$= 300 \times 80 \times NORMDIST(NORMSINV(0.625), 0, 1, FALSE),$$

which gives the value $G(Q^*) = 9{,}101$.

Using this result, the expected profit is

$$\Pi_r(Q^*) = 50 \times 1{,}000 - 9{,}101 = \$40{,}899.$$

2.5. *How about the Manufacturer?*

Thus far we have considered only the retailer's decision. Supply chain management, however, is concerned primarily with improving the efficiency of multiple supply chain partners. Therefore, we extend the discussion to include a manufacturer who sells to the retailer. In our modeling scenario, the manufacturer responds to retailer requests by making units to order at unit production cost M. The manufacturer's profit when the retailer orders optimally is then:

$$\Pi_m = (W - M)Q^*. \tag{11}$$

Note that there is no uncertainty in this expression because the manufacturer produces to order and takes no risk.

For the normal distribution the manufacturer's profit can easily be computed in Excel by the following formula:

$$\Pi_m = (W - M) \times NORMINV(C_u/(C_u + C_o), \mu, \sigma).$$

If the manufacturer's unit production cost is $M = 30$, we can compute this in Excel by writing the following expression in a cell:

$$= 20 \times NORMINV(0.625, 1{,}000, 300).$$

Thus the manufacturer achieves a profit of $\Pi_m = \$21{,}912$.

Now test your understanding by completing the following three sample problems.

2.6. Homework Problem #1: Wholesale Price

For the previous example let the wholesale price W range from 31 to 99. Plot Π_r, Π_m, and $\Pi_r + \Pi_m$. Explain the behavior of the three graphs.

2.7. Homework Problem #2: Postponement

Yeah Inc. is a Canadian wholesaler of brightly colored T-shirts. Yeah orders the T-shirts from a contractor in Bangladesh. The lead time is 6 months and the selling season is 4 months during the summer. The unit revenue is $R = 2$, whereas the unit wholesale price of all colors is $W = 1$. The T-shirts come in four different colors, with specific parameters given in the following table:

Color	orange	yellow	lime green	signal red
μ	800	300	600	400
σ	300	170	200	130
S	0.75	0.80	0.70	0.75

1. What are the optimal order quantities of the different colors? What is the resulting expected profit? Use the "Postponement" spreadsheet to calculate the expected profit of Yeah Inc. when ordering these quantities.

   This spreadsheet calculates the expected profit, using Monte Carlo integration, for any order quantities of each color. It can be found at http://mba.tuck.dartmouth.edu/pages/faculty/dave.pyke/papers/Postponement.xls

2. A local dying company, Pink Ink Inc., contacts Yeah and suggests that it *postpone* the application of the color. This change involves buying uncolored (known as *greige*) T-shirts in Bangladesh. Pink Ink offers to color these T-shirts with a lead time of 3 days, implying that they can be colored to order. Using this method, Yeah will take the risk on the *total* quantity, rather than the quantity of each color. The expected demand for the total number of T-shirts is then 2,100 with standard deviation $\sqrt{(300^2 + 170^2 + 200^2 + 130^2)} = 419$. Unfortunately for Yeah, the unit cost will increase by 10% with Pink Ink. The unit salvage value of uncolored units is 0.80 (achieved by dying all units yellow and selling at yellow's salvage value). Using the postponement strategy, how many uncolored T-shirts should Yeah order? Using the spreadsheet, what is the expected profit?

3. What is your recommendation to Yeah?

2.8. *Homework Problem #3: Evaluating Different Market Structures*

NoNo is a producer of high-end YoYo's (they make only one product) at unit production cost $10. The YoYo's sell only during the summer, and a new model is launched every year. The total production lead time is 6 months.

1. The YoYo is currently sold in 100 different identical retailers. They pay a unit wholesale price of $15 and sell at unit revenue $30. Unit salvage value is $8. Each retailer faces a normal distribution of demand with mean of 100 and standard deviation of 40.
   a. How many YoYo's should each retailer order?
   b. What is the expected profit for each retailer?
   c. What is the manufacturer's profit?
2. Mississippi.com, a large Internet retailer, is planning to move into YoYo's. The company would pay a unit price of $13 and sell at unit revenue $25 (with salvage value the same, at $8), and would expect to get a demand of 5,000 units with standard deviation of 290.

The number of retailers would then be reduced to 50, each with expected demand of 120 units and standard deviation of 45. All cost and revenue parameters would stay the same for the retailers.
   a. How many YoYo's should each retailer order?
   b. How many YoYo's should Mississippi.com order?
   c. What is the manufacturer's profit?
3. Rather than using Mississippi.com, the manufacturer can choose to start up an Internet retailer called Nile.com to sell its YoYo's. Nile.com would then sell at the same unit revenue and have the same expected demand and standard deviation as Mississippi.com. There will, however, be some fixed costs associated with running Nile.com.

What is the maximum fixed cost of Nile.com that makes Nile.com preferable to using Mississippi.com (for the manufacturer)?

3. Supply Contract: Real Option

We now move to a type of supply contract that uses the concept of real options. With this type of contract, the manufacturer offers the following deal to the retailer: Ahead of the season, the retailer buys q call options at unit cost c. Each call option gives the retailer the right to buy a unit of the product at unit exercise price x after the retailer observes the demand. The idea is for the manufacturer to induce the retailer to buy more units, and thus capture more sales, by sharing some of the risk of demand uncertainty with the retailer.

3.1. *Expected Profit/Opportunity Cost*

Because the retailer needs to exercise one option for every unit sold, the retailer's unit revenue will be adjusted down by the exercise price. The expected profit of the retailer will then be the revenue minus the acquisition cost of the options, given by the following expression:

$$\pi_r(q) = (R - x) \min(D, q) - cq. \tag{12}$$

Using our rules of manipulation from the standard Newsboy model, we can rewrite this expected profit as:

$$\pi_r(q) = (R - x - c) ED - \overbrace{E[(R - x - c)(D - q)^+ + c(q - D)^+]}^{g_r(q)}. \tag{13}$$

Let $k_u = R - x - c$ (the unit opportunity cost of buying too few options) and $k_o = c$ (the unit opportunity cost of buying too many options). We then write the expected opportunity cost as:

$$g_r(q) = E[k_u(D-q)^+ + k_o(q-D)^+]. \tag{14}$$

3.2. Optimal Number of Options

This equation clearly corresponds to the Newsboy expected opportunity cost, and hence has the optimality condition:

$$\Pr(D < q) = \frac{k_u}{k_u + k_o}. \tag{15}$$

This can be solved using the corresponding method for the Newsboy model to give the optimal number of options q^* to buy.

3.3. Calculating Expected Profit

The difficult part of the expected profit, that is, the expected opportunity cost, can be found for the normal distribution by the Excel formula corresponding to the Newsboy model (for the case in which the retailer buys the optimal number of options):

$$g_r(q^*) = \sigma \times (k_u + k_o) \times NORMDIST(NORMSINV(k_u/(k_u + k_o)), 0, 1, FALSE). \tag{16}$$

Corresponding to the example for the Newsboy model, the expected profit can be computed by:

$$\pi_r(q^*) = (R - x - c)\mu - g_r(q^*). \tag{17}$$

3.4. Manufacturer's Profit

The profit for using real options differs quite a bit from the Newsboy model for the manufacturer. In this case the manufacturer also faces uncertainty because she does not know how many options will be exercised. Also, it is the manufacturer who is responsible for any extra units and hence will salvage these at the unit salvage value. The manufacturer's expected profit then is:

$$\pi_m(q) = E[(c - M)q + x \min(D, q) + S(q - D)^+]. \tag{18}$$

The first term of this expression is the net revenue received from producing q units at unit cost M and receiving c per unit from the retailer. The second term is the revenue x per exercised option, and the third term is the salvage value S per unit for each option that is not exercised.

For the normal distribution, we have:

$$\pi_m = (c + x - M)\mu - \sigma \times ((x - S)$$
$$\times NORMDIST(NORMSINV(k_u/(k_u + k_o)), 0, 1, FALSE)). \tag{19}$$

3.5. Homework Problem #4: Real Options

For this problem, use the data from the Newsboy example in Section 2.3 ($R = 100$, $W = 50$, $S = 20$, $M = 30$, $\mu = 1{,}000$, and $\sigma = 300$). Assume the manufacturer is considering two alternative real option contracts with $c = 31$ and $x = 20$, or $c = 6.5$ and $x = 48$.

1. For each of the two contracts, answer the following questions: How many options should the retailer buy? What will be the retailer's expected profit? What will be the manufacturer's expected profit?

2. If the manufacturer and the retailer merge into one company that strives to maximize its total profit, how much should this company produce? What is the resulting expected profit?

3. Compare the results for the Newsboy model (the example used in the text) and the results in questions 1 and 2. What are the reasons for the differences?[1]

[1] We thank the students in our Supply Chain Management elective at the Tuck School, Spring 1999, for feedback on this note. Two anonymous referees provided excellent suggestions that have improved this paper considerably.

Appendix. Teaching Note

In teaching this material to second-year MBA students in a Supply Chain Management elective, we required students to read a technical note consisting of Sections 2 and 3 of this paper. The postponement and option problems were assigned for homework after the lecture on this material. We discussed solutions and extensions in the following class. Therefore, the students were able to read the technical note, participate in a lecture/discussion on that material, and then exercise their skills using the problems. In this section, we provide a few additional comments on teaching this material based on our experience.

We began the lecture with a general, qualitative discussion of the characteristics of style goods. Students are asked to develop this list, and they mention such characteristics as high markups, sharp discounting, long lead times relative to the product life cycle, and high uncertainty about demand. They are then asked to suggest products that fit into the style goods category (see the list below). The point of this discussion is to convince them that the Newsboy material is important and potentially very useful.

We then present the model following the basic structure of Sections 2 and 3, taking questions and proceeding as slowly as necessary. Our experience is that students follow this material fairly easily, but it is necessary to take plenty of time presenting it. After a few examples and a brief introduction to the homework, the class ends.

Other Examples of the Newsboy Problem

Early in the lecture, the class creates a list of examples of products or industries that face the Newsboy problem. For the instructor's convenience we list a few here. [This list is based on Chapter 10 of Silver, Pyke, and Peterson (1998).]

1. The garment manufacturer (or retailer): What quantity of a particular style good should be produced (or bought for sale) before the short selling season?
2. The Christmas tree vendor: How many trees should be purchased to put on sale?
3. The cafeteria manager: How many hot meals of a particular type should be prepared before customers arrive?
4. The supermarket manager: How much meat or fresh produce should be purchased for a particular day of the week?
5. The administrator of a regional blood bank: How many donations of blood should be sought and how should they be distributed among hospitals?
6. The supplies manager in a remote region (for example, medical and welfare work in northern Canada): What quantity of supplies should be brought in by boat before the long winter freeze-up?
7. The farmer: What quantity of a particular crop should be planted in a specific season?
8. The toy manufacturer: A particular product shows significant potential sales as a "fad" item. How many units should be produced on the one major production run to be made?

The Wholesale Price Problem

This problem is useful for illustrating double marginalization. Answers to the problems can be found in the spreadsheet at http://mba.tuck.dartmouth.edu/pages/faculty/dave.pyke/papers/Problems.xls

We see from the solution that Π_r is decreasing in W, Π_m looks concave in W, and $\Pi_r + \Pi_m$ is decreasing in W. Also note that the only value for W that will replicate the optimal profit of an integrated firm is $W = R$.

One insight that can be useful to draw in class is that a franchise setup in which the retailer pays a fixed membership fee, while getting lower unit wholesale price W, will create a bigger pie to share between the manufacturer and the retailer.

The Postponement Problem

This problem illustrates the postponement problem. Out of two *pure* strategies, it shows that full postponement is not always the best approach. The third question illustrates that it is not necessarily *all or nothing*.

1. The optimal order quantities are (1052, 464, 747, 509) with corresponding expected profit of $1,819. These are found using independent order quantities from the standard Newsboy problem. However, to compare with part 3, one should use the "Postponement" spreadsheet, which uses a specific set of random numbers. The expected profit in this case is $1,828.
2. The optimal order quantity of the uncolored option is 2,383 with corresponding expected profit $1,730. Again, this is found using standard analytical Newsboy formulas. Using the Postponement spreadsheet yields a profit of $1,738.
3. The smart student will identify the opportunity to combine the two technologies. A close-to-optimal solution,

found by using the Solver on the Postponement spreadsheet, is (875, 270, 557, 357) for the colored items, and 503 for the greige item, with corresponding expected profit of $1,899. Many other solutions, with expected profit values very close to this, are possible. This might seem like a small increase. But when one considers the fact that the industry bottom-line profit averages 3% of revenues, this will have a huge impact on bottom-line profit (a >50% increase). The optimal solution to this combined strategy is characterized in Rudi and Zheng (1997).

The Market Structures Problem

We found this problem useful in showing that the Newsboy model can be used to quantify the effects of different strategies.

For part 1, we follow the simple Newsboy presentation of Section 2.3. We have $R = 30$, $W = 15$, and $S = 8$. Then

$$C_u = 30 - 15 = 15,$$

and

$$C_o = 15 - 8 = 7.$$

The right-hand side of the optimality condition then becomes:

$$\frac{15}{15 + 7} = 0.682.$$

The demand is normally distributed with mean $\mu = 100$ and standard deviation $\sigma = 40$. Then the optimal order quantity can be found by entering the following expression in a cell in Excel:

$$= NORMINV(0.682, 100, 40).$$

The result is $Q^* = 119$.

We can calculate $g(Q^*)$ by writing the following statement in an Excel cell:

$$= 40 \times 22 \times NORMDIST(NORMSINV(0.682), 0, 1, FALSE),$$

which gives the value $G(Q^*) = 314$.

Therefore, the expected profit is

$$\Pi_r(Q^*) = 15 \times 100 - 314 = \$1,186.$$

The manufacturer's profit, for $M = 10$, is:

$$= 100 \times 5 \times NORMINV(0.682, 100, 40).$$

Thus the manufacturer achieves profit of $\Pi_m = \$59,456$.

For part 2, we now have $R = 25$, $W = 13$, and $S = 8$ for Mississippi.com. With mean demand of $\mu = 5,000$ and standard deviation $\sigma = 290$, Mississippi should order $Q^* = 5157$ YoYo's. The retailers have $\mu = 120$ and $\sigma = 45$, and the cost parameters as before. Therefore, each retailer should order $Q^* = 141$ units.

The manufacturer's profit, for $M = 10$, is based on their sales to Mississippi.com and to the 50 retailers. From the retailers, the manufacturer receives a profit of $35,319, using the previous formula, and from Mississippi, the manufacturer receives $15,471, for a total of $50,790.

For part 3, Nile.com would have $R = 25$, $M = 10$, and $S = 8$. With mean demand of $\mu = 5,000$ and standard deviation $\sigma = 290$, Nile should order $Q^* = 5344$. The retailer results would be identical to those in part 2.

The manufacturer's profit on its own sales would be $74,027. From the retailers, the manufacturer would earn profit of $35,319, as in part 2. Thus, the total profit would be $109,356, or a gain of $58,556 over the $50,790 earned from Mississippi. Therefore, the manufacturer could afford a fixed cost of $58,556 to run Nile.com.

The Real Options Problem

The first real options contract ($c = 31$ and $x = 20$) gives $q = 1086$ with $\pi_r = \$39,809$ and $\pi_m = \$21,000$ which, compared to the standard Newsboy model, is worse for both. [Note the correspondence between the model of real options and the returns problem (Pasternack 1985). The unit wholesale price in the returns problem is then $c + x$ and the unit payback for returns is x.]

The second contract, however, gives $q = 1,345$ with $\pi_r = \$42,289$ and $\pi_m = \$22,771$, which replicates the solution of the integrated firm.

It follows that a real option contract can be very valuable if the parameters are set correctly. If time and student background permit, it may be interesting to look at combinations of c and x that will replicate the expected total profit of an integrated firm. Because the expected profit of an integrated firm is concave in the order quantity, the number of options needs to be equal to the optimal order quantity of an integrated firm. To achieve this, we equate the right-hand side of the respective newsboy fractiles:

$$\frac{R - x - c}{R - x} = \frac{R - M}{R - S}.$$

Solving with respect to x gives

$$x = R - c\frac{R - S}{M - S}, \quad \text{for } c \in \left(0, R\frac{M - S}{R - S}\right).$$

References

ANUPINDI, R., AND Y. BASSOK (1999), "Supply Contracts with Quantity Commitments and Stochastic Demand," in *Quantitative Models for Supply Chain Management*, S. Tayur, M. Magazine, and R. Ganeshan (eds.), Kluwer Academic Publishers, Boston, MA, 197–232.

CACHON, G. P. (1999), "Competitive Supply Chain Inventory Management," in *Quantitative Models for Supply Chain Management*, S. Tayur, M. Magazine, and R. Ganeshan (eds.), Kluwer Academic Publishers, Boston, MA, 111–146.

CORBETT, C. J. AND C. S. TANG (1999), "Designing Supply Contracts: Contract Type and Information Asymmetry," in *Quantitative Models for Supply Chain Management*, S. Tayur, M. Magazine, and R. Ganeshan (eds.), Kluwer Academic Publishers, Boston, MA, 269–298.

HAMMOND, J. H. AND A. RAMAN (1994), "Sport Obermeyer, Ltd.," Unpublished Harvard Case Study (9-695-022), Harvard University, Cambridge, MA.

JOHNSON, M. E. (1998), "Mattel: Vendor Operations in Asia," Unpublished Case Study, Owen School of Business, Vanderbilt University, Nashville, TN, and Tuck School of Business, Dartmouth College, Hanover, NH.

——— AND D. F. PYKE (2000), "A Framework for Teaching Supply Chain Management," *Production and Operations Management*, forthcoming.

KRAJEWSKI, L. AND L. RITZMAN (1999), *Operations Management: Strategy and Analysis*, 5th. ed., Addison-Wesley, New York.

LARIVIERE, M. A. (1999), "Supply Chain Contracting and Coordination with Stochastic Demand," in *Quantitative Models for Supply Chain Management*, S. Tayur, M. Magazine, and R. Ganeshan (eds.), Kluwer Academic Publishers, Boston, MA, 233–268.

LAU, H. (1997), "Simple Formulas for the Expected Costs in the Newsboy Problem: An Educational Note," *European Journal of Operational Research*, 100, 557–561.

NAHMIAS, S. (1997), *Production and Operations Analysis*, 3rd. ed., Irwin, Chicago, IL.

PASTERNACK, B. A. (1985), "Optimal Pricing and Returns Policies for Perishable Commodities," *Marketing Science*, 4, 166–176.

PORTEUS, E. L. (1990), "Stochastic Inventory Theory," in *Handbooks in OR & MS, Vol.* 2, D. P. Heyman and M. J. Sobel (eds.), Elsevier Science Publishers, North-Holland, Amsterdam, 605–652.

RUDI, N. AND Y.-S. ZHENG (1997), "Multi-item Newsboy Model with Partial Variety Postponement," Presentation, INFORM Dallas, TX, October 1997.

———, S. KAPUR, AND D. F. PYKE (1998), "A Two-Location Inventory Model with Transshipment and Local Decision Making," Working paper, The Wharton School, University of Pennsylvania, Philadelphia, PA.

SILVER, E. A., D. F. PYKE, AND R. PETERSON (1998), *Inventory Management and Production Planning and Scheduling*, 3rd. ed., John Wiley & Sons, New York.

TSAY, A. A., S. NAHMIAS, AND N. AGRAWAL (1999), "Modeling Supply Chain Contracts: A Review," in *Quantitative Models for Supply Chain Management*, S. Tayur, M. Magazine, and R. Ganeshan (eds.), Kluwer Academic Publishers, Boston, MA, 299–336.

ZEMEL, E. (1998), "Spreadsheet for Postponed Differentiation," personal communication.

Nils Rudi recently joined the faculty of the Simon School, University of Rochester. He is a Ph.D. candidate at The Wharton School, University of Pennsylvania. Before Ph.D. studies, he worked in software development while taking a B.S. at Molde College in Norway part time. His research interests include supply chain management and models of risk pooling.

David Pyke is Professor of Operations Management at the Tuck School of Business Administration at Dartmouth College. His research interests include supply chain management, inventory systems, logistics, manufacturing in China, and manufacturing strategy.

TEACHING SUPPLY CHAIN MANAGEMENT THROUGH GLOBAL PROJECTS WITH GLOBAL PROJECT TEAMS*

LAURA ROCK KOPCZAK
Department of IEEM, Stanford University, Stanford, California 94305-4024

JAN C. FRANSOO
Eindhoven University of Technology, 5600 MB Eindhoven, The Netherlands

In this article, we describe the Global Project Coordination Course, a course in which project teams composed of three students from each of two overseas universities execute company-sponsored projects dealing with global supply chain management issues. The $75,000 to $100,00 contributed in total by the three to four sponsoring companies funds all course expenses. We assess the benefits and challenges of the use of cross-cultural project teams with diverse educational backgrounds. We conclude that the course provides a unique and effective vehicle for furthering students' knowledge of Supply Chain Management and Information Systems, improving understanding of "soft" issues, and training students to work in diverse, global, cross-cultural project teams.
(SUPPLY CHAIN MANAGEMENT, EDUCATION, PROJECT COURSE, INTERNATIONAL)

1. Introduction

This article describes the Global Project Coordination Course (GPC). The GPC is a Master's-level course in which three students from each of two universities on different parts of the globe form a joint project team to work on a company-sponsored project that addresses a global business issue. The sponsoring company contributes $25,000 to cover course expenses for that project. The course was started in 1996 by Professor Hau L. Lee at Stanford University, working with his counterparts at two "partner" universities: Dr. Jan Fransoo at Eindhoven University of Technology and Professor Mitchell Tseng at Hong Kong University of Science and Technology. The course has since been expanded to include the National University of Singapore and the Royal Institute of Technology in Stockholm. Fourteen projects will be completed under the GPC structure in 1999.

We focus here on the section of the course that we teach. This section teams 9–12 students from Stanford University with 9–12 students from Eindhoven University of Technology to work on 3–4 projects dealing with global supply chain management issues. Both Stanford and Eindhoven have a tradition of requiring students to do company-sponsored projects (see Wouters and Van Donselaar 1999 for a description of another project-based SCM course taught at Eindhoven).

Many of our students will take jobs in which they will work in or lead global project teams

*Reprinted from *Production and Operations Management*, Vol. 9, No. 1, Spring 2000, pp. 91–104.

to implement supply chain innovations. These teams will represent multiple sites within the same company, as well as multiple companies within the same supply chain. This course has been structured to simulate this setting to provide students with critical skills required for this type of work. As will be described, we have found the course to be an ideal vehicle for improving students' capabilities in four areas:
- Project management and consulting skills
- Knowledge of supply chain management (SCM) and information systems (IS) theory and how to apply the theory in a real setting
- Understanding of "soft" SCM issues
- Ability to work effectively in a global, cross-cultural project team with a diverse set of skills and knowledge.

The course bears some similarities to a course that is taught at USC (Kumar and El Sawy 1998); in both courses, students learn to integrate SCM and IS concepts and apply them to a real-world project sponsored by a global company. The GPC, however, is unique in three ways. First, students work in global, cross-cultural project teams with diverse educational backgrounds. This simulates the kinds of project teams that they will work in when they graduate. Second, the course goes beyond a 1-day (overseas) field trip to the sponsoring company; there are at least three face-to-face meetings with the sponsor and frequent teleconferences and videoconferences. Unlike the USC course, the GPC commences and concludes with "live" multiday meetings of the project team (companies included), one at Stanford and the other at Eindhoven. In between, the students have weekly or bi-weekly conference calls and videoconferences with the company, and make 2-day visits to at least two company sites in Europe and the United States. Third, since the focus is on SCM, students typically visit or interview multiple companies and multiple sites of a single company and so must understand the different viewpoints of the various companies and sites. They must also deal with issues of trust, confidentiality, and power, and differences in cost accounting systems. The project scope often includes defining how the solution can be "sold" to supply chain partners. We will elaborate on these unique aspects of the course and how they affect learning in Section 4.

In addition to training future practitioners, the Global Projects Course supports our universities' goals of advancing the theory and practice of supply chain management in other ways (see Figure 1). On the research front, by solving a company's specific problem, the course professors develop an understanding of a real-life problem on which to base development of relevant and generalizable theory. It also builds a bond with the company, which fosters continued cooperation, making it easier to work with the company to obtain feedback on ideas, real-world examples and company data as the research progresses.

As we solicit and run projects and execute follow-on research, we consider and pursue opportunities for creating outputs beyond the project report and final presentation. These range from industry presentations and articles in business magazines to presentations at academic conferences and articles in academic journals to development of teaching cases and other teaching materials.

The remainder of the paper is structured as follows. We discuss course logistics in Section 2 and then provide an example of a project that was completed in this course in Section 3. Section 4 describes what and how the students learn. Section 5 discusses how to start such a course. We conclude in Section 6.

2. Course Schedule and Logistics

The schedule for the Stanford-Eindhoven section of the course is shown in Figure 2. The professors start recruiting and defining projects in November, so that they are ready to kick off in the first week of January, at the beginning of Stanford's winter quarter. This can be tricky, as a company must be found that has a project that is appropriate in both scope and

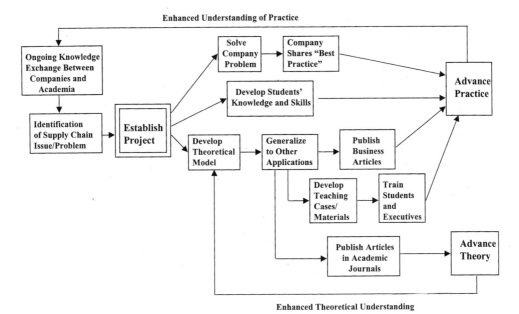

FIGURE 1. How Projects Contribute to Supply Chain Theory and Practice.

timing. Companies must also have the manpower available to support the project. Often the project sponsors are companies that have close ongoing ties to the universities. Both Stanford and Eindhoven have strong ties to industry through supply chain research centers—industry affiliate groups—which they call Forums. (For information on the Forums, visit their web sites: www.stanford.edu/gr/ and www.tue.nl/tm/efgscm/.)

We look for projects that:

1. involve a multiregional supply chain—ideally Europe and the United States or a comparison of U.S. and European supply chains—and so take best advantage of the global nature of the team,

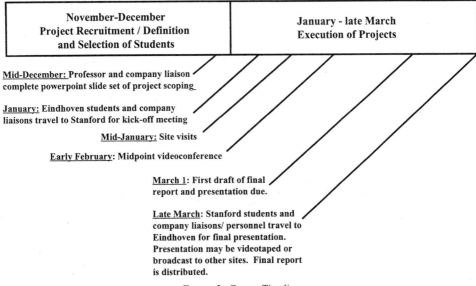

FIGURE 2. Course Timeline.

2. involve both "hard" issues, such as improving physical flows and information flows to improve cost, service and lead time, as well as "soft" issues such as risk-sharing, competitive strategy, and "selling" solutions to partners,

3. require students to understand the viewpoints of multiple companies or multiple sites of a single company in the supply chain,

4. have modest data requirements, with reasonable modeling requirements, and

5. relate to our current or future research interests.

Sponsoring companies and topics are listed in Table 1. We have intentionally solicited projects from different companies each year, to increase the number of relationships that we are developing through the course. We maintain the relationships through periodic informal meetings and through specific opportunities for collaboration, as they arise (e.g., joint research).

We have also sought out projects that relate to our research interests. Specifically, we have done several projects related to innovations in third-party logistics (Hewlett-Packard, Fritz, GeoLogistics, Solectron) and two related to supply chain management in capacity constrained industries (Manugistics, TI, and Nokia). As we do these projects, we look for opportunities to do joint research with the companies in the future.

The $25,000 sponsorship fee is shared by the two universities. The fee covers project expenses such as instructor salaries, travel, communications, and production of the final report. In contrast to some MBA project courses that have been initiated recently (Haynes and Setton 1998), the course is not intended to generate revenue for the school.

Student selection proceeds differently at the two universities. Eindhoven requires students to take the course as part of their postgraduate Logistics and Supply Chain Design degree program. The number of students in this program determines the number of projects to be run. (Typically there are 9–12 students available, allowing 3–4 projects to be run.) The program includes 18 months of courses focused on design of supply chains and their control structures. In addition, students complete three part-time, 2-month projects with companies in parallel to the regular courses and a 6-month, full-time internship after the regular courses. For some of the Dutch students, the GPC is their third 2-month project, and they are fairly

TABLE 1
Examples of GPC Projects: Stanford–Eindhoven Section

Year	Sponsoring Company	Topic
1996	Hewlett-Packard	Distribution in Emerging Markets: Country-Based versus Regional Distribution Centers
1996	Fritz Companies/Yazaki	Third Party Logistics: Inbound Parts Supply to a First Tier Automotive Supplier
1997	Lucent Technologies	Evaluation of Materials Management Methods: In What Environments is 3C Superior to MRP?
1997	Eclipse Group	Supply Chain Consulting: Identification and Characterization of Potential European Partners
1998	Manugistics	Opportunities for Advanced Planning Systems in the Pharmaceutical Supply Chain: the United States versus Europe
1998	GeoLogistics	Conditions for Applicability of Merge-in-Transit-based Distribution
1998	TI and Nokia	Supply of Semiconductors to Nokia: Achieving Flexibility Through Capacity and/or Inventory
1998	Quantum	Disk Drive Service Concept and Processes: How Can Quantum Increase the Value it Provides to OEM Customers?
1999	Ericsson	Evaluation of Radio Base Station Spare Parts Service Concept and Processes
1999	Ericsson	Streamlining Flows of Demand and Forecast Information through Multiple Tiers of the Supply Chain
1999	Solectron	Vendor Managed Inventory: Decision Processes and Plan for Roll-out to Suppliers and Customers

adept at scoping out and developing solutions for real-world supply chain problems by the time they take the GPC. For others, it may be their second project.

A matching number of Stanford students is selected as follows. At Stanford, the course is an elective. Students must submit resumes with a cover letter explaining their strengths and interest in supply chain management. Once projects have been found, project teams with diverse skills and knowledge are created by selecting students with varying work experience, nationality, skills, and knowledge of SCM and IT. Students come mainly from Masters-level programs in Business, Operations Research, and Industrial Engineering. In addition to having SCM expertise on the team, it is advantageous to have someone who has significant work experience to lead the team, as well as someone who is analytical (enjoys modeling), and someone who is strong in strategy and/or marketing.

In early January, the Eindhoven students, professor, and company representatives travel to Stanford to launch the projects. Over 3 days each student team (three students from each university) gets to know one another, learns about the project from the company, develops a work plan for the project, and presents it back to the company for feedback. The work plan focuses on the tasks, schedule, and communications plan. Students also go through an exercise in which they identify their personality type, using the Enneagram system (Baron and Wagele 1994), and brainstorm with members of their team what conflicts may arise because of personality differences and how they can deal with them. Through the exercise the students become aware of how much variation in personality is present among individuals in both cultures. As the groups work together over the semester, the students become cognizant of cultural and individual differences and learn to distinguish between the two.

Either at the kick-off or in the following week, the professors work with each other and with the team to identify theoretical concepts and best practice examples that can be applied and to define how knowledge will be developed within the group. This is important because there will be a difference in knowledge bases between the U.S. and Dutch students, and within the U.S. team. (This will be explained in more detail in Section 4.)

The Dutch students then return home. Over the next 8 weeks, the students visit company and supply chain partner sites in their regions and work independently, communicating with each other and with the company by e-mail, telephone, videoconference, and Internet. Early on in the project, they draw out the physical flows and information flows and characterize the key problems. Gaining agreement between the team and the company regarding this characterization is the objective of the first milestone meeting with the company (after the kick-off). In many cases, it is found that the view of the problem varies across different sites of the company, and even more so across companies.

The students gather sufficient quantitative data to start some of the modeling work. The modeling work is based on knowledge that the students have acquired in earlier classes or models from the academic literature. The modeling work eventually enables them not only to identify solutions to the problems, but also to quantify the relative magnitude of the problems and impact of the proposed solutions. In the final phase of the project, the students draw up proposed solutions to the problems they encountered, possibly by gathering additional information, e.g., at vendors of information system solutions. The last period of the project is spent writing the report and preparing the final presentation. Since the company liaison is closely involved during the entire trajectory, he or she gradually "evolves" with the project team toward the proposed solution. This greatly helps in transferring ownership of the solution from the project team to the company.

About halfway through the course, the students present a PowerPoint presentation to the company liaisons by videoconference. The presentation reviews the project scope, presents intermediate findings, explains remaining work, and previews the format and content of the final deliverables. This is a critical milestone—any problems with project scope or differences in understanding of the deliverables must be worked out at this point.

A draft of the final report and presentation is due March 1. Detailed feedback is given by both professors and by the company within days. This is done via a combination of e-mail and telephone conferences. In our experience, this milestone greatly improves the quality of the final report, because the students do not want to deliver shabby work to the company and therefore treat it as a final report. The scope and structure do not change dramatically from the draft to the final report, but details may change or be filled in, and slide content and the flow of the topics and story line improve significantly.

In late March, the Stanford students, professor, and company representatives travel to Eindhoven for the final presentation. Some companies have flown in up to seven people from around the world to attend the final presentation. If a company site is located at a reasonable driving distance from the Eindhoven campus, the final presentation may be held there. Companies also often ask students to make the presentation a second time at their site (e.g., in the United States, France, or Sweden), so that more people can attend. Related additional expenses are fully covered by the sponsoring companies. Final presentations also may be videotaped and broadcast to remote sites. The other major deliverable is a final report. To make the report easy to read for company executives, the body of the report is structured around the presentation slides, with a slide on the lefthand page and related text on the corresponding righthand page.

The project concludes with a 45-minute debrief session in which the companies, team members, and professors discuss how they as individuals experienced the course (project) and what they would do differently "next time." This is done in a very open and positive way, so that the impressions and perspectives of the different students can come out. After letting the conversation flow for some time, we ask questions such as, "how did the kick-off contribute to the success of the project—what went wrong and what went right?" and "what difficulties did you as a team experience during the project?" Through the session, the students reflect on the process of running a global project, shifting away from the focus on project content that has dominated their thinking as they prepared for the final presentation. We find the students to be quite mature in recognizing their own failings and translate this understanding into an assessment of what they would do differently "next time around." These debriefs have also been instrumental in improving our class over the years.

3. Example: Reverse Logistics at Quantum

In this section, we describe a project in order to give an example of the scope and nature of a typical GPC project in the supply chain domain. The project was carried out for Quantum Corporation, a manufacturer of hard disk drives and addressed their reverse supply chain. The project team consisted of three students from the Eindhoven Logistics and Supply Chain Design program, one from Stanford's Industrial Engineering program, and two Stanford MBA students.

The Quantum project addressed the development of a service product for Quantum. In the current structure, the original equipment manufacturer (OEM) (e.g., Compaq), the OEM's customers, and the hard disk drive manufacturer keep swap stocks to immediately replace a nonfunctioning disk drive with a new or repaired one. The student team designed a new concept, to be presented by Quantum as a service product to the OEM. The concept included reduction of the swap stocks in the system, increasing the frequency of component deliveries, reducing the total flow of broken components through early screening of components that only appear to be broken, and streamlining of the customer interface. The whole concept was packaged as a complete service product, to be offered to the OEM in order to increase consumer satisfaction and reduce costs for both the OEM and Quantum.

The Stanford students visited Quantum's corporate-level service organization, located in Milpitas, California. (The project liaison was a Milpitas employee.) The Eindhoven students visited Quantum's European service site in Dundalk, Ireland. They also contacted some OEMs to get their inputs. The students held regular telephone and videoconferences, sometimes including the Quantum liaison.

Quantum asked the students to look at the problem from four points of view:
1. Marketing: propose a service product and describe its appeal to OEMs and end users;
2. Cost/service: analyze how offering the proposed product would affect costs and service along the supply chain;
3. Competition: assess to what extent the product could be used to create competitive advantage for Quantum; and
4. Business requirements: detail the migration path, including investment requirements and risk.

The assignment required the students to think about the logistics structure of the reverse supply chain, as well as how an improved and more efficient reverse supply chain could assist in better marketing of the Quantum product as a whole. The students did a sound analysis of the logistics system, including a cost estimate of the new operations. This was based on a multiechelon inventory analysis. Using industry transportation cost and inventory carrying cost data, they projected the cost impact of having more frequent, smaller shipments of parts through the reverse supply chain and how costs and benefits would accrue to Quantum, the OEM, and the customer.

During the project, the team diversity led to conflict over the project scope and direction. While the engineers felt the team should focus on a detailed analysis of the supply chain flows, the MBA students did not value that level of detail and concentrated on understanding customer requirements and strategic implications for Quantum. This again was not understandable to the engineers. A significant portion of phone and videoconference time and energy was expended on attempts to reconcile the two viewpoints. With guidance from the professors and leadership of the Quantum liaison, the two sides eventually came to respect and trust each other's work. The team came up with a strong set of recommendations that clearly and thoughtfully incorporated all points of view. The team came to view team diversity as the team's greatest strength. This was a key take-away for the group.

4. What and How Students Learn

In this section, we will discuss how this course supports development of students' capabilities in each of the four areas mentioned earlier:
- Project management and consulting skills
- Knowledge and application of SCM and IS theory,
- Understanding of "soft" SCM issues, and
- Ability to work effectively in a diverse, global, cross-cultural project team.

Project Management and Consulting Skills

Since many courses include group projects that support development of these skills, we will not delve into this aspect here. As will be discussed below, the international setting and global project team do add some nuances that are not present in a typical class project. In working for an international sponsor, teams must work harder to understand the client. For example, a Swedish sponsor prefaced an e-mail with feedback on the midpoint presentation by indicating that the e-mail only included negative comments and that that was a reflection of how they worked, not their level of satisfaction with the students' output. The students found it difficult to figure out which things the client liked and to decide which concepts to develop further. In addition, culture may influence company norms about format and content of slide presentations and report. For example, some European sponsors look for more analysis and detail than would their U.S. counterparts.

Knowledge and Application of SCM and IS Theory

Most projects require the students to perform traditional analyses of supply chain structure, physical flows, information flows, planning and manufacturing cycle times, and inventory policies and how they affect the cost/service trade-off curve. Students typically apply simple inventory models, such as the news vendor model and periodic or continuous replenishment models. They also analyze the supply chain and recommend where inventory control points should be located and how control should be implemented. These types of models were used in an early project that compared the use of country-based versus regional distribution centers for distributing Hewlett-Packard LaserJet printers in Latin America and in Eastern Europe. They were later used in a project sponsored by Texas Instruments and Nokia to address the question of how to achieve flexibility—through inventory or through capacity. Multiechelon models were used in the Ericsson-sponsored project on spare parts and in the Manugistics-sponsored project on pharmaceutical industry supply chains.

Recently, companies have been interested in understanding how information flows can be streamlined to reduce inventory levels and to move the Customer Order Decoupling Point farther upstream. In one project, the students measured the Bullwhip Effect. In the project that Lucent sponsored, students compared supply chain performance under MRP-based procurement to performance under an alternative, pull-based procurement system that generated demand signals for suppliers based on shipments to customers. Companies are also interested in Internet-based solutions and recommendations about software and systems. We have been able to provide this analysis by identifying the project requirement early and selecting a Stanford student who has worked for an enterprise or supply chain software company to be on the project team. Furthermore, since Stanford is in Silicon Valley, it has been easy for Stanford students to visit leading-edge software companies.

The GPC seeks to reinforce, apply, and develop concepts that have already been studied in a lecture-based class. Thus, this class complements other classes that most of the students have taken. (See Table 2 for a listing of the main SCM-related courses at Eindhoven and Stanford and the topics covered.) Some of the students, however, need to play catch-up while in the class. Although this learning process suffices for the purposes of the project, we believe that a regular structured class adds this type of value in a more effective and efficient way.

One issue that we have encountered is a strong tendency for students to favor the literature and theories that are most familiar to them and to reject theories suggested by the other half of the team. For example, while the U.S. students know about postponement, the Dutch students are familiar with the Customer Order Decoupling Point. The concepts are both useful and can be used together, but it can be a challenge to get the teams to accept them. We mention this issue during the kick-off and deal with it to some extent by having students use the same inventory textbook by Silver, Pyke, and Peterson (see Appendix A). We also work with the team early to generate a list of potentially useful theoretical concepts and then provide papers on those concepts for the whole team to read. We also suggest teaching cases and papers about best practices for the team to read. Some of the papers that we have found to be useful are listed in Appendix A. This list corresponds to some extent to the papers that students read in their lecture-based classes. Since the Dutch students read additional papers in Dutch that are therefore not accessible to the full team, our list is understandably U.S.-centric.

Understanding of "Soft" SCM Issues

Recently, companies have been interested in using the projects to address softer supply chain management issues, such as risk-sharing, power, and competitive strategy and and selling proposed solutions to supply chain partners. We have sought out these types of projects, as we feel this is a key area of learning for the students. For example, Texas Instruments and Nokia were interested in how to share risk related to excess capacity and/or inventory. Quantum sought advice on how to create competitive advantage by redefining its service concept and process to increase the value created for OEM customers such as HP and IBM, and Solectron asked the students to make recommendations about how they should present (sell) their Vendor Managed Inventory program to plants, suppliers, and customers.

For these issues, we have not found useful theoretical articles and feel that a "learning-

TABLE 2
Lecture-Based Logistics and SCM-Related Topics and Courses at Eindhoven and Stanford

Eindhoven (Selection)	Stanford
Operations research introduction course • Basic inventory models • Basic queueing models • Linear programming • Project planning	Operations research introduction course • Basic inventory models • Basic queueing models • Linear and dynamic programming
Information models for production and logistics • ERP systems (functional and data modeling) • Workflow control	MBA core operations course • Basic inventory models • Postponement • Capacity planning • Accurate response
Production control • Hierarchical production planning • Workload/leadtime control • Assembly lines	Inventory management course • Basic inventory models • Postponement • MRP/JIT/Kanban
System dynamics • Bullwhip effect • Information distortion	SCM elective • Postponement • Bullwhip effect/information distortion • Vendor managed inventory • Third-party logistics • Tax issues
Goods flow control • Forecasting • MRPI/MRPII/base stock/JIT/Kanban	
Operations research courses on mathematical modeling and simulation	SCM and IT elective • Capabilities of ERP, advanced planning, linking software • Internet-based coordination • Collaborative planning • SC requirements of E-commerce
Design of production control systems Design of distribution control systems Design of warehousing control systems Logistics strategy Logistics organizational design Industrial marketing and logistics Purchasing and supply management	Operations research courses on mathematical modeling and simulation

by-doing" approach is the best way to teach these concepts. In approaching these issues, students interview multiple parties in the supply chain and find they must get around company politics, hidden agendas, biased information, and sloganeering in trying to develop a reasonably accurate representation of the costs and benefits of proposed actions or alternatives. When collecting cost data, they find that the costs are not tracked accurately or in the appropriate buckets and that companies want to emphasize some costs and ignore others. Furthermore, they must deal with the issue of whether they represent the sponsoring company's interests or the supply chain's interests in their analyses and recommendations.

We coach the students on techniques for trying to extract fact from fiction, encourage them to check things by finding data or second sources for information, and challenge them when they take things at face value. We also make sure that they represent the team's views in the final report, indicating assumptions and gaps in data or information. It is helpful to select some team members that are MBA students who have confronted these issues to some extent in case discussions, as well as people with work experience who have dealt with these issues as part of their work.

Ability to Work Effectively in a Diverse, Global, Cross-Cultural Project Team

The GPC balances coaching with a learning-by-doing approach in fostering development of the technical and social skills needed to work at a distance with people from other cultures and organizations. This is a key course goal—at the kick-off, project teams often develop two mission statements: one related to the project and another related to personal development.

During the kick-off, we point out the challenges that students will encounter, and encourage them to strive to detect and correct problems early, before they destroy team cohesiveness and trust. As part of our weekly meetings with the team, we ask them to list current project issues and to categorize them as team-internal, team and company, or team and professor. When we review these issues with them, we stress the importance of spending time on ironing out conflicts and coach them on how to resolve conflicts quickly. Sometimes teams must devote a telephone conference to air grievances and rebuild lost trust; sometimes teams must go back to the company to resolve disagreements on scope and direction.

One issue students must overcome is the technical difficulties of working at a distance. At both the kick-off and the final presentation, half the team is suffering from jet lag. The students also must deal with the time difference throughout the project. Whereas the students plan, at the start of the project, to make productive use of the time difference (9 hours between Stanford and Eindhoven), it usually only leads to delays. During the kick-off, the students plan to update each other at the end of each day, to maximize the effectiveness of the work that their counterparts will do while they sleep. Late updates, however, ensure that possible days of project work disappear like melting ice. Addressing these issues in a regular class is not likely to have much impact on students; in fact, in the introductory sessions we discuss this issue explicitly. However, experience built during the course of the project makes a big impression on the students and teaches them to adjust their ways of working.

Each student team decides how they will communicate. Students find that e-mail, faxes, and phone conferences are useful. Internet-based chat room software, such as that offered by ICQ, Inc., also works well. The Dutch students prefer it to a phone conference because it gives them more time to respond. Although their English is excellent, they appreciate having a bit more time to digest what was said. ICQ software also allows teams at each end of the conference to confer. Some teams initially plan to communicate through videoconferences (PC-based or otherwise), but then abandon them as they find that the hook-ups are less reliable and that communication is impaired by poor (and delayed) sound quality. Some teams set up a web site as a file repository and maintain the latest project schedule and latest versions of trip reports and intermediate outputs on the site.

Every team experiences the need for slack time and contingency plans to overcome the lack of reliability of technology under time pressure. For example, sometimes information faxed ahead of time for a videoconference does not arrive. Sometimes participants donot receive the latest update on where and when a videoconference or teleconference will take place. After experiencing the difficulties of recovering from a lost opportunity, students develop more robust ways of communicating.

Students in the team have different technical backgrounds and different theoretical bases. During the kick-off, we challenge the teams to make use of the strengths of every one of their team members. Good project teams turn their diversity into strength; weaker teams find it a weakness. In general, the Eindhoven students have taken more courses on design of supply chain structures and control systems, and the U.S. students have done more work with strategy, marketing, and IS/IT. This can lead to an "us versus them" situation, in which each side defines the project mission in terms of their own background and strengths. We generally resolve this by having the teams go back to the companies to get clarification of the project mission and direction. (As part of this, we also sometimes need to coach the company liaison, to encourage him/her to provide direction, rather than relying on the team or professors to do this.)

Although using the Enneagram (Baron and Wagele 1994) certainly helps to make some personality differences clear at the start of the project, merely being aware of the differences and knowing some theory regarding how to deal with differences does not prevent significant problems from occurring. The Enneagram characterizes personality types into categories such as Controller, Optimist, Observer, Peacemaker, etc. As the projects progress, students observe their behavior and the behavior of others and notice the conflicts that arise because of differences in approaches relating to personality types. One extreme case we had was a project team with two Controllers. They had difficulty making progress until they dealt with the conflict that naturally arose between the Controllers and between the Controllers and the rest of the team members. Some teams have a different problem—no team leader emerges. By observing behavior, students learn two lessons: first, that individual personality types transcend culture, and second, that personality differences must be dealt with to make the team work effectively and encourage all members to contribute.

Students also read one of three books on working across cultures (Lewis 1998; O'Hara and Johansen 1994; Tronpenaars and Hapden-Turner 1998). On the U.S. side, they then write a short paper on their observations of how the group interacted, tying their observations to concepts discussed in the book, and differentiating between personality differences and cultural differences.

One of the main cultural differences in work style that we have noticed during the last few years is that although the American students tend to be deadline-oriented, the Dutch students tend to plan out the project and strive to make steady progress. Further, work hours tend to be more flexible for U.S. students than they are for the Dutch students. While deadline-driven "all-nighters" are uncommon among Dutch students, U.S. students may work continuously during multiple days and nights to drive a project to completion. This characteristic is probably very much related to their attitudes toward deadlines. The difference in work styles is exacerbated by the fact that the U.S. students have more structure in their schedules— related to midterms, finals, and requirements to attend class—than do the Dutch students. The fairly direct and conflict-inducing communication patterns of both the U.S. and Dutch cultures highlight these cultural differences during many of the projects.

5. How to Start a Global Projects Course

For anyone considering starting a similar course, we would like to offer the following recommendations about finding a partner, recruiting projects, running the kick-off, overseeing the projects, and managing the workload for the professors.

In finding an overseas partner university, it is important that the programs match well in terms of size (number of students who will take the course), technical background of the students (some overlap, some complementarity), and philosophy with regards to the value of interacting with industry. It is helpful if both sides have experience running domestic projects, and if both sides are able to recruit projects. In addition, this course can be part of a broader relationship with the overseas partner university, and of a broader relationship with companies. In our case, this has been one of the key success factors for the course. Stanford and Eindhoven have developed a broad relationship, with a linking of our industry affiliates groups (SCM "Forums"), regular exchange of faculty, and coauthorship of research papers. Most projects are recruited from companies that are members of our Forums.

Sponsoring companies and projects should be chosen wisely—to maximize the benefits, given the intense effort that everyone puts into the course. Projects should line up with the research interests and the knowledge and skills of the professors and students. Partners should be companies—or rather, people within companies—who value the role which academia can play in building knowledge and want to go beyond their day-to-day job and contribute to education and research. Furthermore, the general project scope, site visit dates, and preliminary data requirements should be defined before the kick-off. This will allow the students to make the most effective use of the short project horizon.

The kick-off meeting is critical—professors must make sure that students bond into a team and develop a viable mission statement. A poor start is difficult to overcome. In the past, we have had cases in which the company provided either too little direction or too much information at the kick-off. To balance the objectives, we have the companies present their view of the project for 2 to 4 hours and then leave the students to discuss the project themselves for the rest of the day. On the second day the students again spend some time with the company and some time by themselves and then present back to the company on the third day.

During the course of the project, professors should help the project teams identify and resolve scope changes, technical issues, and interpersonal conflicts early. Professors should do this by encouraging the students to take the responsibility to discuss issues among themselves and with the company, rather than by dictating solutions. Students will resist this at first, as in most educational settings things are laid out for them. In addition, as in all projects, clear, frequent project milestones and open communications channels are prerequisites for success.

The time investment for the professors is substantial. Professors are responsible for recruiting and scoping out projects, making initial preparations with the company liaison, and maintaining contact with the liaison throughout the project. In addition, they arrange for the course logistics—setting up accounts and processes for video- and telephone-based communications, overseeing travel arrangements, invoicing and expense reimbursement processes, and planning the kick-off and final presentation activities. Last, as typical in a project course, professors coach the project teams, meeting with them weekly, reviewing intermediate reports and slide sets, etc. In our experience, running the course with three projects requires about 250 hours for each professor, including about 50 hours spent at the kick-off and final presentation meetings.

6. Conclusion

We have found the GPC, which is based on the experiential learning model (Kolb 1984), to be a useful way to further students' knowledge of SCM and IS theory, improve understanding of "soft" issues, and train students to work in global project teams with diverse backgrounds. This way of teaching is, however, less effective in transferring concepts and more traditional inventory topics. We therefore use it in conjunction with lecture and case-based courses on SCM and IS theory in our program.

After 5 years, we feel the course is running well. We continue to seek projects that are truly multicompany in nature, with intense involvement from multiple companies in the supply chain. We are working on ways to reap further benefits from the course for both the companies and the university programs. Last year, two European Ph.D. students—one specializing in system dynamics and the other in merge-in-transit systems—used data from the Nokia and GeoLogistics projects, respectively, as part of their thesis work. This year, some Stanford Masters students will follow up with a company by doing another more detailed study of one aspect of the project, to meet the requirements of another course. We also will have a Ph.D. student do a more sophisticated analysis of some company data, leading to a research publication. Finally, some of the projects have been described as teaching cases for use in other courses.

As we have built up experience, we have found that an additional benefit of these types of courses has been the way they have allowed us to develop and strengthen the relationships between the universities and industry. These relationships form a foundation that will serve us well as we look for new opportunities to work together to enhance education, research, and practice.[1]

The authors acknowledge the efforts of the faculty who initiated and expanded the Global Projects Course with Jan Fransoo, namely Professors Hau Lee and Mitchell Tseng, as well as all the sponsoring companies who have enabled us to build this successful course.

Appendix A. Useful Articles and Teaching Cases

1. Bertrand, J. W. M., J. C. Wortmann, and J. Wijgaard (1990), *Production Control: A Structural and Design Oriented Approach,* Elsevier, Amsterdam.

2. Feitzinger, E., and H. L. Lee (1997), "Mass Customization at Hewlett-Packard: The Power of Postponement," *Harvard Business Review,* January/February, 116–121.

3. Fisher, M. L., J.H. Hammond, W. R. Obermeyer, and A. Raman (1994), "Making Supply Meet Demand in an Uncertain World," *Harvard Business Review,* May/June, 83–93.

4. Fransoo, J. C. (1998), "European Manufacturing and Distribution of Pharmaceuticals," Teaching Case, Eindhoven University of Technology.

5. Fuller, J. B., O'Connor, and R. Rawlinson (1993), "Tailored Logistics: The Next Advantage," *Harvard Business Review,* May/June, 87–98.

6. Gutgeld, Y., and D. Beyer (1995), "Are You Going out of Fashion?," *McKinsey Quarterly,* 3, 55–65.

7. Holland International Distribution Council (1998), *Worldwide Logistics: The Future of Supply Chain Services,* HIDC, The Hague.

8. Kopczak, L. R., and H. L. Lee (1993), "Hewlett-Packard DeskJet Printer Supply Chain," Teaching Case, Stanford University.

9. ——— (1997), "Logistics Partnerships and Supply Chain Restructuring: Survey Results from the U.S. Computer Industry," *Production and Operations Management,* 6, 1, 226–247.

10. ——— (1997), "Apple Computer's Supplier Hubs: A Tale of Three Cities," Teaching Case, Stanford University.

11. ——— (1998), "Materials Management at Lucent Technologies: 3C vs. MRP," Teaching Case, Stanford University.

12. Lee, H. L., and C. Billington (1992), "Managing Supply Chain Inventory: Pitfalls and Opportunities," *Sloan Management Review,* Spring, 65–73.

13. ———, Padmanabhan, V., Whang, S. (1997), "The Bullwhip Effect in Supply Chains," *Sloan Management Review,* Spring, 93–102.

14. ——— (1997), "Hewlett-Packard Company: Network Printer Design for Universality," Teaching Case, Stanford University.

15. Silver, E. A., D. F. Pyke, and R. Peterson (1998), *Inventory Management and Production Planning and Scheduling,* 3rd ed., Wiley, Chichester.

16. Van Goor, A. R., M. J. Ploos van Amstel, W. Ploos van Amstel (1996), *Fysieke Distributie: Denken in Toegevoegde Waarde,* 3e druk, Stenfert Kroese, Houten.

17. Van der Vlist, P., J. Hoppenbrouwers, and H. M. H. Hegge (1997), "Extending the Enterprise through Multi-level Supply Control," *International Journal of Production Economics,* 53, 1, 35–42.

References

Baron, R., and E. Wagele (1994), *The Enneagram Made Easy: Discover the 9 Types of People,* Harper, San Francisco, CA.

Haynes, P., and D. Setton (1998), "McKinsey 101," *Forbes,* May 4, 130–135.

Kolb, D. A. (1984), *Experiential Learning: Experience As the Source of Learning and Development,* Prentice Hall, Englewood Cliffs, NJ.

Kumar, K. R., and El Sawy, O. (1998), "Extending the Boundaries of Operations Management: An International Field Studies Approach Integrating Information Systems," *Production and Operations Management,* 7, 2, 228–236.

Lewis, R. D. (1998), *When Cultures Collide: Managing Successfully Across Cultures,* Nicholas Brealey Publishing, London.

O'Hara, M., and R. Johansen (1994), Global Work: Bridging Distance, Culture and Time, Jossey-Bass, Inc. Publishers, San Francisco, CA.

Tronpenaars, F., and C. Hampden-Turner (1998), *Riding the Waves of Culture: Understanding Cultural Diversity in Business,* 2nd ed., McGraw Hill, New York, NY.

Wouters, M. J. F., and K. H. Van Donselaar (1999), "Design of Operation. Management Internships across Organizations—Teaching OM by Doing OM," *Interfaces,* to appear.

Laura Rock Kopczak is a Consulting Associate Professor at Stanford University. She specializes in supply chain management and quality management. She is also the Director of Research of the Stanford Global Supply Chain Forum. Her research areas include supply chain restructuring, logistics partnerships and supply chain integration and coordination. Dr. Kopczak has taught courses at several other universities in Switzerland, the Netherlands and Hong Kong. Previous to pursuing her Ph.D., she worked for ten years at Hewlett-Packard Company. Dr. Kopczak holds a B.S. in Electrical Engineering, an MBA, an M.S. in Operations Research and a Ph.D. in Industrial Engineering.

Jan C. Fransoo is an Assistant Professor at the Technische Universiteit Eindhoven in the Netherlands. He holds an MSc in Industrial Engineering and a Ph.D. in Operations Management, both from the Technische Universiteit Eindhoven. Jan Fransoo held visiting appointments at Clemson University and Stanford University. His research interests include production control in the process industries, aggregation issues in production control and supply chain management, and supply-driven logistics. He has published in journals such as *European Journal of Operational Research, International Journal of Operations and Production Management, Transportation Research, Computers in Industry,* and *Journal of Intelligent Manufacturing.*

WARREN ELECTRIC GROUP: AN INDUSTRY ALLIANCE TO TEACH LOGISTICS THEORY MEETS PRACTICE*

F. BARRY LAWRENCE

Engineering Technology and Industrial Distribution Department, Texas A&M University, College Station, Texas 77843-3367, USA

Warren Electric Group (WEG) provided students of a Distribution Logistics course the opportunity to do a "live" project. The classes went to WEG and studied their logistics system. The students learned in a real-world environment, the faculty built stronger industry ties for future research, and WEG gained the students' insights in the course of the project work. The project was unique in several respects. In addition to being a real-world project, it involved the entire class of 50 students. Each class conducted a structured study of the key attributes of logistics and examined the WEG environment in relation to state-of-the-art logistics technologies and methods.
(LOGISTICS, DISTRIBUTORS, WAREHOUSING, INVENTORY)

Introduction

Warren Electric Group (WEG) provided the students of a Distribution Logistics course an opportunity to do a "live" project. As designed, the classes went to WEG and studied their logistics system. The students, faculty, and WEG realized many benefits in the course of the project. The students learned logistics in a "real-world" environment, the faculty built stronger industry ties for future research, and Warren gained the students' respect and their insights in the course of the project work.

The effectiveness of the project was reflected in its results. In their evaluations the students described the project as extremely challenging and eye-opening. They were fascinated by the extent theory permeated the workplace and they found that poor implementation of theory usually resulted in inferior performance. The students also found that having industry leaders attend their final presentations drove them to perform far above their usual standards. The students felt such pressure to perform well that they described the project as the most work-intensive course they had ever experienced.

An Innovative Approach

As this paper demonstrates, the project was unique in several respects. In addition to being a real-world project, it also involved two entire classes of 50 students. Each class conducted a structured study of the key attributes of logistics and examined the WEG environment in relation to state-of-the-art logistics technologies and methods.

---

* Received December 1999; revision received June 1999; accepted July 1999.

This project differed from the typical senior or masters project in the following ways:

1. Undergraduate courses rarely have a "live" class project and, when they do, it typically takes the form of individual students working alone or in small groups (as in a senior design project). This class started as individual groups but advanced to a single delivered study, in which all groups were bound together for the final paper and presentation. One executive commented that he had trouble finding five people who could work together, and he was very impressed by the cooperation of these two classes of 50 students.

2. Masters classes frequently carry out a single-effort project, but the students are more mature than these groups and their numbers are much smaller.

3. In projects of this nature, the company and one or two students usually agree on a single topic for study. This study covered the landscape, so to speak; the project examined all major topics studied in the course and was not designed around any individual student interests.

4. Projects in masters programs and undergraduate study generally match the student and a mentor to the project and they work together to achieve a defined goal. In this project the entire company played host to the classes for a day, educated the whole class on their systems, matched their program to logistics principles, and involved all functions in the presentations.

5. Most projects do not have a day of reckoning, as it were, when multiple stakeholders from the company come to the University and critique the students' work. Occasionally, one or two company representatives have come, but in this project 7 to 10 individuals attended the presentations, including the CEO.

6. Most projects receive only data and assistance from experts in the company. In this project, the company also provided funding, for faculty and graduate student salaries, as well as for all travel expenses.

Many projects contain some of the elements of this class but we have not encountered any others so ambitious or with as many challenges. The project has had a significant impact on the students and their recruiters. The students used the example of this class in their interviews when they were asked about their understanding of the real world and whether they could work well as part of a team. We now place 10 to 20% of our students with consulting firms, and recruiters find this class to be very valuable. Former students have said the project was good preparation for their later work in industry.

Course Goals

The course was designed to cover the basic logistics concepts while providing the students with a learning experience that would take them to a level of understanding difficult to achieve in the classroom. The course/project content was based on three approaches to the environment:

1. *Basic Logistics.* This first, classic approach to logistics is outlined in Ronald Ballou's *Business Logistics Management* (1992), the course textbook. The course interpretation of Dr. Ballou's work was that logistics could be categorized into facilities (warehouses) planning, transportation planning, inventory and materials management, and meeting customer service requirements.

2. *Distribution Logistics.* A second approach, formalized in this class, was called the logistics loop (Lawrence 1999). The logistics loop demonstrates the actions carried out in the distribution logistics function and how they were interdependent and ultimately controlled by an outer information loop (see Figure 1). The information loop tightened the inner policy loop, leading to lower inventory levels and other savings. In effect information could be traded for inventory.

3. *WEG Logistics.* The third approach was defined by WEG, which requested that classes study a recent acquisition, Watson Electric, and help WEG understand how to integrate Watson into its operations. They felt the combination of the two entities had led to considerable

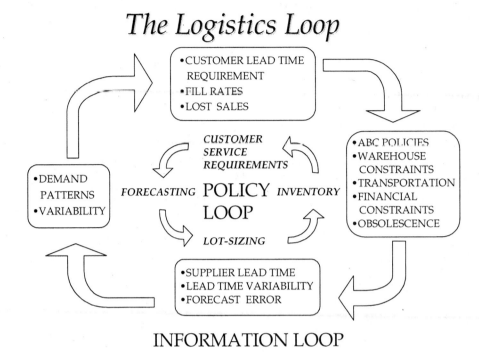

FIGURE 1. The Logistics Loop.

redundancies in their logistics network. They challenged the class to evaluate the system and look for improvement opportunities.

The educational goals reflected the focus on the business workplace as a "live" case-study environment:

- To provide the students with a real-world example to reconcile theoretical constructs with workplace realities.
- To introduce students to industry information sources and their uses in problem solving.
- To raise the level of student performance through the introduction of industry executive involvement.

The project was designed for use in the undergraduate course but could easily be adapted for graduate-level coursework. Two classes of 50 students made the trip to WEG and each class did its own project.

The Project Environment

The format was designed not only to give the students an overview of logistics principles (as in any class) but also to force them to consider practical realities in their studies. Students had to reconcile, in their minds and in their presentation to WEG, why intelligent, successful organizations sometimes choose not to go to that "bleeding edge" advocated by their textbooks and journals. More important, they had to recognize that frequently a company has been better off without the latest technology or craze. The students also were able to explore areas that WEG had not yet adopted that, in fact, may have made sense.

Preliminaries

The first assignment was a case produced in a previous class from the same project design, "TTI's Advanced Inventory Management Program, VMI as a Competitive Weapon" (Lawrence 1998). The case was taught as an active learning experience. The students were instructed to read the case and two or three articles on the electronics distribution industry (TTI's field).

The students wrote a one-page paper on the industry and participated in a class discussion (moderated by an industry specialist), during which additional issues were raised. The case focused on an electronics distributor with considerable logistics problems in transportation, customer service, inventory, and warehousing. Besides introducing the students to the logistics of an important industry group, it helped get them started on researching their own case. The students then spent another week, in groups of two to three members, writing another paper with additional references on TTI itself and suggesting possible solutions to their problems in a case discussion moderated by a TTI executive. This exercise was extremely popular with the students because it helped them understand the upcoming assignment.

In the Field

The second assignment was the field trip to Warren Electric Group (WEG). The class went to WEG's Houston facility, where they participated in several activities. First, Cheryl Thompson, owner and CEO, gave an overview of WEG's strategic plan. She pointed out that WEG was growing fast and the implications of growth for existing operations were very important to the management. The current environment had given WEG considerable opportunity to expand and Ms. Thompson believed the chance for growth would offset the difficulties involved. In addition to its strong market position, WEG had another advantage: the company was one of the largest woman-owned organizations in the country and was able to capitalize on that fact in many of its negotiations.

After Thompson's presentation, a series of Warren executives from different areas of responsibility gave the classes information from their fields. Richard Russell was responsible for the Watson Electric Company acquisition and addressed some of the problems they were encountering in melding the two companies. WEG had identified Watson Electric as the topic they wanted the class to explore, so Russell's presentation held great importance for the students. Other Warren executives spoke next on sales, quality, information systems, and strategic accounts.

The classes were then taken on a warehouse tour of the main facility in Houston and a new one in Deer Park. The following week, classes visited the Watson operations in Dallas (Russell's home base) and Waco, Texas. The classes were divided between the two sets of operations, with the first class focusing on Dallas and the second class focusing on Waco.

The Group Study Areas

The classes were divided into 10 groups each (see Figure 2). The instructor assigned each group a topic to research, using trade journals as their primary sources. They were also expected to study Ballou's (1992) key logistics areas. The students were required to present

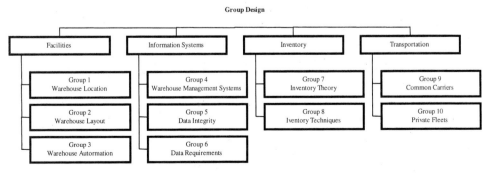

FIGURE 2. Group Assignments.

an oral and written report on the industry "State of the Art" in their particular area. Then they had to present the "State of Warren Electric Group" with regard to the latest technologies and methods they had uncovered. The WEG portion was taken from the field trip to WEG, where company executives reported on the strategic objectives of the company and introduced students to their operations.

Facilities Planning

The facilities planning area was divided into three groups who studied warehouse location, warehouse layout, and warehouse automation. For this portion of the project, the warehouse location issue centered on whether WEG should close some redundant facilities. The issue was very important because customer service was at stake. Warren maintained counter service (a form of retail trade) and "hot-shot" delivery from each warehouse. The counter sales were important because large segments of WEG's customers are electrical contractors. These contractors would send someone to the Warren counter to pick up emergency items; if a warehouse were to close down, then the contractor would feel the need to go elsewhere.

The warehouse layout group studied the philosophies of layout, an area of intense interest to distributors at this time, so information sources were numerous and rich in depth. WEG had laid out their warehouses by following a combination of the popularity, product size, and similarity philosophies. They endeavored to keep the fastest moving products near the shipping area or at least at the end of rows (popularity). They placed heavier items on lower shelves (product size) but frequently kept these products upstairs (a violation of the product-size methodology) to group on similarity. The similarity philosophy can be used with items that were picked together, items that had similar characteristics, or items that came from a common supplier. WEG favored the last approach because they had franchise agreements with Allen-Bradley (a division of Rockwell) and other major suppliers.

The warehouse automation group looked at the potential to automate the large Distribution Center in Houston and the "Super Branch" planned for Dallas. WEG had not yet bar-coded their operations, so the students focused their attention on the ways in which the addition of bar-coding to the information system could enable more advanced forms of technology (cross-docking, forecast sharing, and the use of conveyers or carousels).

Information Systems

The information systems groups focused on moving the company to real-time inventory management. Bar-coding was also a major issue for these groups but they focused less on automation of physical systems and more on information flow. The first group, Warehouse Management Systems, looked into how stock pickers could be routed through the warehouse to minimize costs and maximize output.

The second information systems group looked into data integrity. Because WEG was not then bar-coded, the group was able to demonstrate how bar-coding and automated picking procedures (pick to light, Radio Frequency) could lead to fewer picking errors. When most distribution firms tried more advanced information handling, the first problem to arise was incomplete, inaccurate data. The students would face this problem almost immediately on graduation because bar-coding was sweeping through the distribution industry.

The last information systems group looked into data needs. They explained what sort of data WEG needed to collect to employ state-of-the-art forecasting and purchasing models. Capturing the correct information, in the correct format, and in the proper amount (the number of periods needed for accurate forecasting techniques, for example) was essential for effective decision making.

Inventory

The inventory groups were divided between theory and implementation techniques. The theoretical group studied the principal inventory theories and reported on their strengths and weaknesses. Manufacturers were hotly pursuing Just-In-Time (JIT) and trying to offload their inventory on distributors (Carbone 1996). The assignment challenged the students to understand and explain the impact of JIT systems on distributors as part of the supply chain. The students made Supply Chain Management (SCM) a major focus of their efforts. They also studied Theory of Constraints (Goldratt 1992) and considered it as an alternative for distributors as well as a governing force in the supply chain. Finally, they had to explain the nature of "push" systems (as opposed to JIT "pull").

The implementation group had to look at the methods used to achieve SCM objectives. The group studied strategic initiatives such as Vendor Managed Inventory and Integrated Supply, concerning which WEG is an industry leader, and these had major implications for industrial distribution (Lawrence and Varma 1999). They demonstrated how SCM was affecting distribution and provided the underpinnings for WEG to predict what might be the next set of customer expectations.

Transportation

For the transportation groups, the project divided along the lines of common carriers as opposed to private fleets. WEG heavily used common carriers but also maintained their private fleet for hot-shots, interbranch transfers, or local delivery. The company was interested in better management of the common carriers and vehicle routing for the private fleet. The first transportation group suggested using some of the technology available with common carriers for tracking of shipments in conjunction with their real-time management of inventory. The second group studied some vehicle routing programs and how they could be used to reduce the cost of private fleet operations.

The Project

The deliverable for Warren was a document designed to combine the efforts and recommendations of all student groups. The final book was to be presented to Warren along with a verbal presentation of the results of the project. This proved to be the most challenging and stressful part of the class for the students.

"State of the Art"

After the field trips, the students were given contacts at WEG to provide additional information. The students then wrote research papers entitled "WEG and State of the Art," in which each group described the state of the art in the area assigned. They attached to the paper an assessment of the "state of WEG" as compared to the "state of the art." If WEG differed from what the journals suggested was the cutting edge, the students had to explain why. If they believed WEG should upgrade, they had to explain how and why. If not, they needed to explain why WEG's position was best.

Reporting to WEG

At approximately midsemester the students made professional presentations of these papers and also submitted a hard copy to the instructor. The papers were graded and passed back for revisions. The students then combined their groups to create chapters and recommendations for WEG.

In the final stage of the project the groups merged into "super groups," which produced a four-chapter book that was bound and presented to WEG. The groups included their recommendations to WEG in each chapter. The recommendations had been developed through conversations with WEG personnel, with the WEG people presenting mostly drawbacks to the students' suggestions. In the end the students had to make their own suggestions and defend them.

The finale of the project was a PowerPoint presentation for the WEG executives. A theater at the City Conference Center was reserved and several WEG executives, including CEO Cheryl Thompson, VP John Draper, and Richard Russell, attended the final presentation. The students engaged the executives in several strategic discussions. One issue was the capability of technology to move WEG into a more competitive posture. The students understood the difficulties associated with automation but were convinced there were opportunities for process improvement to be had with new technology. The executives asked for specifics on costs and ideas for implementation.

The presentation also explored the hub-and-spoke method of warehouse replenishment. The students determined that WEG could benefit by relying more heavily on their Distribution Centers and pulling inventory back from the field. The WEG executives agreed with this conclusion and had already held discussions on the topic. The executives and the students then discussed the implementation of this method.

The students made other suggestions that were brought forward and discussed. Both classes presented their findings to WEG. The executives were very impressed and pleased with the outcome. The instructor wrote an academic case based on WEG for the next semester to be taught in the same method as the TTI case. The following semester, Richard Russell and David Russell represented WEG for the company portion of the case exercise and Brian Roy of Rockwell Automation/Allen-Bradley represented the industry viewpoint.

Effects on the Instructor

Class preparation was more extensive for this class than for most undergraduate courses. In addition to the regular grading, testing, and lecturing activities, considerable additional effort was required for a "live" project. The instructor first secured the cooperation of the target firm (1 to 2 days, depending on the firm), then wrote and submitted the proposal for funding (1 day), assisted the firm in planning their site visit (1 day), went with the classes on their trip (1 day), and hosted company executives on the presentation day (1 day).

The project ran smoothly for a number of reasons. First and foremost, the companies took a great deal of pride in presenting an interesting and challenging environment for the students. The partner companies were usually large recruiters and wanted to put on a good show. The students were also intensely interested in impressing potential future employers.

Problems did arise, however, and were addressed early in the planning stages. Although the company executives generally regarded the project as very important, some of their employees had other priorities. The instructor soon realized that if an individual was going to be a major source of information for a group of students, he or she had to understand that the students could not wait 2 or 3 weeks for a response to a request for data. Since the class effectively had only 1 month between the date of the field trip and the due date of first phase of the project, we asked the company executives to prioritize the project before the field trip.

The students also presented a problem. The partner firms were very open about their problems and inefficiencies and were also open to the students' suggestions. The students were often judgmental and occasionally made offensive or arrogant statements to the firm in conversation or in the reports. In some cases, the students had reached the conclusion that they were doing the company a favor instead of the other way around. This problem was the most disturbing aspect of this project. The instructor had to head it off early and repeatedly revisit it with classroom statements pointing out, first, that the company was very successful and, second, that the company was doing them a great favor. The students were directed toward finding the reasons for this success in spite of the company's current process inefficiencies and to ask whether they are, in fact, inefficient. This angle placed the student in the position of reconciling state-of-the-art theory with workplace realities and was the most challenging (and valuable) part of the project.

Warren Electric Group (WEG)' was the second in the series of class projects and provided a new twist by introducing a more complex problem environment. The class learned a lesson with which consultants and researchers are all too familiar—project creep. This project was extremely challenging at all levels and if the companies involved had sought to explore too much territory, the students would have been overwhelmed. The instructor realized that the project parameters must be well defined and achievable for the class in just one semester.

Another problem was that organizing a group of 50 students was extremely difficult and had the potential to get out of control. The students had to be empowered to determine some things for themselves. Groups were given the power to assess their own members so they could control the quality of their area of the project. The course schedule had rigid deadlines because the final project delivered to the company was dependent on all groups coming through with their portion of the project on time.

Adjustments continued to be made, for both classes, principally to maximize the industry interface (field trip and follow-up exchanges) and the final presentation from the students. The structure of the class had become more rigid in deadlines but continued to be as flexible as possible regarding the content. Student creativity was the best way to improve the project and the instructor clearly saw it should not be managed away. Students asked for greater definition at the beginning but, when they finished, they expressed appreciation for the freedom they had been granted.

The course already had a tremendous industry interface, but we continued to enhance it by involving the company in the early planning stages of the project and through designing the class to be closer and closer to the real world. We then chose firms, based on their ability to fit the course-learning objectives. WEG was an excellent choice and at this writing we are completing a large Steel Service Center, Ryerson Tull, that was also able to meet the course objectives in almost every respect.

Our department placed a great deal of value on this class project for several reasons. First, the project increased the bond between the department and important recruiters or companies that invested in research. Second, the class positioned the instructor to write publishable case studies. Third, the proposal included 1 month's funding for the junior faculty member and 4 months' for a graduate student/teaching assistant. Since many universities place a great deal of emphasis on publication and funded research, this project could be helpful in achieving tenure.

The class was designed to work with up to 60 students. Larger classes were possible but the coordination difficulty did increase with class size and anything over 100 students (groups of 10 to 12 students each) would probably not be practical for the instructor or the company sponsor. Smaller classes are easy to implement and could go down to one student per group, although gaining the interest of recruitment-driven firms would be more difficult.

The educational goals were typically met by the project without exception:
- The project had a very strong real-world flavor because of the environment and the involvement of company specialists.
- As stated earlier, the theory taught in class had to be reconciled with the workplace. Students quickly learned that the company had intelligent, hard-working employees and that quick-fix solutions were not acceptable.
- The case usually took on the focus of a specific challenge facing the company and so the students generally directed the project to that problem.
- As part of the class, students were given assignments that required them to use trade journals to explore important topics.
- Student evaluations reflected the pressure they felt to perform above their usual standards because they had to present to the company.

Effects on the Company

The commitment from the company sponsor was significant. Initially, most companies balked at contributing cash, but not time, to the students' project work. The commitment of other resources far outweighed the financial cost to the company, and the total cost (financial and other) was far less than the recruitment value for a major employer. The first objective was to help the sponsor to understand this. Our approach was to ask how much it cost the company to send recruiters to campus and how long it would take those recruiters to reach 100 students in as much depth as the project did. This usually overcame the financial objections.

Most firms have seen other value in having their employees work on the project, such as the growth that came from interaction with the students, and have not contested the actual visit. We realized that this raised an important point: if the company was not a major recruiter, the project might not deliver the value they expected. We encouraged companies to think of recruitment and not the project's outcome as their principal deliverable. Although undergraduate students can be quite creative, they are not professional consultants and the project design is such that they cannot focus entirely on the concepts most interesting to the firm. This mindset has caused the firms to be pleasantly surprised when the students have delivered more than expected, as they usually did.

As stated earlier, the company funded about $10,000 to $15,000 for the proposal, including travel expenses and partial support for faculty/graduate student salaries. They also committed major resources to the student visit, follow-up questions, and final presentation. Recruitment of firms was difficult at first because we did not have a track record, so we chose two firms that had made large donations to the university and had hired many students. We hoped they would step up to the challenge for reasons of recruitment and relationship. They also understood the program and educational process well, having served on many university committees, and could help considerably in getting all the bugs out of the class design. These high-profile firms also made university approval easier.

Since the initial projects, we have been oversubscribed and no longer have to recruit companies. Graduating seniors and word of mouth have brought many others to us. We now select our partners based on the following criteria:

1. Does the company carry strategic importance to the department? Is it potentially a major recruiter, donor, or funded research partner?

2. Does the company introduce a new industry (electronics, electrical, fluid power, etc.) or important discipline (manufacturing, distribution, logistics, etc.) to our students?

3. Does the company understand the required commitment and is it capable of meeting the challenge?

A "no" on question 1 or 2 is acceptable as long as the other is a "yes." No company will be considered that cannot answer "yes" to question 3.

The feedback from the companies has been extremely positive and some have even asked about involvement in grading. We have resisted this concept because it could lead to student protest about biased or unclear grading criteria. It also risks the company's being blamed for a poor grade. Most firms have been adamant about protecting their relationship with the students and have no desire to involve themselves in grading. Their feedback has been very valuable, however, in class design and the students always ask about the company's satisfaction after the class. We are still working to improve the feedback mechanism.

Effects on the Students

The classes were undergraduate junior/senior-level Industrial Distribution (ID) majors. The Industrial Distribution students had a better command of logistics coming into this class than most majors did because they already had completed five or six ID classes. The class took place in the spring semester only and did not continue beyond one semester (i.e., the class did not have two levels). The class met twice a week and had similar test and project-work weights to other courses.

The class had two exams worth 200 points each and a minimum of four case studies worth a total of 100 points that allowed the companies who sponsored the class in the past to come in and interact with the current students. The project was worth 200 points, 100 for the first phase (the state-of-the-art, state-of-the-company survey) and 100 for the second phase (the final presentation and book for the company). The students were allowed to grade their group members on a 0 to 100 scale. The individual team member's assessments of fellow group members were averaged and multiplied times the project grade. If a student project got 90 out of 100 points on the first phase of the project, then 90% of an average group grade of 90 would mean an 81 overall. On the other hand, if the group got no input from a group member and gave him a zero, the grade on that phase of the project for the student was also a zero. The first and second phases of the project constitute 200 points and if an individual angered both groups enough, the students could effectively fail that person. Students have been pushed to failure by group evaluations more than once and each semester several students lost at least a letter grade because of failure to contribute to their groups.

The students found the class to be significantly more challenging than their other courses. Even though the project was designed to be no more work-intensive than any other class project, the students built it into a major undertaking. Some students advised their peers not to take the course in their final semester (while interviewing). Other ID professors were mindful of when the project was due and tried not to schedule major activities at that time because it would have hurt their projects/tests. This simple adjustment took the class out of the realm of just calculating what they needed for a grade and into the potential for embarrassing themselves in front of a major recruiter or future customer.

Student evaluations identified the class as their most challenging and the project as the best thing about the class. When asked, many students claimed that, although the class was their favorite, they would not like to see other classes have a project of that type because they would feel overwhelmed. Students claimed that the project allowed them to put everything they learned in the program to work. They found the meshing of theory and the real world to be the most interesting part of the course.

Completed Projects and Future Plans

The class project has been extremely successful. Some companies have further leveraged the experience by connecting faculty and graduate student projects to it as well. The project was redesigned again for the fall of 1998 with R. J. Gallagher, a large pipe/valve/fitting distributor, to give the students a more structured set of steps for preparing the book and presentation. Deadlines were set for such things as recommendations and the rough draft of the book. Groups were rearranged to handle presentations, the book, recommendations, and a Web site with the project results, which could be accessed through the instructor's and department's Web pages.

The R. J. Gallagher project slightly redesigned the course to take advantage of its Integrated Supply (I/S) contract with a large chemical manufacturer. I/S is an extremely advanced form of Supply Chain Management (Lawrence and Varma 1999) and was a perfect fit for the class. The information systems groups on Data Integrity and Data Requirements were combined, and a new inventory group on I/S and Strategic Alliances was formed.

The I/S group was process based rather than topic based and seemed to work well. It was more challenging for the students because it forced them to integrate their studies into their report. Groups had been able to focus on a particular area before and not understand the system as a whole. I/S was a system within Gallagher and forced students to think in broader terms.

In the spring of 1999 the class took this process focus to a new level. Although Warehouse Location and Warehouse Layout were considered too important to eliminate, we reorganized the remaining groups into process focuses: Inbound Freight and Receiving, Shipping and Outbound Freight, Inventory Processes, Strategic Alliances, Value-Add Processes, and

Information Flow. The Project Company was Ryerson Tull Steel, a $3 billion steel service center. Ryerson had been heavily engaged in the class design and the project was extremely challenging. As of this writing, there is little doubt the students learned more using the process focus but we will have to wait for student and company feedback after the semester to determine whether the methodology was too much for a one-semester class.

Conclusion

Four case studies have been written to date (TTI, WEG, Ryerson Tull, and R. J. Gallagher) and are in varying stages of publication. The case studies are used in the class to further the students' appreciation of logistics and how different product environments affect the logistics process. In the fall of 1999 an international computer software/consulting firm will sponsor a project on Habitat for Humanity. The class will again follow the process design after consultation with Habitat and the sponsor firm. Several other distribution and consulting firms will join the effort.

The class has been an exciting experience for over 400 students (4 semesters) and the faculty of the Industrial Distribution Program. We look to continue it into the future, adding manufacturers and end users to the list of participating firms.

References

BALLOU, R. (1992), *Business Logistics Management*, Prentice-Hall, Englewood Cliffs, NJ, USA.

CARBONE, J. (1996), "Outsourcing, Alliances Change the Rules for Distribution," *Purchasing*, May.

GOLDRATT, E. (1990), *What is This Thing Called Theory of Constraints and How Should It Be Implemented?* North River Press, Croton-on-Hudson, NY, USA.

LAWRENCE, F. B. (1998), "TTI's Advanced Inventory Management Program, VMI as a Competitive Weapon," 1998 *Proceedings of the Decision Sciences Institute*.

—— (1999), "Closing the Logistics Loop: A Tutorial," *Production and Inventory Management Journal*, Spring.

—— AND A. VARMA (1999), "Integrated Supply: Supply Chain Management in Materials Management and Procurement," *Production and Inventory Management Journal*, Summer.

F. Barry Lawrence is an assistant professor with the Department of Engineering Technology and Industrial Distribution at Texas A&M University. He has extensive industry experience in both retail and wholesale sales with published articles in professional, academic, and society journals including *Production and Inventory Management, Journal of Operations Management, Journal of Engineering Technology*, and *Industrial Distribution Magazine*. Lawrence received a B.B.A. in Finance from the University of Texas at Austin, an M.B.A. from Southwest Texas State University, and a Ph.D. in Operations Management from Texas A&M University. Lawrence's areas of interests include logistics and supply chain management, electronic commerce, and specific issues involving inventory and information systems. He has conducted extensive industry studies in the areas of integrated supply for electrical and pipe/valve/fitting distribution; forecasting and logistics for fluid power distribution; warehouse automation and layout for electronics distribution; warehouse and transportation logistics for electrical distribution; warehouse/transportation/inventory management/customer service for steel distribution; and distribution information systems for sporting goods (fishing tackle) distribution.

INNOVATION DIFFUSION AT HEWLETT-PACKARD*

ANDRÉ KUPER AND DWIGHT BRANVOLD

Hewlett-Packard Company, Palo Alto, California 94304, USA

From its origins as Supply Chain Education, a service of Strategic Planning and Modeling (SPaM), the team known as "Innovation Diffusion" has evolved into a premiere consulting organization that provides intellectual leadership to businesses across Hewlett-Packard and Agilent Technologies. This paper traces the evolution of the team, presents its current offerings, and describes its aspirations for the future. In the spirit of Doing Business at Internet Speed, we see an expanding horizon in which the diffusion of breakthrough innovations leading to a portfolio of real options is crucial to business success worldwide.

(INNOVATION DIFFUSION, KNOWLEDGE TRANSFER, OPERATIONS MANAGEMENT, SUPPLY CHAIN MANAGEMENT)

Introduction

The need for diffusion of breakthrough innovations in companies competing in the new age of electronic commerce, especially across product groups at Hewlett-Packard (HP), has become more urgent. Not only has HP acknowledged that innovation is the life blood of the enterprise, the company has established teams of on-site experts to advance this cause. Among the consultants working in this area, the most widely known is a small team called "Innovation Diffusion" that offers a range of services, programs, and interventions from its corporate-level position in the Product Processes Organization (PPO).

This paper tracks Innovation Diffusion back to its origins as "Supply Chain Education," a service provided by Strategic Planning and Modeling (SPaM), a corporate-level consulting organization, since 1992. The shift in emphasis from "education" to "diffusion" in recent years reflects discoveries at many levels—technical, cultural, and structural—and the discovery process itself has been a source of inspiration to the experts who have made the transition together. Our goal here is to understand this transition and develop an appreciation for the extraordinary value creation potential gained by sharing innovations across the company.

What is the difference between the original approach and the new regime? In retrospect, we consider the following distinctions essential:

- *Education.* Traditional education creates a curriculum, which implies fixed content, repeatable delivery, and clear lines of demarcation between teaching and subject matter. Content exists apart from activities required to conduct the business. With this approach,

---

* Received November 1998; revision received October 1999; accepted November 1999.

we begin with a general needs assessment (overlooking the fact that needs are continually subject to change) and develop reusable training programs based on these needs.
- *Diffusion.* By contrast, we use "diffusion" to characterize an approach that is more responsive, dynamic, and flexible. Diffusion involves the immediate application of experience, knowledge, and skill to a unique business situation (in which our initial needs assessment is continually refreshed). There is an emphasis on real-time intervention, which includes cultural and structural components along with technical learning. The content to be embraced in the business situation evolves as we address new realities.

This distinction invites metaphorical thinking. Instead of knowledge engraved on stone tablets brought down from the mountain, consultants and business partners learn together to face reality, translate vision into value, evaluate strategic alternatives, deploy fleets of resources, and practice making a smooth competitive voyage. As the business moves ahead at full steam, often through uncharted waters, visiting a safe harbor to allow time for classroom learning is not remotely feasible (especially as there will be little time to apply formal lessons at sea). What must be understood by the crew gets created while sailing the ship, especially as we navigate treacherous seas, sail through storms, or wait for fresh winds to arrive.

Supply Chain Education

For more than 10 years, Hewlett-Packard businesses have turned to Strategic Planning and Modeling (SPaM) for intellectual leadership in supply chain management, return on assets, and customer service. This consulting team began as a group of industrial engineers and management scientists with a clear mission—to collaborate with researchers in leading academic institutions to develop analytical processes and models that would "catalyze" improvements in HP supply chains. Over the years, their work has been highly successful. Recommendations from SPaM have saved the company millions of dollars while advancing the field of applied research in supply chain management (Lee and Billington 1995).

Supply Chain Education was launched as a service that would disseminate learning derived from SPaM projects. At first, knowledge transfer through traditional education was offered by the consultants themselves, taking advantage of project experience. As demand grew, however, the experts were spending so much time providing education they decided to form a supporting education team. Customer needs drove the development of dedicated resources that would serve managers, business planners, and financial analysts across HP divisions, people responsible for showing a strong return on the dollars invested in their organizations. Of course, people needing to show a return on investment were ready to make the most of training modules and educational resources with proven success at improving financial results across the company.

By launching Supply Chain Education, SPaM addressed certain basic needs. HP businesses made it known they wanted:
- *Access to knowledge and resources for business teams.* To stay up to date on innovations in supply chain management, customers needed easy access to new developments and best practices from different companies and industries, including unpublished information from subject-matter experts.
- *Application of concepts in their business.* Applying knowledge to business problems required managerial support for adjusting project timelines and facilitating cross-functional and cross-business collaboration. When project leaders had difficulty securing management commitment, other functional leaders and supply chain partners were asked to support changes mandated by the results of their project efforts.

Supply Chain Education addressed these needs from the start. Our first step was to provide access to supply chain information and application of knowledge in particular business situations. We determined what training was needed, by whom, and for what situations. We decided that the most cost-effective way to move forward was to involve SPAM experts, as well as their customers, sponsors, and academic partners. On all sides, we developed insights into customer expectations and business needs, competitive factors, infrastructure systems, financial opportunities, barriers, and constraints. We also developed a business plan for the new service, because our goal was to become self-sustaining and profitable. Our assumption was that training, although not a solution to a business problem, is nevertheless a critical element in changing people's behavior.

Addressing the need for access to information and resources, the team developed a computer-based reference tool (Casey and Branvold 1995) and launched a series of conferences in supply chain management to provide a forum for practitioners. Our first, second, and third Supply Chain Management Conferences were highly successful in raising awareness across the company and gaining visibility for the group. We also began developing resources for publication—technical articles, white papers, case studies, and presentations (including slides, audio, and video).

In addition our customers' needs to demonstrate improved financial results were addressed in several ways. We offered businesses the means to:

- *Improve the return on investments in supply chain projects.* Our services helped customers improve their investment returns from supply chain projects and make the best use of the funds provided. We found that traditional education can help project leaders focus on the right issues, deal with barriers, and pursue opportunities through stakeholder involvement. In many cases, we achieved accelerated project completion with improved results.
- *Determine the best leverage points for supply chain investments.* We helped functional staff understand their business from a supply chain perspective and determine leverage points with high investment potential. A common outcome of our education process was to develop agreement on where to invest and whom to involve.
- *Support changes in functional roles.* We convinced management to support changes in functional roles. Our educational service aimed successfully at aligning cross-functional teams to adopt a supply chain perspective on a project or initiative. We found that education helps remove implementation barriers and open opportunities outside the original project scope.

In the realm of application, our workshops developed a common understanding of business problems previously resolved across HP and at other companies. These workshops pointed the way to strategic responses to emerging problems. At first we worked with experts involved in customer projects; our role was to align diverse contributions toward an integrated solution to the problem at hand. It is now apparent that Innovation Diffusion began with our transition from supporting roles in projects and workshops to a leadership role in conducting a discovery process with the business itself.

Transition

As we have seen, the transition to our diffusion model began almost as soon as the group was formed. As Hewlett-Packard moved aggressively with new products and services for emerging and expanding markets, we found that customer needs for the traditional approach began to disappear. An early indication was that demand for training programs we were developing for certain sponsors never materialized. Instead, when business needs arose, customers were motivated to invest in new content to address the specific business situation. The need for "education and training" shifted to an urgent request for fast review and application of innovations in a dynamically changing context. Moreover, the business problems changed in scope and focus. As supply chains became more complex across multiple businesses and partners (who might well compete in other markets), cross-business and cross-functional diffusion became a requirement. HP businesses needed fast and effective gauging of new realities along with responsive strategies in a highly tactical environment. In some cases, customer expectations were not aligned with our new focus. When asked for information about business strategy, supply chain initiatives, and organizational context, one customer said, "We need training! Why don't you just teach us?" And yet, the increasing specialization of SPAM consultants responding to the variety of business challenges warranted a different approach to capturing and diffusing knowledge.

By focusing on *access* and *application* of knowledge to the business situation at hand, our team created a space where discovery and diffusion of innovations could grow. Although the need for access continues, our main impact is in applications. At the same time, our relationships with customers and with partners, in the Product Process Organization and in the world of research, are changing. As specialization increases and new combinations of knowledge and skill are requested, we feel an urgent need for ongoing dialog with customers and experts. Rather than investing in packaged responses to problems, we are working out a repertory of responses that can be applied as problems arise.

Throughout this transition to Innovation Diffusion, we have come to appreciate certain critical success factors. In our team, consultants are urged to:

- Understand customers in depth (especially what is essential to their business success in a particular environment) and provide cost-effective solutions to specific needs.
- Collaborate with customers to develop shared objectives. A clear *Memorandum of Understanding* (MOU) should be created to document project relationships among all participants.
- Ensure that any significant customer interaction has explicit upper-management sponsorship. This should be spelled out in the MOU.
- Develop customized solutions in short time frames. Our recommended approach, prototyping, has been borrowed from software development.
- Maintain a pool of expertise by monitoring practices in companies considered to be role models; for example, develop partnerships across HP businesses, innovative companies, dynamic industries, leading experts, and academic institutions (without overlooking content experts).
- Develop knowledge networks and application processes to address needs proactively. Far greater returns on investment are achieved dynamically than by capturing and repackaging insights after a project ends. Inciting the participants to share insights is a barrier when perceived as an add-on to their tasks. Emphasize integration of knowledge rather than separation from actual project experience.

Open Enrollment Classes

As part of our transition, we have created Open Enrollment Classes that can be attended by any interested HP employee. In effect, we have an ongoing business that could be branded Supply Chain Education. This business responds to personnel turnover and other changes needing training and education, including refreshers. Supply Chain Management at Hewlett-Packard (Kuper 1999) includes modules on Awareness, A Common Supply Chain Language, Basic Supply Chain Concepts, and An Exercise in Inventory Calculation. The class features an exercise based on the *Beer Game* (created at MIT) to illustrate the adverse consequences of independent decision making. Whereas the original *Beer Game* (with its debrief) focuses on understanding the system-dynamics aspects of holding inventory, business needs require a business perspective. Over the years, we have collected illustrations of the "Bullwhip Effect" (Lee, Padmanabhan, and Whang 1999) in various business units.

In this class, we appeal to people's experiences as business managers or consumers to facilitate learning. We deal with the "blame" taxonomy and with supply chain dynamics as drivers of success or failure. Our simulation game is not about winning or being better than others; it simply reveals how the system stacks the cards against individual participants, as in a real supply chain.

Modules on *Basic Supply Chain Concepts* and *A Common Supply Chain Language* are strongly tied to SPaM publications, and this core remains constant to promote a shared organizational understanding. The *Front-End* and *Back-End* modules are customized, however, depending on business needs, and their content is adapted to a specific business situation. This is especially true of *Innovations in Supply Chain Management* and *Application*, the final modules, which are customized to address issues common across small groups. Because of their more frequent occurrence and because of the diverse business backgrounds of participants, we are incorporating fresh insights into our flagship class.

Innovation Diffusion

Moving toward the future, Innovation Diffusion continues to evolve into a leading-edge service that sharpens the customer's competitive edge. We are focused on the process by which future uncertainties resolve into present realities. The metaphor of making a voyage continues to inform our thinking, providing an image of enterprise that moves into currently unknown domains by applying the latest innovations and discoveries. For this reason, the array of services and programs presented here must be considered provisional.

- Inventory-Driven Costs Website
- Transforming Supply Chains for eBusiness
- Product Design for Supply Chain Excellence
- Supply Chain Competitive Analysis
- Forecasting and Planning for Supply Chain Management
- Supply Chain Management Conference
- Inventory-Driven Cost Workshop
- Product Rollover Workshop
- Supply Chain Workshop

The following program descriptions are subject to continual revision as we undergo the transformations of an entrepreneurial journey.

Inventory-Driven Costs Website

Our experience has shown that theoretical concepts must be revealed through frameworks that are easy to understand and use. A good example would be the concept of inventory-driven costs, including depreciation, price protection, obsolescence, and capital investment, which are not owned by a single function or organization. Because accounting systems are historical by nature and do not lend themselves to planning for future uncertainties, a systemwide view of these cost drivers is extremely difficult to develop (see, for example, Hope and Hope 1996).

To help supply chain managers improve their results, our team has created precise metaphors to explain the relationship of inventory-driven costs to profitability:

> Driving along the highway, we move from the past into the future. Making our way in this fast-moving environment, we count on rear-view mirrors to reflect what's already happened and a windshield to protect our view of what lies ahead. We also rely on a good map of the territory to help us find our way. Anyone wishing to reach a strategic destination knows that these familiar devices—mirror, windshield, and map—are indispensable. Supply chain managers need all these tools. In many ways, they improve our ability to measure or estimate uncertainties—including inventory-driven costs—and understand their impact on profitability (Billington and Mora 1995).

A Website based on this metaphor, which uses the multimedia capabilities of the Internet, has allowed our team to diffuse these challenging concepts to a wide audience across HP.

Transforming Supply Chains for eBusiness

This workshop introduces new approaches to functions and businesses (and provides a window on HP initiatives). By focusing on supply chain designs serving electronic commerce in the context of traditional open distribution, the workshop responds to the need for a systems approach to Internet commerce. Originally, it helped business leaders respond to the Dell challenge, often expressed as the challenge of Going Direct. Although customers looking for computer products now associate the "direct model" with lower prices and greater responsiveness, that approach undermines the value proposition of distributors, resellers, and other partners. Distribution and product delivery organizations need help in defining sophisticated supply chain models that support new approaches to value delivery and customer requirements while at the same time improving financial results. We are leveraging innovations across businesses, especially as highly efficient supply chains are developed at HP and in other industries. The business-to-business component of Internet-based commerce is outpacing business-to-consumer by several orders of magnitude. This development changes relationships up and down the supply chain as well as individual contributions to end-user value. We take a different look at the role of the Internet—an information integration tool—as an interface to different players along a supply chain.

In creating this workshop, our team developed both the content and conceptual framework from scratch. Supplementing our own research, we partnered with Stanford University to develop sessions from a global perspective. The following modules are included in the workshop:

- *Assessment* involves exploring the business situation of supply chain partners, including their competitive landscape, business strategies, action plans, and initiatives. The modular approach ensures that content addresses the business needs of a particular audience.
- *Front-End* focuses on electronic interfaces to customers and ways to exploit customer intelligence and relationship management.
- *Back-End* focuses on the "back office support" of the Internet as an enabler of business-to-business communication (the main area of growth).
- *Integration* ensures end-to-end supply chain integration. Here we accommodate one-to-one relationship management and one-to-many relationships across the value chain.
- *Application* includes a design review process that relates knowledge to the business situation and develops the next steps for eBusiness. We introduce tools for conceptual analysis and develop plans for review with peers, decision makers, and experts to share opportunities, issues, and risks.
- *Action Planning* is the module in which next steps are prioritized and ownership and timelines are specified.

Afterward, we evaluate our work with participants and later with stakeholders, project leaders, and sponsors. A postmortem with the workshop team is also part of the process.

Product Design for Supply Chain Excellence

This workshop has been created for a product division interested in helping R&D, Marketing, and New Product Introduction teams focus on how product designs affect supply chain costs and product availability. The workshop covers the basics of supply chain management, then explores case study results on "design for universality" in LaserJet printers. The results of a preworkshop assessment are also presented.

To prepare this new workshop, we interviewed opinion leaders from different functions and analyzed demand patterns, lead time, product structure (fanout), and inventory-driven costs. We found that products lacking a wide variety of options may yet have quite a few stock-keeping units (SKUs), resulting from language and packaging requirements. In such situations, moving from a small set of SKUs to a plan for many more dramatically reduces profitability, unless the product is carefully designed to minimize postponement and supply chain impacts. We also quantify the impact of reducing part lead time mean and variability, to help designers and marketing staff make trade-off decisions early in the product management process.

In addition to achieving functional alignment, we introduce techniques for quick analysis to support design decisions. Because of the cross-functional nature of the workshop, we make sure to obtain joint ownership for these new approaches.

This workshop offers the following modules:
- *Assessment Review* provides an overview of product design decisions and their impact on supply chain responsiveness and costs.
- *Basics of Supply Chain Management* develops a common understanding of basic concepts and how they affect the balance between customer service and inventory costs.
- *Inventory Calculation Exercise* provides a simple way of assessing inventory levels arising from uncertainties in alternative supply chain scenarios.
- *Application of Concepts through the LaserJet Case* is a classic Design for Supply Chain Management case that shows how design decisions (like a universal power supply) affect responsiveness and cost in a worldwide supply chain.
- *Quick Analysis* includes a review and application of tools to improve design decision making.
- *Cross-functional Action Planning* ensures alignment and ownership across functional groups involved in decision making for new products.

Supply Chain Competitive Analysis

Thorough analysis of competitors' supply chains is often requested by our customers. Project managers have a need to understand competitive supply chain data on an ongoing basis. We have developed a framework for acquiring supply chain intelligence, relying on outside resources to gather data while using internal analytical resources to perform the assessment. Even so, there are barriers to competitive assessments, including our current lack of a methodology for using competitor information to understand the strengths and weaknesses of HP supply chains. Moreover, we need a methodology for applying assessments in a business context.

We engaged an experienced manager from the grocery industry to help in developing the methodologies we need. Our purpose is to develop our own competency and install this capability with our customers. A pilot project with a customer entering a new market was used to validate this approach. This service differs from other diffusion offerings in that the process is evolutionary and the deliverables are entirely customized.

Given these business challenges, our analysis consists of the following:
- *Business Strategy and Context Assessment* develops an understanding of strategy, plans, and initiatives supporting the business and their supply chain implications. We develop an agreement on who has to be involved, people who can ensure successful application of the information (or prevent this from happening), identify competitors deserving our attention, and provide an initial review of competitors' supply chains. Continuity is our main focus—how to install ongoing capabilities within the business unit as part of other competitive assessments. If this continuity requisite is not met, the engagement ends.
- *Alignment Workshop* reaches agreement on which questions to ask about which competitors and which "control limits" are needed when these choices require revision. An action plan for working with success measures is the final outcome of this workshop.
- *Competitor Supply Chain Analysis* reveals strengths, weaknesses, opportunities, and threats in light of our competitors' plans, initiatives, and assets. The analysis builds on the focus of interest in our competitors' supply chains.
- *Review Workshop* arrives at a common understanding of analysis results and plans for next steps with agreed-upon ownership and success measures.

Forecasting and Planning for Supply Chain Management

Several improvements in forecast accuracy using improved processes, metrics, and tools have given rise to this workshop. In the Asia Pacific region, for example, a new tool has provided decision makers at the regional distribution center and in all major countries in the region with an instantaneous view of inventory throughout the supply chain and forecasts compared with actual orders. New metrics are used to reward country managers who provide more accurate forecasts. A monthly process has been implemented to support the new tool and metrics. This workshop helps businesses improve forecast accuracy using the principles learned in recent projects. Questions addressed during the workshop include:

- What are the best ways to track forecast accuracy?
- How can decisions between marketing and planning be made efficiently?
- What tools are available to help improve forecasting?
- What are some industry best practices from which we can learn?

The workshop supports cross-functional teams in formulating action plans for improving forecast accuracy through:

- *Preworkshop Assessment* reviews forecasting and planning metrics used by the groups in attendance.
- *Process Mapping* develops an understanding of information interfaces that support decisions. The outcome is to identify opportunities and challenges and define the steps required to address them.
- *Metrics Identification* develops a thorough understanding of which supply chain metrics are successful in the business context at hand.
- *Tool Review* provides an overview of easy-to-use tools for monitoring and improving supply chain performance through forecasting and order-fulfillment metrics.

Inventory-Driven Costs Workshop

A program on channel partnerships was envisioned on the basis of a successful pilot, which involved weekly data sharing and joint ordering from top resellers. Our team provided diffusion of learning in several areas—supply chain basics (Lee and Billington 1992; Davis 1993), countering the bullwhip effect (Lee, Padmanabhan, and Whang 1998), and information sharing in a supply chain (Lee and Whang 1998)—and helped HP account managers and field representatives see the benefits of transforming the pilot into a permanent program. Incremental prototyping based on existing modules was the approach we took to developing the program.

A traditional learning session was followed by a design review and, finally, a commitment to the proposal by all parties. This channel partnership program was successful at cutting inventory-driven costs from the supply chain nearly in half in its first year.

This workshop includes the following steps:

- *Perform Assessment* by conducting a review of the business situation, future scenarios, and key performance measures.
- *Review Results* to develop a common understanding of why inventory-driven costs are important and what can be done to reduce them.
- *Present Supply Chain Basics* to develop a common understanding of the principles of supply chain management.
- *Review* existing plans and initiatives.
- *Develop Action Plans* for reducing inventory-driven costs.

Supply Chain Management Conference

This annual event, the fourth in a series, reflects our evolution to Innovation Diffusion in theme, format, and resources. Originally, we focused on planners and buyers from HP businesses, our original customer base. As requirements changed, however, dependencies on other functions and supply chain partners started to change and with them our intended audience. With each conference, we found we had created a "community of experts," in which customers could showcase successful initiatives, take advantage of resources, and learn from other participants, including SPAM consultants, customers, and partners.

With our fourth conference, "Doing Business at Internet Speed," the evolution of Innovation

Diffusion and Hewlett-Packard have come full circle. In the current 24/7 business environment, there is little time for reflection or formulating a response to new realities while running a successful business. Therefore, the conference as a once-a-year opportunity for dialog has evolved into an ongoing community focused on continuous problem solving. We are developing an infrastructure to support interaction between the members of this community, where everyone plays a role in determining the best response to an emerging business issue. This fresh approach allows Innovation Diffusion to strengthen its role as strategic adviser and provide the leadership customers have requested. Instead of an agenda frozen in time, we are facilitating an ongoing discussion organized by "threads" that unfold at Internet speed.

The conference development process includes the following steps:

- *Surveys* are undertaken to determine customer business needs and interests, so we can develop a design. An outcome is a design committee that ensures customer needs are met at the conference itself. (In the future, information from the community will make surveys less critical for diagnostic purposes.)
- *Framing Business Issues* allows the conference team to identify the primary challenge the company faces. Entering the retail business (1996), meeting the Dell challenge (1997), and understanding the impact of the Internet on our business models (1999) are three examples of major business issues.
- *Understanding Innovations* focuses attention on trends across industries and companies, helping HP business units learn from diverse sources.
- *Success Stories in Hewlett-Packard* reveals who is doing what, why, and how in supply chain management. Community members showcase their successes and exchange ideas with their peers.
- *What It Means to My Business* develops a common understanding of the current situation and identifies what to do, how to do it, and how to measure success. Millions of dollars have been saved by HP businesses applying the lessons advanced in our conferences.

Product Rollover Workshop

This workshop stems from the experience of a product manager who needed to conduct a product rollover in difficult circumstances. Previous rollovers had cost more than planned because of schedule slippages and excess inventory in the channel. A rollover strategy with contingency plans was needed to avoid these costly problems, with agreement on roles and responsibilities from everyone involved.

The workshop develops an understanding of supply chain fundamentals, rollover cost drivers, and strategic issues (including "triggers" for activating contingency plans during the rollover process). We conduct cross-functional planning for the rollover and define roles, responsibilities, handoffs, and timelines. Commitment by all players to strategic and contingency plans is an essential outcome.

Workshop modules were developed through evolutionary prototyping (based on materials from Stanford and UCLA) and incremental prototyping (based on analytical work by SPaM (Billington, Lee, and Tang 1998). Our emphasis, however, is on analyzing past and planned rollovers to ensure common understanding of the issues and action planning for the rollover team. These highly customized modules precede and follow a conceptual framework originally published in *Sloan Management Review*. Finally, an organizational perspective on the experience of HP rollover teams is included for transfer to the business situation we face.

Supply Chain Workshop

This workshop is our most versatile offering for customers and partners. It focuses on implementation of supply chain strategies, including the need to develop support for strategic choices, develop action plans, and solicit feedback for the strategic process. Participants gain a thorough understanding of supply chain issues and what can be done to address them in their own business context. Initiatives we have supported include automated inventory replenishment, cycle-time reduction, improving service levels, collaborative planning, and improving product design for supply chain efficiency.

The need to include supply chain factors in phase reviews is an important consideration that arises from these themes. Traditional factors have included time-to-market and material costs, but costs associated with product design and supply chain performance have usually gone unrecognized. Since designers' performance measures are driven by phase reviews, customers have rarely been able to motivate designers to consider modularity, standard interfaces, and standard parts as ways to reduce total costs. This becomes even more important as product design becomes an outsourced function.

This workshop deals with supply chain cost drivers, ROA, and Design for Supply Chain Management and examines a proposal to include supply chain factors in phase reviews. Workshop sessions are based on standard modules with incremental changes to reflect the customer's business situation. Success is indicated by management commitment to join customer efforts to modify the phase review process to include supply chain considerations.

Customer Partnerships

As we have seen, Innovation Diffusion is driven by customer business needs. By segmenting these needs, we have introduced changes in what we provide in response. Our evolution as a service provider enables us to deal with the challenges customers face and, most important, to respond at Internet speed. Rapid assessment of the business situation, for example, and development of strategic responses has sharpened our competitive edge in providing supply chain and asset management innovations. Beyond our traditional offerings, we offer customized services, new technologies, and refreshed expertise. Acquiring knowledge and experience continuously allows us to create knowledge assets, solutions, and applications as quickly as customer business situations evolve.

Notice the similarities between our diffusion approach and trends in information technology. Large-scale investments in IT infrastructure are being replaced by fast, targeted application of standard products with common interfaces and protocols. Customization is a competitive differentiator, built mostly on the foundationally unique knowledge of expert providers. This new way of working avoids the high failure rate of "big bang" (Schmickrath 1999) projects and the increased complexity of our supply chains. Businesses moving at Internet speed cannot afford a freeze of resources and time during which value is created by multiple players with different faces. Our partners in one supply chain may be fierce competitors in another (and these competitors may contend for the same partners). In a changing world, diffusion of knowledge strengthens our competitive position and becomes essential to successful enterprise-wide relationships.

Our role as a service provider has shifted, as well. Interactions with customers are moving from the operational level to helping business leaders face new realities, develop economic measures of success, and evaluate strategies. From building capability and supporting the allocation of resources to diffusion of breakthrough innovations, we help businesses identify what they need to deal with the current situation, ensure achievement of common goals and objectives, and support strategies created from carefully evaluated alternatives.

Knowledge Assets

With Innovation Diffusion, the development and management of knowledge assets becomes a primary activity. Ideally, we create assets that will have the greatest impact on business results, a "mass customization" approach that is responsive and productive. Within the current 24/7 business environment, however, development seems to require customers and partners. Knowledge creation does not happen in a vacuum (after the innovations have been made) but requires solid grounding in a business situation as well as an understanding of the need for transfer to a larger community. Knowledge must be transformed into deliverables mapped to customer business needs. Our consulting practices are segmented by developmental needs, as well, to make sure we build the necessary assets from which to create a solution for each customer engagement. We continuously evaluate our knowledge assets to determine whether we have what we need to address customer problems and plan our next development efforts. Assets must be tested and evaluated to make sure HP business interests are served when delivering value to customers, external as well as internal.

Capturing knowledge from many sources—academic institutions, SPaM project experience, HP business units, and other companies—is an important aspect of meeting customer needs for dynamic problem-solving capability. Learning with and from the supply chain management community beyond Hewlett-Packard helps us to leverage and manage these assets.

Prototyping

Having discussed customer partnerships and knowledge assets as important aspects of Innovation Diffusion, we now point out the dynamic nature of the development process. Prototyping is essential. No matter which deliverables we consider—seminars, workshops, assessments, conferences, Websites, or other assets designed to guide business teams in addressing their needs—we create prototypes that capture our experience. From prototypes we develop the means to address business problems dynamically, and the process of iterative refinement has served us well in developing approaches that are increasingly effective. What we sometimes call a "solution" does not appear until a prototype has been refined many times and applied repeatedly to the problem at hand.

Prototyping can be accomplished in several ways, but they have in common the developmental technique known as "building a model." Indeed, modeling to capture, extend, and apply knowledge is as important to Innovation Diffusion as it is to analytical disciplines like Systems Dynamics or Decision Analysis. Just as models lead to greater understanding in these problem-solving domains, models lead to effective knowledge assets for improving business performance. As our close association with Strategic Planning and Modeling suggests, we have built a highly successful consulting practice on the development of models to address business situations across divergent business domains. Prototyping is the crucial first step in our modeling approach (Preece 1994).

Three prototyping methods are outlined in Table 1.

- *Rapid prototyping* allows us to develop knowledge from scratch as a response to the

TABLE 1
Prototyping Methodologies for Developing Knowledge Assets

Method	Characteristics	Competencies
Rapid prototyping	• Create knowledge from scratch • Assume business needs are inaccurate or incomplete • Assume knowledge design will be redone	• Ability to develop new subject-matter expertise • Methodology for knowledge development and evaluation • Business knowledge
Evolutionary prototyping	• Reuse modules • Focus on amending and adapting knowledge • Assume knowledge can be applied in a new business context	• Subject-matter expertise • In-depth knowledge of business commonalties and differences • Methodology for evaluation of knowledge in the business context
Incremental prototyping	• Expand modules • Focus on increasing content in a given knowledge design • Assume increase of knowledge	• Continuous growth of subject-matter expertise • Methodology for evaluating and addressing business needs • Knowledge of the developing business

business situation. Business needs may not be accurate or complete, so any intervention undertaken without validation might be a poor investment. Methodology for developing and evaluating knowledge is the competency required. This approach supports assessments or other collaborations with the modeling experts on our team. Transforming Supply Chains for eBusiness (workshop) and Supply Chain Management Conferences derive from rapid prototyping.

- *Evolutionary prototyping* focuses on amending existing knowledge. Reuse of content developed for other projects and transferred to new situations is the competency required. This approach is used for our existing portfolio of knowledge assets and includes using external experts to deliver modules. The Product Rollover Workshop stems from evolutionary prototyping.
- *Incremental prototyping* is used to expand existing modules to include additional elements in an existing knowledge design. New modules may be developed through exchange programs, internal R&D, or evaluation of seminar contributions. This approach has produced Open Enrollment Classes and Supply Chain Workshops.

Customer Engagement Process

Our customer engagement process begins with defining the business context for our involvement, identifying leverage points through prototyping, completing and implementing the knowledge design, facilitating the design review process, planning next steps, and evaluating our results. In many instances, we assume an existing strategic intent, so we work with the customer to determine the primary business issues or initiatives or action plans needed to formulate a strategy.

Defining the business context leads to a shared understanding of objectives expressed in a Memorandum of Understanding. Typically, we interview the most important stakeholders, those who can make the project a success or prevent any implementation. Depending on project scope, prototyping can be part of establishing the business context. Identifying and validating leverage points involve reviewing a prototype knowledge design. Stakeholder review allows us to evaluate the knowledge design. The final design must be approved by the project leader and the sponsor. The design is then implemented, as a workshop, application, or process for addressing business issues. We use design reviews to apply learning directly to the specific business context.

This process allows us to generate "next steps." The project leader has an opportunity to present the plan with an informed audience of players in a facilitated session. Those involved in creating the prototype participate in the review and suggest modifications before making a commitment of support or accepting a new role in the proposed plan. Evaluation focuses on insights by customers on the entire process. We collect customer input at the end of the engagement and some time later. The latter assessment is typically 1 to 2 months later and is driven by the duration of initiatives, response time to issues, or time between plan and implementation. Finally, we need to determine the engagement's return on investment with the sponsor, project leader, and main stakeholders.

Management Support

A major barrier to the success of Innovation Diffusion is alignment with upper-management support. Although workshops are the preferred way of gaining this alignment, some organizations are not ready. They require preparation to ensure the involvement of key stakeholders. Often their participation depends on recognizing symptoms, communicating issues, and persuading managers of the need for alignment. Articles we have developed and published in major journals address these awareness and credibility issues; they advance our marketing efforts while preparing organizations for the involvement of experts.

Another benefit of publication is enhanced credibility as a service provider from within the company. We help organizations along their developmental path with customized workshops featuring publications and other materials that allow people to learn supply chain management concepts. Workshops also provide a mechanism for giving new employees the knowledge to work with their peers.

An Evolving Business

Management of the Product Processes Organization has insisted that we develop Innovation Diffusion as a self-sustaining and profitable business. This gives us the freedom to succeed and grow but requires a different business model than that found in most industrial firms. To be economically viable, we have learned that it is very important to:

- Understand in detail who our customers are, what they need for success in their business, and what would be a cost-effective solution to their needs.
- Partner with customers to develop clear and shared objectives. This is a critical element in the Memorandum of Understanding. The MOU also defines the project relationship between customers, partners, and ourselves.
- Ensure that any significant customer interaction has explicit sponsorship by upper management. This should be spelled out in the Memorandum of Understanding.
- Be able to develop customized solutions quickly, using prototyping as our main development approach.

To maintain a pool of expertise, we track trends and practices in industries we recognize as role models. This requires partnerships and ongoing relationships with HP businesses, innovative industries, industry experts, and universities.

Conclusion

In the spirit of doing business at Internet speed, Innovation Diffusion has been gathering momentum as a leading-edge service that orients businesses toward future success. Our origins in Supply Chain Education are still visible in open enrollment classes, publications, Websites, and other offerings in which reusable learning is captured, packaged, and presented. Newcomers will always need an orientation to technical subjects like supply chain management, forecasting and planning, product design, order fulfillment, and others. This is the domain of "education and training," the field of best practices, in which our subject-matter experts continue to play a significant role at Hewlett-Packard.

The power of Innovation Diffusion is manifest, however, in original approaches to business problems for which we provide (and sometimes invent) a wide range of solutions, from situational analysis to formulation of strategic responses for dealing with uncertain futures. Here the word *innovation* has special meaning. In the quest for significant breakthroughs, Innovation Diffusion begins with an exploration of business needs, collaborates on solutions capable of generating a strong return on investment, builds commitment through management support, and delivers results to the customer's satisfaction and delight.

As we expand our business horizon to embrace a broader range of customers, we intend to remain both effective and profitable. We are working to ensure that customers appreciate the contribution to their business of breakthrough innovations and the value of our ongoing involvement. We recognize that our credibility in offering state-of-the-art services is a requirement for growing our business and a welcome challenge to our problem-solving capability. Making effective use of the approaches, processes, and tools described in this paper, we expect to demonstrate the increasing power of Innovation Diffusion to advance both our customers' and our own business success.[1]

---

[1] For his leadership and sponsorship during our years of existence, the Innovation Diffusion team within Strategic Planning and Modeling expresses its gratitude to Corey Billington, now director of PPO Professional Services at Hewlett-Packard. For knowledge development, editorial insight, and general wizardry in creating this article, we are grateful to Michael Stillman.

References

BILLINGTON, C. AND M. MORA (1995), "Inventory-Driven Costs—The View through the Windshield," *Financial Notes—The Magazine of the Worldwide HP Financial Community*, 1999.

———, H. L. LEE, AND C. S. TANG (1998), "Successful Strategies for Product Rollovers," *Sloan Management Review*, Spring 1998, 39, 3, 23–30.

CASEY, C. AND D. BRANVOLD (1995), "Supply Chain Fundamentals," Windows-based computer reference tool.

DAVIS, T. (1993), "Effective Supply Chain Management," *Sloan Management Review*, 34, Summer 35–46.

HOPE, T. AND J. HOPE (1996), *Transforming the Bottom Line-Managing Performance with the Real Numbers*, Harvard Business School Press, Boston, MA, USA.

KUPER, A. (1999), "Supply Chain Management from the 30,000 Foot Level," published in the library section of www.hp.com/go/supplychain

LEE, H. L. AND C. BILLINGTON (1992), "Managing Supply Chain Inventory: Pitfalls and Opportunities," *Sloan Management Review*, 33, 65–73.

——— AND ——— (1995), "The Evolution of Supply Chain Management Models and Practice at Hewlett-Packard," *Interfaces*, 25, 5, 42–63.

——— AND J. WHANG (1998), "Information Sharing and Supply Chain Management," working paper.

———, P. PADMANABHAN, AND S. WHANG (1998), "Information Distortion in a Supply Chain: The Bullwhip Effect," *Management Science*.

———, ———, AND ——— (1999), "The Bullwhip Effect Exploring Causes and Counter Strategies," published in the library section of www.hp.com/go/supplychain

PREECE, J. (1994), *Human-Computer Interaction*, Addison-Wesley Publishing Company.

SCHMICKRATH, D (1999), "How Do Caterpillars Learn to Fly? Transforming Supply Chains at Hewlett-Packard." *Supply Chain Management Review*, Winter 2000.

André Kuper is a member of Innovation Diffusion, a consulting team within Strategic Planning and Modeling (SPaM), which reports to PPO Professional Services at Hewlett-Packard. His work focuses on accelerating the diffusion and implementation of supply chain innovations. Before joining HP, André worked at the Applied Superconductivity Lab at the University of Twente and at Andersen Consulting in Enschede, The Netherlands, doing research and applying innovations in superconducting technology for the former organization and multimedia self-learning tools for the latter. André Kuper holds Masters in Applied Physics and Instructional Design from The University of Twente, The Netherlands.

Dwight Branvold consults with HP business leaders who need to manage process complexity, supply chain cycle time, customer commitment performance, demand-supply matching, product rollover, inventory-driven costs, and other business uncertainties. As manager of Innovation Diffusion, he has worked with customers in virtually every sector, geography, and market segment across HP and has developed professional relationships with leading supply chain experts worldwide. His team uses these resources to help strategy leaders implement initiatives that meet critical business needs. Dwight joined Hewlett-Packard in 1986 and founded Supply Chain Education in 1992. He has published several articles in the performance technology literature and presented at conferences and seminars on supply chain management. He holds an M.S. degree in counseling from the College of William and Mary and a Ph.D. degree in instructional science from Brigham Young University.

EXPERIENCES WITH THE USE OF SUPPLY CHAIN MANAGEMENT SOFTWARE IN EDUCATION*

ANN CAMPBELL, JARROD GOENTZEL, AND MARTIN SAVELSBERGH

School of Industrial and Systems Engineering, Georgia Institute of Technology, Atlanta, Georgia 30332, USA

This paper discusses four experiments and experiences with the use of supply chain management software, in this case the CAPS Logistics software, at different levels of undergraduate and graduate education at the School of Industrial and Systems Engineering at the Georgia Institute of Technology. We hope that the readers will get an idea of the commitment and resources necessary to integrate supply chain software into the classroom as well as the potential rewards.
(LOGISTICS GAMES, SUPPLY CHAIN SOFTWARE, LOGISTICS EDUCATION)

1. Introduction

In the past decade, society has witnessed unprecedented changes in the availability and use of information technology. The use of e-mail and the Internet has become common place in industry as well as in many households. There has also been an increase in the availability of sophisticated planning tools, especially in the area of supply chain management, with vendors such as i2 Technologies, Manugistics, CAPS Logistics, and Numetrix.

Such changes should affect curricula at all educational levels in order to prepare students for the high tech world in which they will be living. Many people believe, for example, that it is essential that elementary school students are exposed to the Internet. Likewise, we feel, that it is necessary to expose undergraduate and graduate students in industrial engineering, management science, operations management, and operations research to sophisticated planning tools, such as supply chain management software.

This paper discusses four experiments and experiences with the use of supply chain management software, in this case the CAPS Logistics software, at different levels of undergraduate and graduate education at the School of Industrial and Systems Engineering at the Georgia Institute of Technology. We hope that the readers will get an idea of the commitment and resources necessary to integrate supply chain software into the classroom as well as the potential rewards. Our choice to use the CAPS Logistics software was one of convenience; it was available. However, there is no reason to believe that the experiments we discuss cannot be replicated with other supply chain management software.

In each of the experiments, students learn supply chain concepts in an environment that resembles one that they may encounter when they finish their education and go on into

---

* Reprinted from *Production and Operations Management*, Vol. 9, No. 1, Spring 2000, pp. 66–80.

industry. The use of supply chain management software makes teaching supply chain management more flexible and more extensive and provides students with more elaborate problem situations that better represent reality. Most supply chain software has well-developed graphical interfaces to represent the elements of the supply chain being studied. Visual representations help students connect better with the data and the solution methods.

We discuss the use of supply chain software in the form of an inventory routing game, as part of a case study and a design project, and as the basis for a software development class. Each of these situations represents a different level of interaction with the software. The inventory routing game can be used in a single lab session and does not require any previous exposure to supply chain management software. In a case study or a design project, where supply chain concepts are learned through model development, the use of supply chain management software is more involved and requires either previous experience or some form of basic training. Software development requires a much greater time commitment and has to be the focus of an entire class. In this case, students have to be or have to become intimately familiar with the supply chain management software and its capabilities.

The various situations also offer a continuum of interaction with reality. A game is internal to the class, removed from the source of data. A case study represents a company setting, perhaps incorporating some prepared data. In a design project, students work directly with company representatives and the data gathering process. In software development, students must draw from many experiences to anticipate operational reality.

The structure of the remainder of the paper is as follows. In Section 2, we briefly introduce the CAPS Logistics supply chain software. Section 3 describes our experiences with the use of a logistics game for vendor-managed inventory resupply. A supply chain design case study is presented in Section 4. The design project in Section 5 considers standard vehicle routing. Section 6 traces the software development of the inventory routing game used in Section 3. Finally, in Section 7, we summarize the advantages and disadvantages of using sophisticated planning tools in education based on our experiences. In order to facilitate replicating some of the experiments described in this paper, we provide more detailed information on each of them either in Appendices A–D or on The Logistics Institute web page at www.tli.gatech.edu.

2. Supply Chain Software

CAPS Logistics is a market leader in logistics modeling software. Its modeling capabilities are supplemented with a geographic information system (GIS) and optimization functionality. The core of all products is the Logistics Toolkit, which consists of logistically based data structures, modeling tools, and a macro-modeling language (MODL). Menu-driven platforms, created in the MODL language, provide specific modeling structures for a variety of routing and supply chain applications. The Logistics Toolkit allows further customization of each platform so that the models can be tailored to unique logistics scenarios. Logistics entities—such as plants, orders, distribution centers, customers, products, transportation channels, and vehicle routes—are made tangible through the graphical user interface (GUI) and up-to-date electronic maps and roads. CAPS software links with Microsoft Access via open database connectivity (ODBC).

Georgia Tech acquired the CAPS Logistics supply chain software when it joined CAPS Logistics Academic Link program. The Academic Link program offers CAPS Logistics software at no charge to its partners for use in teaching, research, and presentations. More information on this program is available at www.caps.com/partnerclients/academic/acadpart.cfm.

3. Game Session

A simple way to introduce supply chain software in the classroom is by means of logistics games. Logistics games simulate the realities of a particular logistics problem, allowing the

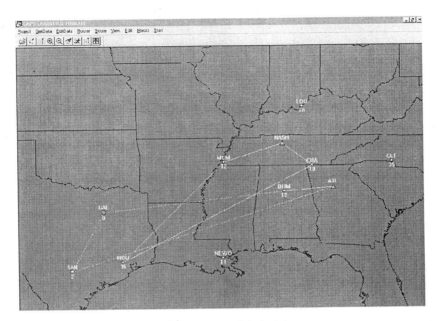

FIGURE 1. Screen capture of the logistics game.

students (players) to develop a thorough understanding of the problem and to design and test various solution strategies in an engaging environment. Since the quality of the decisions made by the player are quantified by a score, students can compete with each other as in other games and make learning more fun.

There are several logistics games publicly available. In Appendix A, we provide a list of the ones that we are aware of and where they can be obtained. The main difference between the logistics game that we have used and the publicly available logistics games mentioned in the appendix is that the one we have used is built on top of commercial supply chain management software. This has the advantage that while students are playing the game and are learning about a specific logistics problem situation, they are also exposed to features of the underlying supply chain management software. Furthermore, the game has a professional user interface and extensive database capabilities, since they are "borrowed" from the supply chain management software (Figure 1).

We have used the logistics game in a master's level class on distribution systems. The class had just started studying routing and scheduling, and the logistics game considered vendor-managed inventory resupply. (Section 6 discusses the development of this logistics game in more detail.) The problem is to minimize the cost of supplying a set of customers over a certain planning period while trying to ensure that customers do not run out of product. When vendor managed resupply policies are in place, the vendor can make deliveries whenever he wants, and he can deliver any quantity that will fit in the customer's storage tank at the time of delivery. All customers use product at a customer-specific rate and have varying storage capabilities. Thus, a planner has to make decisions about who should receive a delivery each day, which vehicles and drivers should be used, what routes should be followed, and what quantities should be delivered.

In the game, the student assumes the role of planner and makes these decisions. The objective of the game is to minimize the total cost over the planning period. The total cost includes mileage costs, drivers' wages (both regular and overtime), fixed costs for using vehicles, and penalties for the length of time that a customer is out of product. At any time during the simulated planning period, the player (student) can construct new routes, provided that there are vehicles and drivers available at the distribution center. This involves using

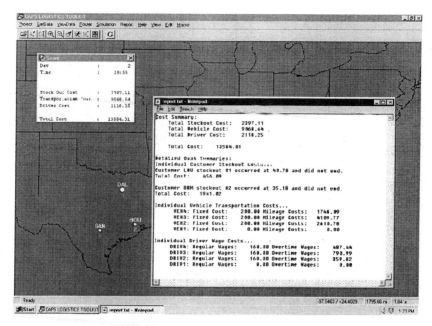

FIGURE 2. Report showing the score of a particular game play.

menus, clicking on customer icons, and entering delivery volumes, as prompted by information on the screen. These routes are executed, the appropriate costs are incurred, the internal database is updated, and the graphical representation of the state of the system changes accordingly. During the planning session it is possible to look at helpful statistics about the customers and their inventories, the vehicles, as well as at information about what has been planned and not yet executed. All of this is an effort to make the game as close to reality as possible so that the students can understand and appreciate the complexity and difficulty of the problem, but in as simple and entertaining a way as possible (Figure 2).

We installed the inventory routing game on several computers in a laboratory setting. Students were divided into groups, and a sample "play" of the game was demonstrated to all of them. They were given 30 minutes to get familiar with the game before playing the game through the entire planning period trying to get the best score possible. While getting familiar with the game, students quickly got a good understanding of the complexities associated with implementing a vendor managed inventory resupply policy by experiencing the impact on cost of different decisions. The graphics helped the students form ideas for routing strategies. From experimenting, they also quickly realized the benefits of planning ahead and considering the long term rather than just the short term, especially when resources are tight. For example, they might plan on sending a truck from Atlanta to Dallas without considering making deliveries to customers along the way earlier than necessary. They often realize a little later, when this truck is on its way to Dallas and all of the vehicles are tied up, that the customers in between are getting close to running out. Experimentation also taught the students what information was important to track for the customers.

Logistics games provide a simple way to help students gain a thorough understanding of complex logistics problems. They experience very directly what makes these problems difficult. By experimenting, they form ideas both on how to and how not to solve them. As mentioned earlier, in our case, they were also exposed, although in a limited way, to supply chain management software.

The overall experience was very positive, even though the students felt that they would have been able to do better and learn more if they had had more time both to practice and to play the game. However, it was clear that the students' understanding of the complexities

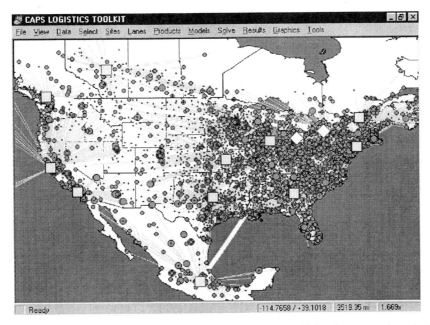

FIGURE 3. Network flow formulation for the supply chain modeling case. Diamonds represent the replenishment depot for Canada and U.S./Mexico. □, regional distribution centers; ○, dealers, scaled according to dollar demand.

of vendor-managed inventory resupply was much greater than could have been expected from lecturing on the subject for the same amount of time. Therefore, it is the intention to develop several more of these logistics games, each addressing a different logistics situation.

4. Case Study Class

A case study concerning the analysis and redesign of a North American distribution system was used as the framework for a focused supply chain modeling course for undergraduate seniors. The format was designed to simulate the work environment that students would soon experience. The professor assumed the role of Vice President for Logistics and the teaching assistant assumed the role of a consultant.

The class was divided into teams of three to five students. All teams were "in training" for the company, temporarily assigned to the VP for Logistics for the length of a school term. Two of the three class projects were designed to use the supply chain software. For that reason, software training occurred in the second week of the 10-week term. The teams remained the same throughout the term. Lectures were provided only when issues arose where the teams required additional education. Teams worked with the software in their own time. No official lab session was established.

The case was based on the supply chain used to deliver service and repair parts to dealers for Ford Motor Company. Drawing upon an existing research relationship with the planning department at Ford, extensive data were available for the case and several decision models had already been developed. Since the term was limited to 10 weeks, it was decided to begin with an established model rather than have students develop their own. The consultant proposed the model, a simplified network flow formulation of the Ford supply chain already implemented in the CAPS software. Students were encouraged to challenge the validity of the model to gain an understanding of the relevant supply chain issues and then to improve and modify it to develop modeling skills. Figure 3 shows the sites and arcs for the network model. In addition, students were furnished with spreadsheets of the data used to establish model cost, demand, and capacity parameters.

The initial project was the same for all groups: determine the number and location of regional distribution centers. The students very much enjoyed the ability to quickly evaluate the effect of moving distribution center locations, both in terms of overall cost and channel decision visualization. Such rapid replication and visualization would not have been possible with a standard paper case.

The second project assigned a different objective to each group, though each was related to the modeling of distribution center to dealer transportation. The network model utilized less-than-truckload (LTL) carrier costs, though most of the dealers received product via multistop routes. One group contemplated how to better consider routes in the model. The second group considered the effect of delivery frequency. The third group determined the merit of using pool points instead of LTL carriers.

Ideally, the initial project would have familiarized students with the software, allowing them to modify the proposed model as needed for the second project. However, the students had not grappled enough with the model in the first project. As a result, they were not able to fully utilize the software capabilities in the second project.

It became clear that the initial project should have been more narrowly defined, allowing the students to implement some simple ideas and concepts and to compare these to the default options provided by the software. In this way, the students would have gained confidence in their software application skills. Course evaluations resonated with this idea. One pointedly said that the class should have started with a "case that was simple enough to have a correct 'answer' so that students would get feedback as to whether they were using (the software) correctly or not."

When students are supposed to adapt and/or develop a model for advanced case analysis, then they need to begin by constructing the model—in their words, "to start from scratch." Though more time consuming, the students would acquire software modeling skills and become more versed in the technology. This interaction with the software should take place in a defined lab session where a "lab advisor," with advanced knowledge of the software, is available for consultation.

Despite struggles with the second project, students warmly welcomed the integration of software with the case study. One student wrote, "The [software] exposure was very beneficial. We were introduced to a real world technology and how to apply it to a real world problem." Software enabled a case study with a mixture of rich data and advanced modeling technology from which the students gained insight on how to approach supply chain problems.

5. Design Project

A design project—or independent study—affords the opportunity to immerse the student in supply chain software. With more focus and a longer time scale than a case, a project allows enough time for effective self-paced learning. Students reap the benefit of this training by evaluating many more solutions and scenarios than would be possible without software.

A design project is part of the core curriculum for industrial engineering undergraduates at Georgia Tech. Titled Senior Design, this project-oriented class is taken during the student's final two quarters. The students are organized into groups of no more than five. Projects are selected from a list of company-submitted proposals, which describe a problem and designate a company representative. One faculty member is assigned as advisor for the group, matching expertise with problem definition.

To illustrate the integration of supply chain software with a Senior Design project, we follow one group through the 6-month process. This particular group of five students chose to work with the Atlanta region of the American Red Cross. The Red Cross suggested to investigate the distribution of blood and blood components to 115 hospitals throughout the state of Georgia. Currently, hospitals place orders daily. Deliveries are either made with Red Cross vehicles that are manually routed each day or sent directly via a courier service or taxicab. Red Cross sought a framework to guide the manual process. Moreover, they aimed to lessen reliance on the expensive courier service. The project targeted these two objectives.

After consultation with the faculty advisor and company representative, data requirements were outlined, and solution approaches were proposed. Route data sheets used by the dispatcher were collected for a 2-week period, capturing order quantities, load/unload time, driving time, and distance between stops. Vehicle, driver, and courier cost parameters were collected to value solutions for this fortnight scenario. Current routes establish a baseline for assessing solution approaches. Space-filling curve (SPC) and nearest neighbor route generation heuristics were proposed.

The group initially planned to evaluate solutions manually using trip mileage technology (at the website www.mapquest.com) and a matrix lookup. The faculty advisor suggested CAPS Logistics software for both route generation and route evaluation.

By the end of the first quarter the group had invoked the software's geographic information system (GIS) functionality to geocode hospitals—translating the address into latitude–longitude. The geographic representation provided a visual understanding of the delivery problem and vector coordinates for the heuristic algorithms. This hour-long process would have been onerous without the software.

At the beginning of the second quarter, students began entering the 2-week order scenario. The need to define orders and vehicles for the software focused the modeling effort. The students had to understand hospital order timing, distinguishing AM and PM orders. Forced to match orders with vehicle characteristics, they determined that vehicle capacity was not a limiting factor since Red Cross vehicles can handle significant peaks in order quantities. Instead, route length in time was the crucial constraint. Software functionality also prompted consideration of time windows. Students determined that although time windows may be important for operation, they were not required for developing the planning framework. Though these issues may have arisen anyway, the software provided a natural setting to guide students through the key modeling issues.

The final report recommended a mixture of the two heuristics as a framework for manual routing. The SPC heuristic was used to route two vehicles for AM deliveries in the Atlanta metropolitan area. They determined that SPC is appropriate where the road network is dense. The nearest neighbor heuristic was used to set the fixed route basis for PM deliveries throughout the entire region (see Figure 4). Eight trucks are used for these routes. Based on results for 2 weeks of orders, the annual transportation cost was reduced by nearly 9%, from $631,000 to $577,000. Routing vehicles over an electronic road network provided credibility for Red Cross managers. Moreover, the software allowed swift, detailed examination of multiple days' solutions. Creating the same visualization and credibility would have been a monumental task without the use of software.

During job interviews, students working on this project have found companies to be very interested in this software experience. In addition to logistics insight, students developed GIS skills and understand of the geocoding process and other issues related to using electronic road networks.

It was observed during the course of the project that students needed a fair amount of time to experiment and familiarize themselves with the supply chain software functionality. Translating raw data into the right form for the software takes time, several weeks in this case. The benefit is that once data are formed appropriately, solution adaptation and replication is speedy. As with the controlled game environment, interaction with many solutions develops insight rapidly. Since this final phase is where much of the supply chain intuition is developed, keeping to an aggressive schedule is worthwhile.

6. Software Development Class

The final example of the use of supply chain software in the classroom is a 10-week course devoted to the development of a logistics game. The objective in the course was to design and implement a logistics game for a complex logistics problem. The game had to have a

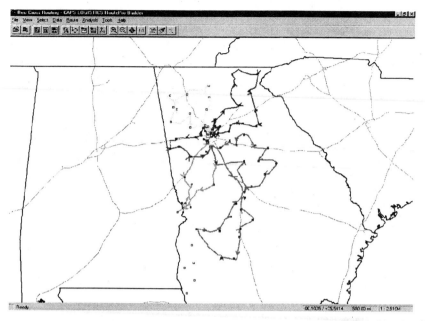

FIGURE 4. Fixed route structure for Atlanta Red Cross deliveries.

graphical interface that would visualize the state of the system as it evolves over time and had to allow a decision maker (the player) to influence the behavior of the system. To achieve this, the class combined a simulation with the visualization and database capabilities of the supply chain software. During the course, students learned more about the specific logistics problem, logistics software, discrete event simulation, interface design, and software engineering. The level of understanding of the supply chain software necessary for this course goes well beyond that required for the earlier examples.

The logistics game developed is the inventory routing game mentioned in Section 3. The group started by developing a thorough understanding of vendor managed inventory replenishment systems by identifying the key objects and relationships involved in such a system. It is essential to understand the relation between usage patterns, vehicle capacities, tank capacities, routing decisions, travel times, etc., in order to create an effective and realistic simulation. Creating state transition diagrams that describe every possible interaction was time consuming, but it was important in obtaining an understanding of how all the factors were related. While doing this, the group identified what data are needed to initialize the simulation, what data are needed to describe the "state" of the system, and what data would need to be maintained. With this in mind, they created an appropriate relational database structure.

After designing the basic interactions to be modeled in the game and creating the database, the class was divided into two groups. One group was assigned the task of developing the simulation (done in C++). The main task of the simulation is to generate the next event based on the current state of the system and the current set of specified routes. The second group was charged with using the supply chain software to create the user interface and to maintain and update the data representing the state of the system.

One of the primary tasks of the group designing the user interface was to represent the "current state of the system." This is a nontrivial task in a complex system, because it typically requires a large amount of data to specify the state of the system. Choices include how to convey as much information as possible through the choice of colors, shape of icons, size of icons, and limited statistics. For example, what information should the size and color of the icons representing the customers give? In the finished game, the color and size indicate whether a customer is using product (small and green), whether a customer's inventory is below some specified threshold (medium and yellow), or whether the customer is out of product (large and red). Another issue was how to handle and display the routes. Should all routes that have been planned but not yet executed be displayed? If they are, the user can quickly see what has been planned, but it may also lead to a possibly crowded screen. In the finished game, only the routes currently being executed are shown, with solid links between the customers that have already received a delivery and dashed links between customers that have not yet received a delivery. Another key task was determining how to guide a novice player through the game by offering enough "help," while not making it annoying for more experienced players.

By the end of the quarter, both groups had their respective parts of the game in place, but there were still some outstanding issues regarding the information passing between the two parts that needed to be worked out. One class member from each group worked on the project during the next quarter to get the game fully functional.

Maybe even more so than in the previous examples, it took the students a long time to get to the point where they felt comfortable enough with the software to carry out the required tasks. Members of the class received basic training on the software early, but did not really start using it until the design of the game was completed. A better understanding of the software early on would have helped in the design of the simulation. It may also have been better to create the teams early on, so that they could have started discussing implementation choices and done some initial coding before the design of the game was complete, increasing the chances of having a working prototype by the end of the quarter.

Using the supply chain software helped speed up the development greatly. Furthermore, being able to call on existing "tools," especially for graphics, enabled the creation of a game that looks professional. The built-in macro language made designing database updates that translate into changing icons and colors on the screen relatively simple. The internal database structure of the supply chain software was easy to use and made maintaining and checking data values fairly straightforward.

Ideally, the inventory routing game would be made available as an executable for students (and others interested) to use at home. Unfortunately, the CAPS Logistics Toolkit does not support the creation of such an executable at the moment. Therefore, the use of the game is currently limited to computers with a license to the CAPS supply chain management software.

7. Conclusions

Overall, our experiences with the use of supply chain software in undergraduate and graduate education have been positive. We conclude by summarizing the advantages and disadvantages of using sophisticated planning software in the class room as we see them. First and foremost, students seem to like it. As a consequence, students participate more actively and absorb more of the material presented to them. Second, the use of sophisticated software allows the instructor to illustrate the material using realistic size instances that reflect the true complexity of the planning problems. Furthermore, using planning software makes it easy to experiment with various instances as well as various solution strategies, all of which lead to a more thorough understanding of the planning problem at hand. Third, most sophisticated planning tools have graphical user interfaces that visualize instances and solutions. Such visualizations are informative and facilitate understanding specific characteristics of the problems. (A picture is worth a thousand words.) Finally, students are exposed to the type of sophisticated software that they may encounter when they finish their education and go into industry. In fact, it increases their chances of finding a job, since many of the companies appreciate experience with sophisticated planning tools.

On the other hand, there are also some disadvantages to the use of sophisticated planning tools. First, as was the case with the supply chain software used in the experiments described in this paper, we are typically dealing with commercial software. This means that the use of the software may not be free of charge, that the use of the software may be restricted, that there may be complicated licensing issues, or that the vendor is only prepared to provide support and training at a cost. Second, the use of software requires appropriate computing facilities and computer support staff. Third, in most cases the use of software, especially sophisticated software, requires a large upfront time investment on the part of the instructor. Many academic institutions do not have a reward structure, in terms of tenure and promotion, that entices faculty to undertake such efforts. Finally, courses involving the use of sophisticated planning software may need to be structured differently. The single biggest complaint from students was that there was not enough time to learn how to use the software. This is not surprising given the complexity of sophisticated planning tools. It would be nice if students could familiarize themselves with the software at home, but this is usually not possible since it is commercial software.

Following is a set of appendices providing more information about other logistics games (Appendix A), our procedure for developing a game using supply chain software (Appendix B), and descriptions of the format of the case studies we have made available (Appendices C and D). The data sets for the case studies are Microsoft Excel documents and do not require CAPS or other supply chain management software to view them or to use them.[1]

[1] We thank the people at CAPS Logistics for the support that they have provided during the activities discussed in this paper.

Appendix A

Logistics Games

The most famous logistic game is probably the Beer Distribution game developed by John Sterman at MIT (Sterman 1989, 1992) (learning.mit.edu/pra/tool/beer.html). It can be played using paper and a few supplies or online using the version implemented at the University of Indiana (Jacobs 2000) (jacobs.indiana.edu/beer). The game involves four entities: a retailer, a wholesaler, a distributor, and a factory. The objective is for each player (entity) to minimize costs, where costs are based on inventory carrying costs and backlog charges.

Jackson and Muckstadt at Cornell University have developed several simulation games, including a distribution game (www.orie.cornell.edu/~jackson/distgame.html), a transportation game (www.orie.cornell.edu/~jackson/trucks.html), and a warehouse location game (www.orie.cornell.edu/~jackson/whsloc.html). The games in this suite are easy to understand, take little time to get started, and are nice graphically. The distribution game involves both a supplier and a central warehouse and requires the user to make supply decisions to meet random demands at multiple locations. The transportation game is concerned more with learning how to make effective routing and scheduling decisions for trucks given a set of demands. The warehouse location program allows the user to locate warehouses, as well as plan truck routes. Also available on Jackson's website is a sampler of multimedia virtual tour of a factory (Jackson and Muckstadt 1990) (www.orie.cornell.edu/~jackson/plnttour.html).

Robert Grubbstrom from the Linköping Institute of Technology in Sweden has developed the international logistics management game (a demo is available at www.ilmg.com). It involves up to seven competing companies, production in four regions, multiple modes of transportation, varying wage and production levels in different markets, and allows communication among the players (companies).

Lean Production is an interactive simulation game modeling a bicycle factory and its supply chain. The game includes a logistics planning and control system based on the MRP II concept and an integrated controlling information system including business planning and performance indicator systems (Zapfel and Piekarz 2000) (www.ifw.unilinz.ac.at/lean.html).

The number of computerized logistics games appears to be increasing, since two more games "in-progress" were found in a web search. The Michigan Interactive Logistics Simulation game developed by Dennis Severance and David Murray is in the process of being made playable online (mis.huji.ac.il/Mils). The Canadian Professional Logistics Institute is producing an interactive CD that simulates a logistics problem considering seasons, shelf-life, and international suppliers and customers. It is not available yet, but the samples viewable on the web at www.loginstitute.ca/cdrom.html look impressive.

Appendix B

Developing a Logistics Game

In this appendix, we provide more details about the development of the inventory routing game, for those interested in creating logistic games themselves.

At the heart of the game is a relational database that stores all the information necessary to describe the state of the system, the planned routes, and the executed routes. The database is initialized with the data describing a specific problem instance. To facilitate playing different instances, an Access database was designed to store all the data necessary to describe an instance. Given a sample Access database, anyone should be able to easily create an instance that represents a variation of the problem in which they are interested. This instance can then immediately be used in the game. In the game, the user selects which Access database to import and the data are imported into the CAPS internal relational database via ODBC. As soon as the data are present in the CAPS database, the user will see a visual representation of the initial state of the system via the graphical interface. The CAPS internal database stores a lot more information than the initial Access database, since the game needs to keep track of the changes that will occur during the planning period as well as the planned and executed routes. This includes, for example, whether each customer is using product or not and where each vehicle is heading from and to.

While playing the game, part of the information stored in the CAPS database is represented graphically on the screen, such as customer locations and partial information concerning their status (above safety stock, below safety stock, or out of product). In addition, the user can use the on screen menus to query the CAPS database and get more detailed information on the customers, vehicles, products, and drivers.

At the start of the game, the user must decide which events (vehicle departs from plant, vehicle arrives at customer, customer starts using product, customers hits safety stock, etc.) will force the simulation/game to pause, so the user can see and evaluate the new state of the system and, if the need arises, can plan new routes. After these decisions are made, the simulation is initiated. This means that all the information in the CAPS database is written out to text files. These text files are used by the simulation to create an initial event queue. The simulation is written in C++ and converted to a dynamic link library (DLL). The game itself is written in MODL, the macro language provided with the CAPS logistics toolkit. At appropriate points in time, the game calls the simulation functions. As in a standard discrete time event simulation, the event queue contains all of the known upcoming events for each customer, ordered by their estimated time of occurrence. When the simulation is called it advances its internal clock until the first event occurs that is of one of the types specified by the user as a stopping event. At this point, the simulation hands back control to the game and passes back an array of values describing what event has just happened and at what time the event took place. Using this information, the game updates all of the time-dependent information in the CAPS database, such as anything involving usage, to give it the appropriate value at the current time. Other information in the array includes which customer, vehicle, and driver (if any) were involved in the most recent event and relevant volumes. This allows CAPS to determine which parts of the planned routes have now been completed and how and when this happened. After the CAPS database has been updated as a result of the event information, the screen is redrawn to reflect the new state of the system. Also included in the array are the values representing the three parts of the score: the driver cost, reflecting hourly wage and overtime costs; the vehicle cost, reflecting a fixed cost for usage and a per mile charge; and stockout costs, reflecting a per unit charge for any customers having deficient inventory. After the database is updated and the screen redrawn, the user has the ability to use the menus to look up information or create any new routes before selecting *resume*. After selecting resume, certain parts of the CAPS database are rewritten to text files, and the control is handed over to the simulation. To maintain the event queue, the DLL for the simulation is not freed until a complete play of the game is complete. Effectively, the simulation just resumes after every event beyond the initial one. The game proceeds in this same way with control passing back and forth until the user decides to end the game or the playing horizon (specified in the original Access database) is reached.

From the above discussion it is clear that we have relied heaviliy on two features of the CAPS Logistics Toolkit: the internal database and the graphics capabilities (including the use of menus, etc.). To reproduce this game or to create one similar to it, institutions that do not have access to the CAPS Logistics Toolkit need access to other supply chain software that can provide similar functionality and features, or need to implement these themselves in standard programming languages such as JAVA. However, the use of a standard programming language will increase the development time significantly.

Appendix C

Inventory Routing Problem Instances

The IRP is concerned with the repeated distribution of a set of products from several facilities to a set of customers over a given planning horizon. The facilities can produce these products at given rates and have ample storage capabilities for the products. The customers consume products at a given rate and have limited storage capabilities. A fleet of vehicles is available at each of the facilities as well as a set of drivers. The objective is to minimize the overall costs during the planning period.

The following data have been collected for two real-life instances of the IRP and are available on The Logistics Institute web page at www.tli.gatech.edu/research/casestudy/cs.htm in the form of several Excel workbooks.

Customers

- ID: an identifier for each customer—such as a business name or city where it is located.

- X: longitude coordinate.
- Y: latitude coordinate.
- OPENTIME: time a customer starts using product each day (using a 24-hour clock, like all times).
- CLOSETIME: time a customer stops using product each day.
- OPENWINDOW: time a customer starts being able to receive deliveries each day.
- CLOSEWINDOW: time a customer stops being able to receive deliveries each day.
- FIXEDSTOP: fraction of an hour required to make a stop at a customer, not including fill time.
- MATEVEHCLASS: type of vehicle able to make delivery at a customer.
- PRODTYPE: type of product that is used by a customer (limit of one currently).
- PRODMEAN: mean rate at which customer uses product per hour when time is between open time and close time.
- PRODSTDEV: standard deviation of this usage rate (not used currently).
- PRODCAPACITY: the limit on how much inventory of a product can be held at a customer.
- PRODSS: "safety stock" for inventory of a product. It is often set so that when inventory falls below this level, this is a trigger to plan a delivery to the customer.
- PRODINV: initial inventory of product at a customer.
- PRODSOCOST: when customer runs out of product, this is the "cost" per unit that the customer would have used if sufficient resources were available.

Drivers

- DRIVERID: an identifier for each driver.
- HOMEBASE: home facility associated with a driver.
- OPENWINDOW: time a driver can start driving each day (not enforced).
- CLOSEWINDOW: time a driver must return to the home plant each day (not enforced).
- REGTIMEWAGE: wages earned per hour of regular time work.
- OVERTIMEWAGE: wages earned per hour of overtime work.
- MATEVEHDRIV: type of vehicle that a driver is able to drive (not enforced).

Facilities

- ID: an identifier for each plant such as the city where it is located.
- X: longitude coordinate.
- Y: latitude coordinate.
- OPENTIME: time plant starts producing (the same for all products currently).
- CLOSETIME: time plant stops producing (the same for all products currently).
- FIXEDSTOP: fraction of an hour required to make a stop at a plant while driver is on a tour, not including reload time.
- FAILUREPARM: parameter for describing frequency of failure in production process (not used).
- MATEVEHCLASS: type of vehicle that is able to pick up product from a plant (not used).

Products

- PRODUCTID: an identifier for each product.
- FILLRATE: number of units of product per hour that can be pumped into a vehicle at the plant.
- DISPENSERATE: number of units of product per hour that can be dispensed from a vehicle to a customer.

Facproducts

- ID: unique record number representing a plant/product pair.
- FACILITYID: an identifier for a plant, must match an ID on FACILITIES worksheet.
- PRODUCTID: an identifier for a product, must match a ProductID on PRODUCTS worksheet.
- PRODRATE: number of units of the product that is produced per hour while plant is producing.
- PRODINV: initial inventory at a plant of a product.
- PRODCAP: limit on amount of inventory of a product that can be maintained at a plant.

Vehicles

- VEHICLEID: identifier for each vehicle.
- HOMEBASE: home facility associated with a vehicle.
- MAXVOLUME: limit on amount of product that a vehicle can hold.
- SPEED: speed at which vehicle drives on average, used to compute travel times.
- FIXEDCOST: cost charged for using a vehicle during the time horizon.
- COSTMILE: cost charged per mile driven on a vehicle.
- PRODUCTID: an identifier for a product, must match a ProductID on PRODUCTS worksheet.
- MATEVEHDRIV: "type" of vehicle (not used).
- VEHFAILPARM: parameter for describing frequency of failure in delivery process (not used).

Instance

- INSTANCEID: identifier for instance.
- TIMEHORIZON: number of days game will be played.
- DRIVLIMIT: driving below this limit will be charged regular wage, above this will be charged overtime wage.
- USAGECHINT: (not used)
- STOPOPEN: (not used)
- STOPCLOSE: (not used)

The following basic questions related to the inventory routing can be investigated:

1. How would you decide which customers should receive a delivery on a day to make sure none of them would run out of product? Would you just look at current inventory or would you look at distance from the plant as well?
2. Which customers do you think would be good choices to be on a route together? What factors would you use to make such a decision?
3. If you were a planner trying to make a schedule for these customers, is there any other information that you think would be helpful?
4. If you were making a schedule for delivering to these customers, how far do you think you would plan ahead to make sure you wouldn't let anyone run out of product? 1 day? 2 days? Why?
5. For a given dataset, which appears to drive the total cost more: stockout cost, driver costs, or vehicle costs? For each of these, if it represented the only cost involved, how would this change your delivery policy?
6. Time horizon is listed as a characteristic of the instance. How do you think strategy would be different if time horizon was 3 days versus 33 days? Why?
7. How do small delivery time windows for customers complicate the problem? Do small windows for using product really affect things?
8. Do you think it would make the problem easier or harder if all customers had product capacity the same size as vehicle capacity? Why?
9. If you consider the stochastic information about customer usage rate, such as customer specific standard deviation, would this change your answer to question 1, and if so, how?
10. If safety stock is used as a signal to start planning a delivery to a given customer, how would you suggest setting this level? What factors would you consider besides usage rate?

Appendix D

Supply Chain Design Case Study

The supply chain design case study focuses on the distribution of automotive parts and supplies to the Ford authorized dealers throughout North America. Ford is faced with pressure to provide excellent customer service, which means timely distribution of parts to the dealers, with minimal logistics investment, both in capital and operations. The design of supply chain infrastructure will have a strategic impact on this objective.

Ford authorized parts flow through supply chain infrastructure that has been used for years and consists of a National Replenishment Center (RC), several Regional Distribution Centers (DCs), and Dealers. The following data have been collected to assist in the evaluation of the existing supply chain and in the construction and analysis of alternative supply chains:

Dealers

- Location: latitude, longitude, and zip code
- Current primary DC
- Current route assignment
- Demand
- Average shipment size

Regional Distribution Centers

- Location: latitude, longitude, and zip code
- Material handling cost
- Fixed cost
- Inventory cost

National Distribution Center

- Location: latitude, longitude, and zip code

Products

- Weight
- Value

Lanes

- Distance
- DC replenishment time, including handling and transportation
- Origin-destination cost quotes for truck and rail
- Carrier contract rates for multistop routes
- LTL cost (nondiscounted) for average shipment size

These data, as well as a more thorough description of them, are available on The Logistics Institute web page at www.tli.gatech.edu/research/casestudy/cs.htm in the form of several Excel workbooks.

The following basic questions are related to the supply chain:

1. Does the current supply chain have the right number of distribution centers and are they placed in the correct locations?

2. Consultants have performed an analysis assuming dealers are allocated to the nearest distribution center. Does such an allocation result in minimal supply chain costs? If not, how should the dealers be allocated to distribution centers?

Other issues that may be addressed are as follows:

1. Dealers are typically visited on multistop routes from a distribution center. There are basically two approaches to modeling multistop deliveries in a network flow structure (the basis for most supply chain design models): (1) fixed dealer clusters, and (2) individual dealers, where the "route costs" are suitably divided over individual dealers. How does the chosen approach affect the resulting supply chain? How should the "routes cost" be divided over individual dealers?

2. Ford makes regular visits to the dealers. It is currently assumed that each dealer is visited three times a week. This allows the computation of average shipment sizes by calculating the overall demand and dividing by the delivery frequency. Average shipment sizes have been used in the supply chain design process. Is this realistic? How does it affect the resulting supply chain?

3. Ford is considering changing to every day delivery. How is this going to affect the costs?

4. Ford is considering the use of pool points. Pool points are locations that provide a similar function as a distribution center, namely transhipment, but without any storage facilities. Pool points can be thought of as parking lots where trailers or loads can be exchanged. Is this a viable option? Where would you locate pool points? How would you operate a supply chain including pool points?

5. Up to now we have not discussed issues related to inventory costs at the distribution centers. How can these be incorporated in the models?

References

Jackson, P. and Muckstadt, J. (1990), *Llenroc Plastics: A Case Study in Manufacturing and Distribution Systems Integration*, Technical Report 898, Cornell University Department of Operations Research and Industrial Engineering.

Jacobs, B. (2000), "Playing the Beer Distribution Game Over the Internet," *Production and Operations Management*, 9, 1, 31–37.

Sterman, J. (1989), "Modeling Managerial Behavior: Misperceptions of Feedback in a Dynamic Decision Making Experiment," *Management Science*, 35, 321–339.

Sterman, J. (1992), "Teaching Takes Off: Flight Simulators for Management Education," *OR/MS Today*, 40–43.

Zapfel, G. and Piekarz, B. (2000), "The PC-Based Simulation Game Lean Production for Controlling the Supply Chain of a Virtual Bicycle Factory," *Teaching Supply Chain Management*, Vol. 2 of *POMS Series in Technology and Operations*.

Ann Campbell is a Ph.D. candidate in the School of Industrial and Systems Engineering at the Georgia Institute of Technology. Her research focuses on integrating inventory and routing decisions, and is motivated, in part, by her work with Praxair, an international industrial gases company that has adopted a vendor managed inventory replenishment policy.

Jarrod Goentzel received his Ph.D. from the School of Industrial and Systems Engineering at the Georgia Institute of Technology. His research focused on supply chain design and was motivated, in part, by his work with Ford Customer Service parts distribution in North America. He is currently Director of Product Management for supply chain products at Baan Company.

Martin Savelsbergh is Associate Professor in the School of Industrial and Systems Engineering at the Georgia Institute of Technology. His research focuses on computational integer programming and computational logistics. His current work includes projects in mixed integer optimization, vendor managed inventory replenishment, and dynamic and stochastic vehicle routing.

TEACHING SUPPLY CHAIN MANAGEMENT WITH AN INTEGRATED BUSINESS CURRICULUM AND SAP CLIENT/SERVER PARADIGM*

R. S. M. LAU, ROBERT E. ROSACKER, AND STEPHEN L. TRACY

Operations Management Department, University of South Dakota, Vermillion, South Dakota 57069, USA

Department of Accounting, University of South Dakota, Vermillion, South Dakota 57069, USA

Business Research Bureau, University of South Dakota, Vermillion, South Dakota 57069, USA

This paper describes our experience of developing and implementing an integrated business approach to undergraduate curriculum modifications using SAP R/3, an enterprise resource planning software system, as a teaching tool. Students are now exposed to integrated business concepts by taking a required, new sophomore-level course in Integrated Business Solutions and by completing the normal series of required business core courses, in which each course has been modified to include work directed at reinforcing integrated business concepts. In addition, two separate Enterprise Resource Planning (ERP) tracks have been developed. Track one requires the completion of two elective courses emphasizing the technical and implementation issues associated with SAP system implementations. Track two involves the completion of a supply chain management course incorporating the SAP Supply Chain Optimization, Planning, and Execution (SCOPE) initiative.
(SUPPLY CHAIN MANAGEMENT, ENTERPRISE RESOURCE PLANNING, INTEGRATED BUSINESS SOLUTION, BUSINESS CURRICULUM, SAP)

1. Introduction

In today's dynamic and ever changing business environment, the communication and interaction between manufacturers and customers are necessarily important to gain competitive advantage. Manufacturers must be closely linked to both suppliers and customers to be responsive enough to customer requirements. Service organizations are no exception, because their customers demand faster responses, accurate records keeping, and better services. To achieve this improved delivery performance, there is a great need to have a more efficient planning and control system to enable the optimal synchronization of all the processes of the organization (Watts, Kim, and Hahn 1992; Rajagopal and Bernard 1993; Tan, Kannan, and Handfield 1998).

With purchased materials and services accounting for 60 to 70% of the cost of goods sold for an average manufacturing company (Chase, Aquilano, and Jacobs 1998, p. 466), supply chain management is one of the most discussed topics among practitioners and academics

---

* Received November 1998; revisions received March 1999 and September 1999; accepted October 1999.

today. The basic premise of supply chain management is to apply a total systems approach to managing the entire flow of information, materials, and services from raw material suppliers through production/distribution facilities and warehouses to the end customers. In addition to achieving manufacturing excellence to gain competitive advantage, businesses are also in need of a number of internal and external reporting mechanisms to satisfy many constituencies' requirements and for managerial decision making. As a result, the major challenge for businesses worldwide is integration across the supply chain, especially in the area of information systems. In recent years enterprise resource planning (ERP) has emerged as a strategic tool to integrate and synchronize all necessary functions within an organization to reduce cost and lead time, which are essential for gaining competitive advantages in this changing business environment.

Although there have been enormous changes in the business world, business schools across the country have been slow to revise their curricula to reflect the changes. The traditional approach to business education is to produce functionally oriented graduates, such as in the areas of accounting, finance, and marketing. Although many business faculty members have admitted that this approach can only satisfy marketplaces that no longer exist in the modern, international environment, little action has been taken because most of us still think and act functionally. In this paper, we describe our experience of developing an integrated business curriculum and using SAP R/3, an ERP software system, as a teaching tool. The new curriculum design has provided our students a smooth transition to learn the concepts and practices of supply chain management. We hope our experience will stimulate more discussions on how to reengineer the existing business undergraduate curricula to better prepare our students to meet the needs in the modern workplace.

2. The Rise of ERP Systems

ERP systems have evolved as a strategic tool in recent years because of continuous improvement in the available techniques to manage businesses and the fast growth of information technology. The growing complexity and the reengineering of business processes are also drivers for ERP. Today ERP can trace its roots back to the 1960s, when material requirements planning (MRP) was used as a proactive method of inventory management and a production planning tool. The basic concept of MRP is to explode the end-item demand into a detailed schedule of purchase or production orders by considering data input from the master production schedules, the bill of material, and inventory records. MRP employs a simple logic but the magnitude of data involved makes it computationally cumbersome; it has gained acceptance only to the extent that computer technology has improved over time.

MRP is a reasonably good technique to managing inventory and for planning purposes but it has two major drawbacks. First, MRP does not consider many constraints that are commonly found in the production system; that is, MRP assumes a fixed production lead time and an infinite capacity. Second, MRP does not take into account other resource constraints or its impact on other functions, other than manufacturing, of the same organization. A modified MRP logic, also known as Closed-Loop MRP, was later developed to address this problem by incorporating a module of capacity requirement planning (CRP).

Eventually, an integrated manufacturing management system, known as manufacturing resources planning (MRPII), was evolved in the 1980s to provide better integration between manufacturing and other functions in the organization. A variety of functions can be linked together in MRPII, including business planning, production planning, master production scheduling, material requirements planning, capacity requirements planning, and the execution system for capacity and priority. Outputs from these systems are integrated with other financial reports, such as the business plan, the purchase commitment report, shipping, and budgeting. However, the focus of MRPII is still on those manufacturing activities, and the integration of information is still quite limited in scope and timeliness.

The complexity of business processes has led to the development of truly integrated solutions that are commonly known as ERP systems, which attempts to integrate the suppliers and customers with the manufacturing information. On the most basic level, ERP is a complex software system that ties together and automates the basic processes of business from taking customer orders to monitoring inventory levels to balancing all financial records. An ERP system can be considered as an automated record keeper or spreadsheet that can tally up a company's resources (such as raw materials and production capacity) and commitments (such as orders), regardless of whether the data are maintained in an accounting, manufacturing, or materials management system. ERP software accomplishes this task by digitally recording every business transaction a company makes, from the issuance of a purchase order to the consumption of inventory, and continually updating all connected systems to reflect each transaction. ERP systems are often described as "a transactional backbone" that gives companies access to the information they need to make more knowledgeable decisions or to support other more task-specific applications, such as electronic commerce or supply chain planning software (Minahan 1998).

The other powerful driver for the rise of ERP is that the pace of change in business is simply becoming too fast for companies to rely on traditional ways of integrating different special-purpose systems together. Many companies today are still using mainframe systems that were built with layer upon layer of custom interfaces dating back a few decades. There has been no central planning to link together all the different systems of software logic. As a result, none of these systems has been designed to communicate with others. Information departments often need to write custom software programs that act as primitive conversation starters to share the data. The results are predictable—a tangled web of customized connections and interfaces that must be maintained and/or torn apart and rebuilt each time the system is changed.

As companies attempt to integrate more and more independent legacy systems and information, they find themselves unable to respond quickly enough and thus spend an increasing amount of time and money customizing and maintaining the various systems. As information is inextricably linked to the core processes of the business, system gridlock means business gridlock. Many companies are stuck in "a quagmire of incompatible architectures and hard-to-maintain but harder-to-eliminate legacy applications" (Koch 1996). Slow information system changes also mean slower product introductions and longer lead times for getting a worldwide view of inventory to those who need the information for decision making. Instead of fighting a losing battle to overhaul the existing computer systems, many companies have decided to turn to ERP software for creating a single, new computing standard across the company, thereby eliminating the need for patchwork integration.

Despite complicated, expensive, and long implementations, the sales of ERP systems have grown enormously, amounting to around $100 billion a year (Davenport 1998). According to a recent Booz Allen & Hamilton study, more than 70% of Fortune 1000 companies have either begun implementing an ERP system or plan to do so over the next few years (Minahan 1998). Smaller firms are expected to adopt similar plans as prices for ERP packages drop and larger companies start demanding their suppliers be ERP compliant.

3. Why Teach Supply Chain Management with SAP?

An effective way to learn supply chain management is to have a thorough understanding of many basic business processes as a whole. Recognizing the importance of an integrated systems approach to managing the complicated business environment, our school initiated the teaching of integrated business solutions in the spring semester of 1998. Our integrated business curriculum uses SAP R/3, the ERP client/server software system developed by SAP AG to achieve tight integration across all functions within an organization. However, companies can no longer rely solely on improved internal efficiencies to be competitive; they must also monitor thousands of external data points and react quickly across their entire supply chain. The new SAP SCOPE (Supply Chain Optimization, Planning, and Execution) initiative, introduced in late 1998 by SAP AG, provides the necessary information infrastructure to support and respond in real time to changing external market conditions. As a direct result of their exposure to new business education methods and SAP, our students have found themselves in demand and immediately marketable to employers.

About the SAP R/3 Client/Server System

SAP is a fully integrated software system supporting the entire range of standard business applications over a multitude of diverse computer platforms. This platform has been selected and implemented by numerous international companies including such notable multinational firms as IBM, Microsoft, Coca-Cola, and General Motors. The best features of the SAP system are full integration and the information is reconcilable or is reconciled automatically (Williams and Hart 1997). It offers business organizations, regardless of size (small, medium, or large), the opportunity to create and access a companywide, "real-time" database on any combination of computer systems (e.g., mainframe IBM, midrange AS/400, or PC-compatible server). SAP R/3 systems are immediately updated on a transaction-by-transaction basis and they are capable of delivering accurate companywide data and information in common currency and language to desktop computers and their support software (e.g., Microsoft Office suite).

SAP R/3 uses a three-tier, client/server structure: presentation server, application server, and database server (see Figure 1). The system is built around a comprehensive set of application modules (such as financials, human resources, manufacturing and logistics, and sales and distribution) that can be used either alone or in combination. The modules can be used to support processes that span different functional areas in a company. Because the modules are integrated and use a common database, transactions processed in one area immediately update all other areas.

With the new release of the SAP R/3 client/server system, SAP users can now enter the world of electronic commerce through the Internet and their intranets. For example, sales executives or representatives can pull out their laptop computers anywhere in the world, connect to the Internet, and initiate customer purchases using Internet-enabled workflow and electronic forms. Employees can also initiate business-to-business procurement activities and MRO (maintenance, repairs, and operations) purchases on the Internet. The filled-out forms route themselves to the appropriate corporate departments over the SAP system. Then all relevant inventory checking, financial, and distribution processes are performed automatically by the SAP system.

After firmly establishing itself as the leader in the market for ERP software, SAP AG is now moving into the supply chain management arena. The move is a direct response to the criticism that, whereas most ERP systems can compile vital information into a single, companywide system, they lack functionality in key areas, such as transportation planning, electronic commerce, and communication exchanges between businesses. This gap has spawned a new breed of software, known as supply chain management software, the most popular of which are application software from companies such as i2 Technologies and Manugistics. Supply chain management software systems allow users to control their supply chains more effectively than the traditional MRPII or even ERP systems (although ERP-type transactional systems are still required in companies operating supply chain management software).

These supply chain management systems take in data from ERP orders or past sales history and create forecasts to help plan the demand. They also take into account the constraints of real-world manufacturing environments, allowing buyers, materials managers, and production planners to develop realistic schedules that can fulfill new orders with existing resources.

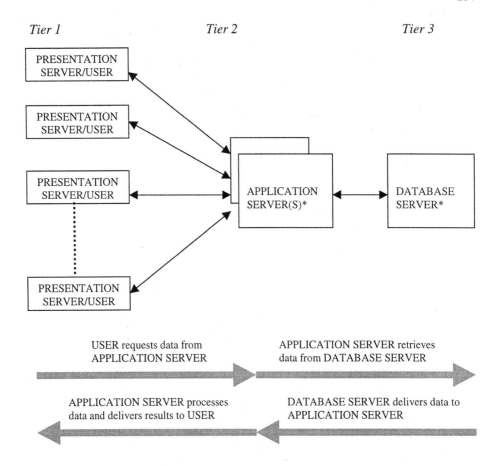

* For a complex environment, there could be many application and database severs linked together.

FIGURE 1. Three-Tier Client/Server Structure.

Not surprisingly, supply chain management software is currently in great demand. A recent study by consultants AMR Research suggests that the supply chain management software market is worth around $1.8 billion and given an anticipated compound annual growth rate of 50%, should see that figure increase to $13.6 billion by 2002 (Crabb 1998).

SAP AG is serious about supply chain management because that application represents 30 to 40% of its potential users and their needs. As a result, SAP AG has undertaken one of its largest development projects ever in SAP SCOPE. As part of its SCOPE project, SAP AG also created a supply chain advisory board composed of 25 SAP R/3 customers and formed the SAP Supply Chain Competence Center to aid the implementation of advanced planning and optimization systems. SAP also plans to spread its expertise in SCOPE by training its business partners to use the TeamSAP education and implementation processes, educating its customers through workshops, and by teaching college graduates at the new Supply Chain Information Institute (Mills 1998).

The SAP SCOPE project includes the introduction of several real-time supply chain applications that can be integrated with its SAP R/3 system and other ERP systems. These supply chain application modules include Business Information Warehouse (BW), Advanced Planning and Optimizer (APO), Sales Force Automation, and others. BW allows users to integrate company-specific information along with commercially available business information, such as market

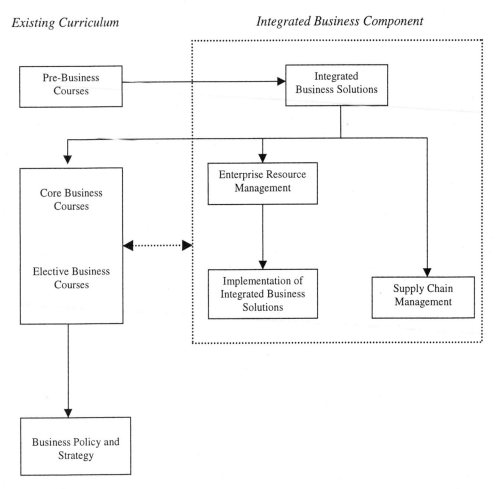

FIGURE 2. Integrated Business Curriculum Design.

research, demographic, and company benchmark data. APO includes five main elements: supply chain cockpit, available-to-promise, advanced planning and scheduling, forecasting, and supply chain planning interfaces. These application elements are indispensable tools for effective management of the entire supply chain. Finally, Sales Force Automation allows salespeople to collect data from both home-base servers and the Internet to provide comprehensive customer data for timely decision making. Each of these application modules is essential for effective management of a supply chain. As SAP AG continues to emphasize and support them, our faculty and students will benefit from using SAP R/3 software as a teaching tool in the integrated business curriculum.

4. Developing an Integrated Business Curriculum

To fully appreciate the concepts and practices of supply chain management, an integrated business curriculum must first be put in place. From the beginning of the development process of an integrated business curriculum, we have carefully evaluated and balanced the needs of the business community, faculty, students, and our unique curriculum requirements. The new curriculum design emphasizes the needs for both technical competence of SAP as well as the concepts and practices of supply chain management. Figure 2 illustrates how the new curriculum helps achieve our objectives. The dotted area represents the added integrated business solutions components to our existing business curriculum. Students may choose one of the two paths to undertake the study of integrated business solutions: (1) by completing a three-course series that emphasizes the technical and implementation issues of enterprise resource planning software, especially SAP R/3; or (2) by completing a two-course series that emphasizes the concepts and practices of supply chain management. The descriptions of these options of study are further elaborated later in this paper. As a result of the added course requirements, fewer credit hours will be required for business and advanced free-elective courses.

There are several obvious reasons that our first SAP track emphasizes the technical and implementation issues surrounding integrated business solutions. First, it is difficult to, and no one should, overlook the fact that the business world has seen an increased use of computer technology for the creation, storage, and dissemination of business information. Concurrently, many major firms have been actively engaged in mergers, creating increasingly larger national and multinational conglomerates. These two forces, individually and in combination, have fostered a need for better and more extensive companywide information systems, systems directed at and capable of blending data and information across the various business disciplines. These modern state-of-the-art information systems must be understood and appreciated by their users. For many years, business education has already responded to these changes by incorporating more computer technology requirements in the existing curricula. These efforts, however laudable and forward thinking they are, are still not sufficient to prepare business students for an extremely dynamic, complex, and multifaceted business world.

Second, SAP software has provided a well-received solution to the information needs of today's businesses. SAP R/3, the client/server version represents the most popular integrated information system currently marketed. A direct result of this phenomenal success has been the creation of a classic mismatch between supply and demand, in which the need for experienced SAP personnel to support implementations and/or to operate installed SAP information systems vastly exceeds the available supply—clearly a "good news, bad news" scenario. On the "good news" side, this shortage in the marketplace has created tremendous opportunities for management and computer consultants. On the "bad news" side, the shortage translates to a critical marketing issue for SAP AG. If a base of trained and proficient consultants/employees does not exist, sales will slow because of the long times required for installation as a result of all qualified personnel being engaged. Furthermore, installation delays have the potential to translate into horror stories. Reports of installation misadventures can adversely affect future sales as potential customers become concerned with the availability of qualified consultants or employees. Some of our new courses are designed to address this critical, immediate need for competent, technical personnel for SAP implementation.

Our second SAP track, the Supply Chain Management paradigm, is directed at enabling the teaching of supply chain management concepts within an integrated business curriculum. Although the two-pronged rationale detailed earlier also applies to this educational model, our real target is to use the broader inclusion of integrated business solution's instruction (using SAP as the training tool) within student educational experiences as a foundation, permitting us to emphasize the operations of an organization, as well as between organizations—the very essence of modern supply chain management.

Curricula Revisions

Revisions to the undergraduate curriculum are twofold. First, a new, three-course sequence (BADM 201 Integrated Business Solutions → BADM 301 Enterprise Resource Management → BADM 401 Implementation of Integrated Business Solution) has been developed and added to our existing curriculum. This three-course sequence will, for all intents and purposes, function as a single continuous course, traversing the sophomore, junior, and senior years. Each course progressively builds on and expands the knowledge base acquired in the prior course(s). After completing this three-course sequence, students are quite capable of understanding and using the SAP R/3 system and competent enough to work on some SAP implementation projects. Alternatively, students may elect to take a Supply Chain Management course in lieu of the last two courses, which emphasize the technical and implementation issues of SAP system. In addition, moderate but substantive changes have been integrated into the material delivered and methodologies used in the required business core courses. This approach allows our students to appreciate their functional contributions to the total business and specifically to the supply chain.

The instructional materials contained within the three-course sequence (or two-course sequence for the Supply Chain Management option) are interrelated to, but not redundant to, that covered in the business core courses. Hands-on experiences in a team-oriented format, within a business case context, are employed in each new or modified class. A single business case is used throughout the undergraduate program of study building toward an implementation scenario in the capstone undergraduate course. Here are the brief descriptions for the four new courses in integrated business solutions.

INTEGRATED BUSINESS SOLUTIONS—BADM 201 (SOPHOMORE-LEVEL). This required course introduces the fundamental concepts and importance of integrated information systems in the modern, international business environment. It provides conceptual foundations and hands-on experiences supporting the development of advanced concepts in junior- and senior-level courses. Specifically, the course uses the SAP paradigm as a model for discussing and building integrated business solutions. It provides an introduction to the SAP information system through hands-on experiences and an exhaustive analysis of an implemented case company. Finally, the course affords a solid introduction to how integrated business solutions and the SAP system are employed in effective business management, including specific discussion concentrating on the concepts and methods of supply chain management.

ENTERPRISE RESOURCE MANAGEMENT—BADM 301 (JUNIOR-LEVEL). Reengineering of business processes has been a prerequisite for successful implementations of ERP systems and supply chain management software. The rationale, methods, and procedures commonly employed in reengineering and deploying enhanced business management processes in the modern, international business world constitute the foundation materials for this elective course. Reengineering of many business processes is a constant in the modern business environment and reengineering concepts currently represent one of the preferred methods for enhancing a company's bottom line.

Specific instruction is directed at business processes executed in the SAP R/3 system through study and analysis of event-driven process chain (EPC) diagrams. EPC diagrams use events to show the logical and sequential relationships between SAP R/3 system functions and business processes. The EPC methodology, a product of the ARIS Toolset from IDS Scheer, enables students to become familiar with information technology–modeling tools that assist in business process reengineering. The use of EPC models in systems analysis and design is a useful framework for problem formulation for any type of integrated business solution. In summary, this course uses a case methodology and hands-on SAP-integrated business solution's experiences surrounding the analysis, documentation, implementation, and use of student-developed reengineered solutions to common business processes.

IMPLEMENTATION/CONFIGURATION OF AN INTEGRATED BUSINESS SOLUTION IN AN SAP ENVIRONMENT—BADM 401 (SENIOR-LEVEL). In this course, all of the integrated system's concepts and hands-on experiences provided to students throughout their program of study are brought together through a team project and simulation activities requiring students to analyze, document, and implement an SAP-based integrated system. The EPC methodology is used to identify and refine possibilities for improving business processes and value-added tasks. The intent is to give the students a "real-world" look and experience with the migration of a case company from its current, heterogeneous business information environment to a fully functional integrated business solution.

SUPPLY CHAIN MANAGEMENT—BADM 402 (SENIOR-LEVEL). Although BADM 301 and 401 have been designed to address the critical, immediate need for competent, technical consultant(s) for SAP implementation, many students can benefit from learning a more holistic view of organizations. BADM 402 Supply Chain Management is designed to place more emphasis on the concept and practices of supply chain management and less emphasis on the system implementation issues of SAP. The course design is driven by the observation that use of the SAP R/3 system can only create better intraorganizational information for decision making, but there is an even greater need for interorganizational communication throughout the supply chain. In addition to the topics usually covered in a traditional supply chain management course, SAP APO (Advanced Planner and Optimizer) will be used as a teaching tool. Newly introduced in 1998, SAP APO provides a complete suite of advanced supply chain planning tools for real-time planning and decision support. Special topics, such as Theory of Constraints and supply chain optimization techniques, will also be included in this course to address different strategic and operational issues of supply chain.

Required Business Core Curriculum Classes

Required sophomore-, junior-, and senior-level core courses in the current undergraduate curriculum include work in the areas of accounting, finance, management, management information systems, marketing, and production. Each of these required business core courses has been modified to include a 2-week integrated business solutions module designed to bring out the integration points between the core discipline and the overall business system. Integration points among these disciplines are first introduced to the student in the required BADM 201 course and reinforced and expanded on within each respective required core course. These modifications are designed to ensure that students may still gain a minimum level of integrated business concepts, even if they choose not to pursue further studies in the BADM 301, 401, or 402 courses.

5. Implementation of Curriculum Revisions

The process of implementing the integrated business curriculum involved two teams of faculty and staff. The SAP Concept Development Team involved the Dean and two professors who had the most knowledge about and experience with SAP systems. They were responsible for the conceptual development of the SAP-integrated business solution's project and for ultimately negotiating, obtaining, and executing the SAP University Alliance Agreement in late 1997. The SAP Concept Development Team members continued their leadership roles at this juncture by forming an interdisciplinary SAP Curriculum Team and providing the necessary ongoing management and direction to the SAP Project.

The SAP Curriculum Team members have been responsible for all aspects of the integrated business solution project throughout its duration, including the approval of project expenditures and the completion of all deliverables required with respect to this project. These individuals were identified by the SAP Concept Development Team as those persons in possession of the personal and educational characteristics ensuring that implementation of these substantive changes in pedagogy stood the highest possibility of success and presented the greatest opportunity for replication.

Implementation Outcomes

The first integrated business solutions class was conducted during the spring semester of 1998. It was designed to be the equivalent of the BADM 201 Integrated Business Solutions course; however, it was held as a readings class because it was directed at, and available only to, graduating seniors. Course enrollment was 15 students and all of them successfully

TABLE 1
BADM 201—Student Evaluations[a]

Classifications	Quality of the Course	Usefulness of the Course
Total ($n = 71$)	3.92	3.92
By gender		
• Female ($n = 25$)	3.68	3.92
• Male ($n = 46$)	4.04	3.91
By academic standing		
• Junior ($n = 25$)	3.56	3.76
• Senior ($n = 39$)	4.05	3.95
• Graduate and others ($n = 7$)	4.43	4.29

[a] A scale of 1 (Poor) to 5 (Excellent) was used for evaluation purposes.

completed the requirements of the class. The course was modeled after WB100 (R/3 Business Process Overview Workshop), a three-day, first-level SAP professional training course.

During the summer of 1998, several sections of the BADM 201 Integrated Business Solutions were completed. Three sections were offered during the 4-week June summer session, one section was offered during the 4-week July summer session, and four sections were offered during a 1-week, special 40-hour session conducted the week before commencement of fall semester. Total enrollment for all sections was 152 students, with each enrollee successfully completing the course requirements. Several sections of this course were team taught by faculty members of the SAP Curriculum Team and this method of instruction was deemed successful and identified by the students as highly desirable.

A survey was taken in the four 1-week, team-taught sections of BADM 201 for evaluation purposes. Students gave very positive responses, respecting the instructions and training they received from the course. When asked if they would recommend this course to other students, 69 out of 71 (97.2%) survey respondents indicated they would. On a scale of 1 (Poor) to 5 (Excellent), the students were also asked to rate the quality and usefulness of each major functional segment [e.g., materials management (MM), human resources (HR), financial (FI), managerial accounting (CO), and production planning (PP), etc.] of the course. Table 1 reports survey results for the overall quality and usefulness of the course by two classifications: gender and academic standing. Simple statistical tests (ANOVA and t test) revealed no significant differences in the mean responses relative to gender. Academic standing seemed to play a role in how the students rated the overall quality of the course ($p = .013$). Graduate students generally rated higher than the seniors and, in turn, the seniors rated higher than the juniors for the overall quality of the course. One explanation for this observed pattern is that the more business courses one takes, the more likely one will appreciate the value of integrated business solutions.

For the fall semester of 1998, 133 students registered for the BADM 201 Integrated Business Solutions classes and 93 students registered for the BADM 301 Enterprise Resource Management. Enrollments for new elective courses have traditionally averaged less than 35 students per class. The new, 2-week integrated business solution's segments in the business core courses were implemented in at least one section of each business core course, for experimental and evaluation purposes during the fall semester of 1998. The experience gained from these new course materials will be used for future modifications of our business core courses. For the spring semester of 1999, the first section of BADM 401 has been offered, thereby completing the first track-one's series of courses for the SAP system. BADM 402 (Supply Chain Management) will be initially offered in the spring semester of 2000, thereby enabling the completion of the first track-two's sequence of courses.

TABLE 2
Supply Chain Management Course Outline

1. *Emerging Topics in SCM*
   - Globalization and logistics network issues
   - Information systems and e-commerce
2. *A Systems Approach to SCM*
   - Strategic issues in resources and capabilities
   - Implications of Theory of Constraints on supply chain design
3. *The Role of Information in SCM*
   - ERP and supply chain software
   - SAP R/3 system—MM, PP, SD modules
   - SAP SCOPE initiative and SAP APO
4. *Materials Management*
   - Inventory management and risk pooling
   - SAP B2B procurement
   - Optimization techniques
5. *Supply Chain Integration*
   - The bullwhip effect
   - Distribution strategies
   - Computerized beer game
6. *Strategic Partnership and Outsourcing*
   - Developing and maintaining supply chain relationships
   - Vendor-managed replenishment
   - Third-party logistics

Supply Chain Management Course Design

This new introductory course in supply chain management embraces an integrated systems approach to managing the full business process: from procurement, production, and distribution, to final delivery of goods and services. One special feature of the course design is that information technology is emphasized throughout the course and the SAP R/3 system is used primarily as a supply chain–planning tool for real-time planning and decision support. In particular, the MM, PP, and SD modules of SAP are used to track the entire business process. With SAP APO, SAP has combined the ERP execution power of the R/3 system with advanced data analysis and supply chain management tools. However, beyond a regular version of the R/3 system, SAP does not provide any support for the SAP Advanced Planner and Optimizer (SAP APO) to the University Alliance members. Even without direct access to the SAP APO module from our R/3 system, some latest practices of supply chain management, such as Web-based business-to-business (B2B) procurement process, can still be shown interactively using SAP's live demonstration on the Web. As a result, authorized users are able to log on the demonstration system through the SAP Web site to take advantage of many useful features of SAP for demonstration and evaluation purposes.

In addition, this course uses a computerized beer game to illustrate the dynamic nature of a supply chain. The beer game is a role-playing simulation developed at MIT in the 1960s to illustrate the advantages of taking an integrated approach to managing the supply chain. The game also demonstrates the critical value of sharing information across the various supply chain partners. The Windows-based version of this simulation game has been developed and is available to the users of the book by Simchi-Levi, Kaminsky, and Simchi-Levi (2000).

The objective of this course is to provide our students with state-of-the-art models and tools in procurement, operations, and logistics. Students are evaluated based on their performance in two examinations (counted toward 50% of the course grade), SAP assignments (25%), and case studies and simulation (25%). To ensure that the students can effectively learn the theory and practices of supply chain management, the course is further organized into six major components for course delivery (see Table 2 for details).

6. Conclusion

The integrated business curriculum, supported by our newly formed university-industry partnership, has significantly impacted the design and delivery of our business curricula. Our business faculty members have redesigned the undergraduate curriculum to include integrated business solutions using SAP software as the training tool. During the implementation process, we realized that the strategic issues of ERP systems have a more profound impact on our students than the technology issues. From the design to the delivery of our integrated business curriculum, the emphasis of our integrated business curriculum is not on the SAP R/3 software per se but rather we focus on business processes, enterprise resource management, and supply chain management concepts. Simply training students how to use or implement SAP software systems will not effectively address or solve any of the many substantive problems and issues that a business faces. As a result of the new integrated business curriculum, career prospects and employment opportunities for our students have been substantially improved. Building on this integrated business curriculum, the design of the new supply chain management course can now effectively address the critical issues regarding interorganizational communication throughout the supply chain.

References

CHASE, R. B., N. J. AQUILANO, AND E. R. JACOBS (1998), *Production and Operations Management: Manufacturing and Services*, Irwin McGraw-Hill, Boston, MA, USA.
CRABB, S. (1998), "Supply Chain Software: The Six-Figure Solution," *Supply Management*, 3, 20, 14–17.
DAVENPORT, T. H. (1998), "Putting the Enterprise into the Enterprise System," *Harvard Business Review*, 76, 4, 121–131.
FISHER, M. L. (1997), "What is the Right Supply Chain for Your Product?" *Harvard Business Review*, 75, 2, 105–116.
KOCH, C. (1996), "The Integration Nightmare: Sounding the Alarm," *CIO Magazine*, 10, 4, 44–54.
MILLS, E. (1998), "SAP Pushes Supply Chain Integration System at Conference," *InfoWorld Electric* (http://www.infoworld.com/cgi-bin/displayStory.pl?980311.emsap.htm).
MINAHAN, T. (1998), "Enterprise Resource Planning: Strategies Not Included," *Purchasing*, 125, 1, 112–127.
RAJAGOPEL, S. AND K. N. BERNARD (1993), "Strategic Procurement and Competitive Advantage," *International Journal of Purchasing and Materials Management*, 29, 4, 13–20.
SIMCHI-LEVI, D., P. KAMINSKY, AND E. SIMCHI-LEVI (2000), *Designing and Managing the Supply Chain*, McGraw-Hill, Boston, MA, USA.
STARR, M. K. (1997), "Pedagogical Challenge: Teaching International Production and Operations Management Courses," *Production and Operations Management*, 6, 2, 114–121.
TAN, C. K., V. R. KANNAN, AND R. B. HANDFIELD (1998), "Supply Chain Management: Supplier Performance and Firm Performance," *International Journal of Purchasing and Materials Management*, 34, 3, 2–9.
WATTS, C. A., K. Y. KIM, AND C. K. HAHN (1992), "Linking Purchasing to Corporate Competitive Strategy," *International Journal of Purchasing and Materials Management*, 28, 4, 2–8.
WILLIAMS, K. AND J. HART (1997), "SAP: Connecting the Enterprise," *Management Accounting*, 78, 10, 51–54.

R. S. M. Lau is an associate professor of operations management at the University of South Dakota. His current teaching and research interests are in the areas of operations strategy, supply chain management, and enterprise resource planning and applications. His work has appeared in many refereed journals, including *Logistics and Transportation Review*, *International Journal of Production Research*, *International Journal of Operations and Production Management*, *International Journal of Quality and Reliability Management*, and others.

Robert E. Rosacker is an accounting professor at the University of South Dakota. He obtained his Ph.D. degree from the University of Nebraska–Lincoln. His teaching and research interests are in the areas of management information systems (SAP), government information and benefit delivery systems, and electronic benefit transfer systems for welfare recipients.

Stephen L. Tracy is the Director of Business Research Bureau, which serves South Dakota through the operation of a Research Division, Information Services Division, State Data Center, Small Business Development Center, Family Business Initiative, and other various contracts. In addition to his duties at the Business Research Bureau, he serves as the Director of the SAP University Alliance Program. The Alliance Program has established the University of South Dakota as one of the premier schools providing an Enterprise Resource Planning–based education.

TEACHING SUPPLY CHAIN MANAGEMENT TO BUSINESS EXECUTIVES*

THOMAS E. VOLLMANN, CARLOS CORDON, AND JUSSI HEIKKILÄ

International Institute for Management Development, Chemin de Bellerive 23, CH-1001 Lausanne, Switzerland

By focusing on the management of entire value chains, supply chain management has gained increasing popularity in management research and in the teaching of global businesses. The right practices can take companies to great heights; lack of attention can draw companies close to peril. In teaching supply chain management to business executives, there are four major issues that need to be highlighted: flawless execution of operations, the change from supply to demand focus, outsourcing and supply base development, and partnership implementation. This article explains these four issues, and the material that is developed at IMD to teach each of them.
(SUPPLY CHAIN MANAGEMENT, DEMAND CHAIN MANAGEMENT, SOURCING, PARTNERSHIPS)

Introduction

The supply chain management teaching approach at the International Institute for Management Development (IMD) was developed within the Manufacturing 2000 research project (M2000). M2000 was a major collaborative research project between industry and IMD. The primary mission of M2000 was "to continuously redefine the nature of manufacturing activities and enterprises by identifying the changing requirements for manufacturing excellence and the appropriate organizational responses."

Most recently, our M2000 work focused predominately on supply chain management. Our guiding tenet was that supply chain management is a vehicle of corporate transformation–large-scale change–the objective of which is the coordination of change across companies and business units in the whole supply chain.

In M2000, we replaced the term supply chain management with demand chain management. Why? Because in our view, the chain focus should start with the customer and work backwards, instead of starting with the supplier/manufacturer and working forward. The focus needs to be on the final customer and the ways in which the overall chain can optimize the flow, produce maximum benefits, take out any unneeded transactions or other costs, and continually improve the bundle of goods and services provided–to all members of the chain.

Teaching demand chain management to business executives means discussing it from a number of perspectives. Demand chain management integrates several managerial concerns: flawless execution, move from supply to demand chain management, outsourcing and supply

*Reprinted from *Production and Operations Management*, Vol. 9, No. 1, Spring 2000, pp. 81–90.

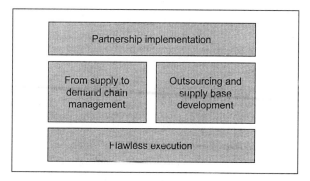

FIGURE 1. The conceptual framework for teaching demand chain management.

base development, and partnership implementation. Figure 1 illustrates this conceptual framework.

Flawless execution is an absolute prerequisite for ambitious demand chain management. The move from supply to demand chain must be dictated by the distinct customer needs focusing on a particular business unit. The issues in outsourcing and supply base development are concerned with core competency development and the choices that need to be made by the firm to focus its resources. And finally, customer and supplier partnerships with aggressive improvement agendas are the vehicle for transforming the demand chain.

Flawless Execution

In good demand chain management, flawless execution is imperative. It focuses performance measurement on several levels of operations and between two or more partners in the chain. Flawless execution begins with good performance in terms of internal measures, such as ability to keep the production schedules, perfect order fulfillment, quality, and productivity improvement. This internal focus is next expanded to see what are the world class manufacturing techniques that are being implemented, such as total quality management (TQM), Total preventive maintenance (TPM), 5s,[1] and empowerment. But focusing on the internal operations of one company is not enough. Good performance in demand chain partnering assumes joint operations between one or more companies to satisfy the customer needs of the whole chain.

A good example of the need for the chain based on flawless execution is seen in fast moving consumer goods. One ultimate measure of chain perfection is the extent to which products are not available on the supermarket's shelf when the consumer wishes to buy them. This goal needs to be met while simultaneously reducing the inventories in the entire pipeline. The emphasis on flawless execution is well illustrated in the teaching case Unichema. This case serves as an excellent starting point for a program or course module in demand chain management.

Case Unichema: *Prerequisites to Demand Chain Partnering.* The Unichema case is about a Netherlands-based division of Unilever that manufactures specialty chemicals. The firm is facing globalization of competition, lower than desired returns on investment, and an internal turf war between logistics and sales over who should be the primary contact point with customers. There are new customer demands for just-in-time (JIT), technical support, vendor managed inventories, faster delivery times, etc. And there is insufficient knowledge of how the customers use Unichema's products. The company also has one problem that is less

---

[1] The 5S's stand for Hiroyuki Hirano's *Five Pillars of the Visual Workplace*. The S's stand for Japanese words, but Western companies have chosen their own meanings to describe industrial housekeeping. For example, Boeing's version of the S's are *sorting, sweeping, simplifying, standardizing,* and *self-discipline.*

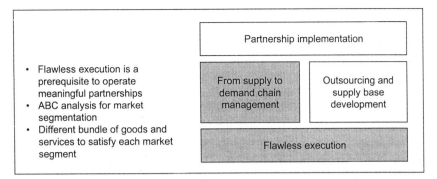

FIGURE 2. Case Unichema puts the focus on demand and flawless execution.

common. It fully recognizes that the solution to its problems can not be found only in cutting costs. Unichema realizes that it must focus on new ways to create value with customers.

Analysis of the case includes Pareto or ABC analyses, which are based on classifying customers by sales in Dutch Guilders, and products by shipments in tons. Classification is the right idea, but it needs to be based on the right criteria, such as contribution margin or—even better—on a surrogate for return on investment in this case, since the firm has high fixed assets. The primary lesson is this: the ABC analysis is a method for establishing market segmentation, and it becomes readily apparent that it will take a different bundle of goods and services to optimally satisfy each market segment.

The Unichema case also focuses on the performance of some production units. The firm is making far too many mistakes in a situation in which flawless execution is a prerequisite to being able to operate meaningful partnerships. The point is that flawless execution is the ante to play in the partnership game. Without it, no customer can depend upon a supplier to meet their commitments, unless costly buffers are kept to guard against the uncertainties in production.

Unichema is an effective kickoff case for demand chain thinking. It sets up the need to tailor-make unique demand chains for particular market segments, and it points out that partnerships cannot be established without flawless execution of operations (Figure 2).

From Supply to Demand Chain Management

The demand chain management concept extends the view of operations from a single business unit or a company to the whole chain. Essentially, demand chain management is a set of practices aimed at managing and coordinating the whole demand chain, starting from the end customer and working backward to raw material suppliers. There are two fundamental objectives: (1) to develop synergy along the whole demand chain, and (2) to start with specific customer segments and meet their needs rather than focus on internal optimization.

A common view of the supply chain is that it is essentially a streamlined pipeline that processes raw materials, transforms them into finished goods, and delivers them to the customers. More realistically, a demand chain is much more complex than that: business units are supplied by and supply a multitude of other business units, with third-party providers supporting the linkages between them (with transportation, warehousing, logistics, manufacturing planning and control systems linkages, and information management).

In demand chain management the bundles of goods and services are customized for each customer segment and individual customer partner. Moreover, the bundles are continuously evolving because of joint improvement efforts between customers and suppliers. The manufacturing planning and control systems that support this environment tend to be based on "groupware" that allows partners to look inside each other's systems and coordinate their actions based on knowledge of plans and inventory availability—instead of on forecasts.

Information systems linking companies are extended from the transactions phase into the knowledge phase. In the future they will focus on communication and open-ended dialogue between the companies. This dialogue will take place in real time, at the detailed level between those who execute the manufacturing planning and control system, with no need for the decision making to traverse hierarchical levels.

Case Heineken: The Match between Meeting Customer Needs, New Ways of Working, and Information Systems. The Heineken case is subtitled: "Customer-Driven Supply Chain Management Transformation." The case can be taught by first focusing on the enormous amount of physical movement involved in the supply chain for beer. A can of beer is roughly the same size and weight as a mobile phone, but the latter is roughly 1000 times more expensive. The volume of beer that Heineken produces in a year, 64 million hectoliters, is more than anyone can imagine; but if it were put in 33-centiliter bottles and lined up, the string of bottles would go around the world 30 times. Heineken is the largest shipper over the North Atlantic, filling 300 containers each day.

The learning issues in the case can be grouped into three sets: the customers pull (primarily the leading Dutch retailer Albert Heijn), the financial problems that lead to an internal restructuring ("People Make Heineken"), and systems and the use of information. The customer pull originated from a list published by Albert Heijn of their 10 "mega-losers," including Heineken beer. The "People make Heineken" initiative came from a consulting study after ABC costing showed that no money was being made in the domestic market. The starting point for the work with information systems came from a study by the management consultant Nolan Norton, which found Heineken paying twice for one-half functionality and that 110 of the 125 terminals hooked to the main frame were in the computer department.

At first, Heineken did not see the three sets of problems and their solutions as connected. But that should come as no surprise, because it is only when they are tightly connected that the right course of action becomes clear. If the results from the consulting studies are only seen as a need to reduce costs, then the result is the all-too-typical head count reduction. But in this case the changes in the way people work need to be driven by the need to respond to customer dictates, supported by new information systems. Albert Heijn asked Heineken to deliver beer anywhere in Holland in less than 24 hours (instead of the former 3 days), and this drove the improvement. The beer company re-engineered the processes and systems that connected it with Albert Heijn. Major performance improvements followed.

The overall learning points from the Heineken case can be captured as follows: start with the market place and work backwards to determine the necessary changes in processes, working practices, skills, competencies, and supporting information systems. The real pay-offs in information systems come from systems linking companies—not those that focus exclusively on internal optimization. The most effective integration is cross-company and across the demand chain (Figure 3).

Case Mabe Estufas: Supply Chain Partnering for Fast Market Development. The Mabe case is based on a demand chain partnership that begins with Mabe, a Mexican producer of white goods. Mabe wants to enter the US market; at the same time, General Electric (GE) is searching for a partner to leverage their excellent brand name in electric ranges to gas ranges. The combination of Mabe and GE allows for a very fast development of the market, and the firms achieve a dominant position in the US gas range market.

The case discussion starts with a Strengths, weaknesses, opportunities, threats (SWOT) analysis of the partnership for Mabe. Typical strengths include good brands, high quality, consumer acceptance, growth, low labor costs, an excellent and loyal work force, good market share, a favorable plant location, and a strong partner in GE. Weaknesses include the potential dominance by GE, and the current problems with the supplier base, which include the suppliers' inability to meet the newly increased demand for Mabe products, and the

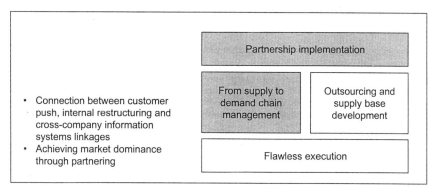

FIGURE 3. The Heineken and Mabe Estufas cases point out the connection between customer needs, information infrastructure, and partnering.

problems associated with supporting Mabe in new product introduction. The opportunities for Mabe include further growth, including expansion into the Latin American market with GE's strong brand and excellent products, leveraging its buying power and logistics volumes, and increasing its dominance of the Mexican white goods market.

The next questions are how GE has been able to help Mabe and what Mabe has, in turn, provided for GE. The result will usually be a long list of what GE has provided, such as the brand name, product design expertise, physical distribution, connection and management of the supplier base, best purchasing terms and conditions, credit, and the GE management techniques such as "workout." The Mabe list starts out shorter, so it may be useful to ask why GE decided not to go it alone. At the end of the discussion, it is clear that Mabe offers GE a substantial risk reduction. The risks for GE entering Mexican operations are large, since GE has limited knowledge of the culture, political environment, or Mexican labor rules.

Outsourcing and Supply Base Development

In demand chain management, the dual objective of cost reduction and value enhancement means that some best practices focus on simplifying the chain; others attempt to improve the effectiveness of the entire chain. In the first category are programs to reduce both the customer and supplier bases. For example, British Petroleum Exploration and Chrysler Corporation reduced their numbers of suppliers from 20,000 to 3600 and from 2500 to 1140, respectively. A frequent result, as seen in the automotive industry, is the creation of tiers of suppliers. Some car manufacturers have extended this concept: they ask a single supplier to take over a major portion of the car, providing, for example, the car's front "corners" from a through-the-wall plant, with minimal transactions.

Outsourcing implies that a supplier develops and continually improves competencies, assets, and infrastructure to provide a certain bundle of goods and services. But changes in a company's focus of activities, even as part of an outsourcing initiative, should aim at improving the effectiveness of the entire demand chain. The changes need to have a strategic or overall focus, beyond just spinning off units or adding operations or processes piecemeal.

Two central propositions favor outsourcing. First, a supplier can do the same activity at least as well as we can do it—and we do not see this particular activity as being central to our long-term competitiveness. If someone else can provide this activity on a cost-effective basis, and give us reasonable assurance that they will continue to do so, then we can devote our attention to activities that are more central to our distinctive competency. Second, specialization in the demand chain increases speed and flexibility. In order to benefit from this increased potential, companies in the demand chain need to manage virtual relationships,

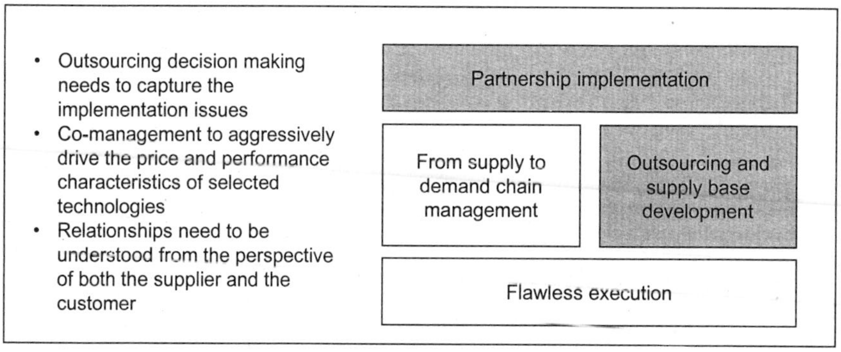

FIGURE 4. The Du Pont and Nokia Mobile Phone cases point out that effective outsourcing and supply base development integrate strategic and operative considerations.

to jointly develop competencies for the whole demand chain, and to locate and remove inflexibility from the chain.

Case Du Pont: Outsourcing and Subcontracting. At the end of 1996, various business units at Du Pont were making outsourcing decisions that seemed inconsistent with each other. Something done in-house on one site was performed by a third party in another. Yet, despite discrepancies, managers provided consistent guidelines: "If it's a core competency, you keep it. If it's generic, you have the option to go outside." The case describes Du Pont's make-or-buy decisions and offers plenty of food for discussion of what are really the important drivers of good outsourcing decisions.

In its polymer business, Du Pont's European operation considers the compounding of special compounds a core competency, both for competitive and economical reasons. However, prior to 1996, they outsourced part of production. The situation is different in the US. There, Du Pont continues to outsource compounding, as US union agreements mean that all chemical company employees are paid under the same guidelines. There it makes economic sense to outsource as much compounding as possible.

In the company's resin creation business, there is a set of complex outsourcing decisions. With small lot sizes, where the product is not proprietary, Du Pont sends its customers directly to an outside supplier and takes no responsibility for product quality. However, the company makes an exception for key customers who refuse to take products not manufactured by Du Pont: in such cases, Du Pont makes the small lots in-house. Similarly, outside contractors make products that are unique and have only small sales volumes, although for key customers, the company guarantees "in-house" quality.

Defining core and noncore competencies may be critical to determining the future direction of the business, but it does not mean that all noncore activities should be outsourced. Du Pont uses outside suppliers in manufacturing, but maintains its distinctive competencies in product development and sales and technical support. However, the company's outsourcing decisions take other factors than competencies into consideration, such as local economics of the business, the future of the industry, and environmental and regulatory issues.

Case Nokia Mobile Phones: Developing Agile Supply Base. The Nokia Mobile Phones case augments the supply base development perspective presented in the Du Pont case (Figure 4). The immediate concern of the case is the development of good demand chain management practices and mutually beneficial demand chain partnerships in high-growth, high-technology industries.

Nokia Mobile Phones defines the company's distinctive competency as the development and manufacturing of mobile phones. In its business, technology-related competencies rapidly develop from "distinctive" to "widely available." Nokia follows a strategy of not being vertically integrated, because this could easily lead to possessing "parasitic" competencies. For the mobile phone manufacturer, differentiation means designing and manufacturing cellular phones and finding and comanaging the best suppliers for each product generation. Comanaging with the suppliers means aggressively driving the price and performance characteristics of selected technologies.

The case holds a lens to three of Nokia Mobile Phones' supplier relationships: GWS Perlos, Elcoteq Network and Rohm Electronics. The first two relationships illustrate not only the various factors that influence the development of customer-supplier relationships, but also show how the relationships need to be understood from the perspectives of both companies. The third part of the case explains how Nokia formed and developed the partnership with Rohm Electronics to improve the supply line between Nokia's Bochum factory in Germany and Rohm Electronics' local operation.

Case Thomas Medical Systems: *Outsourcing Technology Clusters.* The Thomas Medical Systems cases (ABC) describe a major multinational company competing in the medical equipment business. The case focuses on X-ray equipment and the development of a new product for cardiovascular X-ray. The A-case depicts interaction with one supplier where Thomas starts with a desire to purchase assemblies rather than items—in order to move up the value chain—to provide more integrated solutions to hospitals. But as would be expected, the devils are in the details. The supplier firm does not have compatible CAD/CAM systems, they have a different approach to engineering design and database maintenance, and their competence in areas such as assembly have been seriously overestimated. The A-case illustrates what happens when one tries to implement an outsourcing program without a clear outsourcing policy.

The B-case develops the policy—which is a good first step—but clearly leads to many new questions. The questions focus on how long will it take to implement the policy and what is required from the outsourcing partners to meet Thomas' wishes. The C-case shows two more examples, the need to refine the policy, and to administer it with discretion. But it reinforces the need to develop a clear outsourcing policy and not to approach outsourcing on an ad hoc basis.

Implementing Demand Chain Partnerships

Many companies find that although it is relatively easy to start a partnership, sustaining it over a long period of time is a much more difficult proposition. What happens after the first gains are made, once the interface between the companies has been rationalized and all the basic transactions simplified? How do you sustain a sense of urgency?

Companies can only sustain a demand chain partnership over time if there is continuous transformation. Both partners have to commit to an aggressive improvement agenda, and once they have achieved the initial objectives outlined in that agenda, they need to draw up the next targets for the cooperation.

Given the heavy demands of time and resources required to manage a full partnership, companies must decide judiciously whom they want to partner with and at what level. The Swedish building contractor Skanska started a partnership program with its 10 major suppliers in order to change the way of working with their suppliers. The partnership with Rockwool was the first of Skanska's partnerships, and the Skanska and Rockwool case describes how the two companies made it work. Another case, about Dutch companies TeStrake and SDI, and Du Pont, illustrates that complexity in managing partnerships grows when moving to higher level of partnering with several companies involved.

Case Skanska and Rockwool: *Making the Supply Chain Partnership Work.* The case describes a demand chain partnership between Skanska AB, the leading building contractor in Sweden, and Rockwool AB, which produces insulation materials. The development of productivity in the Swedish building industry was poor in the booming market of the 1980s. The collapse of the building volumes in the beginning of the 1990s forced Skanska to take

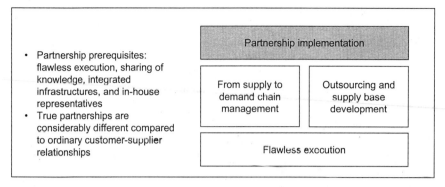

FIGURE 5. The Skanska & Rockwool and TeStrake cases show that long-term partnering requires continuous renewal of an aggressive improvement agenda.

strong actions to improve its efficiency. Cost cutting, reduction of the number of personnel, internal time based management (TBM) and TQM efforts were necessary, but not sufficient. Skanska foresaw more long-lasting results in the rethinking of the demand chain, which required Skanska to look for closer cooperation with its key suppliers.

The case highlights a number of issues—growing in complexity. Both firms need to understand what benefits might accrue from developing a well-functioning demand chain partnership. Skanska wishes to simplify its demand chain and cut its costs by reducing the number of suppliers and building partnerships with 10 major suppliers, vastly reducing the transactions by using electronic data interchange, and most importantly, finding ways to reduce overall costs. The company expects a much larger volume to flow directly from suppliers to building sites—and not through the retailers.

From Rockwool's angle, a much-reduced group of retailers will service the Skanska account, which implies specialization on the retail trade. Issues that typically come up in the case discussion center on the relative risks and burdens for each firm. Most participants will believe that it is much riskier for Rockwool than for Skanska, since retaliation of the retailers on Rockwool for entering this agreement (which seems to cut them out) will be anticipated. Is it worth taking this risk with a customer who represents 5-10% of sales volume?

Potential strategic implications are much larger than the share of sales might suggest. Rockwool can take the challenge of partnering with its largest customer. Together with Skanska, it can change the rules of the business and become dominant in its business by being the first company able to play efficiently under the new rules (Figure 5).

Case TeStrake: Beyond Early Supplier Involvement. The TeStrake case is about a Dutch company that is trying to work in a new way with a consortium of suppliers. The aim of the Dutch firm is to develop new products rapidly and cost effectively by leveraging the best in each supplier. TeStrake and another Dutch firm, Stork Digital Imaging (SDI), are developing an ink jet color printer for very high-resolution printing on cloth and paper. Working on the project are SDI, the lead company, TeStrake, a third subcontractor (here, "supplier B"), and DuPont, the marking agent for the combined enterprise (DuPont makes the inks for the printer).

TeStrake and SDI are working on a printer project called the AX4. As DuPont refines its sense of its customers' requirements, TeStrake and SDI need to change the design of the AX4. Consequently, the project runs significantly over the cost budget and comes late to market. What were the problems with the AX4? It took too long, it cost too much, communication problems plagued the companies, the companies significantly underestimated system integration, market information was inadequate, and when problems came up, the firms fell back to old ways of negotiating. TeStrake was not involved early enough in the product design and no real trade-off existed between the technical specifications, development cost, and the product cost. Too much time elapsed before the companies understood the extent of the cost overruns and the large uncertainties were resolved last instead of first. How could the problems have been avoided? What are the companies doing differently on the next product development project, the Production Ink-Jet Printer (PIP)? In PIP, the companies involve the suppliers much earlier. SDI tries to get fixed cost estimates much earlier. The development costs are not open-ended. The companies share the risks (and the rewards). Negotiation becomes periodic, instead of continuous. The companies change their approach to prototypes dramatically: they resolve major uncertainties early, even if early resolution might increase the overall time. They freeze design specifications early on, and the time to market drives development.

Key Lessons

At IMD we are finding the ideas of demand chain management as particularly important to our executive audience. Demand chain management is the best opportunity to create competitive advantage in today's world. We believe that anyone in the commodity business deserves it! The way to not be in the commodity business is to develop new bundles of goods and services—to move up the value chain—to help customers better achieve their objectives. This implies careful segmentation of markets and specific demand chains to provide the bundles for each segment. Moreover, demand chain management is not a one-time dictate. A demand chain partnership must include an aggressive improvement agenda. The operative question always remains: What is next? What is the next cost saving or value enhancement? But these need to include the entire chain—not optimizing one party's performance at the expense of another.[1]

[1] Manufacturing 2000 was a 7-year research partnership (1991-1998) between IMD, Lausanne, Switzerland, and the following firms: Andersen Consulting, Australian Manufacturing Council, Bally, Bell Packaging Corporation, BP Chemicals, CMB Packaging, Digital Equipment Corporation, Du Pont De Nemours International, Exxon Chemicals International, GKN Automotive, Heineken, IBM, Johnson & Johnson, KNP BT, Mandelli, Nestlé, Nokia Mobile Phones, Philips, Siemens, SMH, Sony Europe, Volkswagen/Audi. We are grateful to these companies, as well as to the other companies described in the case studies for their contribution.

References

BECHLER, K., M. STANFORD, D. A. MARCHAND, AND T. E. VOLLMANN (1995), "Heineken Netherlands B.V. (A): Customer Driven Supply Chain Management Transformation," IMD Case Study POM 176.

———, D. A. MARCHAND, AND T. E. VOLLMANN (1995), "Heineken Netherlands B.V. (B): Transforming IS/IT to Support Supply Chain Management," IMD Case Study POM 177.

HEIKKILÄ, J., T. E. VOLLMANN, AND C. CORDON (1996), "Skanska & Rockwool: Making the Supply Chain Partnership Work," IMD Case Study POM 184.

———, ———, AND ——— (1998), "Nokia Mobile Phones: Supply Line Management," IMD Multimedia Case Study POM 201.

JULIEN, D., C. CORDON, AND T. E. VOLLMANN (1997), "TeStrake: Beyond Early Supplier Involvement," IMD Case Study POM 202.

———, T. E. VOLLMANN, AND C. CORDON (1998), "Thomas Medical Systems' Outsourcing Policy (A), (B) and (C)," IMD Case Studies POM 205-207.

VIVANCO, L. M., C. CORDON, AND T. E. VOLLMANN (1996), "Mabe Estufas (Mexico): Developing Suppliers for Profit and Growth," IMD Case Study POM 186.

———, ———, AND ——— (1996), "Philips Consumer Electronics Company (USA): Developing Your Customers to Manage the Demand Chain," IMD Case Study POM 188.

———, ———, AND ——— (1997), "Outsourcing and Subcontracting at Du Pont Europe," IMD Case Study POM 191.

——— AND P. V. JENSTER (1996), "Unichema," IMD Case Study POM 185.

Useful Books and Articles for Supporting Supply Chain Management Teaching

COLLINS, R. S., K. BECHLER, AND S. PIRES (1997), "Outsourcing in the Automotive Industry: From JIT to Modular Consortia," *European Management Journal*, 15, 5, 498-508.

DAVIS, T. (1993), "Effective Supply Chain Management," *Sloan Management Review*, 34, 4, 35-46.
DYER, J. H. (1996), "Does Governance Matter? Keiretsu Alliances and Asset Specificity as Sources of Japanese Competitive Advantage," *Organization Science*, 7, 6, 649-666.
——— (1996), "How Chrysler Created an American Keiretsu," *Harvard Business Review*, 74, 4, 42-56.
FISHER, M. L. (1997), "What is the Right Supply Chain for Your Product?" *Harvard Business Review*, 75, 2, 105-116.
HAKANSSON, H. AND I. SNEHOTA (1995), *Developing Relationships in Business Networks,* Routledge, London.
KUMAR, N. (1996), "The Power of Trust in Manufacturer-Retailer Relationships," *Harvard Business Review*, 74, 6, 92-106.
LAMBERT, D. M., M. A. EMMELHAINZ, AND J. T. GARDNER (1996), "So You Think You Want a Partner?" *Marketing Management,* 5, 2, 24-29.
LAMMING, R. (1993), *Beyond Partnership: Strategies for Innovation and Lean Supply*, Prentice-Hall, London.
LEE, H. L., V. PADMANABHAN, AND S. WHANG (1997), "The Bullwhip Effect in Supply Chains," *Sloan Management Review*, 38, 3, 93-102.
———, ———, AND ——— (1997), "Information Distortion in a Supply Chain: The Bullwhip Effect," *Management Science,* 43, 4, 546-558.
LEVY, D. L. (1997), "Lean Production in an International Supply Chain," *Sloan Management Review*, 38, 2, 94-102.
LEWIS, J. D. (1995), *The Connected Corporation: How Leading Companies Win Through Customer-Supplier Alliances,* Free Press, New York.
MOODY, P. E. (1993), *Breakthrough Partnering: Creating a Collective Enterprise Advantage*, Omneo, Essex Junction.
VOLLMANN, T. E. (1996), *The Transformation Imperative: Achieving Market Dominance Through Radical Change,* Harvard Business School Press, Boston.
WOMACK, J. P. AND D.T. JONES (1996), *Lean Thinking: Banish Waste and Create Wealth in Your Corporation,* Simon & Schuster, New York.

Thomas E. Vollman is professor of manufacturing management at IMD. His research interests include manufacturing planning and control, performance measurement, supply chain management, and enterprise transformation.

Carlos Cordon is professor of manufacturing management at IMD. His research interests include manufacturing management and supply chain management.

Jussi Heikkilä is research associate at IMD and PhD candidate at Helsinki University of Technology. His research interests include supply chain management and project management.

INTEGRATION, GLOBALIZATION, AND CUSTOMIZATION: LOGISTICS MANAGEMENT EDUCATION IN ASIA PACIFIC*

PETER GILMOUR

Graduate School of Management, Macquarie University, N.S.W. 2109, Australia

This paper describes the logistics management education programs at the Graduate School of Management at Macquarie University in Sydney, Australia. The programs include a Master of Management degree in Logistics and Operations Management, a Graduate Certificate in Logistics Management and logistics streams in a Postgraduate Diploma in Management and an MBA. These programs are taught on the University's Sydney campus and in the facilities of its strategic alliance partners overseas: the Hong Kong Management Association in Hong Kong and the Straits Times in Singapore. Emphasis is placed on the importance of participative learning for the student body of mature-age full-time managers and part-time students. A range of different teaching devices to facilitate high participation levels are described. Local cases have been written that are taught in conjunction with managers from the companies about which the cases have been written. Cases are linked with video interviews and video "plant tours." They are also linked with field visits. The Internet is used to access strategic supply chain frameworks for self-evaluation and benchmarking. Computer-based (for example a SAP demonstration and a spreadsheet model for aggregate planning) and manual (for example the "beer game" and a JIT simulation) exercises highlight specific supply chain concepts. The key role of the concepts of integration, globalization, and customization in the design and structure of these programs is emphasised.
(LOGISTICS EDUCATION, SUPPLY CHAIN MANAGEMENT EDUCATION, MANAGEMENT EDUCATION, INTEGRATION, ASIA PACIFIC REGION)

Introduction

Managing and teaching logistics in the Asia Pacific trade block presents a number of differences to the other two major world blocks, North America and Europe. All economies in the region, with the exception of Japan, are economically relatively small; all except Australia, China, and India are geographically small; all are substantially focused on external trade. A particular characteristic of this external trade is that most of it involves trans-sea movements. Asia is also used by many large companies as a sourcing hub for worldwide operations. Scale can be achieved only by complex, cross-national, trans-sea, cross-cultural supply chains. Integration across countries with a great diversity of management skills and applications of technology are required; the same supply chain may include horse-and-cart transport, manual handling, handwritten documentation, floor-stacked storage in Bangladesh and internet data transmission, automated warehousing, and cross-docking in Singapore. In

---

* Received December 1998; revision received May 1999; accepted September 1999.

Asia Pacific integration and globalization (or at least regionalization) are essential to success. Coupled with a worldwide trend toward customization, this makes for a challenging environment within which the logistics professional must work. Education in the systems-based concepts of logistics, communication technologies, warehousing, and transport technology, cross-cultural management, and decision making is increasingly important for the logistics managers in the region to succeed.

This basic level of operational complexity together with the recent economic slowdown in the area provides the potential for logistics management to be a strategic driver for success for companies in the Asia Pacific region. Li & Fung, a multinational trading company based in Hong Kong, is an example of one company in the region that is using supply chain skills to drive substantial growth (Hutcheon 1991; Magretta 1998). Li & Fung sells garments and "hard goods" such as toys and luggage to about 500 European and U.S. retailers. To do this it coordinates the activities of a worldwide network of 7,500 suppliers. "We might buy the yarn in Korea, have it dyed and woven in Bangladesh and do the sewing in Thailand. We mix and match at every stage," explained Dr. Victor Fung, the chairman of the company (Fung, 1998). Effective coordination of these supply chains allows the customers to get quick response. "Five weeks after we have received the order, 10,000 garments arrive on the shelves in Europe, all looking like they came from one factory, with colors, for example, perfectly matched. Just think about the logistics and the coordination" (Magretta 1998, p. 106). "This is a very low barrier to entry business," he continued. "We contract with our manufacturers [suppliers] for between 30 and 70 per cent of their capacity. This creates scale, which together with our IT, reputation and network provides Li & Fung with a high barrier to entry" (Fung 1998).

The success of Li & Fung involves integration, globalization, and customization: the ability to integrate with suppliers and customers over a global network to provide exactly the needs of each customer. These elements also are the foundation for the logistics teaching program at the Graduate School of Management at Macquarie University in Sydney, Australia.

The Logistics Teaching Program

Macquarie University is named after Major-General Lachlan Macquarie (1762–1824), Governor of the colony of New South Wales from 1810 to 1821. It was established in 1967 and now has 13,000 students in eight schools. The Graduate School of Management is located in a complex of purpose-built buildings on its own grounds on the eastern edge of the University's 400 hectare site in North Ryde, a northwestern suburb of Sydney, 11 kilometers from the city center. In addition to teaching in Sydney, the graduate degree programs of the School are offered in Hong Kong and Singapore. Whereas marketing and administration in Sydney are done by the School's own staff, these functions overseas are done through strategic alliances: in Hong Kong with the Hong Kong Management Association and in Singapore with the Straits Times. These third-party operators also provide the teaching facilities.

Almost all students in Sydney and all students in Hong Kong and Singapore are full-time managers and part-time students. Their average age is 35 and they typically hold middle management jobs. Current enrollments total 1,650 in Sydney, Hong Kong, and Singapore. The graduate degree and diploma programs offered are a Postgraduate Certificate (3 course units), a Postgraduate Diploma (6 course units), the Master of Management (10 course units), the MBA (16 course units) and the DBA (4 course units and a dissertation). Students are accepted into these programs based on their management experience, academic records, and referees' reports. Applicants without degrees but with substantial management experience can be accepted into the lower-level programs. Upon completion of a lower-level program students can continue to the next highest program, depending on their performance record.

TABLE 1
The Master of Management in Logistics and Operations Management

Master of Management Core Units
   Marketing Management
   Human Resource Management
   Accounting for Management
   Information and Decision Analysis
   Strategic Management
   Strategic Behavior
Logistics and Operations Required Units

Logistics Management
The ability to supply customers with the right goods and services in a timely fashion is providing organizations with a source of significant competitive advantage. These customers may be internal customers who require raw materials, parts, components, or services to be procured for them. The may be external customers who are themselves purchasing goods and services. The unit examines the overall trade-off between total logistics cost and customer service, which is at the heart of managing logistics operations. Within this framework the details of this logistics system are considered: the impact of technology—barcodes, paperless systems, RF; ecological considerations; the physical elements—transport, warehousing, materials, handling, order processing. The way that effective logistics must cross functional boundaries and its contribution to strategy implementation is also examined.

Logistics and Operations Strategy
A carefully developed operations strategy is needed to enable an organization to establish the processes and facilities required to produce the goods and services targeted by the corporate strategy. A sustainable long-term competitive edge can be generated if logistics operations are managed strategically to generate the time and place utility required by these goods and services. Students taking this unit will examine in detail the operations and logistics strategy employed by one participating organization. Teams will work closely with managers from this company on the various component areas of their operations and logistics strategy together with its integration with the organization's overall strategy.

Management of Service Operations
It is only over the past decade that worldwide research activity has developed a theoretical basis for the effective management of service organisations. This unit develops this theory and applies it to the management of local service organizations. Most successful service organisations have a clearly defined service concept and an effective service delivery system to meet and exceed customer expectations. They also have the capability to measure the performance of the service delivery system and relate this to service level objectives. This unit will examine these concepts in detail and apply them to a range of local organizations with the use of recently written local case studies and discussions involving Australian managers of service firms.

Technology Management
This unit explores the way in which technology development supports the nonmarketing elements of the value chain—inbound logistics, operations, outbound logistics, and service activities. The use of information systems, the development of equipment and facilities, and the application of appropriate management concepts (such as total quality management) will be explored as technology-oriented ways to integrate these activities. Also examined in the course will be the role that technology can play in the development and implementation of corporate strategy.

Logistics streams exist for the Postgraduate Certificate, the Postgraduate Diploma, and the Master of Management. In Hong Kong and Singapore a Master of Management in Logistics and Operations Management is offered. The structure of this program is shown in Table 1. Units that deal entirely or partially with logistics management are: Logistics Management, Logistics and Operations Strategy, Operations Management, and Technology Management.

Each unit offered comprises 40 contact hours and the expectation that the student will do another 120 hours of self-directed study, which includes reading, syndicate preparation of case studies and assignments, research and compilation of projects, and exam preparation. The 40 contact hours are delivered in two standard formats: the first is "one night a week" and the second is a "block." In Sydney the teaching calendar is four 10-week terms separated by an exam week and a week's break. Many units are taught one night a week from 6 to 10 P.M. for the 10 weeks. The alternative format is five full 8-hour days. These five days can be five consecutive days or the same day for 5 weeks, although the most common format is Friday, Saturday, and Sunday of one week and Saturday and Sunday of the next. Teaching in Hong Kong and Singapore is all in the block format. This is because all the teaching is done by Sydney-based faculty who fly in for 10-day periods. The block format in these two locations varies slightly because of the custom in Hong Kong of working on Saturday mornings. A block in Hong Kong might be Friday night (3 hours), Saturday morning, all day Sunday, Tuesday, Thursday, and Friday nights, Saturday afternoon, and all day Sunday. In Singapore Saturday morning classes substitute for the Friday evenings. For block classes prereading is sent to the students about 6 weeks before the block and they have a project to complete 6 weeks after the block as well as an exam about 3 or 4 weeks after the class sessions.

Components

These students are fitting in University around full-time work commitments—they may be sitting in class at 10 P.M. after having been at work since 7 A.M. that morning. Many have young families. All are enthusiastically climbing the corporate ladder. Given this situation it is essential to provide a participative learning experience. With the depth of managerial experience in the student group, high levels of participation have substantial pedagogical benefits. Barnes, Christensen, and Hansen (1994), among others, enumerate the benefits of the active learning experience provided by the case method of teaching (Taylor 1997). There are, however, cultural influences on participation. When the participative nature of the program was explained, a new student in Hong Kong responded, "We hear you and we understand what you are saying. We will try our best [to be participative]. But it is not in our culture."

Case Studies

A range of case studies have been written on supply chain issues for organizations in Australia, Hong Kong, China, and Singapore. These cases are used as practical extensions to short theory-based sessions. They are listed, together with the teaching objective of each, in Table 2.

These cases are taught in either of two ways. The first is the traditional method in which the students read the case and consider prepared questions about the case before the class session. At the class session the lecturer asks particular members of the group questions that relate to a prepared teaching structure. The main points of the session are summarized by the lecturer on the white board. In many of these sessions a manager "from the case" has been invited to the session. He or she listens to this first part of the session—the lecturer must be firm in not allowing the students to ask this person questions at this stage—then is asked by the lecturer to comment on the class discussion, to answer questions, and to bring the class up to date on the current situation at the company. The first section, the class discussion, might take around 45 minutes and the second section with the visiting executive may also be about the same length. In situations in which it is difficult to arrange a visitor—teaching the Walls (China) case to a class in Sydney, for example—a prerecorded video interview with a key manager from the company is shown. These are typically recorded by the academic who wrote the case either in the University's studio or on-site in the manager's office. The class session is concluded by the lecturer summarizing the main logistics issues to be learned from the case.

The second method used to teach cases is to have the students work in syndicate groups before the class session. Each syndicate is told to read the case and think about all the questions for the case (typically four or five, but can be as many as nine). For the class session

TABLE 2
The Use of Case Studies[a]

Case	Country	Focus of the Case	Year	Length (pages)	Source
Walls (China) Co[b]	China	Logistics operations startup Global sourcing Logistics operations in a developing country	1996	28	Council of Logistics Management, 2803 Butterfield Rd., Oakbrook, IL 60521 USA
Owens Corning Fiberglas[b]	China	Logistics facilities location Local outsourcing	1998	24	Peter Gilmour
Yokogawa Electric	Singapore	Multinational JIT	1994	17	Peter Gilmour
Kodak CDC Singapore[b]	Singapore	Global logistics Global network design Central control	1996	31	Peter Gilmour
Caltex Australia[b]	Australia	Cross-functional integration Supply chain positioning	1997	27	Peter Gilmour
Bougainville Copper Ltd	PNG	Global supply options Use of supply systems	1993	19	Peter Gilmour, *Logistics Management: An Australian Framework*, Longman Australia, Melbourne, 1993, 53–71
SEC (Vic)	Australia	Supplier relations Supply system design	1991	18	Peter Gilmour, *Operations Management in Australia*, Longman Aust., Melbourne, 1991, 170–187.
Linfox	Australia	Strategy formulation Third-party operations	1991	13	Peter Gilmour, *Operations Management in Australia*, Longman Aust., Melbourne, 1991, 281–293.
Amway[b]	Australia	Strategic facility location Distribution center design Use of warehouse technology	1993	22	Peter Gilmour, *Logistics Management: An Australian Framework*, Longman Australia, Melbourne, 1993, 144–165.
Parfums Christian Dior	Hong Kong	Global supply chain Operations Warehouse consolidation	1998	22	Peter Gilmour
Southcorp Wines	Australia	Capacity planning Forecasting	1995	24	Peter Gilmour
CIG	Australia	Supply chain design Asset management	1991	16	Peter Gilmour, *Operations Management in Australia*, Longman Aust., Melbourne, 1991, 188–203.
Merrell Dow	Australia	Outsourcing options Order processing Inventory management	1993	17	Peter Gilmour, *Logistics Management: An Australian Framework*, Longman Australia, Melbourne, 1993, 283–299.
Australian Co-op. Foods	Australia	Delivery scheduling DC design	1993	12	Peter Gilmour, *Logistics Management: An Australian Framework*, Longman Australia, Melbourne, 1993, 355–367.
HK Sports Institute[b]	Hong Kong	Service concept formulation Service delivery system design	1997	26	Peter Gilmour
Repco	Australia	Inventory management Slow moving parts Setting service levels	1993	12	Peter Gilmour, *Logistics Management: An Australian Framework*, Longman Australia, Melbourne, 1993, 388–399.
AWA Limited	Australia	Warehouse centralization Warehouse layout	1996	21	Peter Gilmour

[a] All these case studies are written by Peter Gilmour and are available, unless otherwise indicated, by writing to: Professor Peter Gilmour, Graduate School of Management, Macquarie University, NSW 2109, Australia.
[b] Video interviews have been made of senior executives of these companies to use in conjunction with the cases.

they are asked to present their answers to one of the questions they are assigned. Each group is given between 5 and 7 minutes to make their presentations; then the remainder of the class session will follow as before.

The visiting manager is an important component of these class sessions. He or she enables the students to link the concepts around which the case was written with the practical challenges of implementing them. In almost all cases the visitors really enjoy the experience. Students do, however, tend to focus on the negative aspects of the case: what is wrong and what they can propose to correct things. It is often worthwhile when the lecturer introduces the visitor at the beginning of the session or thanks him or her at the end of the session to highlight the progressive aspects of the company's operations.

A video interview is a good, but second-best, substitute for the class visitor. Although most lecturers are not professionally trained journalists, these videos can be produced quite quickly and to a good standard. Most have been recorded by the University's audio-visual section, either in the campus studio or on-site. Occasionally overseas they have been recorded on a single handheld video camera without lighting. The quality in these cases is not as good but is acceptable.

On some occasions audioconferences have been used as a substitute for the class visit and videoconferences have also been used. For audioconferences a loudspeaker microphone is attached to a telephone in the classroom. The case is discussed by the class and the students asked to write any questions they have on slips of paper. Then the call is made to the "manager from the case" and the students come to the microphone one at a time to read their questions; the sound quality is such that the entire class can clearly hear the "visitor's" answer. When an Australian manager is discussing a case with Hong Kong or Singapore students, the time difference of 3 hours together with the weekend scheduling for most classes means that the guest participates from home on a weekend evening. This requires a certain amount of good will on the guest's part.

Field Visits

Most units in the logistics area have a field visit as an important element. Recent visits have been to the Amway of Australia DC (distribution center), the Australian Co-Operative Foods milk and dairy products manufacturing plant and DC and to the Bowin Design's space gas heater manufacturing plant. For each of these, the visit combined the opportunity to inspect the physical facilities with a subsequent class session on a case written about the company's operations. Before the visit students have read and thought about the questions for the case. They have also been given a list of things to look for during the visit (Upton and Macadam 1997).

During the visit the hosts answer questions about the operational aspects of what the students are seeing but not the issues that are addressed in the case. These are considered, with the help of the visiting manager, in the later class session.

For a number of the cases a video plant tour or DC tour has been made. In most cases the voice-over has been done by the manager responsible for the facility. Production has been done by the Macquarie University and Hong Kong Management Association's audio-visual departments. These are used when a field visit is not possible, for example when the Amway of Australia case is being taught in Hong Kong or Singapore or when the Hong Kong Sports Institute case is being taught in Singapore or Sydney.

Internet Analyses

A Web site has just been set up with the aim of developing, over time, a substantial data base on the logistics operations of companies in Australia, Hong Kong, and Singapore. This database will be used for both teaching and research.

A problem with traditional data collection methods is the substantial time lag for the respondent between submitting the data and receiving feedback on their analysis. The design of this Web site is such that the confidentiality of individual data sets is maintained but the respondent can obtain, immediately, summarized information (averages and ranges) on the total database and on segments of interest, such as the same industry sector.

The exact structure of the Web site is still being developed but two data sets have been installed for use in the course unit in logistics strategy. The first is a strategic framework that was developed by a joint Macquarie University and Andersen Consulting research team (Gilmour, Harrison, and Moore 1998). The second is an adaptation of a database generated by the World Class Logistics research at Michigan State University (Michigan State University 1995). These two databases have been used for teaching in the past but the amount of effort required to input the data has had a significant negative impact on the efficacy of the session. Using the Web site the data are input by each student prior to the session and the entire session itself used for analysis and interpretation. Data collected are automatically allocated to strategic dimensions, which can then be used by the participant to evaluate the strategic positioning of his or her organization.

Exercises

A number of exercises are regularly used. These include:

- SAP demonstration. SAP A.G. (Systeme, Anwendungen, Produkte in der Datenverarbeitung) has provided the university with a full version of their ERP software. In 1998 a group of final-year undergraduate computer science students prepared a demonstration package of the supply chain elements of SAP for the Graduate School of Management's logistics teaching program. With one student per terminal, using the demonstration users guide and some assistance, the exercise takes about $1\frac{1}{2}$ hours. This demonstration can also be used in Hong Kong and Singapore.
- The Sterman Beer Game (Heineke and Meile 1995, pp. 101–111). This exercise is based on the systems principles of industrial dynamics (Forrester 1958). It shows rather dramatically the fluctuations in order quantities and inventory holdings that occur over 35 periods in a four-tier supply chain—retailer, wholesaler, distributor, and factory—when communication between the tiers is minimized. The exercise takes about 2 hours to run in teams of eight or nine.
- "Fabulous Fabrications." An adaptation of the game developed by Hewlett-Packard and John Deere to examine JIT operations. A "product" is made by a sequence of workers placing cardboard on each side of a styrofoam block attached first by a rubber band and then by masking tape. Colored circles are drawn on each side using a fixture. These are made first in batches of eight, then in batches of four, and finally one at a time; in every case in the sequence of red, green, red, blue, red. Production is aimed at meeting the demand of a customer who is placing orders, in a predetermined color sequence, every 20 seconds. This exercise also takes about 2 hours and again quite dramatically shows the advantage of having a supply chain that is flexible and short.
- "Calamity cartage" (Gilmour 1993, pp. 206–212). This is a transport planning exercise which takes about 1 to $1\frac{1}{2}$ hours, depending on the number of participants. Each player has a truck loaded with banana passionfruit in Brisbane. Markets exist at 10 cities across Australia with a fixed-price export contract available in Perth on day 6 (the last day of the game). Each day the truck can be driven a maximum number of kilometers to the market of the player's choice where the banana passionfruit can be sold at night. The instructor works out the price each night depending on the size of the market and the amount of fruit sold into it.
- Ripco spark plugs (Gilmour 1993, p. 243). This is an inventory management exercise. Given two periods of initial data and a forecast, the students have to decide how many units they will order in the next period. After deciding, the instructor tells them the actual demand for that period and the forecast for the next. The objective of the game is to minimize the sum of ordering and carrying or stockout costs over 13 periods. The

tendency is to order something each period. If they work out an economic order quantity first they can ascertain that this is not the best strategy.
- Logistics planning simulation exercise (Gilmour 1993, pp. 281–283). Using a deck of cards for two random variables, breakdown frequency and repair time, this exercise simulates (in $\frac{1}{4}$-hour increments) the operation of three forklift trucks in a warehouse over a $7\frac{1}{2}$-hour day. The performance of the system is evaluated by calculating the utilization of the repair shop, the downtime for each fork, the average queue length at the repair shop, the average queuing time, and the average downtime.
- Aggregate planning. An Excel spread sheet has been prepared to assist students to use the data in a case on manufacturing lawn mowers (Gilmour 1991, pp. 108–122). They use the software in the School's computer laboratory or can download it for use on their own PCs or laptops. The objective is for each student to prepare and analyze an aggregate plan and a master production schedule for Victa Lawn Mowers.

Resources

The development of business education in Australia, in particular, and in Asia, in general, has followed the English model with a heavy emphasis on economics. Integrating economics into a management program has become the dominant approach only over the last couple of decades. This has meant that the development of particular areas of management have often relied on the research interests of a single faculty member. The logistics programs described in this paper were developed by a single individual, including writing all the cases listed in Table 2 and developing or modifying the exercises described in the paper. Similarly the logistics programs at the RMIT University in Melbourne and the National University of Singapore have been developed by a single faculty member. Both Australian programs, at Macquarie and at RMIT, have been supported to a minor extent by the professional associations, The Logistics Management Association of Australia and the Charted Institute of Transport. The new program at the National University of Singapore has been given seed money by the Singapore Trade Development Board. In the current climate of economic rationalism, the bottom line is that the development of a logistics educational program by an individual is feasible if the program then generates sufficient student enrollments.

Objectives

Most of this teaching is set within the overall context of the trade-off between the total cost of the system and the level of customer service that it can deliver. This trade-off is examined at three levels (Gilmour 1993, ch. 1). The first is the operational level of the trade-offs between the elements that comprise the supply chain: for example, information can replace inventories; fast response can replace warehouses. Next are the trade-offs between the traditional functional areas, manufacturing efficiencies and field inventories for example. The last level is the relationships that exist between separate entities in the supply chain, such as suppliers, manufacturers, retailers and third-party providers of transport, warehousing, and information. The objective of the logistics teaching programs at Macquarie University is to examine the practical implications for management of all these interrelationships.

Achievement of these objectives is influenced by cultural factors. Chinese companies, particularly family (privately owned) companies, tend to be quite bureaucratic; the owner/manager decides the strategic direction of the firm and the middle managers have no role or expectation of participation in the formulation of strategy (McGraw 1998). For many students in Hong Kong and some in Singapore who work for these companies the concept of using logistics as a strategic capability is different to grasp. Most Australian students, on the other hand, either already have an input into strategy development in their current work positions or expect this to be the case in the near future. For them the strategic role of logistics is easier to conceptualize.

TABLE 3
Graduate Logistics Programs in the Asia Pacific Region

University	Degree	Objective	Duration
University of Technology Sydney	Master of Mgt (Supply Management)	The Master of Management Program aims to develop new skills and understanding of the diverse field of buyer and supplier relations. A complex cross-disciplinary field, this Program is designed to help the supply practitioner and those responsible for managing supplier relationships understand the scope of their involvement in both local and international markets. The overall aim of this Management Program is to enable the practitioner to refocus their organization's supply management activities into a strategic force.	6 semesters part time
Monash University Melbourne	Graduate Diploma of Logistics Management	This course offers comprehensive study of all the logistics elements from procurement to distribution to customer service. It covers both operational and strategic responsibilities and links together supply, materials, and distribution management issues in the value chain. Subjects may also be taken as single units without the option of progression to higher level courses.	2 years part time
Monash University Melbourne	Master of Business (Logistics Management)	The overall aim is to provide a comprehensive intellectually demanding and up-to-date understanding of logistics management concepts; improve the professional expertise and effectiveness of participants in their current workplace and create career advancement opportunities.	2 years part time
RMIT University Melbourne	Master of Business (Integrated Logistics Management)	This postgraduate course is an integrated program offered by combining key elements from the Masters Programs presented by the Graduate School of Engineering and the Logistics Management Group within the Graduate School of Business. The focus is management of total costs over the life cycle of major capital investments, such as defense, infrastructure, and mining.	12 months full time or 30 months part time and distance education
RMIT University Melbourne	Master of Business (Logistics Management)	This postgraduate course builds on the Graduate Diplomas offered by the Logistics Management Group and focuses on the strategic aspects of logistics management, questioning, and analyzing the role of logistics in the development of the supply chain. The course is a rigorous but practical management program that has been designed for operational managers and is led by industry experienced and qualified staff.	12 months part time
Curtain University Perth	Master of Commerce (Logistics Management)	This course has been designed for professional logistics specialists who are interested in developing careers in logistics management and/or in logistics. Areas of study will relate to transportation, physical distribution, warehousing, material and inventory management, purchasing, manufacturing, location modeling, retailing, and information system linkages for government and private industries on a national and global basis.	2 years full time
National University of Singapore	Master of Science (Logistics)		
Hong Kong University of Science and Technology	Graduate Diploma in Transportation Logistics Management	This course has been designed to retrain existing logistics and transportation staff working in industry.	1 year part time

TABLE 4
Job Titles of Hong Kong Students

Document Control Manager	WKK Technology Ltd
Supplies Officer	HK Government Supplies Office
Station Manager	Kowloon-Canton Railway Corporation
Export Manager	Bowden Industries Ltd
Logistics Planning Manager	Procter & Gamble HK Ltd
Logistics Manager	Olivetti Personal Computer Far East Ltd
Accountant	Kumagai Gumi (HK) Ltd
Purchasing Manager	Barncy Technology Limited
Sales Manager	Esquire Travel Agency Limited
Parts Administrator	GE Medical Systems China
Accounts Manager	Protech Property Management Ltd
Manager Merchandise	HK Seibu Enterprise Co Ltd
Sales Manager	Carreta Meadows Wye Forwarding
Senior Engineering Manager	Nice Industries Ltd
Head, Materials Management	Ciba Specialty Chemicals
Manager New Products	Marco Polo Hotels
Purchasing Executive	Components (Far East) Ltd
Assistant to General Manager	Paget Enterprises Ltd
Distribution Centre Manager	Olympus HK Ltd
Assistant Manager	Nanyang Brother Tobacco Co Ltd
Warehouse and Distribution Manager	Parfums Christian Dior (HK) Ltd
Shop Manager	Hong Kong Telecom
Business and Logistics Manager	McPhersons CPG Ltd
Supply Chain Manager	Quaker Oats Asia Inc
Deputy Manager	Banque Indosuez
Assistant to Managing Director	Wui Long Holdings Co Ltd
Warehouse Manager	Schick International Ltd
Accounts Manager	Wai Ming Finance Ltd
Senior Manager	Fleet Trans International Co Ltd
Marketing Operations Manager	Breakthrough Ltd
Logistic Manager	East West Ltd
Field Services Manager	The Hong Kong Jockey Club
Manager Business Operations	The Industrial Bank of Japan Ltd
Logistics Officer	Sony International (HK) Ltd
Professor of Medicine	The Prince of Wales Hospital
Construction Manager	Hung Mau Realty & Construction Ltd

Conclusions

Although this paper has concentrated on one particular graduate program in logistics management, a number of others do exist within the region. These are shown in Table 3. Most are in Australia. The program at the National University of Singapore is housed in the Production Engineering School, in contrast to all the others that are in business or management faculties. It is not surprising that the focus of the NUS program is on technology, that is, technology as applied to the infrastructure required by logistics systems as well as the technology associated with the communication needs of the system. As seen from Table 3 the number of graduate programs is quite small. A much larger number of undergraduate and postsecondary programs exist. A listing of these offerings in Australia is regularly published by the Logistics Management Association (Logistics Management Association of Australia 1997). A number of other universities in the region, such as the Hong Kong University of Science and Technology, offer undergraduate programs in logistics.

An ability to integrate supply chain operations over considerable geographic distances and in a way that will deliver to stakeholders a customized service has growing appeal to a wide range of organizations in the Asia Pacific region. (This range is shown in Table 4, which lists the job titles and companies of the 1997 intake of the Master of Management in Logistics and Operations Management in Hong Kong.) The design and teaching of the logistics programs in the Graduate School of Management at Macquarie University are aimed at employing the concepts of integration, globilization, and customization to enable organizations to gain competitive advantage through innovative but judicious supply chain operations.

References

BARNES, L. B., C. R. CHRISTENSEN, AND A. J. HANSEN (1994), *Teaching and the Case Method*, 3rd edition, Harvard Business School Press, Boston, MA, USA.

FORRESTER, J. (1958), *Industrial Dynamics*, Massachusetts Institute of Technology Press, Cambridge, MA, USA.

FUNG, V. (1998), personal communication, November.

GILMOUR, P. (1991), *Operations Management in Australia*, Longman Cheshire, Melbourne, Australia.

—— (1993), *Logistics Management: An Australian Framework*, Longman Cheshire, Melbourne, Australia.

——, N. J. HARRISON, AND P. MOORE (1998), "The Role of Logistics in the Formulation and Deployment of Strategy: An Empirical Analysis of Australian Packed Consumer Products Manufacturers," *International Journal of Logistics: Research and Applications*, 1, 3, May–June 1997, 263–80.

HEINEKE, J. N. AND L. M. MEILE (1995), *Games and Exercises for Operations Management*, Prentice Hall, Englewood Cliffs, NJ, USA.

HUTCHEON, R. (1991), *A Burst of Crackers: The Li & Fung Story*, Li & Fung, Hong Kong.

Logistics Management Association of Australia (1997), *Logistics Education Directory* 97–98, Logistics Management Association of Australia, Sydney, November 1997.

MAGRETTA, J. (1998), "Fast, Global, and Entrepreneurial: Supply Chain Management, Hong Kong Style," *Harvard Business Review*, 76, 5, September–October 1998, 102–114.

MCGRAW, P. (1998), "Line Manager Perceptions of Human Resource Values and Practices in Hong Kong," *Proceedings Sixth International Human Resources Management Conference*, University of Panderborn, Germany, June 22–25, 1998.

Michigan State University (1995), *World Class Logistics: The Challenge of Managing Continuous Change*, Council of Logistics Management, Oak Brook, IL, USA.

TAYLOR, D. H. (1997), *Global Cases in Logistics and Supply Chain Management*, Thomson Business Press, London, UK.

UPTON, D. M. AND S. E. MACADAM (1997), "Why (and How) to Take a Plant Tour," *Harvard Business Review*, 75, 3, May–June 1997, 97–106.

Peter Gilmour is Professor of Management and a former Director of the Graduate School of Management at Macquarie University where his teaching responsibilities are in the areas of logistics, technology, and operations management. Professor Gilmour has had extensive consulting experience in Australia and overseas. Before joining the Graduate School of Management at Macquarie, he was Senior Lecturer in Administration at Monash University. Earlier in his career, he taught at the Graduate School of Business at Michigan State University while gaining his Doctorate, and was Research Fellow in Business Logistics at the Graduate School of Business Administration, Harvard University, and Visiting Scholar at the Graduate School of Business Administration, Columbia University, New York. He has also held positions in systems analysis and distribution planning with Mobil Oil Australia in Melbourne and New York. He has written thirteen books, including *Logistics Management: An Australian Framework*, *Total Quality Management: Integrating Quality into Design, Operations and Strategy* (with Bob Hunt), *The Management of Technology* (with Bob Hunt), *Operations Management in Australia*, *The Management of Distribution* (two editions), *Physical Distribution Management in Australia* (two editions), *The Management of Technology*, *Australian Marketing Casebook* (three editions) and *Moving Goods and People*, and also a number of monographs and professional papers.

PRODUCTION AND OPERATIONS MANAGEMENT SOCIETY

The Production and Operations Management Society (POMS), created in 1989, has been building an international network of practitioners and academics to advance the state of the art in production and operations management. The activities of the society include the following:

- *Production and Operations Management*, a premier journal of research and novel applications
- *POM Chronicle,* a quarterly newsletter
- Annual meetings
- Specialized conferences and seminars
- An online computerized placement service
- Education and curriculum development

Membership benefits also include the journal, the newsletter, reduced registration rates for the meetings, and other services offered by the society. Annual membership dues are $65 ($20 for students and retired members). If you would like to become a member, please send your name and address by mail or fax to: POMS Executive Office, College of Engineering, Florida International University, EAS 2460, 10555 West Flagler Street, Miami, Florida 33174, USA. Phone 305-348-1413. Fax 305-348-6890.

Call For Papers - Focused Issue of *Production and Operations Management* on the e-Business and Supply Chain Management

The web is having unimaginable impact on how firms interact with each other and their customers. Stumbling blocks for supply chain integration such as high transaction costs between partners, poor information availability, and the challenges of managing complex interfaces between functional organizations are rapidly dissolving on the web. Digital exchanges are making transaction costs insignificant, moving vast quantities of complex information is becoming cheap and easy, and web-centric software that facilitates collaboration are simplifying interfaces. Tools in each of these categories are rapidly maturing, fundamentally changing supply chains.

In recognition of these developments, *Production and Operations Management* will publish a focused issue on **e-Business and Supply Chain Management**. We seek papers that present leading edge research on this rapidly evolving topic. The possible paper topics are vast – for example:

- Integration of supply chain planning and procurement
- Models for B2B exchanges
- Analysis of auctions
- Impact of information intermediaries on supply chains
- Web-centric product design
- Order fulfillment and returns management in B2C
- Forecasting and inventory management in B2C

Papers must clearly address e-business related topics, but may employ any scientific research method including mathematical modeling, empirical analysis, or rigorous case techniques.

To submit a paper for publication in this focused issue, send five copies of the manuscript to one of the two focused issue editors. Manuscripts must be received by **November 30, 2000**. All papers will be reviewed within four months of receipt.

Focused Issue Editors

M. Eric Johnson
Tuck School of Business Administration
Dartmouth College
Hanover, NH 03755
m.eric.johnson@dartmouth.edu
phone: 603-646-0526; fax: 603-646-1308

Seungjin Whang
Graduate School of Business
Stanford University
Stanford, CA 94305-4024
whang_jin@gsb.stanford.edu
phone: (650)723-4756; fax:(650) 725-0468

Call for Papers for Special Issue of
Production and Operations Management on
Beyond ERP: The Supply Chain and the World Wide Web

Editors: Mark L. Spearman and Kalyan Singhal
Deadline: September 30, 2000

The advent of the Internet will have a profound impact on the way commerce is transacted. Since the rise of enterprise resources planning (ERP), all eyes are now on how this paradigm will be transferred to the Web. Unfortunately, there are significant problems with ERP that must be addressed before it can realize the full potential of the Internet. Within ERP is the older model, MRP II (manufacturing resources planning) that was built upon a simple model of MRP (material requirements planning). MRP, developed more than 30 years ago, made several simplifying assumptions in order to make the computations feasible. One of these was that lead times are an attribute of the part in question, not the condition of the facility. This assumption leads to inflated planned lead times which, in turn, leads to long flow times. This artifact has been perpetuated to the present day and lies at the heart of the material planning module of the most popular and comprehensive ERP systems today. Many ERP systems attempt to "fix" this problem by utilizing an "advanced planning and optimization" (APO) system that usually performs a capacity check of the material plans. Unfortunately, such an approach is ad hoc in its very nature (done after the material plans are already infeasible) and greatly adds to the complexity of the system. Oftentimes such systems must maintain a complete model of all of the work in process in the line as well as data for the status of each process station.

We are seeking papers in the following areas:

- Web-based ERP
- Simple and robust models for production planning and scheduling
- Supply chain management (i.e., multi-echelon) with capacity considerations
- Algorithms used in advanced planning and optimization systems
- Combining ERP and lean manufacturing
- Experiences and case studies of ERP
- Cross-functional integration with marketing and finance
- Integrating web based ERP with central data warehouses

Please send five copies of your double-spaced manuscript by **September 30, 2000** to Kalyan Singhal, Merrick School of Business, University of Baltimore, 1420 N. Charles Street, Baltimore, MD 21201, USA. Phone 410-837-4976, e-mail: Ksinghal@ubmail.ubalt.edu.